Ballet's Magic Kingdom

Ballet's Magic Kingdom

Selected Writings on Dance in Russia,
1911–1925

Akim Volynsky

Translated, Edited, and with an Introduction and Notes
by Stanley J. Rabinowitz

Yale University Press
New Haven and London

Frontispiece: Yury Annenkov, *Akim Volynsky*, 1921 (From Yury Annenkov, *Portrety* [Petrograd: Petropolis, 1922], 41).

Published with assistance from the foundation established in memory of William McKean Brown.

Portions of this book originally appeared in slightly altered form as "Against the Grain: Akim Volynskii and the Russian Ballet," Dance Research *14, no. 1 (Summer 1996): 3–41, and "The House That Petipa Built: Visions and Villains of Akim Volynskii,"* Dance Research *16, no. 1 (Summer 1998): 26–66, and are reprinted by permission of the journal, the Society for Dance Research, and Edinburgh University Press.*

Set in Adobe Garamond type by Keystone Typesetting, Inc.
Printed in the United States of America by Sheridan Books, Ann Arbor, Michigan.

Library of Congress Cataloging-in-Publication Data
Volynskii, A. L., 1863–1926.
[Selections. English 2008]
Ballet's magic kingdom : selected writings on dance in Russia, 1911–1925 / Akim Volynsky ; translated, edited, and with an introduction and notes by Stanley J. Rabinowitz.
p. cm.
Includes bibliographical references and index.
ISBN 978-0-300-12462-0 (alk. paper)
1. Ballet—Russia (Federation)—History and criticism. 2. Ballet—Russia (Federation)—History—20th century. 3. Ballet dancers—Russia (Federation)—History. I. Rabinowitz, Stanley J. II. Title.
GV1663.V65 2008
792.80947—dc22
2008020365

A catalogue record for this book is available from the British Library.

This paper meets the requirements of ANSI/NISO Z39.48–1992 (Permanence of Paper). It contains 30 percent postconsumer waste (PCW) and is certified by the Forest Stewardship Council (FSC).

10 9 8 7 6 5 4

For Evelyne Tiersky Pini, whose elegance and joie de vivre are what so much of this book is about,

and for Mark Canner, whose remarkable literary sweep and critical insight inspired me through every stage of this book from beginning to end

The ecstasy that lifts us to the sky
dominates over all canons of beauty.
—Akim Volynsky, 1924

Contents

∗∗∗⁖∗∗∗

Part 2. The Book of Exaltations: The ABCs of Classical Dance (1925)

Acknowledgments

The longer the gestation period, the greater the debts, and for a project that has been over a dozen years in the making, the gratitude runs deep. This book's official inception and protracted execution coincide with the final stages and gradual termination of my parents' long lives, so it seems fitting to begin my acknowledgments by thanking them, sadly in absentia, for the unflinching support they perennially provided me with both in good times and bad. My decision in 1998 to turn into a book my initial and modest forays into Volynsky's dance writings and the vibrant world of Saint Petersburg ballet that he chronicled for fourteen years preceded by only a few weeks my father's mental decline and entry into the nursing home, where he died seventeen months later; Yale's interest in publishing my manuscript (news of which my mother celebrated by having a second cigarette that day) came five weeks before she died at age ninety-seven in the summer of 2006.

The date of the beginning of this labor of love is exactly traceable to a letter I received in 1993 from the then, and current, editor of the lovely publication *Dance Research,* Richard Ralph. Having read my earlier work on the life and achievements of Akim Volynsky, in which relatively little was said about his career as a ballet critic, Dr. Ralph inquired about whether I might like to extend my research and do something on that topic for his journal: the rest—as the saying goes—is history. If the initiator of a journey deserves unique pride of place in its outcome, as I believe should be the case, then I am happy to say that my debt to Richard Ralph is substantial indeed. The author of a second letter of inquiry about my involvement with Volynsky's ballet writings warrants special mention and profound gratitude—the venerable Arlene Croce, former dance critic for the *New Yorker*. Her curiosity about any possible further plans I had to expand my work in this field and, subsequently, in what is now a fateful phone conversation, her encouragement to forge ahead with it, led to my conviction that the subject warranted a full-length study and that I (bless her!) was the one to do it.

And, by the grace of God, do it I did, but not without the wisdom and generosity of a group of people whom it is my genuine pleasure (and relief) to thank publicly at long last. My Russian-born colleagues and friends Viktoria Alexandrovna Schweitzer, Tatyana Yurevna, and Inna Petrovna Babyonyshev endured with patience and tact my numerous questions, occasionally accompanied by odd bodily demonstrations, on matters of meaning and style in their native language, though in a highly technical area that tested the limits of even their vast knowledge (they passed with flying colors). The admirably bilingual Irina Klyagin, whose special area of expertise is Russian ballet, laboriously examined rough drafts of my translations, particularly of *The Book of Exaltations,* and provided invaluable advice on how to handle in English scores of tricky, at times seemingly incomprehensible, patches of Volynsky's notoriously dense prose. Harry Haskell examined my manuscript and made valuable suggestions as to how I might improve it. I gratefully acknowledge other Amherst College colleagues who helped me in various ways: Stephanie Sandler (now of Harvard University) early on shared with me her knowledge of ballet; the writer Carl Vigeland (now of the University of Massachusetts at Amherst) made available to me during many lunches his expertise in the world of publishing; Rebecca Sinos provided useful information for several references to ancient Greek civilization; Helen von Schmidt read my introduction and, with her trained editorial eye, indicated several infelicities; Dale Peterson, my longtime friend and literary fellow traveler, followed with interest and typical intellectual insight the long and windy road of this journey; and, most especially, Catherine Ciepiela again and again provided exquisite critical advice and emotional uplift when both were sorely needed. Fortunate is the person who is surrounded by such knowledgeable and supportive colleagues, and lucky is the professor who has had as the dean of the faculty a person of such high academic and administrative caliber as Lisa Raskin. Through her nine-year tenure, Dean Raskin offered every possible means of support available to her to create the conditions necessary for me to conduct my work with a sense of material security and psychological comfort, and I am ever grateful for the time she always found to deal respectfully and empathetically with my needs. I am also delighted to thank Amherst College for awarding me in 2000 a grant for my research from the H. Axel Schupf '57 Fund for Intellectual Life as well as a senior sabbatical fellowship during the spring 2003 semester. In a world where so much of any writing project is dependent on the field of information technology, three Amherst College specialists made available their much-needed expertise: Paul Chapin, Debra McCulloch, and Jayne Lovett. When I think of the hours Jayne devoted to helping—with extraordinary aplomb and serenity— such an impatient and technologically unsavvy person as myself, I can only marvel at the contribution she has made to seeing my work come together at its final stages. Judi Kolenda, administrative assistant of the Russian Department, pitched in at critical times as well.

To my great fortune, three eminent figures to whose careers dance is central played an instrumental role in bringing my project to its current state. Tim Scholl early on urged me to take on the task of introducing Volynsky to an English-speaking audience, and since then he has been tirelessly available to help me in almost every aspect of this project. Lynn Garafola has been my good angel from the time she first served as a reader of my work for *Dance Research;* for years our foremost American expert on Russian ballet has guided and mentored this formally trained Slavist in countless ways, and whatever shortcomings there may be in this book, they certainly cannot be attributed to the lack of care and attention that Professor Garafola has lavished on my writing. Robert Gottlieb came into the picture when my major work on Volynsky was largely completed, but for four years thereafter he generously took time from his busy schedule to advise and inspire me. I am both grateful and flattered that he has become an interested party in this endeavor.

At Yale University Press, my editor Jonathan Brent, his assistant Annelise Finegan, and manuscript editor Susan Laity worked with me in a consummately professional manner, and I am deeply in their debt for their efforts.

Finally, two people who have been dear friends and to whom I take the deepest pleasure in dedicating this book. From Amherst to Avignon, Boston to Bologna, French-born Evelyne Tiersky Pini for thirty-five years has shown respect and affection for who I am and what I do; my endless encounters with ballet's French terminology continually brought to mind Evelyne's voice and the extraordinary culture she represents. Mark Canner, reader and literary mind par excellence, has for twenty-five years inspired me with his knowledge of books and love for "the pleasures of the text," which are second to none in my experience; his willingness to impart his exquisitely developed taste has been as appreciatively received as it has been generously offered.

A Note on the Text

As was standard in Russian newspapers, Volynsky usually referred to his subjects by either last name alone or by last name and first initials. In the interest of readability, throughout the text I have silently added first names for dancers, composers, and other figures of the Russian art world and substituted first names for initials in essay titles—for example, "Tamara Karsavina" for "T. P. Karsavina."

In addition, I have made excisions in some of Volynsky's articles and reviews, as well as more substantial deletions in his *Book of Exaltations*. A respected expert on dance, who some years ago read my translation in its original, uncut version, reported having found the book to be "very woolly" and claimed that reading it was "like falling into a bog." "Brilliant," "abstract," "tendentious," "difficult" were some of the adjectives used to describe this reader's reactions to Volynsky's work, and they are, alas, accurate. Volynsky tended to be didactic and long-winded, and because the chapters of *The Book of Exaltations* were originally presented as a series of lectures at his School of Russian Ballet, these tendencies were exacerbated. In the interest of space, yet with a pang of regret, I have removed those sentences, paragraphs and, in some cases, entire sections (equaling about a quarter of the original) where Volynsky is at his most verbose and prolix, and where the information is the most repetitive.

The meanings of certain dance terms vary slightly according to time and school. Volynsky's usage reflects that of the Russian school in the first decades of the twentieth century.

Except for citations in the notes, which follow the Library of Congress transliteration guidelines, my transliteration of Russian names adheres to a modified system, dependent on custom and readability. The common masculine ending "ij" appears as "ii" in the note citations and as "y" in the text. The double letters "ej" and "aj," most frequently encountered at the end of masculine first names, are given as "ei" and "ai," respectively, as in "Sergei" and "Nikolai." The final letter of the Russian alphabet, given as "ia" in the note citations, is written as "ya" in the text.

All translations are my own unless otherwise indicated.

Introduction

Akim Volynsky and His Writings on Dance

Dance was the last form of artistic expression to engage Akim Volynsky (1861–1926), perhaps Russia's most erudite and influential humanist scholar and critic of the late nineteenth to early twentieth century. For forty years he devoted himself to the propagation of culture with an all-consuming passion that verged on the fanatical, and ballet was the last arena in which he fought his never-ending battle for an elevated aesthetic consciousness. By the time he made his debut in 1911 as a dance journalist for the widely circulated Petersburg daily *Birzhevye vedomosti* (The Stock Exchange News), to which he contributed regularly until the Bolsheviks terminated the publication in early 1918, Volynsky was already known as the author of prodigious writings on literature, the fine arts, and philosophy, many of which had initially appeared in the early modernist journal *Severnyi vestnik* (Northern Herald), which he edited from 1891 to 1898.[1] Journalism, with its penchant for short forms of written expression that can reach a wide audience and provide a forum for argumentation and polemic, appealed to the crusading and proselytizing Volynsky from the start. His first publication was an angry letter to the editor of the Jewish newspaper *Rassvet* (Dawn) in 1880, followed some years later by a rather tendentious article on Baruch Spinoza for a similarly low-circulation Jewish magazine, *Voskhod* (Sunrise), in 1885; his last writings, on ballet theory and performance, appeared in *Zhizn' iskusstva* (The Life of Art)—the liveliest and most popular arts review in Petersburg (at that time called Petrograd)—between

1920 and 1924, by which time Volynsky had become the leading dance writer in Russia.² Yet less than two years later, Volynsky's reputation began to fade as, feeling out of step with the new, postrevolutionary society, he shunned active participation in it, although his fame has revived somewhat since the fall of the Soviet Union in the early 1990s.

Who *was* this long-forgotten, often controversial author and thinker whose activities centered on so many forms of artistic expression, and who, during the final phase of his life, between 1911 and 1924, composed almost four hundred articles on ballet criticism in addition to one of the most remarkable books ever written on classical dance, *The Book of Exaltations* (1925)?³ And how did his initially obscure forays into nonmainstream publications on rather specialized philosophical topics culminate in his position as Russia's most famous —and feisty—ballet authority, about whom the famous choreographer Fedor Lopukhov reflected late in life: "How damned keenly (Volynsky) understood and felt the ins and outs of our art"?⁴

Born Chaim Leib Flekser in 1861 to a Jewish family of booksellers in Zhitomir, Ukraine, Akim Lvovich Volynsky began to use his literary pseudonym— derived from the province of Volhynia, where he grew up—in 1885; "Chaim Leib" was dropped earlier and disappeared permanently. Volynsky's upbringing reflected the enclosed tradition of Orthodox Judaism; he studied biblical Hebrew, the Bible, and the Talmud, continuing, in ways which would have far-reaching implications, his forbears' reputation as the "people of the Book." But at fifteen the boy was already demonstrating brilliance in philological and literary studies, and in 1879 he moved to Saint Petersburg to continue his education. There he received his degree as a lawyer (which in part explains the combativeness and argumentativeness of his discourse), and there he lived until his death. Having escaped the confines of the provincial community that nurtured him through his mid-teens, Volynsky devoted his intellectual life to a sustained and quite conscious attempt to destroy all orthodoxies, for which he would pay a high personal and professional price. Yet for all his rejection of the power of the rabbinate, Volynsky felt a strong bond to Judaism and religion. The ballet historian Vadim Gaevsky, writing recently about *The Book of Exaltations,* ties Volynsky's final published work precisely to this earliest phase of his emotional and intellectual development when he argues: "Apparently in the word *book* Volynsky invested a certain prophetic, partly biblical meaning (*bible* means 'books'). And the very emotions (exaltation and enormous anger) that every one of his books manifests bears the stamp of Old Testament prophesies."⁵ Indeed, for all Volynsky's disdain for Old Testament moral severity and authoritarianism, the tone and slant of his writing contained a patriarchal, semantically certain quality; for all his self-projection as the radical revisionist of received truths, his tastes ran to the classical. And nowhere would these qualities be better exemplified than in his work on ballet, which Volynsky read as a text. As noted by the critic Galina Dobrovolskaya, "What was innovative in Volynsky's analysis was that at the center of his attention stood not the scenario, not even the music, but rather the dance 'text' of the ballet, the professional facts about its performers and their unique personalities, which unfolded in their dancing."[6]

Volynsky plunged headlong into the cultural wars that began to rage in Russia in the early 1890s when in 1891 he assumed the role of editor of *Severnyi vestnik* and quickly became the country's first modernist critic. Here he came face to face with the young generation of Russian decadents and symbolists, who in large measure owed to Volynsky the crucial exposure they needed to launch their careers, whether through his help in publishing their work or in his reviews of it in his eagerly awaited monthly column "Literary Notes." Volynsky both encouraged and legitimized the younger generation's emancipation from the older by showing that they could approach the intellectual level of their predecessors' writing while simultaneously usurping, even transcending, its authority. Apropos of his newly chosen vocation as critic, Volynsky declared—with the fierce determination and self-righteousness that typify all of his subsequent undertakings—that he intended to "pursue a specific profession, [which] means, to adopt a definite principle of life, a specific plan of action. . . . How can one possibly work without a clear worldview, without substantiated and demonstrated ideals, without broad philosophical convictions?"[7] This worldview led Volynsky to offer his single-handed challenge to the then-reigning positivist-materialist tradition in Russian thought and reflected his loyalty to a higher plane of existence based on metaphysical contemplation and spiritual self-perfection, a view that was profoundly influenced by his study of idealism.

Volynsky's evolving credo was inspired by Immanuel Kant (who, along with Spinoza, was his favorite philosopher), whose transcendental idealism and concept of the unknowable *Ding an sich* (thing-in-itself) explained for him the fundamental components of the human condition in all its metaphysical and mystical implications. As opposed to the materialists, Volynsky believed that art was important for its connection to the spiritual: it allowed one to know better the divine and moral planes of existence, a concept that sustainedly preoccupied him. "Aesthetic consciousness of the lofty," he wrote in 1889, referring to Kant's *Critique of Pure Reason,* crosses over to the sphere of moral consciousness. It is mystical in its very essence."[8] Aesthetics and morality are profoundly interrelated; both reflect, and are inspired by, the sacred. In article after article, Volynsky argued for the independent role of creativity in human development, never failing to state his preference for the beauty of art over the beauty of nature, for the superiority of the ideal to reality, and for the triumph of spirit over matter. Retrospectively evaluating Volynsky's accomplishments, the critic M. Korolitsky argued, "He looked at creation as an object of scholarly analysis and, accordingly, he promoted a precise ideal of aesthetic beauty, of aesthetic images, and of broad cultural and philosophical ideas."[9] Underlying Volynsky's work is a passionate defense of the single idea that beauty (as he understood it) will save the world, not as an end in itself but as a means to achieve wholeness, harmony, and moral perfection. To return criticism to principles that acknowledge the role of art in divining genuine beauty, exposing the innermost dimensions of human existence, and leading humanity to the ideal, Volynsky acknowledged his strategy "not to recount but to judge." The key to appreciating Volynsky's critical legacy and its inherently spiritual quality is his insistence (uttered during the throes of his career as dance journalist, by the way) that "my criticism in its very essence is the contemplation of aesthetic phenomena through the prism of theology [read, 'idealism']."[10] Somewhat earlier, in describing one of the major characters in his book *Leonardo da Vinci* (1900)—the narrator and expert who guides the reader through the labyrinth of art—Volynsky was surely being self-referential when he wrote: "He is not a writer, not a literary critic; it would be more accurate to call him a dreamer of the old-fashioned visionary kind."[11] Consequently, Volynsky's writing cannot be seen as "objective" or "rational" in the usual sense of these words. His partisan brand of criticism and his championing of the role of impatient advocate carried away by his own "theological" insights precluded Volynsky from ever composing with complete scholarly cool and detachment. Rather, his work may be viewed more as a *meditation* on the subject at hand from the point of view of, in Volynsky's own words, "unchanging values."

If these values—a belief in the supremacy of "high" European, especially classical Greek, culture as the spring from which all great aesthetic and intellectual achievement flows and a loyalty to supra-empirical ideas as the source of human thought and activity whose essence art needed to capture—remained constant throughout Volynsky's career, the works in which they were propagated varied enormously. Philosophy and literature constituted Volynsky's earliest intellectual home; books on these subjects, largely compilations of previously published essays, flowed from his pen with stunning rapidity: *Russian Critics* (1896), *N. S. Leskov* (1898), *The Struggle for Idealism* (1900), *The Kingdom of the Karamazovs* (1901), *The Book of Great Anger* (1904), *F. M. Dostoevsky* (1906). Interest in the fine arts followed. First was the magisterial *Leonardo da Vinci*, about which the writer and critic Marietta Shaginyan claimed: "Russia never had a book which was at once so controversial and so monumental";[12] later, his heretofore unpublished, possibly his longest, and certainly his last tome, on Rembrandt—which, movingly, returned the exhausted and (privately) anti-Soviet Volynsky to where his serious intellectual activities had begun: the seventeenth-century Holland of his beloved Spinoza.

And then came dance, beginning in 1907. Volynsky had become involved in theater through a brief stint (1905–1906) as director of repertoire for Vera Kommissarzhevskaya's noted Petersburg company, during which he experienced the challenges and problems associated with the stage, especially with scenic art. The next year he undertook a four-month excursion to Greece that completely changed the direction of his scholarly interests, moving him away from literature, fine arts, and theater to the study of ballet. Always one who traced the earliest sources of artistic expression, even traveling to the place of its origins, Volynsky (who had read Nietzsche's writings on the cult of Dionysus and its relation to Greek tragedy) visited all the known archeological sites of the Dionysian cult, often by foot, and came to the conviction that among the elements of contemporary theatrical spectacle, balletic dance alone preserved the character of the Hellenic sense of plastic art. His explorations also led him to plunge into serious study of ballet and, concomitantly, to demonstrate— with his trademark passion for, and high-strung aesthetic sensitivity toward, his subject—that modern ballet was ultimately classical in its mechanics and feeling. A statement from a letter he wrote during his travels demonstrates the depth of Volynsky's affection for Hellenic culture and the impact it would have, especially on his attitude toward dance; these remarks place him squarely in the tradition of Russian intellectuals who looked to classical civilization for artistic inspiration and even for fabrication of Russia's national identity. "I am in Greece, on the Acropolis . . . and believe me: nothing in my literary and scholarly work has as yet provided me with such abundance and such rapture as that with which I've been seized in Athens. . . . Something large, new, fresh, and refreshing flowed into my soul, and I see ahead of me the kind of work I had never before imagined but without which one cannot take a step in the area of those ideals with which I have lived all my life."[13] And where else but in his adopted city of Petersburg, filled with magnificent neoclassical architecture, could ballet be expected to recapture its original vocabulary and syntax? And who else but this former literary and art critic, so long comfortable with his role as a defender of the true faith and resurrector of forgotten traditions, should be the one to lead this newly adopted struggle on the dance front?

But Volynsky's foray into the uncharted territory of ballet criticism had practical and psychological roots, as well as purely scholarly ones. For in a sense, professionally he had almost nowhere else to go. After the demise of *Severnyi vestnik* in early 1899, its publisher even feared for Volynsky's well-being, predicting, "I don't know how he'll survive here—alone, impractical like a small child, proud, indigent, and refusing to complain to anyone about

anything. He'll spend whatever he earns on books and he'll literally go hun-
gry." His former friend and supporter, the writer and founder of the Russian
symbolist movement Valery Bryusov, expressed a widely held sentiment when
he railed in 1904: "Why does this phantom from the grave, this corpse who has
retained only the outer appearance of life, come to our war counsels, our
lectures, our festivities?"[14] Virtually driven out of literary publishing by his
unrelenting attacks on almost everyone in the field, including his closest associates and collaborators, Volynsky found himself deprived of any forum for his
ideas except the occasional lecture. But the adverse effects of his growing
isolation from learned and intellectual circles, fueled by his brand of off-
putting pontification–cum–oracular assuredness, might be countered by activities in a new public forum, in which he could direct his energies and
channel his prophesies as a passionate advocate of cultural revival to a new
constituency. And that forum became ballet, for few would argue that from
around 1908–1909, with the formation of Sergei Diaghilev's Ballets Russes and
the related exodus of such giants as Vaslav Nijinsky, Mikhail (Michel) Fokine,
Tamara Karsavina, and Anna Pavlova, Russian classical dance, with its tradition of technical virtuosity and choreographic excellence, was ripe for redefini-
tion and resuscitation.

   Actually, the need for revival had originated somewhat earlier. The image of
the dying swan, centrally featured in Fokine's 1907 "new" ballet of that name,
provides a fitting metaphor for the situation in the world of academic classical
dance, which had been dominated by Marius Petipa until his own choreographic swan song in 1903. It was this event, preceded by the death of the
theater's "second" ballet master, Lev Ivanov (another Volynsky favorite), in
1901, and the ensuing scramblings to find a suitable successor at the Maryinsky
that threatened the stability and signaled the dissolution of the old order. (This
turmoil largely continued until the appointment of the dancer-choreographer
Fedor Lopukhov as artistic director in 1922 began to put the theater on a more
even keel.)[15] Many have written about the sparkling genius of Petipa, the
Frenchman turned Russian who brought balletic art to unprecedented perfection and popularity at the imperial capital's premier venue for ballet performance. But the most succinct comment about the precarious fate of the great
tradition which the ballet master had established over a period of thirty-five
years may belong to Lynn Garafola, who wrote: "By 1900 . . . as Petipa's creative
powers waned, Imperial technique congealed in the habits of his earlier master-
works: it became an academic language that brooked no departures from its
laws. The syntax and vocabulary that had been Petipa's means were now ends
in themselves, constraints upon expression rather than instruments of it."[16]
The end of Petipa's "golden age" threatened to shift the center of gravity of
Russian ballet away from the Maryinsky as the cradle of inspiring choreo-

graphic activity, as the institution lost ground to other theaters and companies, local and foreign, whose innovative art appeared unwelcome there.

Enter Volynsky.

"Underappreciated, undercut ballet establishment yearns for defender to re-invigorate excitement about its previous glory"; "undermined, underemployed critic seeks opportunity to re-ignite his mission to raise the public's aesthetic consciousness, preferably by inculcating in it the joys and challenges of dance performance." It was this extraordinary encounter between "the betrayed and abandoned," this fortuitous marriage of true minds, that would produce a body of writing about balletic art that for the first time in dance criticism reflected the thinking of a specialized reporter and educated scholar and theoretician, rather than a gifted amateur. Virtually alone among serious observers of ballet—"that pure magic kingdom of beauty" as he once called it—Volynsky felt no need to travel to Paris (or elsewhere) to cover Diaghilev's Russian Seasons, against which he conducted a tireless polemic from afar; indeed, his last trips abroad were to Milan in 1909 to accept honorary citizenship for his Leonardo book, and to Berlin in 1913.[17] He preferred instead to remain in Petersburg and support the "loyal," home-grown talent in the grandest house in the land, built in 1860 and named after the tsarina Mariya, wife of Tsar Alexander II. Russian classical dance (no less than Petersburg's Imperial Theater), whose pristine beauty and resplendent purity Volynsky alone seemed to appreciate, was left to be defended by none other than himself; even his kindred spirit André Levinson (1887–1933), who had earlier exhibited a similar, if less vituperative, disapproval of Diaghilev and Fokine's transformation of dance into extravagant visual spectacle, had emigrated to Paris. This is not to say that Volynsky's praise for Petipa's classical technique would be unequivocal —he occasionally found it overwrought and exaggerated, although he sounded almost lyrical compared with, say, Benois, who wrote in 1902: "We won't deny Petipa's talent, but we must nonetheless admit that [his] art is far from genuine. It is merely academic design that is nicely delineated but lacking in any soul or artistic temperament."[18] Nor do I argue that Volynsky's position vis-à-vis the conventional and narrowly academic Maryinsky troupe lacked its own radicalism: he aimed to restore its clearly (and deservedly) eroded preeminence by changing its direction not toward some unknown utopia via avant-garde technique but rather back to its former perfection through the return to what he believed were ballet's ancient roots. His revolution called for Hellenist restoration, not modernist innovation; his clarion call became "Back to the future!"

After his life-altering sojourn to Greece, Volynsky continued to occupy himself with literary matters—translating, editing, composing introductions to various and sundry volumes—as he would even through the postrevolutionary period, when, for example, he found himself working beside Levinson in the publishing house Vsemirnaya Literatura (he in the Italian section, Levinson in the French). But beginning in 1908, Volynsky threw himself almost completely into the serious study of dance with all the vast scholarly erudition and irrepressible enthusiasm at his disposal, even at one point working with no less an authority than the dancer and pedagogue Nikolai Legat, from whom he learned all the classical exercises and to whom he remained forever loyal. Word about Volynsky's interest in dance matters spread, and in 1911 he began serving as ballet critic for *Birzhevye vedomosti,* a newspaper committed to reporting on current artistic events at the highest level.

The dates here are significant—indeed symbolic. For Volynsky's connections with the dance world traverse exactly the period (to recall the title of Tim Scholl's excellent book) "from Petipa to Balanchine"—that is, they begin immediately after the former's death in 1910 and terminate just at the latter's emigration from Russia in the summer of 1924. During that period, with hyperactive regularity, Volynsky fired off reviews dealing with individual artists and performances, continuing his job after the demise of the newspaper two years later, when he moved over to *Zhizn' iskusstva.*[19] Yet Volynsky's dance journalism, especially during the twenties, constituted more than a motley array of reports on current productions. His endeavor was more comprehensive, his writing more programmatic. The nature of Volynsky's approach—the essence of his project—as a dance critic was of a different order, as witnessed, for example, in the opening salvo of an article he wrote in 1915 on Konstantin Skalkovsky, his (as he brashly proclaimed) much inferior forerunner. Somewhat disdainfully, he states: "The serious art of ballet still lacks a body of criticism. Contemporary journals haven't devoted to it any articles whatsoever, obviously considering it a phenomenon of lower aesthetic value as compared to literature and other forms of artistic creation, and so having no interest among the public."[20] Among other goals, Volynsky's dance writings—those which most often approach the genre of essay rather than newspaper column—would constitute the individual bricks by which a *theoretical* foundation of ballet would be systematically built. His debut piece for *Birzhevye vedomosti* (and the opening selection of this collection), "Dance as a Solemn Ritual," can be read as Volynsky's credo for all that follows: it already demonstrates a commitment to viewing ballet as adhering to a larger system, the movements of which could—indeed, needed to be—read as symbols of a higher order of being. "There is not a pas," Volynsky contends, "without a thought behind it—or, to put it more accurately, every pas in ballet, because of its combination of lines and movements, carries with it a specific idea from the world of the soul and the imagination." Such original thinking about the transcendental quality of ballet not only precipitated those immediate, often lyrical responses to a given performance, hurriedly though thoughtfully produced on the nearest typewriter, but it eventually resulted in extended reformulations of ballet's very foundations, exhaustively articulated in Volynsky's crowning achievement, *The Book of Exaltations.*

It is important to note that Volynsky's infatuation with Hellenism and his dream of establishing its links, and relevance, to the modern context, reflect a larger movement in Russian culture. In this respect, his dance writings, permeated with deep longing for world, and especially classical, culture, contain as much value for the cultural historian as they do for the ballet aficionado. By the turn of the century Nietzsche's writings, most notably his *Birth of Tragedy,* had captivated Russia's literary intelligentsia; the symbolist generation whose thinking Volynsky had echoed in the 1890s was mesmerized by the German philosopher's interpretation of Greek civilization for it comported with their similar attempts at recapturing the lost wholeness of humanity's spirit and the centrality of myth to spiritual renewal. Already in 1900 Volynsky was asserting: "When it has restored its link with religious consciousness, poetic consciousness will one day become as it was in ancient Greece, man's finest activity."[21] For writers like Alexander Blok, Fedor Sologub, and Vyacheslav Ivanov (the most influential of them all in this context), the aspect of poetic activity that would revive (if not replace) religious consciousness and restore life's unified wholeness was theater. As Greek tragedy most naturally expressed this ancient people's deepest religiosity (with the tragic chorus embodying the Russian spirit of collectivity known as *sobornost'*)—so argued Ivanov in his seminal work *The Hellenic Religion of the Suffering God* (1904)—so the contemporary stage, by returning to its roots in ancient drama, could facilitate the human community's approach to the ideal world of the past. For many, theater was nothing short of a liturgical act through which, claimed Georgy Chulkov, "we should rise to heights which we are not capable of attaining in everyday life."[22] A whole current of experimental drama, including that of Kommissarzhevskaya's company, stressed the genre's purely religious design. "Kommissarzhevskaya's theater," wrote the critic Alexander Red'ko in his evaluation of the period, "turned itself into a church, in which the producer and the actors celebrated exactly like priests in the traditional church, in the name of the infinite power guiding the world."[23]

Yet though moved by the same impulse to reestablish the inherently mythical basis of art by recapturing the Greek past, Volynsky short-circuited the Dionysian decadence associated with Nietzsche and changed the emphasis from the theater of drama to the theater of dance. If, in Ivanov's view, the dramatic could reunite life's disparate, contradictory elements into an indissoluble unity, then for Volynsky it was the balletic which vouchsafed the attainment of such harmonious perfection. Downplaying the human word as the only form of expressing thoughts and feelings, Volynsky instead emphasized the silent, though eloquent language of the body. Chulkov's admonition about rising to customarily unattainable heights Volynsky takes literally in his paean to verticality, invoking Kant, who defined standing as the human spirit's victory over nature. Not verbal communication but rising on the toes "represents [our] highest conceivable and imaginable expression" ("The Toes"), or, in other words, elevation equals the profoundest manifestation of beauty.

Ancient drama, with its contemporary overlay of Nietzschean libidinal paganism, was inimical to Volynsky's project for human transcendence: "After the winds and storms of sexual passion, after the extensive flood of all manner of eroticism onstage," contended Volynsky in "What Will Ballet Live By?" ". . . a new and fresh historical dawn will arise. A new sun will shine and with its brilliant rays illuminate all the summits of human engagement." That dawn he saw as classical dance; those rays emanated not from Ivanov's "suffering god" Dionysus but from the Sun god himself, Volynsky's beloved Apollo. "When people learn to dance to the accompaniment of Beethoven's music, as once King David danced in frenzied religious ecstasy to the music of a prayerful chant," declared Volynsky in a 1908 interview on Isadora Duncan, "then they'll be very close to a new moral truth, to a new wholeness of mind and heart—to the final gesture of history. This will mean coming (back) to Apollo, to the vibrant, efficacious, and purifying Apollo, as the ancient Greeks said: purified from all the chaos of truth and untruth, which is called the orgiastic temperament of Dionysus."[24] The kingdom of Apollo need not, as Nietzsche had contended, submit to the kingdom of Dionysus.

So convinced was Volynsky of the "purifying" Apollonian nature of classical dance that his reverence for the Sun god took the form of a ballet libretto—unique to his 1923 oeuvre—entitled "The Birth of Apollo," which (according to the essay's opening lines) was first imagined during his travels through Greece, though finally published sixteen years later. Proof of the scenario's long gestation may be seen in Volynsky's conception of the role of Leto, tailor-made for Ida Rubinstein, who accompanied him on his Greek odyssey and soon afterward gained the reputation as "a dramatic mime with the highest degree of expressiveness," the words he used to describe Leto. Or in the dance performed by the Egyptian woman in the first act—"with a wonderfully graceful back, assuming exquisite profiles and three-quarter poses"—which sounds exactly like the Assyrian dance Fokine choreographed for Karsavina in 1907 and later incorporated into *Egyptian Nights*. In any case, Volynsky's impressive, indeed overwhelming, erudition clashes with the practicalities of realistic dance production. With its call for Pelasgian giants, Ninevite merchants, Nubian traders, Babylonian envoys, Semitic women, Ethiopian slaves, various priests and hunters, not to mention Apollo himself (leading twenty-four warriors!) and his mother, Leto—all of whom perform a dizzying array of ancient Greek hyporchema (choral songs and dances) as well as ethnic and classical dances—this gargantuan production demonstrates how Volynsky's fastidious and overly ambitious classical scholarship invariably interfered with more streamlined and flexible interpretations of classicism.

Yet more important to contemplate may be not the negative qualities of Volynsky's overloaded, pedantic imagination but rather how this fiercely ret-rospectivist mind-set sought new possibilities for classical ballet and antici-pated, albeit with entirely different results, Balanchine's Diaghilev-produced, Stravinsky-composed work on a similar theme, *Apollon Musagète* (1928). I shall return to the Volynsky-Balanchine connection later; suffice it to say at this point that for all Volynsky's desire to reform the Petipa tradition and for all his much-vaunted criticism of the Ballets Russes's lavish renditions, his proposal for "The Birth of Apollo" recalls precisely the old-fashioned quality of Petipa's lengthy productions, as well as such Diaghilev exports as *Cléopâtre* (1909), *Schéhérazade* (1910), and *Daphnis and Chloë* (1912), which bear the stamp of Fokine's collaboration. Volynsky's imagined Greece partakes largely of a fin-de-siècle exoticism rather than the scaled-down purity and uncluttered simplicity he elsewhere lauds as central to the Hellenic ideal, especially in *The Book of Exaltations.*[25] Yet contradiction is not unknown to Volynsky's writing; indeed, seen early on in his attitude toward Fokine, it forms one of his constants.

Their radically different approaches to Hellenism not only allow us to grasp the mutual antipathy that existed between Volynsky and Fokine, they also help us understand more acutely many of the critic's objections to the ballets he was reviewing. We must always remember that Volynsky's vision of ballet was frozen in a form of idealized beauty that tended to blind him to the fluctuating ebbs and flows of modern times and made any brand of dance experimentation anathema. Fokine, of course, was among the earliest post-Petipa reformers of choreographic art (the Moscow-based Alexander Gorsky was another, though he was less frequently vilified by Volynsky). For Fokine history was not an end but a means by which "he searched for the harmony in the contemporary perception of reality and tried to saturate ballet with events and personages that would respond to his peers' own sensibilities."[26] What Levinson, with the same baffled incredulousness that characterizes Volynsky's writing on the subject, lamented as the abandonment of classical ballet's genuine essence "for the aesthetic diversions of the new ballet masters, for the playthings of precocious symbolism and restless frivolity," was to Fokine an attempt to recognize and incorporate in his work "the entire practice of art of that time, its contra-dictory and complex creative life, when interest in history and historicism was combined with the stylization and dramatization of art—with more re-fined forms."[27] Volynsky's article "The Innovator" shows a largely principled disagreement over Fokine's faulty knowledge of classical sources. (We must remember that he knew firsthand only the choreographer's Russian productions.) Like Levinson, Volynsky took the position that Fokine's flawed recreation of ancient dance stemmed from an overly hasty assimilation of the subject matter combined with a lack of respect for the wonders of antiquity; Volynsky refused to accept Fokine's rebellion against what the young choreographer deemed an almost fetishistic truthfulness to the literal rendition of historical detail.

Yet however much Volynsky disparaged Fokine's ill-conceived experiments because they "were not based on the historically unfolding structure of the pas and (therefore) violated the immanent logic of ballet's development," the latter's attempted reforms were not so egregious that Volynsky wasn't occasionally willing to forgive and forget.[28] The critic fully appreciated Fokine's skill and creative energy, though his praise was later informed by his growing nervousness about the fragile state of dance in the young Soviet Union and his desire for the choreographer to come home. Implicit in his comments as well was Volynsky's respect for Fokine's prestige and unquestionable status, both of which, he believed, could return Russian ballet to its former preeminence as well as to its legitimate sources. Fokine rejected any suggestion of becoming Volynsky's ally in this endeavor; indeed, his hostility toward what he perceived as the critic's artistic blindness was as deep as any enmity or crudeness Volynsky had ever demonstrated toward him. "He combined in his writings," raged Fokine, "the most shop-worn technical dance terms (without any knowledge of them) with philosophical and deliberately foggy emissions in abstract concepts."[29]

It was Volynsky's obstinate veneration of classical dance—banishing from its realm those traces of contemporary styles and trends which informed Fokine's choreographic vision—that permeates (and, arguably, limits) his ballet reviews. This worship, it is true, might have restricted the critic's judgments, closing them off to the original artistic expression that any "deviating" interpretation displayed; but it is just this highly personalized view of the academic canons, based on deeply felt assumptions of what acceptable ballet performance should be, that gives Volynsky's writing the immediacy, passion, and range of scrutiny that make it so exhilarating and exasperating to read. Intense, visceral response most often enhances, rather than compromises, the intellectual acuity of this dance journalism. The totality of emotional investment in Volynsky's critical posture meant that his eyes and ears were everywhere; he examined with the kind of minute detail normally associated with textual analysis every facet of a given performance while also paying close attention to the history of previous productions. The music, costumes, makeup, sets, choreography, and human body in its every expression and gesture all fell within the critic's purview, and he examined them with a perspicaciousness heretofore unknown in ballet criticism.

With what erudition and evocative detail Volynsky writes about Schumann's pianistic lyricism ("Schumann, Ballet, and Fokine"), Glazunov's symphonic harmony of movement ("*Raymonda*"), and Tchaikovsky's graceful melodic lines ("*Swan Lake:* The Swan in Music"), always arguing for the centrality of music to dance. There were other composers he praised (Adolphe Adam, Léo Delibes), and those he excoriated (Ludwig Minkus, Cesare Pugni); but the key criterion here was what the French call *dansant*—the ability of the music to support dancing. This is why, despite his acknowledgment of Stravinsky's undeniable talent, Volynsky panned *Firebird* and *Petrushka,* which premiered at the Maryinsky during the 1920–1921 and 1921–1922 seasons ("Stravinsky's Ballets"). Viewed by many as a symbol of the theater's recovery and its forward-looking direction after the atrocious years of revolution, civil war, and various other calamities, Leonid Leontiev's Fokine-inspired *Petrushka* and Fedor Lopukhov's original rendition of *Firebird* (which the choreographers had seen in Fokine's versions in Paris) inspired in Volynsky the same negative reaction as the works' Ballets Russes debuts had in Levinson. Wrote the latter, presaging Volynsky's position: "Stravinsky's *Firebird* is interesting, though not *dansant,* and his *Petrushka*—a wonderful example of musical representationalism— renders the ballet itself superfluous."[30]

Volynsky rarely ignores costumes, makeup, and set design—here his previous experience at Kommissarzhevskaya's theater stands him in good stead— and his insistence that these components be "balletic," that is, that they highlight the singular properties and merits of the dancing, is difficult to dispute. But some of his descriptions so excel in the vividness and scrupulousness of their visual detail that the reader feels like an active witness to the performance itself. Such is the case in his reviews of the Korovin-designed *Little Humpbacked Horse* ("A Kaleidoscope of Attire") and *Sleeping Beauty.* The former's glowing hues of yellow, gold, red, and chestnut brown (which "shout at you too much") are as cheerfully dazzling as the latter's washed-out dark green, milky pale white, and monotonously pink tones ("the colors [are] inseparable from those of the dancing . . . [and] must sing, shine, and entice") are limpidly dull. And while Volynsky insisted in the *Sleeping Beauty* review that "clothing in dance must be . . . obedient to all the choreography's demands," in the area of costume he tolerated on certain occasions a freedom of creation that encouraged not the binding repetition of history but rather the liberating imagination of fairy tale. Yet fairy-tale visions could go too far, and in the critic's earlier review of *The Little Humpbacked Horse* ("The Tsar Maiden") Korovin's vividly rendered sets are faulted for their insufficiently elevated nationalism "in the Byzantine style" and their excessively nonliteral rendition of Moscow, where "it is impossible to avoid a cross."

These delicately nuanced appreciations of costume and stage design pale next to Volynsky's unforgettable rendition of Lev Ivanov's *Nutcracker* ("one of the finest ballets in the world," he proclaimed, revealing another similarity with Balanchine), reimagined almost a dozen years after he had first written about it (in 1912) for a 1923 review of a new and thoroughly inadequate production at the Maryinsky ("A Wretched Housepainter"). The several pages of purely rhapsodic prose in which Volynsky re-creates the enchanting intricacies of the costumes and props in the scene of the Dance of the Snowflakes ("the bits of fluff fall[ing] from above—wet, viscous, moist"; "the ice-like stalactites, which are also trimmed with light snow") induced the ballet scholar Roland John Wiley to claim recently: "Translation cannot do full justice to Volynskii's remarkable language, with its elaborate imagery, now poetic, now graphic, now alliterative, now enriched with the vocabulary of danse d'école. . . . He was a writer with a refreshingly lucid grasp of the artistic effects [of ballet]."[31]

Ballet's aesthetic impact could best be gauged in its choreography, and Volynsky's ballet criticism was at its most trenchant in its discussion of the steps and formations, the gestures and groupings of the dancing he observed. "Volynsky ceased perceiving choreography as merely the decorative embellishment of a production," argued Dobrovolskaya in her assessment of the critic's originality, "but rather considered it as the main component which discloses the [production's] content and expresses the basic idea of the author."[32] An appropriate appraisal, reflecting the importance of Volynsky's literary background to his dance writing. Reading ballet, as one would a written text, he looked for its *author*—a highly original position in his day, when the choreographer (commonly called the ballet master) was taken merely as the provider of a scenario's visual adornment through the arrangement of stage dancing. The centrality, the inviolability of the dancing forms the nub of virtually every review Volynsky wrote, no more exquisitely than in his eloquent portrayal of the work of Mathilde Kshesinskaya, Olga Preobrazhenskaya, and Nikolai Legat in *Harlequinade;* his detailed evaluation of the staging of act 2 of *Giselle,* in (the aptly titled) "Elegy"; his lovingly fervent elaboration of a variation in *Don Quixote;* and his lavishly discriminating commentary on the White Swan adagio in *Swan Lake* in "The Swan in Motion." With these in mind, it is hard to take seriously Fokine's dismissal of Volynsky as a person who "introduced into his writings on ballet unbelievable falsity, pompous nonsense, and complete muddle."[33] Quite the contrary. Volynsky's meticulous attention to the mechanics of ballet is continually filled with unexpected comparisons and bold insights; he combines—and delicately balances—the often unfettered exuberance of aesthetic delight with the intellectual self-control that produces choreographic snapshots of photographic precision.

But choreography's enchantment comes from more than the superb workings of the arms and legs, the feet and hands; it flows from what Volynsky called "the body's graphics," and his reviews never fail to stress the human figure, which held for this student and scholar of Leonardo da Vinci a special, even obsessive fascination. If not always the absolute perfection, then at least the harmonious coordination of all the body's features, including the face, the eyes, the back, the hair, was needed to guarantee the full "emotionality" of genuinely effective dance performance. Alertness to these features, and to the success with which they reflect the requirements—at times the very meaning— of the dancing, yields descriptions which may be pithy or elaborate, but are always expressive. Sometimes a single line can evoke an entire picture: of Evgeniya Eduardova, Volynsky wrote, "The delicate features of her snow-white face radiate gently from under her dark makeup" ("*Eunice*"); of Evgeniya Biber, "Her body is too massive and does not give the impression of the swaying of a gentle breast" ("The Russian Dance"). Other times Volynsky draws up a bill of particulars that especially annoy him, such as the impersonality of Taisiya Troyanovskaya's eyes (with their cold glance), her unchanging smile, and her heavy head (in "*Sleeping Beauty*"). Or he becomes eloquent, as he does about Olga Spesivtseva's "exquisite body structure, the exceptional shape of her leg, the gradual tapering downward of her figure and the resilience of its ascent, the amazingly straight back and her absolutely delicate and sinuous waist, the plaintive curve of her neck and resplendently playful eyes" ("Two Schools of Classical Dance"). Or he composes an entire article on a single feature, as he does in "Dancing Hands."[34]

Pervading these observations is Volynsky's original view of the dancer's body as a unique professional instrument; but let us also note that the body is decidedly female and that for Volynsky, as later for Balanchine, ballet was woman. His reviews continually assert that the ballerina's performance does not constitute a part of the ballet but is the ballet itself. Challenging the more stereotyped portrayals of ballerinas in the past, Volynsky's portraits resemble a gallery of highly individualized personalities with unique talents and complex inner worlds, thereby buttressing his argument that the revival of ballet would emerge from the multifaceted forms of Petersburg's great female dance tradition. Earlier Volynsky had laid out his basic position on the female's superiority to the male when, in his extended preface to the 1909 Russian edition of Otto Weininger's controversial *Sex and Character,* he claimed: "Woman is less differentiated than man, more integral and unified in her polarly contradictory elements, and therefore her very sexuality is not a self-contained, predatory force but something complex, simultaneously corporeal and spiritual. . . . And as the inspirer of art, of thought, of life, as the object of all religious cults and the central figure of the greatest artistic creations, has she not already disclosed that mysterious essence of hers, which is responsible for her genuine ideal semblance?"[35] Precisely at this time Volynsky transferred this "ideal semblance" to the world of ballet and discovered that the art of dance is woman's most natural arena. And from the ancient worship of Greek goddesses to Volynsky's modern cult of the female dancer, the path is straight and unambiguous, even if there is an occasional detour to the art of a performer whose work technically falls outside the sphere of ballet but who represents exquisite femininity in motion (as we learn in Volynsky's writing on Isadora Duncan). The physical and emotional center of each production, the ballerina transforms dance movement into dream; upon her hangs the effect and meaning of the entire piece.

In descriptions whose expressiveness virtually leaps off the page, we see how the ballerina embodies the special object of Volynsky's veneration, the center of his aesthetic fascination. Before us spring up, in Dobrovolskaya's words, "the fast-moving, passionate Pavlova, soaring above the ground; the miniature, refined Preobrazhenskaya—the very poetic embodiment of music; Kshesinskaya —crude but captivating any hall with the charm of her personality; the poetic, elegant Karsavina."[36] Pavlova was Volynsky's unquestioned favorite, certainly among the "older generation," and the standard by which he judged everyone else. Though she had left the Maryinsky in 1908, before Volynsky began writing about dance, Pavlova did appear there during his tenure as ballet critic, and he composed several impassioned pieces for each of her performances. Her presence is as palpable when she is not the subject of his review as when she is, whether in a past performance Volynsky had not personally witnessed or when being compared with the dancer under review (such as Elizaveta Gerdt or Elsa Vill). Yet it was to the younger Spesivtseva, "the weeping spirit" who was the incomparable and final prerevolutionary Giselle (Volynsky's favorite ballet), that the critic devoted his most inspired writing: he exalted her long neck and face, the tautness of her legs, her dignified beauty, the grace of her posture. And although by late 1923 Volynsky had begun to cool toward her, Spesivtseva's departure to the West after the 1924 season dealt him a blow from which he never recovered. Nor, incidentally, did he recuperate from another trauma the same year, the tragic death of the young dancer and new star in the Russian firmament, the partner of George Balanchine whose talent both men greeted with equal enthusiasm: Lidiya Ivanova. For the one, Ivanova embodied the exemplary academic ballerinas of old on whom he had pinned his final hopes for the rebirth of classical dance in Russia; for the other, she signaled the emergence of innovative possibilities in the interpretation of choreographic art, new directions for classical dance movement.

The brief, intense relationship between the venerable critic and the up-and-coming choreographer sheds light on the final phase of Volynsky's career, when, with increasing stridency, he attempted (unsuccessfully) to create ballet in his own image. The two men breathed the same air of excitement and ferment that pervaded postrevolutionary Petrograd's dance atmosphere; both were nurtured by the same Russian soil in which the art of animated form had flourished for over two generations, but which currently seemed to be stagnating. How full of approval and expectation was Volynsky for his designated successor to Boris Romanov, whose "Dance of the Buffoons" he had earlier lavished with similar praise in his article "T. P. Karsavina." Concluding his 1922 review of *The Nutcracker,* Volynsky wrote: "I must mention the great success provoked by a still quite young and unusually musical artist. Balanchivadze [Balanchine] dances the buffoon with a hoop, in essence a trepak, with an energetically expressed and folksy rhythm. He stands in the hoop slantwise, in profile to the audience, and totally sparkles in the silvery design of his costume. His face is deathly pale from agitation. The youth is tall and full of wild intensity. He waves the hoop and tosses it under his feet. Then he encircles himself with it and rushes downward like a hurricane. In his day Romanov won fame for this number, but now Balanchivadze has gained the upper hand with his young, lively, and superbly disciplined talent. Several details of his trepak are full of surprise. But their forethought and complete harmoniousness with the dance's overall character force me to assume the inspiration of an experienced teacher here. Could it be [Alexander] Shiryaev? I cannot imagine anyone else."[37]

Dobrovolskaya has suggested that this teacher was probably Balanchine himself, but the point is that Volynsky's legendary critical eye had already discerned in this eighteen-year-old what would later become his hallmark traits: the keen musical sense, the intense and disciplined energy, the original interpretive power.[38] But it was just this youth's originality that felt stifled (indeed, offended)—less by the retrograde intolerance of Volynsky's criticism than by the inept conservatism of a new facet of Volynsky's activities, his pedagogy. True, Volynsky's vicious lambasting of Lopukhov's experimental *Dance Symphony* in early 1923 especially antagonized the forward-looking Balanchine, a participant in the production; but it was the critic's forays into dance instruction in his recently founded (1920) School of Russian Ballet (later called the State Choreographic Technical College) that produced the greater animus.[39] Volynsky's enterprise became the rostrum from which he could realize his dream of preaching the gospel of cultural revival, this time to a live audience. A pedagogue and orator by nature, Volynsky lectured regularly at the school (whose number grew from one hundred to three hundred in just five years) on subjects ranging from the aesthetics, ethics, and techniques of classical dance to its psychology and philosophy. Additionally, courses were offered on music theory, literary history, the artist's anatomy, the history and aesthetics of costume, biomechanics, and other subjects—all of which allowed students to come to the theater fully armed with a knowledge of culture that had hardly been the norm previously.

Through his close contacts in the ballet world, Volynsky managed to attract Preobrazhenskaya, Vaganova, and Legat (who had previously instructed Pavlova, Karsavina, Lopukhov, and Vaganova herself) as teachers. But Volynsky's sanctimoniously proclaimed mission to make "choreography . . . facilitate the emancipation from the everyday nightmares of the past" and have it become "once and for all moralistic and heroicized in all directions,"[40] besides smacking of rhetorical pretentiousness, fell pitifully short in practice. In a review which finds a 1923 recital of Volynsky's students crude and stodgy, the normally reticent (in print) Balanchine exhibits a contempt that presages his mood as he left Russia the following year, never to return. What he witnessed, Balanchine reported, "produced a stifling impression that is difficult to disavow: the press has forced us to expect from [Volynsky's] school a solution to all of Russia's ballet problems, but what we saw was the total collapse of such hopes. To have reforms one must have reformers, but in the Technical College there are none, and to the host of Petrograd ballet studios yet another one has been added— with the blaring name Choreographic Technicum—yet at its feet stands a broken trough."[41] Volynsky waited until January 1924 to counterattack, responding to the "chutzpah" of this "raw youth" ("who has begun to burn out, to become lifeless and to completely fade from the stage of the Maryinsky"), in a mean-spirited (and certainly unknowing) "going-away present," which scathingly concludes: "Choreography is saved, but where is orthography: poor Balanchine! I couldn't finish his remarks. . . . They form a kind of verbal fabric that is muddled, semi-literate, nervously shrill. . . . These poor kids! These poor analyzers!"[42]

Alas, Balanchine's words were prescient; the days of Volynsky's school were numbered, and it was forced to close in the autumn of 1925 because of its unprofitability and loss of distinguished dance faculty. Yet the legacy of that institution lives on permanently in Volynsky's remarkable *Book of Exaltations,* his most lasting contribution to the study and practice of ballet, "dedicated to the students of the school of Russian Ballet" and consisting largely of the lectures he gave there. Published in a print run of three thousand copies (and reissued after a sixty-seven-year hiatus in an edition of five thousand), the book immediately became a collector's item. And although it received no recognition in reviews or later studies, for many who knew *The Book of Exaltations* then and read it now, Volynsky's novel work contains considerable appeal. Among distinguished volumes devoted to Russian ballet technique—Liubov Blok's *Classical Dance* comes to mind—none compares with *The Book of Exaltations* in theoretical boldness and philosophical scope. For Volynsky's tome, though conceived in part as a primer (and thus its subtitle "The ABCs of Classical Dance"), transcends the category of mere teaching manual or practical handbook (such as Vaganova's *Basic Principles of Classical Ballet*); presenting ballet as a noble profession and craft, it embraces the psychology, the philosophy, the ethics of classical dance, as well as its technology and aesthetics. And in its propagation of the premise that ballet consists not only of forms but of poetic images and abstract ideas, *The Book of Exaltations* reaches the level of ideological treatise, becoming a kind of song of songs written by a passionate balletomane in a metaphorical style inseparable from the book's essential message, namely that ballet is a form of poetry.

In order to understand and write about this pinnacle of human expression one must, Volynsky implies, possess a richness of language equivalent to the nuanced subtlety that classical dance itself represents. "Volynsky," suggests Gaevsky, "to a large extent created that literary as well as professional language in which ballet criticism began to expound. In this sense *The Book of Exaltations* is also a dictionary, a lexical manual, and guidebook."[43] Again and again the encyclopedist Volynsky demonstrates an interest in the semantics and etymology of words, underscoring the profound (though unexpected) interconnectedness between the terminological and the philosophical, philology and aesthetics. Words like *apperception* and *contraposto,* not to mention the Romance roots of so many balletic terms or the Greek origins of numerous theatrical expressions (*hyporchema, orchestra*), achieve an almost spellbinding effect, though none approaches the incantatory repetitiveness and associative breadth of the book's title, the virtually untranslatable *likovanie.* No single dictionary definition fully captures the meaning of *likovanie* as Volynsky uses it. The noun *lik*—from the same root as the modern Russian word for face (*litso*)—indicates a deeper meaning or essence, such as image, and its current usage translates as "the representation of a face on an icon." Thus, in writing his portraits of Russian ballerinas, Volynsky sought to establish not their (exterior) stereotyped litso, but rather their (interior) personalized lik. One obsolete and interesting usage of *lik* translates as (church) "choir," retaining the word's current religious connotations; it also delectably connects to the Greek root for *choir* (*chor,* Russian *xor*), which Volynsky sees at the base of the word *choreography* (and which he often spells without the connecting "o" so as to stress its Hellenic origins). The more widespread appearance of *lik* comes in the verb *likovat',* "to rejoice," "to triumph," recalling the transcendent rapture felt during a church service performed by a choir and connoting a higher, exalted state of being. In his usage of *likovanie* Volynsky fundamentally introduces a neologism, combining the various senses of joy, ecstasy, worship, exultation, and not least of all uplift—all possessing the crucial sense of raising and soaring above. For these reasons, the word *exaltation* seems maximally to capture all the complex coloration of Volynsky's intentions in his hymn to the sublime art of dance.

No thinking about classical ballet in Russia has ever been expressed in such elaborate language, so rich in metaphor and lofty in tone; no description of the mechanics of dance contains quite the polemical fervor or comprehensiveness of approach as one finds in *The Book of Exaltations*. Its pages not only consist of material dealing with the distinct features and forms of balletic movement but also contain short prose poems, from two to five pages in length, with such titles as "Earth and Sky," "Elevation," "The Clock's Chimes," "The Ballet Libretto," "The Ballet Master." In "Myth and Fairy Tale" Volynsky reimagines the role of the ballet master as an independent force and creative visionary in choreographic art; in "Male Dancing" he reinstates respect for the artistic possibilities of the danseur's role, which he accuses Petipa of undervaluing. In other pieces, such as "Ballet" and "Verticality," Volynsky reveals his penchant for declaiming as fact that which flows from his spiritualistic imagination, steeped in the tradition of Kantian idealism. Often ignoring the concrete data of observation or the demands of materialism, a practice which acquires special poignancy against the backdrop of the pending onslaught of rigid Soviet Marxism that was beginning to permeate all facets of Russian life, Volynsky's criticism is not beyond subordinating historicism to an ecstatically perceived idealist (counter)utopia, wherein reigns his original, highly subjective, dreamscape of ballet. *The Book of Exaltations* often makes less sense as an explanation of historical reality than as a moral vision: the origins of ballet have nothing to do with antiquity, and the balletic forms and positions Volynsky traces to ancient Hellas recall Greek vase painting as much as theater, frozen sculpture as opposed to scenic spectacle. This mystical union of past and present, this fusion of two loves—Greek antiquity and ballet—stems rather from Volynsky's long-held antipathy toward materialism and his escape into a visionary idealism of which he had long dreamed. An earlier-formulated belief that "only idealism—the contemplation of life through the idea of the spirit, through the idea of divinity and religion—can explain art," properly orients us to the conceptual framework of Volynsky's *Book of Exaltations,* as it does to his previous writings on literature, philosophy, and fine arts.[44] As noted above, Volynsky fervently opposed Lopukhov's venturesome *Dance Symphony,* yet this title applies remarkably well to his own unconventional work, which is nothing if not a qualitatively new hybrid creation filled with poetic forms that exceed the limits of traditional writing on ballet. An unorthodox creation rigidly orthodox (and deeply flawed) in its understanding of, and loyalty to, Hellenism as the single spring from which serious modern dance must flow—yet another of the numerous paradoxes that characterize Volynsky and his work.

The metaphysical quality of pirouettes and entrechats? Or, to quote Gaevsky, "Prophecy and ballet? Oracles and battements, tendu, the first position of the legs, the second position of the arms, grand plié . . . ?"[45] Odd though this combination may (and at the time did) seem, it fits centrally into Volynsky's premise that art is fundamentally mythopoeic, and that dance in particular contains and therefore must recapture what to him were its classical, mythical roots. Obsessed with the sensual and erotic and with favoring discontinuity in the dance line, Volynsky's much-despised modern ballet ignored what he believed was the exquisite geometry of classical dance—its "Apollonian . . . certainty of form."[46] Clear lines, clean edges, and precise rhythms; a severe and exact style that moves straight upward to the vertical—all of this assumed mystical dimensions for Volynsky and reflected a mind-set deeply influenced by the symbolist outlook. Such dance, which the Russian ballet needed constantly to achieve, reflected the striving of the heroic will toward heavenly beauty and moral perfection: it plumbed the mysteries of the ancient past to which modernity is still tied. All this in turn allowed for the possibility onstage of miracle—the miracle of transforming the merely mortal and human into the eternal and divine. Many can argue that in trying to provide such a theoretical foundation for Russian ballet—awaiting, as Gaevsky puts it, its "second coming"—Volynsky too narrowly stressed the classical, too inflexibly, and misguidedly, interpreted the "Apollonian." But it may be more productive to contemplate the fact that this same impulse toward Apollonian myth attracted Balanchine and resulted in his groundbreaking *Apollon Musagète*. And after reading *The Book of Exaltations,* it is hard to imagine that it was not Volynsky but Stravinsky who wrote the following: "I am thus brought face to face with the eternal conflict in art between the Apollonian and Dionysian principles. The latter assumes ecstasy to be the final goal—that is to say, the losing of oneself—whereas art demands above all the full consciousness of the artist. There can, therefore, be no doubt as to my choice between the two. And if I appreciate so highly the value of classical ballet, it is not simply a matter of taste on my part, but because I see exactly in it the perfect expression of the Apollonian principle."[47]

Curiously, the publication of *The Book of Exaltations* signaled both the high point and the nadir of Volynsky's position in Petrograd dance life: the critic's private mythology of ballet's magic kingdom, of dance as an art that occasionally seems to have been more imagined than observed, could not withstand the public realities that threatened it. So stung was Volynsky by Spesivtseva's departure that in his magisterial swan song to ballet she receives no mention.[48] His closest friend and soulmate, Nikolai Legat, losing out to Lopukhov (despite Volynsky's strong support) as director of the Maryinsky, had emigrated in 1922, and all hopes of his return were dashed when in 1925 he defected to—of all places—Diaghilev's troupe, where he taught for a year. The loyal Vaganova moved over to teach at the famous School on Theater Street after Volynsky's institute shut down. And in late spring 1924, Volynsky lost his job at *Zhizn' iskusstva* to the young critic Alexei Gvozdev, so irritating had his presence become. And, of course, there was the frightening reality and crushing inevitability of Soviet life itself: shortly after Lenin's death in January 1924, new and competing mythologies—the worship of the everyday over the empyrean—began taking hold, culminating, symbolically, in the renaming of "Peter's creation" ("Petra sozdan'e," to recall Pushkin's *Bronze Horseman*) as Leningrad.

Volynsky carried on, though he retreated to his scholastic world of research, withdrawing irrevocably from the bustling realm of cultural life to which he had devoted the past forty years. Shortly before his death of heart failure on 6 July 1926, he completed his ambitious study on Rembrandt, which still exists as an unpublished typescript in his Moscow archive. That Volynsky should have been working on this project during his last years seems appropriate—like the widely criticized Rembrandt in his late phase, the uncompromising Volynsky also realized that fidelity to aesthetic principles far outweighed any recognition he might win. And the often subdued colors and somber moods of the Dutch master conformed to Volynsky's current, albeit expertly disguised, frame of mind. For beneath his frenetically active exterior there lay private despair. Shortly before he died, Volynsky movingly wrote an autobiographical sketch, which contains the following: "I look onto the street from my window under the roof, and I am filled with sickening indignation over everything. I reach for the newspaper, and it falls from my hands. There is not even a place in my soul for ridicule because there is absolutely nothing to jest about. I'd cry over the situation, but my eyes are dry from bitterness. . . . My soul wants to escape and hide somewhere under pure skies, where one can live and breathe."[49]

No sky was purer, no life more engaging, no breathing more inspired than in the world of classical dance. For this perpetual outsider, who often viewed himself (and was himself viewed) as the wandering Jew, the Don Quixote, the Quasimodo of contemporary Petersburg artistic life, the resplendent beauty of ballet served as his most promising entrée into the enchanted realm of high Russian culture. And it is more than probable that Volynsky's extravagantly formulated musings about female balletic art may derive as much from (frustrated) erotic pleasure as from intensely felt aesthetic delight. To be sure, the road was long and often painful from the boulevards of shtetl Ukraine, where the Jewish girls "whose unswerving gait with its sprightly step in the Jewish style haven't the slightest hint of graciousness in their mannerisms," to the luminous elegance of Petersburg's prima ballerinas, whose Slavic beauty the assimilationist establishment critic longed to possess.[50] But Volynsky made the journey and left a written legacy that has been unjustly neglected. Those who agree with Edwin Denby that "a dance journalist's business is to sketch a lively portrait of the event he is dealing with[;][h]is most interesting task is to describe the nature of dancing . . . [and] to be enlightening on general questions of theater dancing, its heritage . . . and to awaken interest in dancing in intelligent readers," will admit that Volynsky's ballet criticism occupies a very special place in that genre.[51] Often controversial and wrong-headed, Volynsky's opinions reveal unflagging respect for the high purpose of balletic art, treating it not as an ornament or a merely decorative feature of civilized society but rather as the pinnacle of cultural achievement. The style and approach of Volynsky's writing on ballet may occasionally seem outdated, but its mission to promulgate the wondrous and inspired beauty of this art and argue for the scholar-critic's role in enlightening, if not creating, dance's audience, is as fresh—and as necessary—as anything that might be written today.

Notes

Unless otherwise mentioned, original documents are from the Rossisskii Gosudarstvennyi Arkhiv Literatury i Iskusstva (RGALI) in Moscow and are cited and numbered by collection (fond), inventory (opis'), and file (ed. khr.).

1. For an extended discussion of *Severnyi vestnik* and Volynsky's role in it, see Stanley J. Rabinowitz, " 'Northern Herald': From Traditional Thick Journal to Forerunner of the Avant-Garde," in *Literary Journals in Imperial Russia,* ed. Deborah A. Martinsen (Cambridge: Cambridge University Press, 1997), 207–227. The year of Volynsky's birth is given variously as 1861, 1863 (the most widely used), 1864, and 1865. The most accurate source available claims that his birth date was May 5 (new style), 1861, for which see *Russkie Pisateli 1800–1917: Biograficheskii Slovar'* (Moscow: Sovetskaia Entsiklopediia, 1989), 480–481. For the most comprehensive study of Volynsky's life in English, see Stanley J. Rabinowitz, "A Room of His Own: The Life and Work of Akim Volynsky," *Russian Review* 50 (Summer 1991): 289–309.

2. The only previous studies in English of Volynsky's dance criticism are my "Against the Grain: Akim Volynskii and the Russian Ballet," *Dance Research* 14, no. 1 (Summer 1996): 3–41, and "The House that Petipa Built: Visions and Villains of Akim Volynskii," *Dance Research* 16, no. 1 (Summer 1998): 26–66, both of which also contain select translations of his work.

3. A complete inventory of Volynsky's published articles on ballet is available in *A. L. Volynskii: Stat'i o Balete,* ed. G. Dobrovolskaia (Saint Petersburg: Giperion, 2002), 358–379. Dobrovolskaya lists 359 separate items as follows: 270 pieces in *Birzhevye vedomosti* (1911–1917); 5 pieces in *Strana* (1918); 76 pieces in *Zhizn' iskusstva* (1920–1924); 8 pieces from various years in eight different publications.

4. Lopukhov quoted in Valeriyan Bogdanov-Berezovskii, *Vstrechi* (Moscow: Iskusstvo, 1967), 259.

5. V[adim] Gaevskii, *Dom Petipa* (Moscow: Artist. Rezhiser. Teatr, 2000), 153. Much of my thinking about Volynsky as a ballet critic has been inspired by Gaevsky's pioneering work, first in "Akim Volynskii i peterburgskii balet," his introduction to

the recent republication of *The Book of Exaltations* (*Kniga Likovanii* [Moscow: Artist. Rezhiser. Teatr, 1992]), 5–22, and later in his expanded version of this work in the chapter from *Dom Petipa,* "*Kniga Likovanii* Akima Volynskogo," 151–172.

6. Dobrovol'skaia, *Volynskii: Stat'i,* 21. Dobrovolskaya's book appeared just as this volume was nearing its conclusion, and I am extremely fortunate to have obtained it when I did for the invaluable information it provided me in the final stages of my own writing.

7. A. L. Volynskii, letter to L. Ia. Gurevich, 4 November 1887, in Arkhiv L. Ia. Gurevich, RGALI, fond 131, op. 1, ed. khr. 104.

8. Volynsky quoted in P. V. Kupriianovskii, "A Volynskii—Kritik," in *Tvorchestvo pisatelia i literaturnyi protsess* (Ivanovo: Ivanovskii Gosudarstvennyi Universitet, 1978), 61.

9. M. S. Korolitskii, *A. L. Volynskii: Stranichki vospominanii* (Leningrad: Academia, 1928), 22.

10. A. L. Volynskii, letter to N. S. Leskov, 16 July 1892, quoted in P. V. Kupriianovskii, "Iz literaturno-zhurnal'noi polemiki 90-kh godov," in *Russkaia literatura XX veka: Dorevoliutsionnyi period (Sbornik statei)* (Kaluga: Tul'skii Gosudarstvennyi Pedagogicheskii Institut, 1971), 12; Volynskii, letter to A. N. Soldatenkova, 8 February 1916, in Arkhiv A. L. Volynskogo, RGALI, fond 95, op. 1, ed. khr. 220.

11. Volynsky quoted in Olga Gerdt, "Entuziast i Romantik," *Sovetskii balet* 2 (1986): 40. The original citation is to be found in A. L. Volynskii, *Leonardo da Vinci* (Kiev, n.p., 1909), 78.

12. M. Shaginyan, *Literaturnyi dnevnik* (Moscow: Krug, 1923), 23.

13. Volynsky quoted in Elena Grekova, "Staryi entuziast," in *Pamiati Akima Volynskogo,* ed. P. Medvedev (Leningrad: Academia, 1928), 49. Many artists of this period indoctrinated themselves in Hellenic culture, and some, such as the Mir iskusstva (World of Art) painter Leon Bakst, wrote about their travels to Greece, for which see his *Serov i ia v Gretsii: Dorozhnye zapisi* (Berlin: Slovo, 1923).

14. Gurevich's statement comes from her letter to E. I. Meshing, March 1899, in Arkhiv L. Ia. Gurevich, RGALI, fond 131, op. 1, ed. khr. 55; Bryusov's remark is found in "Kniga velikogo gneva," *Vesy* 2 (1904): 67–68, under the pseudonym "Avreli."

15. From 1902 until 1917 the director of the imperial theaters was Vladimir Telyakovsky, a former colonel in the Russian army. Following the Revolution, Russian cultural institutions were in chaos until the early 1920s, when the Bolsheviks began to establish themselves firmly in power. Following some protracted wranglings, during which Volynsky supported Nikolai Legat (and Legat supported him) for the directorship of ballet at the Maryinsky, soon to be renamed the Kirov, Lopukhov was appointed to the post, which he held on and off until 1956. The old system of imperial theaters was terminated after 1917, when their overall control was put into the hands of the Soviet government.

16. Lynn Garafola, *Diaghilev's Ballets Russes* (New York: Oxford University Press, 1989), 35.

17. A. L. Volynskii, "Solveig," *Zhizn' iskusstva* (3 October 1922): 2.

18. Benois quoted in Dobrovol'skaia, *Volynskii: Stat'i,* 23. The original source is A. Benua [Benois], "Novye teatral'nye postanovki," *Mir iskusstva* (1902): "Khronika," 28.

19. With the exception of a one-page "News of the Season" in November 1919, Volynsky ostensibly wrote nothing between May 1918 and May 1920. No writing on ballet exists between July 1920 and March 1922. The fact that during the years in question, only

five pieces on Russian dance by Volynsky have been found to exist may be explained less by the dearth of performances during that time of political and economic turmoil than by Volynsky's activities in launching his School of Russian Ballet, for which see below.

20. A. L. Volynskii, "Baletnaia kritika: K. A. Skalkovskii," *Teatr i iskusstvo* 22 (1915): 185. Volynsky's claim here is not entirely accurate. Alexander Benois was writing seriously about ballet in *Mir iskusstva* as early as the first issue in 1902, adopting a quasi-liturgical view of dance which has much in common with Volynsky's views on the subject. See also A. Benua [Benois], "Beseda o balete," in *Teatr: kniga o novom teatre* (Saint Petersburg: Shipovnik, 1908), 97–121.

21. For a particularly helpful discussion of this phenomenon, see *Nietzsche in Russia*, ed. Bernice Glatzer Rosenthal (Princeton: Princeton University Press, 1986). Volynsky's statement is quoted from James West, *Russian Symbolism: A Study of Vyacheslav Ivanov and the Russian Symbolist Aesthetic* (London: Methuen, 1970), 134. The original source of the quotation is from Volynsky's article "Dekadenstvo i simvolizm" in his *Bor'ba za idealizm* (Saint Petersburg: N. G. Molostvov, 1900), 320.

22. Chulkov quoted in West, *Russian Symbolism*, 143. The original source of the quotation is from Chulkov, "Pokryvalo Izidii," in his *Sochineniia*, vol. 5 (Saint Petersburg: Shipovnik, 1912), 131.

23. Red'ko quoted in West, *Russian Symbolism*, 141. The original source of the quotation is A. E. Red'ko, *Teatr i evoliutsiia teatral'nykh form* (Leningrad: M. and S. Sabashnikovy, 1926), 35.

24. N. Molostvov, "Aisedora Dunkan, Beseda s A. L. Volynskim," in *Aisedora. Gastroli v Rossii*, ed. T. S. Kasatkina and E. Ia. Suritz (Moscow: Artist. Rezhiser. Teatr, 1992), 112. The original source of Volynsky's remarks is "A Volynskii o tantsakh Dunkan," *Obozrenie teatrov* (30 January 1908): 12.

25. One is reminded here of Balanchine's repartee with a reporter upon landing in Moscow in 1962 with his New York City Ballet company, as reported in the *New York Times* of 14 July 2001: "When their plane landed in Moscow, an interviewer in the crowd waiting at the airport said, 'Welcome to Russia, home of classical ballet.' Balanchine replied: 'I beg your pardon. America is the home of classical ballet. Russia is the home of romantic ballet.'"

26. Dobrovol'skaia, *Volynskii: Stat'i*, 29.

27. André Levinson, *Ballet Old and New*, trans. Susan Cook Sumner (New York: Dance Horizons, 1982), 36.

28. Gaevskii, in Volynskii, *Kniga Likovanii*, 292.

29. Fokine quoted in Dobrovol'skaia, *Volynskii: Stat'i*, 31. The original source of this comment is M. Fokin, *Protiv techeniia. Vospominaniia baletmeistera* (Leningrad-Moscow: Iskusstvo, 1962), 153.

30. Levinson, *Ballet Old and New*, 74.

31. Roland John Wiley, *Tchaikovsky's Ballets* (Oxford: Oxford University Press, 1985), 387.

32. Dobrovol'skaia, *Volynskii: Stat'i*, 23.

33. Fokin, *Protiv techeniia*, 153.

34. A. L. Volynskii, "Tantsy ruk," *Birzhevye vedomosti* (28 January 1913): 5.

35. A. L. Volynskii, "Madonna," in Otto Weininger, *Pol i kharakter*, ed. Volynskii (Saint Petersburg: Pospev, 1909), xxi–xxii. Compare this with Balanchine's statement in his letter of 1 August 1961 to Jacqueline Kennedy: "But woman is always the inspiration.

Man takes care of the material things and woman takes care of the soul. Woman is the world and man lives in it. Woman makes the earth into a home for man. Even in art, it is woman who inspires man. God creates, woman inspires and man assembles. I firmly believe that woman is appointed by destiny to inspire and bring beauty to our existence" (quoted in Charles M. Joseph, *Stravinsky and Balanchine: A Journey of Invention* [New Haven: Yale University Press, 2002], 25).

36. Dobrovol'skaia, *Volynskii: Stat'i*, 21.

37. A. L. Volynskii, "Mozaika postanovok," *Zhizn' iskusstva* (4 April 1922): 2. Much of what we know of the Volynsky-Balanchine relationship comes from Yuri Slonimsky's article "Balanchine: The Early Years," *Ballet Review* 51, no. 3 (1964): esp. 40–46. Toward the end of his life Balanchine recalled Volynsky with unjust exaggeration: "There was a famous critic in Petersburg, his name was Akim Volynsky. I knew him well. He was drawn to ballerinas and created a whole ballet theory out of it: that in ballet, eroticism is the most important thing, and so on. In his reviews he described how big the thighs of his favorites were, things like that" (*Balanchine's Tchaikovsky: Interviews with George Balanchine by Solomon Volkov* [New York: Simon and Schuster, 1985], 145).

38. Dobrovol'skaia, *Volynskii: Stat'i*, 334.

39. Elizabeth Souritz provides valuable information on this production, known also as "The Magnificence of the Universe," in her *Soviet Choreographers in the 1920s*, trans. Lynn Visson (Durham, N.C.: Duke University Press, 1990), esp. 65–66. Most recently Stephanie Jordan has written on Lopukhov in *Fedor Lopukhov: Writings on Dance* (Madison: University of Wisconsin Press, 2004).

40. Gerdt, "Entuziast," 40.

41. G. Balanchivadze, "Unterofitserskaia vdova ili kak A. L. Volynskii sam sebia sechet," *Ezhegodnik gosudarstvennykh akademicheskikh teatrov* (Winter 1923): 7.

42. A. L. Volynskii, "Gore mne," *Zhizn' iskusstva* 3 (1924): 13–14.

43. Gaevskii, *Dom Petipa*, 154.

44. A. L. Volynskii, *Bor'ba za idealizm* (Saint Petersburg: M. G. Molostvov, 1900), v. Along these lines, it is useful to ruminate on the description of Volynsky as ballet critic in Sholem Asch's 1929 novel *Petersburg*. Volynsky and Asch knew each other in the teens, and Asch recalls his old friend in the character of Boris Abramovich Levinstein (echoes of Levinson?), who closely parallels Volynsky's aesthetic stance vis-à-vis ballet. After distinguishing church mice, theater mice, and cabaret mice, the narrator of *Petersburg* introduces Levinstein: "In spite of its consequence the cabaret mouse lives a solitary life, wanders as if in a dream through the world of reality, and is distinguished from all other species of the mouse world by its unquenchable thirst for the aesthetic. . . . And as the cabaret mouse can find comfort for its thirsty soul only in abstract forms, it looks forward to world redemption through the ballet—in its opinion the most appropriate vehicle for the rhythm of modern life (it must be noted, however, that this particular cabaret mouse derived its scanty livelihood from the ballet, which it helped to popularise in the drawing-rooms of Petersburg by means of elegant essays" (Sholem Asch, *Three Cities*, trans. Willa Muir and Edwin Muir, vol. 1: *Petersburg* [London: Gallancz, 1934], 136).

45. V. Gaevskii, "Azbuka Akima Volynskogo," *Nezavisimaia gazeta* (5 August 1992): 7.

46. The phrase is borrowed from Tim Scholl's *From Petipa to Balanchine* (London: Routledge), 81.

47. Gaevskii, *Dom Petipa,* 169; Stravinsky quoted in Scholl, *From Petipa to Balanchine,* 93–94. The original source of the quotation is Igor Stravinsky, *An Autobiography* (1936; New York: Norton, 1962), 99–100.

48. The composer and musicologist Valeriyan Bogdanov-Berezovsky, who spent considerable time with Volynsky and Spesivtseva in the early twenties, when the three would meet often at her apartment, reported that the critic was wildly infatuated with the ballerina; yet, though Spesivtseva had him firmly in her clutches, she did not acknowledge or reciprocate Volynsky's deep feelings: "[Volynsky] was already an old man, unattractive, wrinkled, with considerably thinned-out gray hair, a slightly sagging lower lip and a penetrating glance that seemed less to photograph, than to X-ray you. . . . Next to the incomparable beauty of Spesivtseva he produced the impression almost of a Quasimodo. Yet it was precisely thus. His love was passionate and powerful. . . . He was tormented by her, he tried to get closer to the object of his adoration . . . he tried to evoke her interest in him" (*Vstrechi,* 255–257).

49. A. L. Volynskii, "Moi portret," typescript dated 12 January 1926, in RGALI, fond. 95, op. 1, ed. khr. 95, 6. The piece has been published in *Minuvshee* 17 (1994): 280–292.

50. A. L. Volynskii, undated letter (from the mid-1890s) to N. M. Minskii, Arkhiv Z. A. Vengerovoi i N. M. Minskogo, Institut Russkoi Literatury, (Pushkinskii Dom), fond 39, op. 1, ed. khr. 361.

51. Edwin Denby, "Dance Criticism," in *Dance Writings,* ed. Robert Cornfield and William MacKay (New York: Knopf, 1986), 534.

I

Reviews and Articles

Dance as a Solemn Ritual

T he ballet season has begun with *Swan Lake,* in which the young ballerina Tamara Karsavina performed twice. The public is clearly interested in ballet, and among various segments of the Petersburg population word is spreading about the talented artists who are appearing on the ballet stage. For anyone following the fate of the European theater, this phenomenon is cause for enormous joy. It shows that a society exhausted by the prosaics of ordinary words and gestures has instinctively begun to search for an answer to several new conceptual interests in the design of balletic dance. So-called classical dancing, with its special forms, from the alpha of ballet, pointe, to the head-spinningly complex and elementally captivating fouetté, constitutes the focal point of the enormous wealth of plastic ideas whose true substance remains unexamined and unsolved. In ballet literature from Jean-Georges Noverre to Carlo Blasis to the present day, there has not been one attempt at making sense of this vast mosaic of forms or at parsing them and explaining in a comprehensive, sustained, and logical way their conceptual thematics and the full variety of their intellectual and emotional features. And yet there is not a pas without a thought behind it—or, to put it more accurately, every pas in ballet, because of its combination of lines and movements, carries with it a specific idea from the world of the soul and the imagination, which at times ascends infinitely over its trivial content, as this content is set forth in the libretto. There is a component of feelings and moods here that cannot be translated in any other way than in dance: on pointe or demi-pointe, in gently languid arabesques, in the finest fabric of chimerical adagios. When the idea of ballet is expressed in simple language, the current attraction to it will become clear. This attraction relates not to ballet's plot, which in most cases is mediocre; not to its music, which is almost always irritating by virtue of its simplicity; not to the vulgar apparatus of its stage sets and costumes but rather exclusively to the dancing itself and to the marvels of its plastique—its harmonious movement—and the brilliant illusion of its forms. We don't always acknowledge this with complete comprehensibility, but it is so. Dance is beautiful in and of itself, but when such powerful talents as Anna Pavlova and Mathilda Kshesinskaya [Mathilde Kshessinska] or such perfect classical ballerinas as Vera Trefilova swirl onstage, or when Olga Preobrazhenskaya [Preobrajenska], with her enormous sense of rhythm, gives herself over to the silent music of movement, the phenomenon of dance arises before us in all its genuine magnificence. Passions without any clamor are heard through the mechanics of forms, which magically replace one another onstage. The quivering of flight, the whirlwinds of double and triple tours, the boundless enthusiasm of the technically almost unfathomable fouetté—a whole new world unfolds before our eyes grandly, delicately, and in the glow of a kind of higher mathematics of correctness and charm.

And the dancing of the corps de ballet, the one and only Russian corps de ballet! A certain uncomplicated dance figure, repeated dozens of times and reproducing the general scheme, acts on one's delicate nerves with the richness of individual nuances that are peculiar to the corps de ballet's male and female dancers. And it is impossible to tear oneself away from this beautiful spectacle, musical in concept and harmoniously symmetrical in its construction. Of course, solo dances and the dances of the corps de ballet are rarely connected to one another by a unity of mood and idea, but I am now speaking of the corps de ballet as a set scenic force, which future reforms will have to raise up considerably. Here is where the movements of the dancers, all the while pre-serving the discipline of classical technique as they weave and unweave, strike us with their self-control and absence of any hurriedness or tension; there is not the slightest constraint among the contiguous or juxtaposed pairs who are dancing together or opposite one another. Everything is strictly in place, mea-sured, firm, and in harmonic accord with the rhythm and tempo of the music that flows from the orchestra. If the ballet finds the moral substance that naturally belongs to it, if all that is unnecessary and arbitrary is discarded from it—all that divertimento rubbish which turns the serious art of dancing into cheap entertainment for an unexacting public—if, finally, the sickeningly ba-roque quality of the theater in general undergoes a restructuring, then a new place will be given to the corps de ballet, perhaps a new orchestra, and its dancing will immediately gain in its significance and its unique importance.

From the corps de ballet emerged the soloist and, with him, the entire ballet, as previously the actor was born from the Greek chorus; and from the lyric and rapturous dithyramb in honor of Dionysus arose—as indicated by Proclus*—the dramatic dialogue and the dramatic scene. And for all the imper-fections of contemporary ballet stagings, it is impossible not to feel as one sits in the theater that when the corps de ballet is dancing (a corps de ballet, by the

---

*A fifth-century B.C. Greek philosopher.

way, that in Petersburg possesses enormous strength) a theatrical phenomenon of the highest order and significance is unfolding before us. In a reformed ballet Pavlova will dance against the background of a single large collective idea of this art, like a harmoniously developing, melodious, and gripping emotion, and Karsavina—the essence of the purest femininity—will rise for one poetic second like a gentle puff of smoke from the corps de ballet masses and will immediately hide and melt into its stormy waves. One must remember that the form of dancing and its idea constitute one inseparable whole, that ballet's substance is determined by its classical design, that the regeneration of ballet on this basis is possible only under one condition: there must exist a normal and judicious atmosphere in which the entire canon, the whole gamut of movements peculiar to the human body can be displayed. From the form of balletic dancing, which, fortunately, has not yet been routed by the barbarity of ignoramuses of the old or the new aesthetics, one must proceed to its possible themes. Otherwise stated, the choreographer's work requires a poetic sensitivity not only to the design of dance but also to those conceptions which might enrich and inflate it. The entire flesh and blood, the very essence of future dance, revolves around this.

If the form of ballet is ideal, then it follows that its theme must have a similarly ideal character. It is impossible to transmit anything ordinary, or any kind of prosaic combinations in this form, because the essence of ballet—dancing on pointe with feet turned out, this entire gleaming fantasy of poses and movements—is totally unnecessary here. Prosaic needs do not require any artificial movements for their expression. For the resolution of simple and real problems on the level of movement, the ordinary use of our extremities is sufficient without any pretension to refined stylization, with the blunt walking on the heels—toes forward—in the Hottentot* style. Here ballet develops along the same line as verbal speech and musical conceptions. If transmitting ordinary things in poetic form seems comical to us, if we cannot help but laugh with Tolstoy at the pompous rhetoric of the old opera with its gushing fountains of endless melodies,† then it is also impossible not to see as foolish the inappropriate application of the precious jewel of choreographic poetry to themes that deal with our everyday troubles and cares. This is why the so-called dramatization of ballet, in the contemporary sense of this word—so elementary and trivial—must in the most disastrous way be reflected on that which is the most vivid and brilliantly eternal in it: the fantasy of its forms. This dramatization

---

*A reference to peoples of southern Africa, known less pejoratively as Khoikhoin.
†Volynsky is doubtless referring to Tolstoy's scathing critique of opera, ballet, drama, and symphonic music in his iconoclastic aesthetic treatise *What Is Art?* (1896).

needs to reduce the fantasy to a minimum, to distort its Olympian features and curtail the marvelous fullness of its self-contained mathematicalness.

Such dramatic ballets as, for example, *Eunice* and *Egyptian Nights,* by the young but already coarsely inflated and unenlightened ballet master Mikhail Fokine, show how instead of pure elements of dance we have things that are supremely mediocre and untalented precisely because they lack what is most important and necessary—the constantly vacillating play and magical beauty of balletic form. We don't see the fantasy of an exceptional creator of the stage, in the exact sense of this word; instead we see a person who has combined dramatic pantomime with the ideal goals of balletic art. These are variations of dances on themes taken from the everyday routine of life, and thus in their essence these character and genre dances, though they occasionally show passion and personality, undoubtedly lack the mysterious sparkle of great, otherworldly thought. There is no delirium of exalted ideas that modern-day Greeks, looking back at the sublime art of their ancient tragedians, call Apollonian obsession, Apollonian enthusiasm. Fokine should present his pantomimes or such conceptually faultless and bold pieces as the *Polovtsian Dances* from Alexander Borodin's *Prince Igor* outside of ballet. But for balletic creation in its new lines and directions, he lacks a lively, poetic imagination. Here we need the outstanding talent of a modern ballet master who has accumulated various bookish and journalistic words; we need a new Noverre, a Noverre of a new intellectual epoch, of bold and inspired strivings in the kingdom of dreams and in the unbounded spheres of contemporary mythology, who divines the variegated crystals of holy liquids and utopias.

Balletic dance is necessary for life's myth, as Aeschylus and Sophocles understood this word. That which lies within man, beyond the deceptive cover of his three-dimensional aspirations and ideas, that which his heart deeply feels and which is approximately transmitted in the comprehension of his abstract thought is what we need to call his mythological essence. This essence is perceived more widely and more subtly in the world of ever newer ideas that are being introduced by the organic and historical development of individual people and the popular masses. But it is not only perceived and unraveled in its ideal content through our brain; it itself passes into life, constantly bursting into it with streams of radiant revelations that create what we usually call art. Art is based on myth. It springs out of it as from its eternally spiritual kernel, becoming more complicated and enriched by the hues of everyday life and by the accessories of historical reality. Refracted in the diversity of life's phenomena, art exudes the majestic tendencies of its living soul and inner truth, which is at the same time the truth of man's religio-philosophical, social, and plastic consciousness in the given stages of its moral and intellectual growth. Art and myth are always inseparable.

The diverse forms of balletic dance are the living language of our ideal and mythological essence. Broken into parts and sparkling in each detail of the complex kaleidoscope of our life, this ideal essence of man demands for its expression nothing supernatural and exclusive. In every feeling a mythological moment is present that is transmitted by the harmonious movement of ballet. The Olympic gods are only the outer reach of the ideal likenesses of the ancient world, and the dancing of ancient Greece—in Dionysus's orchestra or on the sacred road from Athens to Demeter's temple in Eleusis*—was nothing other than the graphic and passionate representation in plastic forms and signs of that which burned within. The religious pulse of the entire nation was communicated by the sacred rite of dance. It was filled with euphony and rhythm in the tragedies of Aeschylus; it boiled and foamed with the naturalistic technique in the dramas of the satyrs,† which, alas, have not entirely come down to us; it splashed with the spurts of mirth and laughter in the comedies of Aristophanes. Clement of Alexandria‡ speaks of this religious rite of dance. It is even heard in the philological structure of Greek speech, in which there passes the strictest boundary between words that express our ordinary everyday movements without any distinct rhythm and tempo and words that are intended to reflect the poetry and plastic form of the myth of the human soul and of history, divested of its random external coating. This is the way it used to be and always will be. The mythology of contemporary humanity must also be presented by the solemn ritual of modern dance: in the movements, both monumental and tender, that are concealed in the body and soul of every living individual who has not permanently distorted and perverted his or her ideal image. These new forms of modern dance are already taking shape and swarming before our eyes because, more and more clearly through the fog of mistakes, weakness, and delusions, the great myth of the contemporary historical moment is emerging. It is enough that a small stone be thrown into this element of ideas and light for these vital and marvelous forms of the new movement to crystallize definitively and permanently so that the new solemn ritual of dancing may begin.

And so, for the rebirth of modern ballet that has come to us from Italy and France, what is necessary is not the dramatization but, I would say, the mythologization of dance, in the deepest meaning of this word. Dance itself, with

---

*In ancient Greek drama, the orchestra was where the chorus danced. Eleusis was the site of secret forms of worship (which became known as the Eleusinian Mysteries) in honor of Demeter, the goddess of the hearth and sister of Zeus.

†In productions of classical Greek drama, a trilogy of tragedies would be followed by a satyr play, which presented a comic, usually obscene treatment of the same themes.

‡The second-century Athenian Clement was one of the most famous scholars of the early period of Christianity.

its complex figures and designs, should neither flounder nor fail in its poetic stylishness and ideality but on the contrary reveal itself even more unrestrictedly than before, more freely, richly, and variegatedly, to confront new intellectual and spiritual phenomena. In the sphere of movement, the individual beauty of balletic dance, which inexhaustibly develops from within its own self according to the intended law of ideal technique and the infinitely diverse impulses and tasks of musical rhythm, befits irrational myth. To dramatize ballet would be to reduce it to pantomime.

When one speaks of ballet today, one has in mind Russian ballet, with which the entire world is occupied. The Italian press recently noted with great sympathy the budding talent of Karsavina and Pavlova, who in a short time have acquired a wide-ranging popularity. But one cannot say that the interest elicited by Sergei Diaghilev's entrepreneurial activity has had a particularly beneficial influence on ballet's development or on the growth of its artistic forms and talents. It is impossible to observe any new and serious trends in Russian ballet, and everything that has been done in this field over the past years not only is far from perfect, it at times produces the impression of cheap gymnastic exercises in the style of Isadora Duncan, which do not deserve serious critical attention. What is worth keeping an eye on in the Petersburg theater, ignoring the sentimental vulgarity of the old subjects, is the dancing of the ballerinas, the soloists, and the corps de ballet. We brush aside the unbearable cacophony and the vulgar motifs of the orchestra but follow with delight the dancing cascade of forms in which there is a unique beauty that is not connected to either the text of the ballet's libretto or the cheap music of the old composers. How sad that such an exceptional talent as Trefilova has left the stage. Her dancing was the genuine embodiment of the brilliant fantasy of the old ballet in faultlessly pure form and sober clarity reminiscent of Pushkin's verse. Just now, when for the future growth of ballet's poetry one needs to engage in the study and critique of her form and her inspired, palpitating sculpture, it is especially appropriate to lament the disappearance of this first-class ballerina from the contemporary stage. She has taken with her the secret of perfect dancing, which operates through means that are unique only to it. With the delicacy of her execution, which produces a magical impression, we have a coherent discourse of movement that is elegant, harmonious, and sinewed. The alternation of forms that arise one after another is as quick as lightning. And there is nothing superfluous from other areas of art and from realms that, though not belonging to ballet, are still somehow connected to it, such as expressive drama. That's the nature of her dancing. To transfer this magic of plastic images into the language of the intellect, we have an eloquent marvel in the area of speculative aesthetics, an exposed riddle of mute but lissome beauty—a marvel of the highest culture and the loftiest and most indispensable intelligence. And it becomes immensely sad when one thinks that not only Trefilova but Pavlova as well has abandoned serious balletic work. I fear that in her wanderings on European and American stages, her enormous talent, if it is not totally vulgarized, will lose something of the spontaneous energy and passion that made her so wonderful only a few years ago.

Pavlova's dancing lacks Trefilova's lightness, but for that reason what fire and passion we find in it, and how much genuine pathos and inspiration is expressed with such balletic taste and tact. She flies across the stage like a whirlwind, and if her encounters with the floor, firmly on her toes, seem occasionally cumbersome and strained, if at times she indulges in something taken from the realm of dramatic pantomime, she for all intents and purposes always remains a remarkable balletic talent in the strict sense of the word. For Fokine's productions, with their feeble inventions in dance form, Pavlova is too important, too full of balletic traditions, too, I would say, saturated with the angst of stormy and passionate movement. She is great for pantomime and sufficiently smart, sensitive, and fresh not to blend with the elegant routine of the old ballet that no longer produces any impression.

I won't say anything now about Kshesinskaya's talent. Like any powerful artistic force, she has her committed supporters and die-hard opponents. Kshesinskaya stands at the center of the entire legend of Russian ballet, and it is not surprising that her name evokes strong passions. I shall also not speak about several other notable new talents who are making their first steps in ballet but who promise much for the future, such as Karsavina. One needn't rush to judgment about fledgling talent; one should watch and wait. Ballet is not dying but growing. And along with it grows that which lives and reveals its powers in the atmosphere of the current historical moment, under the sign of new ideas, in light of a new mythology. We are witnessing the growth of new solemn rituals of movement, language, and sound.

—"Sviaschennodeistvie tantsa," *Birzhevye vedomosti* (18 September 1911): 6

"Coppélia"

With its fundamentally dancelike rhythm and tempo, Léo Delibes's music can't help but act infectiously on a ballet artist. His mazurka, czardas, and waltz in act 1 almost by themselves are transformed into lively human movements. But for all the distinctness of its melodic texture, for all the facility of its instrumentation—which at times creates in the orchestra the effects of a true colorist—Delibes's musical creation is nonetheless not a natural background for genuine classical dancing. Dispersing into a variety of acoustic themes that have no connections among themselves and that, though vivid, lack inner substance, the music provides an occasion only for a series of divertissements that have no connection to the libretto. Character dances alternate with classical dances without any rational continuity. And if the former, given the distinctive rhythm of the orchestral melody, seem natural and appropriate, then the latter produce the impression of cold designs which operate outside the atmosphere of the given music and act upon the eye solely by the charm of their pattern and lines.

How much inferior in this sense to Tchaikovsky! In his ballet music, despite a certain sugariness and sentimentality complicated symphonic ideas never cease to ring and palpitate, from which the beauty and wonder of balletic dance emerge almost by themselves. With such music the technique of complex movement, which is so unlike the chaotic motion of real life, stops seeming like the inert mechanics that are essentially accessible to everybody. Reflecting one of the beautiful phantoms of our heart, the music here lightly and naturally intertwines with the classical dancing, which is as ideal as the music itself. Thought that words cannot capture, shielded by a cloud of thrilling mood, rises before our eyes coated with something unusually alive and alluring. In motion and sound, which are transformed by stylization, thought acquires the vividness of poetic hallucination and materialized wonder.

What is beautiful about the music of *Coppélia* is only that which is uncomplicated and does not require the art of classical ballet in the strict meaning of the term for its transmission. Thus, the waltz of jealousy in act 1 produces an extremely gentle impression. The conventional salonlike lyricism which sounds quietly and tenderly, the coquettish caprice and anger that are transmitted in a beautiful, gently wafting melody—all these constitute an unmatched motif for dancing onstage. For a lyrically talented ballet dancer this is a moment of creativity and poetic inspiration. Unfortunately, I have to report that neither Elena Smirnova nor Elsa Vill, who performed alternately in the role of Swanilda, created anything outstanding in this waltz. As a ballet dancer Smirnova is too heavy. She overcomes complex choreographic difficulties with obvious struggle, and this creates a discouraging impression onstage. Her dances on pointe could be heard in the farthest corners of the Maryinsky's enormous hall, and her pirouettes seemed like gymnastic stunts, behind which could be felt a strong will headed toward the breaking point, which yet lacked poetry and inspiration. Her arabesque is nothing more than imitation without little of the firmness, aplomb, and fading of the figure and pose in which the supreme ecstasy of the dance mood is transmitted. An uninterrupted succession of balletic steps without a breathing spell or meaningful pause works on the eyes like a needless bustle, elevated to the stage through an actor's willfulness. Delibes's waltz completely disappears in Smirnova's execution precisely because the elegance and lightness of rhythmical movement that are required here are absent in her crudely realistic and strained art.

In Vill's execution the waltz produced a far more subtle impression. The dancing of this young and talented soloist contains a great deal of captivating freshness. She playfully flits across the stage, obviously experiencing the joy of a fast-moving, devil-may-care push-off to her leaps. She doesn't quite have the temperament for complex classical variations and adagios, but in the uncomplicated and colorful quasi-balletic dances she is able to evoke amusement and good cheer in the audience. A joyful rhythm bubbles and boils in her strong body. Almost out of the hall's line of vision, Vill nonetheless "with her quick little foot beats her foot"* in order to release that dancelike musical figure quivering in her soul. It is a charming and purely balletic talent that does not soar particularly high but is vibrant and lissome. And yet Vill dances Delibes's waltz too affectedly: it is exaggerated in its salonlike melancholy and delicacy. She is more agreeable than Smirnova in this dance, but a completely different form of talent is needed here, one that burns with fragrant hues and the purest female eroticism.

Another marvelously conceived dance in act 1, the Ballad of the Ear of Corn, also perishes. Both dancers fail to cope with their task: to show their art in the dancing of the adagio, in which everything—every movement, every detail—is in the limelight, hinders or assists the creation of the whole picture. The music fades: one's visual interest is so great, and it so completely consumes our attention, that nothing is heard. Our hearing ceases to resonate for the time being. The dancer, supported by her partner, twists and untwists her pliant torso. Now she rotates in an intangibly quick pirouette, now she lifts herself on one toe and freezes with arms stretched in the air like an ancient statue. She soars over the stage amid waves of the lightest vapor, with an expression of ecstasy on her face. In the adagio the whole art of classical dance comes together; many years ago Blasis considered it the ballet dancer's best and most critical test. In Pavlova's dancing it was possible to see in our own time a genuine adagio in all its beauty and perfection. The plastic tableaux, which had frozen as if outside time, outside its headlong flight, replaced one another with a silence and unflickering quietude of astonishing charm; and after such marvels of balletic art it is almost not worth speaking about Smirnova's and Vill's

---

*A quotation from Pushkin's verse novel *Eugene Onegin*.

adagio. They did what they could but just weren't up to the poetry of this kind of dancing.

In the second act Smirnova and Vill, after the naive pantomime of the doll's resuscitation, first danced the Spanish dance and then the Scottish one, though despite their efforts to create an impression of something fiery, they performed tritely.

The last act of *Coppélia* constitutes an alternation of an infinite variety of divertissements, which lack any intimate connection with the ballet's overall conception. Here the dancing of Dawn, the Prayer, and Hymen, performed by the best talents of the corps de ballet—among whom is the young talent Elizaveta Gerdt—radiated freshness and beauty. Agrippina Vaganova danced the Work variation with exquisite delicacy and resilient virtuosity. The ballet concludes with a coda, the general dancing of all present. The individual features of the separate variations that had already appeared before our eyes were combined and deleted with complete and obtuse indifference. The sense-less chaos of onstage movement that lacked any inspiring and connecting idea was echoed in the orchestra by a tempest of sound, hideous in its conven-tionality, in which nothing remained of the rhythmic design or vivid sculpture of its chief musical themes.

Everything was dispersed and scattered in the cold emptiness of purpose-lessness and lack of ideals.

— *"Koppelia" Birzhevye vedomosti* (17 October 1911): 5–6.

Tamara Karsavina

"The Trial of Damis"; "The Nutcracker"

T he *Trial of Damis* is a little encyclopedia of old dances, primarily of French origin, that, thanks to Alexander Glazunov's marvelous music and a performance by the Maryinsky Theater, creates quite a lively impression. Elements of classical dance are barely observed: everything is reduced to the noble elegance of salon entertainment with a minimal system of plastic figures in the balletic sense of the word and a maximal play of affected poses that relay the sweet lyricism of aristocratic flirtation. Before the spectators' eyes pass such dances as the courante and the musette,* which are not complicated in their technical composition and do not demand any special lightness or flight. Pointework is totally absent. The ballerina's shoe is visible, and its heel, which flashes in the uncomplicated figures of the Spanish saraband or the French farandole, constantly reminds us that in this courtly form one should not seek the grand moral fiber of classical choreography. Here we have the style and not the stylization, the rhythm and the poetry, of intimate experience in the irreproachably cultured form of this famous epoch. If the astonishing music of Glazunov were to stop for one minute, these dances would lose all their charm. They are born from private sentiments, whereas classical dance gives birth to music, requires from it the richest symphonism, and guides it. Developing out of a person's great need to show his mythological essence, his second, inner, godlike "I," in the gesture of movement and to transform and dissolve his materiality into something distinctly ideal, each feature in classical dance is full of abstract content and timeless thought.

Classical dance is, first and foremost, theatrical dance—unconnected to any particular kind of real life and speaking only to the universal imagination; it is hierurgical and religious in the deepest and freest meaning of the word, as were, without exception, the theatrical dances of ancient Greece. But the elegant varieties of the French salon minuet, which are insignificant in their structure, personified from without, and rather vacuous in their content, are the natural property of society halls or modest stages: they are hardly designed to be dealt with critically in the area of ideas. Moreover, in the intimate dances created by the genius of French society, a certain coloratura of movement is required as an example of the glorious arabesque of classical dance, but with a tinge of inevitable prettiness, a ceremonious bowing and glissades terre-à-terre, a gentle hint of elevation and large-scale theatrics in hardly noticeable flights of individual balletic steps.

The young ballerina Tamara Karsavina performed last night in *The Trial of Damis*. Her delightful gift is growing before our eyes: in two or three years she has won the passionate sympathy not only of the Russian public but of the European one as well. I have had the chance to read the extremely sympathetic comments about Karsavina in Italian reviews and the genuine raves about her in English and French writing. On her first trip to Paris, Karsavina succeeded so much "in having the public fall in love with her" (in Alexander Benois's expression), that Anna Pavlova, who was dancing after her, had to make every effort to achieve her deserved success. Of course, Pavlova did achieve it because there is no audience in the world that is not aroused by the genius of her

---

*The courante is a dance that originated in the seventeenth century; the musette is an ancient French folk dance.

balletic art. But there is something uniquely edifying in the skirmishes of a fledgling talent with one of such enormous power and consummate structure.

Such a struggle always anticipates the birth of something that does not yet exist in art: a new line of creativity that will one day have its brilliant apogee and reach its definitive, radiant pinnacle. Karsavina immediately became conspicuous alongside Pavlova, but her talent flourished and expanded in an atmosphere of different aspirations and amid other ideological horizons. From her art, which we still cannot say is perfect, flows a gentle ecstasy—something devoutly pure and beautiful. She delights and moves. Even the touch of dilettantism that one sometimes feels in her dancing gives it a special and charming innocence, which usually disappears with increased experience on the stage. Karsavina's talent is that of a classical ballerina in the strictest sense of the word. In spite of all the obvious, and even somewhat excessively soothing, femininity characteristic of her dancing, the ideal technique of classical choreography, at its most difficult and most intricate, shines with beauty and perfection in her execution. She dances incomparably on pointe, and her pirouette is extremely beautiful. The lyricism of ballet she transmits with a faultless virtuosity that puts her alongside Pavlova and Kshesinskaya, despite the enormous difference of these talents in every respect. Her adagios are picturesque, more in the pictorial than in the sculptured sense: amid the ritual of innocently pure and solemn movements, the ballerina's thin face—with its delicate tan and the dark halo of her hair—burns with inspiration. There are moments when you don't see the dancer at all. You see a woman in the glamour of an irresolute but truthful sensuality, rooted to the spot and melting in the emotions of her soul. The sensitive European public at once submitted to the charm of Karsavina's thrilling femininity.

The Petersburg public, much more virtuous than its Parisian counterpart, in spite of its reputation for intolerance loves Karsavina and her dancing with a heartfelt tenderness. Too sophisticated for the democratic masses, this artist is completely inaccessible to the Frenchified crowd that occupies the orchestra and not so long ago ruled the fate of the Maryinsky Theater with an iron fist. That powerful hold has been decisively broken by the storm of new currents in the theater, and around the name of Karsavina—thank God!—no suspicious passions are seething. Her star is shining in a clear sky, higher than the dark clouds that have shrouded the artistic fame of other, more fiery talents.

In *The Trial of Damis,* Karsavina dances the paspieds, the musette, the farandole, and the variation of Camargo. If these dances had been transferred to the intimate stage of the Hermitage,* to the beautiful setting of the halls of

---

*The Hermitage contains a small performance space, known as the Hermitage Theater, in which ballets and other musical performances are still given today.

the palace, they would have acquired greater plasticity and musicality. In the cold baroque of the Maryinsky, on its enormous stage, Petipa's ballet miniature loses its refined, salonlike color.

The ballet lacks the choreographically primitive charm that is maintained in the strict proportions of space, rhythm, and decorative hues. The dance space is too large, the environment lacks an effectively constructed evocativeness. Karsavina dances to the precise melody of the orchestra, but often the movement of her legs—despite the clarity and chic of her fine pas de bourrée and the distinct swish of her glissade—disappears in the lifeless emptiness of the enormous theatrical shed. Karsavina should dance among the new sets painted by Benois's delicate and intelligent brush and then we would have a genuine re-creation of the style of Watteau and Lanceret* in a choreographic version illuminated by the picturesque colors of a talented artist.

In *The Nutcracker,* the charming ballet of Petipa and Tchaikovsky, Karsavina dances the Sugar Plum Fairy magnificently and beautifully. In the pas de deux of the second act the artist rises on pointe and, holding her body absolutely rigidly, glides across the stage with awe-inspiring lightness: such is the gripping illusion of choreographic conjuring. In actuality, the artist is standing on a delicate little beam, a narrow stick that floats imperceptibly even to the sharpest eye. But the public thinks that the ballerina is gliding! The entire *Nutcracker* is filled with wonders, and the charming marvel of the frozen pose created through the rhythm of an inner mood and life that gives the illusion of movement gently fuses with the endless mosaic of other beautiful marvels of this cheerful ballet.

Evgeniya Eduardova dances the Spanish dance, Chocolate. Elsa Vill and Vasily Stukolkin, those talented comics of the ballet stage, perform the Chinese dance, Tea, with infectious joy. Vill is charming. Her caricature is at times unequalled. If I am not mistaken, her feet are the daintiest and smallest, and how they sing and laugh! In the dance of the clowns Boris Romanov demonstrates the marvels of his fabulous technique; no one can perform it with such passion and genius. The public unanimously applauded the artist not for his talent, which is evident, but for the technique of his daring leap and his playing with the glittering hoop, which crumples in his hands like a ribbon and doesn't disturb anything.

Between the first and second acts of *The Nutcracker* the artists of the corps de ballets, all in white tunics, dance the Waltz of the Snowflakes to Tchaikovsky's melodious music. Against the background of the forest young beings,

---

*Antoine Watteau was a French painter (1684–1721) of the Rococo period whose major influences were the commedia dell'arte and the opera ballet. Eugène Lanceret was Evgeny Lanceray, a graphic artist associated with the Mir iskusstva group.

beautiful and aerial, are amusing themselves. They whirl lightly, like fluff from the mouth of the wind god Aeolus, fusing with the melody and rhythm of the music; and if you allow yourself to divert your attention momentarily from the instruments, it can seem as if it is they who are singing and playing. The music imperceptibly flows into the harmonic forms of the movement. But the movement itself is marvelously transformed into the most delicate tune for the inner ear. Our visual and acoustical impressions are fused perfectly together.

—"T. P. Karsavina. *Ispytanie Damasa; Shchelkunshchik,*" *Birzhevye vedomosti* (24 October 1911): 2–5.

Mathilda Kshesinskaya

"Swan Lake"

A mong the figures of contemporary ballet on the Maryinsky's stage, Mathilda Kshesinskaya constitutes a phenomenon of exceptional interest. Her name enjoys great fame, her talent—unusually brilliant and of the highest caliber—is recognized by all. Not only the technique of her dancing, for which nothing is too difficult, but its overall character produces a captivating impression: it excites and holds you in complete thrall, even though ballerinas of no less talent are dancing alongside her. She is always at the center of the action onstage. Something great and unique to her alone carries her artistic personality to extraordinary heights; it obliterates all fear and makes moot all competition and comparison with other forces in the ballet world. She is so much an individual, so unlike anyone around her, that in criticizing specific details of her choreographic art one does not for a moment lose the sense of the unfolding charm that characterizes her original talent overall.

There is no beautiful contour to her arch. A ballerina almost always dances facing the public rather than showing gliding, sharp, sparkling lines of action in profile. Despite a blindingly beautiful take-off, Kshesinskaya's dancing appears to be concentrated on one spot and thus creates the impression more of a frozen frame than of an inspired quivering of forms to the melody and rhythm of the music. One doesn't feel psychological impetuosity in her flight. Moreover, this dancer does not depart from her toes, dancing all the time on pointe without either getting tired herself or fearing that she's tiring the spectator. Yet Kshesinskaya's dancing is nonetheless a real marvel of balletic art with which no clichéd or routine dancing can compare. She is more a brilliant orator of choreographic ideas and forms than an artist in the direct and exact sense of the word. Kshesinskaya is able to jolt the audience as no one else on the contemporary stage can by the purely external power of her art. Her dancing glistens with hues of rhetorical brilliance. It is not the rhythm of ideal form, restrained and precise, that has pride of place here, but her hyperbolism, her inspired exaggeration and her sweep—wild, crude, and brimming with passion.

Pavlova speaks and sings in her dancing. Her ebullient personality, full of fire and light, does not prevent her from magically falling into the flow of the pure modern figures that flow one from the other with the same lightness and naturalness with which ideal similarities of mathematics conceptually grow and silently combine in their beautiful dance of elevated and looping truths.

Kshesinskaya prophesies. She lifts herself on her toe with such force, with such external passion, that the idea of slightly touching the floor, which is supposed to introduce an animation of gentle universality into the dance movements à terre, completely vanishes in her impulse to perform a movement or gesture on a colossal scale. With her plane foot, almost without an arch, her dancing—always on pointe—produces the impression of a smooth flow of forms, with no springy bending of the knee as she moves and no gentle gracefulness and quivering surge on the surface, and it does so via the powerful and solemn play of its vigorous hues. Her double and triple turns create a genuine whirlwind on the stage. In her solo dancing, in her leaps en avant, which are accompanied by the most difficult cabrioles, Kshesinskaya is unmatched. At such times her face, with its features of captivating intellectualness and special and magnetically attractive beauty, and its clever and penetrating eyes, which are never silent, reflects the poetry of the elevated moment. The mute plasticity of this remarkable artist, who breaks all the canons and patterns of classical discipline, is full of an inner noise and murmuring, full of thunder, full of great and subtle ideas that are transmitted to the public and ignite it with unheard-of ecstasy. Sometimes the public, seized by the rhetoric of her choreographic genius, gives way to the uncontrollable pathos of the impression it has experienced, forcing Kshesinskaya to repeat several times a variation she has successfully performed. And with this the dancer's enthusiasm grows and grows.

The fouetté is the apogee of Kshesinskaya's choreographic art. Left foot on pointe, the dancer with her right foot makes complete circular rotations, not stopping for a second and not moving from her place. Essentially uncomplicated, the step, which consists of two tempos that are usually done to the accompaniment of unpleasant, marchlike music, takes on interest and significance only in connection with the quantity of rotations the artist produces. The frequent, rapid, cyclical movement, without interval, produces an indissoluble whole that is not communicated by words, and an irrational impression of momentary frenzy that can be beautiful. Konstantin Skalkovsky writes that the talented ballerina Emma Bessone did fourteen fouettés in *The Harlem Tulip** and Pierina Legnani in another ballet (I don't recall which) did thirty-two circular rotations without moving an inch from her place! Kshesinskaya, who certainly dances no worse than Legnani, is her equal in the virtuoso execution of this difficult choreographic trick. She does it to perfection, with a mastery that transforms it into a genuine masterpiece. This is the power of an enormous stylistic talent, which gives a final picturesque touch to legendarily bold dancing. The artist here allows a gradually increasing quivering of dance rhythms into the movement, which, fixed on one point, produces an impression of something endless. Without an internal movement, which has the same irrational character, the fouetté would be merely a trick of mindless acrobatics. But in Kshesinskaya it is the finishing touch of her remarkable art, her rhetorical art which exists on a large scale.

In *Swan Lake,* Kshesinskaya dances Odette, the queen of the swans, and Odile, the daughter of the evil genius who looks like Odette. In scene 2 of act 1[†] there is a lovely grand pas of the swans in which the artist provides a series of beautiful and vivid poses. She radiates here with unusually painterly pirouettes avec attitude, which create the impression of inspired, statuesque figures. Kshesinskaya dances the final coda of this act in a rapid tempo through which the passionate burning of her inner pulse is vividly conveyed.

In act 2 Kshesinskaya dances a pas d'action. Her pantomime is superb. In contrast to the dancing, which does not always harmonize with the requirements of artistic measure, the play of her expressive face is of the most refined artistic quality. Nothing is superfluous, and there is no affectation. This is not a demonstrative, naively graphic pantomime that substitutes for words but rather the natural and simple kind that reflects emotion as it accompanies speech, no matter how it may be expressed. In Kshesinskaya's acting there is no conventional balletic pantomime: with the stylized gesture of her hand she is able to say everything that is necessary, everything required by the lyricism of the moment by means of the inner pathos of a balletic figure. In *Esmeralda,* for example, the artist's dramatic talent reaches extraordinary heights in this regard. I have never seen a more poetic expression of speechless love and jealousy on stage. The gypsy cries without tears by means of her darkening eyes. You feel her heart as if it is beating right next to you. In the artist's eyes, raised to the sky,

---

* *The Harlem Tulip* is a fantastic ballet in three acts, choreographed by Lev Ivanov and Petipa. The Italian dancer Emma Bessone danced the main role at the Maryinsky in 1887, and again in 1890–1891.

† Volynsky refers throughout to a three-act version of *Swan Lake* in which the first scene with the White Swan (act 2 in the four-act version) is scene 2 of act 1, the Black Swan scene (act 3 in the four-act version) is act 2, and the White Swan finale is act 3.

there is so much faith, so much intelligence and resignation, that you unwittingly, boundlessly surrender to the scenic illusion of a suffering girl, though everything around her in the last act discourages you with its stiltedness. Once when I pointed out this beautiful moment in Kshesinskaya's acting to an aging lover of ballet (not a balletomane), indicating the pious harmony of her marvelous genuflection, the cantankerous old man told me that the artist was copying the divine Zucchi.

Alas, I have not had the occasion to see that famous ballerina on stage. But I can explain such a lapse of critical judgment about a first-class dancer only by personal ill-will: a huge number of mediocre people and an enormous amount of envy and spite surround Kshesinskaya's powerful talent. A similar storm at one point raged around the glorious name of Mariya Savina when her talent was in decline. However, we can say with certainty that Kshesinskaya does not imitate anyone. Such complete creativity, with its vividly individual stamp, develops from within, inspired by free thought and personal artistic temperament.

Several moments in act 2 of *Swan Lake,* the throwing of the body into her partner's arms; the quick and bold head-spinning fouetté—which, by the way, was performed this time without the usual animation, and not even completely correctly—elicited tumultuous ovations from the theater. Here Kshesinskaya was at the height of that elevated and genuinely classical art, in which the rather crude Italian conceptions, brilliantly recast in the style of French exaltation, become the instrument for transmitting the real and ideal movements of the human soul. In her par terre dancing, just as in the dancing constructed on the ethereal rhythms of elevation, Kshesinskaya, for all the imperfection of the structure of her legs, must be recognized as a great artistic figure of truly phenomenal power.

I still have not said anything about the other performers in *Swan Lake.* The ballet is beautiful in its music and dancing, produced by such virtuosos as Petipa and Ivanov. There are some charming character dances in the ballet (the Venetian dance, the Hungarian dance, the mazurkas), in which the best talents of the corps de ballet and most gifted soloists participate. Olga Fedorova danced the czardas to the thunderous applause of the entire hall. The young artists Evgeniya Biber and Evgeniya Lopukhova performed the Spanish dance —but about this aspect of Tchaikovsky's beautiful ballet I will write another time. I want to devote my current article to Kshesinskaya's first appearance in one of her best parts. She has just returned from London, where she performed in the same ballet (in Diaghilev's company), apparently with great success. But, frankly speaking, European criticism is not distinguished by any particular authority on questions of balletic art. In the ensemble of the Maryinsky Theater's entire troupe you can see more vividly the brilliance and significance of such talents as Kshesinskaya, Pavlova, Trefilova, and Preobrazhenskaya. When examining the enormous amount of newspaper and magazine articles on the topic of the Russian ballet abroad, with rare exceptions have I found in them nothing but commonplace generalities and an inflated style.

—"M. F. Kshesinskaia (*Lebedinoe ozero*)," *Birzhevye vedomosti* (5 December 1911): 6.

Schumann, Ballet, and Fokine

R obert Schumann's *Carnaval* is one of the greatest pieces of piano music of the nineteenth century. It is full of psychological moods, to which the musical elaboration adds a special brilliance. With its diversity of features and themes, which are enveloped in individually drawn characteristics, and with its elegant poetry of musical and rhythmic designs, the whole work produces an impression of incredibly subtle thought whose contours are lost and blurred in the disturbing vagueness of a generally dreamy meditation. Everything is here—emotion, spirit, playfulness, and a weaving of apparitions as frail and fragile as a dream.

The musical scene that opens *Carnaval* is repeated in the final victory march of the Davidsbündler* versus the Philistines. The epic, statuesque rhythm essentially contrasts with the rapid motif of the waltz at the end. The lyricism emerges and sounds like the psychological musical basis of the entire work. And immediately after the Introduction comes the small but apt reference to Pierrot.† Weighty octaves depict all his awkwardness; there is no dance rhythm here at all. To the loser Pierrot, Schumann juxtaposes the happy Harlequin. His musical character is given on the level of gentle youthful yearnings. The composer notes that the emphases must be conveyed with unusual softness. And although Harlequin dances, spins around, and does light jetés, the dance material inserted into this part of *Carnaval* is nothing more than a kind of concentration of rhythmical chiaroscuros. It is important to note and follow this. The figure who stands at the center of *Carnaval*, and who naturally gravitates toward comic ballet, is full of fire and din in his purely

---

*The Davidsbündler were members of an artistic society (Davidsbund) invented by Schumann as a foil to the conservative music establishment.
†Pierrot, Harlequin, Columbine, and Pantalone are all figures of the Italian commedia dell'arte, celebrated during the Venetian Carnavale and similar festivals.

musical portrayal, which is outside the physical aim of dance. In dance the poetic flavor of this portrayal disappears.

The Noble Waltz follows.* Schumann himself was a brilliant dancer. We find in his letters witty descriptions of female traits of dancing. Fixed on the page is the astonishing charm and flavor of lovely, intimate, and far from theatrical ball dancing. The rhythmics are of a refined type and express a richly sexual character. I would go even further: there is a certain premonition of Tristan's longings here.† In the radiant dance tune there are undeveloped and unexplored motifs that gravitate toward the kind of thought and spirit which seek an inner rather than an outer language for their poetic realization. Although marked in tones of pure choreography, this moment also emerges in an obscure haze of psychological mood.

Finally, the main patterns of this poem for piano begin to take shape: Eusebius and Florestan.‡ In Eusebius's treatment everything is based on the melodic factor. The rhythmics of the movement provide no motifs for dancing. And the alternation of passionato and adagio completely removes the musical image of Florestan from the milieu of dance concepts in general. The echoes of Schumann's *Papillons* here have the character of subjective lyricism.

The motifs of vague but sweet dream spread from all sides. Coquetry and flirtatiousness are noted in the character of the sharply etched musical phrases. If one wants to convey this character in dancing, one inevitably winds up with caricature, which is not what Schumann had in mind. In Schumann this pungency is softened by supplanted associations, which are as delicate and fine as smoke. The graceful echo of the sketch Coquette and the musical riddle of *Carnaval* follow. Mysteriously thrilling sounds accompany the idea of the beloved woman and continue throughout the entire piece. And the internal motif of love prepares for the appearance of the butterflies (*papillons*). They have just gnawed through their cocoons and rush though the air on their fluttering little wings. The musical score projects a tenderly nightmarish and ethereally spiritlike movement that is so rapid and so "beyond feasibly" fleet that physical figures are really out of the question here.

The chaos of the auditory elements of the Dancing Letters also seems

*The score of *Carnaval* is divided into sections—the Noble Waltz, Coquette, the Dancing Letters, and so on—whose names were kept by Mikhail Fokine and Léon Bakst, who put together the libretto, with the exception of "Pantalon and Columbine," which they renamed "The Encounter of the Lovers."
†A reference to the medieval legend of Tristan and Isolde, in particular to Richard Wagner's opera about the tragic lovers.
‡Eusebius (representing the thoughtful side of Schumann's nocturne) and Florestan (representing the compulsive side) along with Estrella and Chiarina complement the commedia dell'arte characters and were added to the ballet by Fokine and Bakst.

impossible to arrange in any external form. The sketch is filled with the poetry of E. T. A. Hoffmann, which lies outside the sphere of classical scenic choreography. One must stress the pitch and character of the sounds—not their rhythmic design but their internal symbolism. But this task is totally beyond the means of dance.

Chiarina and Estrella are the music parallels of Eusebius and Florestan. A mood of radiant emotions and distinct lyrical moods sounds in Chiarina's composition. Estrella provides a particularly clear musical opening into the soul of Schumann. At one time, when his relationship with Clara Wieck had been clarified, he was overcome by a passionate feeling toward Ernestine von Fricken,* the prototype for Estrella. The element of psychological agitation predominates in her character, expressed in the harmonic scheme of the entire sketch. Especially typical is the abruptly terminated end of the piece and the constantly returning dominant, which gives the whole melody a tint of turbulent perplexity.

The Encounter of the Loved Ones is one of the best parts of *Carnaval.* After the delicately sounding introduction, which depicts the far-off noise of the carnival's gaiety, comes the duet. The dance is only a vision of a far-off reality. The whole matter is in the cooing of love and the distinct advancing of the canon that constitutes the main part of Reconnaissance. Toward the end there is an echo of the same drone of the bell and the noise of the carnival somewhere far off beyond the horizon.

Pantalone and Columbine are emerging and diverging musical lines, delicate, light, and capricious, among the most charming components of sound but with no dance rhythm whatsoever. After that there is a certain Germanization of the romantic lyricism. The German Waltz is Schubertian in style. The intimacy is evident. And suddenly there is the image of a man, enigmatic and legendary, who has sold his soul to the devil, the image of Paganini. In this spot Fokine mounts Harlequin's dance, with pirouettes, batteries, and entrechats six. Yet Schumann notes here something more deeply intellectual: an inclination to brilliant technique as something self-contained. Harlequin's leaps reduce the significance of the magnificent idea of this moment.

Recognition, Promenade, and Pause take the piece to the end. It concludes with marvelous material. We have before us the satirical treatment of seventeenth-century dance with a sharp challenge and the revolutionary battering ram raised for the destruction of the old sacred cows. The scene from the Introduction alternates with the theme of the victory procession in ternary

---

*Von Fricken was a friend of Clara Wieck, Schumann's wife-to-be. She captivated Schumann when he first met her in 1834, and the two were briefly engaged until he broke it off.

meter which provides a particular acuteness and combat fervor to the appearance of the young protestors. Schumann wanted to emphasize the closeness of the introductory and concluding sections of the poem. The gaiety of the carnival is only a detail of the picture drawn in psychological tones.

Such is the musical structure of *Carnaval* in its most general contours. Everything in it is enveloped in psychology, everything in it develops by means of juxtapositions. The brilliant Harlequin is juxtaposed with the difficult Pierrot. The dreamy and ecstatic Eusebius appears next to the tempestuously romantic figure of Florestan, in whom everything is fervor and flight. This is a graphic reflection of the bifurcation that passed through Schumann's own soul and was imprinted in remarkable musical images under the strong influence of Jean-Paul Richter.* Chiarina and Estrella are a new contrast of antithetical female characters of striking power and brilliance. Finally, the human art of Chopin is juxtaposed with the devilish genius of Paganini, and the Noble Waltz is contrasted with the German Waltz, from which emanate the sentimental dream and reverie in the Germanic style. Everything is built on contrasts. Everything speaks to the mind and ear. The music of *Carnaval* is tied to the subtle sound of the piano and the most delicate harmonic lyricism. Nothing here can or really wants to be materialized in a visible image. As I have said, dancing would only consolidate a fluid idea that provides nothing specific but rather suggests a whole world of mood.

Nevertheless, Fokine wants to pour this light, this air, and these silvery, heavenly mirages into the form of ballet. A man of large-scale temperament, but insensitive to the ethereal and imponderable values of poetry, the young ballet master has essentially provided here a rather superficial pantomime. To talk of ballet in this case—whether old or new—is absolutely out of the question.

In Schumann's *Carnaval*, as in Carl Maria von Weber's *Invitation to the Dance*, the music and psychology are everything. And the dancing—whether it be semi-character, genre, or tap—is only a detail, only a symbolization via gestures of mute pantomime of what the piano already expresses completely. Indeed, one is left feeling extremely unsatisfied by Fokine's pantomime. He has taken something great and brilliant, Schumann's Romanticism, Schumann's metaphysics, Schumann's entire fantasy, and broken it into bits, scattering it across the stage in pantomimic bric-a-brac. But those baubles float like splinters on the performing embankments of the boundlessly beautiful sea of sound. There are no real dances. And they are not necessary on the broad scale of ballet.

---

*The German novelist and humorist Jean-Paul Friedrich Richter (1763–1825), more commonly known by his pseudonym Jean-Paul, enjoyed enormous popularity during the early decades of the nineteenth century.

In Fokine's interpretation Harlequin is the inspirer and initiator of the revolutionary march against the Philistines. His affair with Columbine is situated in the center of the pantomime. But what occurs between the Introduction and the concluding part of the piece is no more than the mystical alternation of illusions and carnival apparitions. The spirit of Schumann himself casts its spell and tugs at everything in the symbolic bifurcation of Eusebius and Florestan. According to the overall scheme as well as the historical data certified by the composer, they were the first and foremost Davidsbündler.

Karsavina plays Columbine. In a skirt with light flounces covered with beautifully drawn little cherries, a light kerchief, and nightcap, she makes a most charming genre picture. With Harlequin she dances several pas de deux on pointe that are delicate, soft, and graceful. Her childlike gestures are affecting, and her sparkling, delicate feet, shod in dark shoes without heels, are beautiful. Vera Fokina and Evgeniya Biber mimic Chiarina and Estrella.

On *Eunice* and *Chopiniana* next time.

—"Shuman, balet i Fokin," *Birzhevye vedomosti* (20 February 1912): 4–6.

"Eunice" and "Chopiniana"

Mikhail Fokine's production of *Eunice* belongs to his first attempts in ballet. Rumor has it that the young artist himself understood the glaring failures of his production, and thus it would be hard to criticize the piece completely since its own creator has already repudiated it. Criticism needs to be well-disposed toward unquestionable talent. Moving artistic talent through analysis onto the correct path, criticism must not discourage it with cavils and catcalls. The general public, which all meaningful newspaper and magazine writing has first and foremost in mind, understands everything with crystal clarity without superfluous words: it hasn't confused the new *Eunice* with the old *Giselle*. The public has learned not to value dancing à la Duncan with a dash of classical ornamentation particularly highly. It clearly sees the confused chaos of Fokine's compilation of balletic themes.

Vera Fokina dances Acis, and Karsavina Eunice, and I have heard that Pavlova danced Acis at the first performance. I can believe that it was good. Before Fokina, I saw the young and talented dancer Liudmila Schollar do Acis, and I liked her dancing a lot. If it weren't for the harshness of its overly expressive posing, as if Schollar were deliberately challenging the public; if it weren't for its shamelessly obvious flirtation with Isadora Duncan's intimate choreography, Schollar's dancing would have been totally beautiful. The extraordinarily lovely structure of her legs and body, which exude energy, gives her movements on stage their unusual distinctiveness. Fokina performs the role of Acis not badly, but too fussily and heatedly, with sharp angles rather than distinctly flowing lines. That is why, for all the inner passion one feels in it, Fokina's dancing confuses more than it arouses, it ill-disposes more than it positively disposes.

It makes little sense to speak of Karsavina as Eunice. The role of the slave girl is not for her gently lyrical and dulcet talent, which lacks passion and drama. Evgeniya Eduardova, Anna Ivanovna Fedorova, and Olga Yakovleva dance the Egyptian women, and Eduardova looks beautiful. The delicate features of her snow-white face radiate gently from under her dark makeup. Her figure is draped stylishly and tastefully: a real dancing beauty from Egypt!

Chopiniana is a charming miniature and Fokine's best creation on the Maryinsky stage. But I don't see any new directions here. This is the same classical dancing that has been around for centuries, which no passing business enterprises and cheap, fashionable trends aimed at the wasteland of public indifference can destroy. There are in classical dancing great ideas and the genius of classical culture, which has survived the storm of historical havoc and transformation. Unfortunately, Fokine's miniature is presented onstage with insufficient expressiveness. There is no adequate partner for Karsavina, no Nijinsky. One senses a great talent in the young dancer Petr Vladimirov [Pierre Vladimiroff], but he's got a long way to go to reach Nijinsky. Nijinsky's dancing overflows with color, reminiscent of the color of the Umbrian primitives. And their most subtle notes contain a certain mystery. Karsavina's partner should return to her!* As should Pavlova to dance the mazurka. Vaganova dances with extraordinary elegance, but Pavlova dances better.

—*"Evinka* i *Chopiniana," Birzhevye vedomosti* (8 March 1912): 4.

---

*Vaslav Nijinsky had been dismissed from the Imperial Ballet in 1911 because of "immodest" apparel (he refused to wear the customary trunks over his ballet tights) and spent the remainder of his career in the West.

Errors of Creation

On "Papillons" and "Islamey"

P *apillons* is one of Schumann's earliest works. Despite being somewhat musically unoriginal, it is still interesting for its vague reveries and subtle experiments in pianistic sound. This is a sketch for the future *Carnaval*. In the poem's alternation of light and dark motifs we note the psychological bifurcation—the concept of Eusebius and Florestan—which is one of the fundamental bases of Schumann's early work. As in *Carnaval* certain shades and acoustical secrets envelop all the musical images. There is no genre picture here whatsoever.

The first waltz of the piece is completely Schubertian in its melodic design. Schubert and Jean-Paul Richter were the main figures in Schumann's early creative development. Schubert's radiant image was reflected in the charming conception of Eusebius, and Jean-Paul Richter provided the poetic motif for Florestan. The quiet light of reconciliation and meekness, and the wings of the spirit hovering over the world's mysteries, delusions, and magic of daring thought—these are the elements that from childhood developed and took shape in the German composer's soul. A musical hypnosis and literary mesmerism poured from all sides into his soul and into that Romantic epoch.

Yet already in that first waltz something distinctively Schumannesque is heard, as it is plagued with a mysteriously prolonged sound. Something large and original is noted that leads Schumann beyond Schubert and Weber, beyond the first Romantics who introduced the themes of dance poems into the pianistic repertoire. They influenced the formation of choreographic numbers in his early works—the waltz, the polonaise, and various marchlike concepts. But the dance form is only a framework for Schumann, only a substructure for his constructions of sound. It is, rather, the acoustical vehicle for the manifestation of personal psychology.

We should note that in this first waltz the motif of the old Grossvaterland is heard, a naively patriarchal dance with which the free shafts of the new intellectual movement—the defenders of the new ideas and forms in music—will later wage a bitter war. It is as if we note a historical frame within whose borders life never ceases creating phenomena of the highest order.

After the insignificant number that follows the waltz there comes a small piece of central importance. Fokine heard the theme of Pierrot here, but the ballet master has unquestionably made a gross error. The octaves, noted by a heavy marcato, do not produce the impression of acrobatic gaiety. The theme itself has too weighty and too German a character. Something fantastic is heard. And the low octave reflections only embolden the feeling of something genuinely fairy-tale-like and authentically folksy, which is not bound to the absurdly clowning figure of the romantic Pierrot. According to Schumann's own directions, the comic masque of "the gigantic boot" from Jean-Paul Richter's novel *The Stormy Years of Youth* is reproduced here.

Having arrived at the ball, a youth sees among the other whimsical masquerade figures a gigantic dancing boot, which he himself puts on. In German folk mythology the boot plays a well-known role. It is sufficient to recall the "seven-league boots" that cause every German youngster's heart to flutter. Now here is a moment for creative choreography. Here one should have devised a German folk dance and placed it at the center of the masquerade. Old dances alternate with new ones. In the broad arena of folk humor a struggle of two generations seethes with the heavily, weightily, but confidently dancing honest German boot. The waltz, the Romantic reworking of the polonaise, the marchlike fervor of the rhythmic lines and musical laughter, in the area in which Schumann was Beethoven's best heir, his scherzi—here are the timbres of national revival, here is the task before which the entire absurd tragedy or, better, the clownery of Pierrot, is only street trash in the eternal beauty of the brilliantly conceived idea. Not having grasped the folk German Aryan melodies of *Papillons,* Fokine has produced a romantic buffoon, and by doing this he has made Schumann into a saccharine painter of a salon masquerade.

A polonaise filled with love, then a stormy polonaise with changing rhythms, a simple waltzlike piece, and a waltz with a purely intimate dance theme, soft and loud echoes of the gaiety of a ball—this is how the separate parts of *Papillons* alternate with one another. In the last number once again the waltz is woven into the motif of the Grossvaterland.

The historic frame of the entire work is rounded off. The seventh at the end is dispersed in the dying quiver of the piano strings. This is the most romantic and most extraordinary moment in *Papillons:* everything here is connected to the soul of the piano. To detach this ending and the sextuple that precedes it from the noble and glorious instrument is, I think, to display insensitivity to Schumann's poetic genius. Orchestration is absolutely unnecessary here because pianistic patches of light either turn into coarse instrumental lines or completely disappear from the acoustical visions which make the piece especially valuable to us.

In one of his letters (1834) Schumann speaks about the fact that in *Papillons* he used the text of Jean-Paul Richter's novel. "I adapted the text to music," he wrote, "and not the other way around. Otherwise I would have wound up with a hollow enterprise." If Fokine had looked at his task the way Schumann did, he would have subjected his music to the idea of ballet dancing and he would probably have wound up with something meaningful. He would then have utilized the profound motifs of the two struggling worlds in the national coloration of native German choreography. But instead of a lively creation, Fokine has given us something completely half-baked. First of all, there is no Pierrot in Schumann's work. Pierrot appears later, in *Carnaval.* Second, in terms of chronology and, of course, its musical character, *Papillons* precedes rather than follows *Carnaval.* In Fokine's conception the butterflies congregate on the flame of a candle brought by Pierrot into the garden after the masquerade ball! From where, I ask, does this cheap romantic nonsense, which is unworthy of Florestan's mighty fantasy, emanate? Third and finally, where did Fokine find butterflies in Schumann? They're not there! "Butterflies" are only a symbol of the winged thoughts that fly from the soul of the artist who gives birth to them with his unqualified genius.

Mathilda Kshesinskaya played one of the butterflies, but I value her enormous talent too much to speak of it in this context. By her presence she only rends the flimsy plaiting of transparent threads by which the episodes of this trivial pantomime are sewn together.

Besides *Carnaval,* about which I have already written in detail, and *Papillons,* Fokine has also staged Mily Balakirev's *Islamey.** This work was written under the influence of Chopin and Liszt in 1869, when pianistic literature in Russia was in its embryonic stages. It also constitutes a creation of the ultimate world of fantasy, in which sound and inner psychological theme are inseparably fused. The whole piece is built on two themes, with the versatile refraction not only of feeling but also of harmonic and melodic beauty. This is the true source of all intoxicating orientalisms. The basic motif is that of the circular dance, which Balakirev heard in the Caucasus. His reworking of this motif is filled with such exclusively personal emotions that it is almost impossible to imagine a public bacchanalia here. In the acoustical variations one more easily sees a single body that sings and sounds like a string in the play of different feelings, from innocent chastity to the raging but internal excitement of passion. For this complicated forms of balletic adagio and expressiveness would be appropriate.

Balakirev was drawn to orientalism not by its expression of power but by its unexplored intoxicants of musical harmonies and by the finest and most delicate lines, which are far more complex than any of the crude conceptions of the splendor of Eastern life in the spirit of the bad illustrations to *A Thousand and*

* Balakirev's *Islamey: An Oriental Fantasy,* based on Russian folk motifs, was choreographed by Mikhail Fokine and premiered at the Maryinsky Theater in 1912.

One Nights. And indeed Balakirev's piece suffers terribly not only in its transfer to the stage, with that most banal bacchanalia, but in its transfer to the orchestra, even though it is done to a large extent skillfully and ingeniously. The chaotic dancing, which lacks distinct figures and lines, only ruins the impression of this wonderful, integral musical fantasy.

Fokine has singled out the bacchanalia as his favorite form of balletic creation. His *Polovtsian Dances* are as wild as a bacchanalia. In Aristophanes' comedy, in which one needed to choreograph the cordax,* he again provides a bacchanalia. In *Schéhérazade* there is also a bacchanalia, and in *Islamey* there is a frenzied bacchanalian raging. Finally in *Tannhäuser* we have the inevitable bacchanalia. Here his bacchanalia lacks both thought and content, yet Wagner himself indicated the theme for such a dance, which Fokine should have worked out carefully. A strictly delineated theme is needed here, but there is no theme in the obstreperous dancing of Fokine's corps de ballet. The real hero of the production was the extremely talented artist Boris Anisfeld. His sets for *Sadko* and *Islamey,* in the vividness of their colors and imagination, are a major phenomenon in the world of theatrical design.

—"Oshibki tvorchestva: O'*Babochkakh*' i '*Islamee*'," *Birzhevye vedomosti* (12 March 1912): 6.

The Little Dove

"Harlequinade"

In *Harlequinade,* Olga Preobrazhenskaya is less solid than in "The Butterfly's Caprices." Given her talent, she is at her best when she is required to express intimate, personal emotion in the plastic forms of dance. If one places her alongside Mathilda Kshesinskaya or Anna Pavlova, the major features of her uniqueness come into view: that special charm of her beauty and style that makes her such a prominent figure in Russian ballet. Kshesinskaya is illustrious as a person who glows with fire. The line of her dancing, with its breakneck movements, almost always deviates from the norms of strict choreography. She need only emerge from the wings and the audience's entire attention is focused on her. Via fragments of broken, almost mangled, movement, she achieves extraordinary effects. Among ideal forms of balletic dancing a kind of satanic power gyrates, tearing asunder the harmonious connections between these

---

*An obscene dance in ancient Greek comedy.

forms and creating a whirlwind of leaps and jumps that are almost impossible to follow. In Pavlova as well everything is monumental, enormous, and luminous, and it is hard to imagine a more accurate pattern of dancing. Absolutely nothing can be added or subtracted. But for all the sharp precision of every one of her balletic steps, all her movements are filled with passion. Leaving the ground, she extends her body along a straight, almost horizontal line, with a stormy and fitful look on her face. And in the movements à terre her excitement and enthusiasm not only fail to disappear, they come across with special clarity.

From your first acquaintance with Kshesinskaya's and Preobrazhenskaya's dancing you are conscious of enormous figures, of living monuments of extraordinary stature and historical significance. Everything in them exudes genius. In Pavlova, moreover, this genius is cast into faultless, almost mathematically perfect form, and its fire flickers among the waves of movement that synchronize with the rhythm of the music. In Kshesinskaya, however, everything is disharmonious, everything flows beyond the spherical patterns of balletic technique. She throws the compasslike correctness of choreographic lines into the chaos of reveries and the vortex of emotion. Preobrazhenskaya's style is completely rococo. The small size, the short legs with slightly pudgy calves, the contours of her head and shoulders, the expression of her face, with the fervently intelligent gleam of her somewhat mocking eyes—everything in this artist exists on the scale of intimate charm. And if one were to see her outside the theater, in the hustle and bustle of the street where everything is huge and enormous, she would seem especially small, even insignificant. She wouldn't engage you, wouldn't hold you, wouldn't give you pause.

From the first sound of the violin Preobrazhenskaya is utterly transformed. Everything speaks and sings in her. Her sharp movements, which are not cast high or far, are so permeated by the beat of the music that it would almost be possible, if one weren't hearing the instruments of the orchestra, to divine the rhythm and melody of the musical accompaniment by them alone. Something small in terms of size, but full of gentle harmony, something eternally radiating with joyful little lamps flutters and whirls across the stage. Here is the poetry of personal emotion, the good-natured humor of a joke registered with feminine grace, and the depths of the most authentic, most genuine art in every turn of her body—an art that is first-class not in power but in quality. Preobrazhenskaya completes the wonderful trinity of the ballet stage, Kshesinskaya, Pavlova, Preobrazhenskaya, who, in terms of their significance and their technique, cannot be found anywhere in Europe. There is nothing monumental in Preobrazhenskaya. But no such flight exists even among the powdery rays of the golden deity who burns above us. Everything is rounded in the lines of her microscopic form. Yet nonetheless, before us is a remarkable theatrical force in the entire fullness of its own seemingly inimitable individuality. In *Harlequinade,* Preobrazhenskaya is less than Karsavina but, of course, is wonderful in her own way. In the presence of the graceful Harlequin, Nikolai Legat, who glides over her like an eagle, she seems like a little dove, fluttering across the stage in gentle movements. Holding her in the air during the transports of the second act in poses of gallant flexions possible only for Legat, her partner does not allow us to feel the slightest tension. It is as if the ballerina is as light as a feather. The adagio comes off faultlessly. But Preobrazhenskaya's variation sparkles with rare beauty. She jumps on her toes with an almost inaudible touching of the floor. Doing a gentle plié, she suddenly turns her body into an arabesque. And rising on pointe, she completely freezes for a moment with remarkably steady aplomb. Then, like down, she slowly lowers herself into fourth position on her knees. And the theater, from top to bottom, rumbles with applause.

In the first act of *Harlequinade* the orchestra performs a serenade, at the end of which the audience responds with a genuine ovation and demands an encore. The conductor rises from his place and bows deeply. At one of the recent performances, he pointed to the stage with his hand in the direction of Legat and several other dancers. But without a doubt [the conductor] Riccardo Drigo could only have meant Legat because at this moment in the ballet he is especially wonderful. In makeup that produced the impression of a satin mask he first dances and rotates in small jumps, then freezes in place, bending his torso over a mandolin. The chords flow as if they are coming from Harlequin's fingers, not from the orchestra behind the stage. And two burning eyes add the impression of heightened drama and emotion. In general, Legat performs perfectly in this act. We have before us an Italian clown with consciously caricatured movements expressing a tempestuous temperament. When Pierrette comes out onto the balcony, his hands, raised upward, describe several disconnected figures in the air. He is terribly impatient. He is waiting for Columbine. And when she appears he trembles with excitement and his hands perform movements filled with supplication. Legat's pantomime is full of life—a reincarnation of such beauty, fullness, and inner surge that the impulsive storm of applause was directed not only at the talented conductor.

—"*Golubok,*" *Birzhevye vedomosti* (18 October 1912): 5.

The Russian Dance

"Die Puppenfee"

⚜

I n *Die Puppenfee*,* Evgeniya Biber dances the Russian doll. Unfortunately, I can't praise this young ballerina's performance: it lacks the hues of Slavonic gaiety and folk color. The Russian peasant woman needs to be aroused earlier. Otherwise, though she is obedient to the magic bow, she won't break into dance straight away. Her shoulders are already shaking, and excitement heaves in her chest, but she still balks, dawdles, idles as she resists the clinging youth. And suddenly she can no longer endure it and starts to move. Her legs are almost invisible; with its proud head fixed in a braid, her body sways rhythmically; and her handkerchief shows up white in her hand. And the youth scurries about her, producing pretzels, first in a prisyadka,† then throwing his knees forward, and then tossing his legs high. The peasant woman keeps moving, sliding, and diving nearby.

The Russian folk dance must be studied now with careful attention because in the not-too-distant future the theater will deal with it fully. In order to lift the crumbled structures of scenic art from the ashes and breathe new life into it, we need to bring together the colorful mosaic of Russian dance and on that basis construct not only a folk but a national dance in the broad sense of the word. Classical dances of ancient times, no less than the movements of contemporary ballet, grew out of folk dancing. The recast folk dances came to life for theatrical religious rites in honor of Dionysus. The same thing must happen with Slavonic folk dancing. And as soon as a revolution of thought sweeps away the shaky foundations of present-day theater, work—idealistic in outlook —will immediately start on the materials of Slavonic choreography. From this native wonder, cumbersome and weighty in form, will then emerge its religious beauty and pure aesthetics. We need to guard the gold of folk dance as if it were the pupil of our eye. We must not overlook a simple feature. Everything is enormously important, for it is hard to foresee where the stream of dance symbols will spring from, where and when the column of dance idealism's

---

*Joseph Bayer's ballet *Die Puppenfee* (The Fairy Doll) premiered in 1888 at the Vienna Court Opera.
†The prisyadka is the famous Russian dance done in squatting position in which the legs are thrown forth alternatively.

smoky forms will swirl with special radiance. That is why, to return to the pretext of my current remarks, I have to say that the russkaya* in *Die Puppenfee* doesn't come off well. Biber is too heavy for this dancing. Her body is too massive and does not give the impression of the swaying of a gentle breast. Scoffing slightly at the little rolls, Biber immediately starts dancing at a rather tempestuous tempo, throwing out her feet, which are shod in totally masculine boots. She conveys her emotions, but all this is unattractive and not in the spirit of the Russian woman, in whom there is no weighty pathos. An Italian woman, dancing a tarantella, on the other hand, would flaunt her coarse cynicism. Thus on Capri, the famous Carolina grants her partner a fleeting sensation as he thrusts at the soft round part of her thigh. But the Russian woman immerses herself in purity. Her partner circles over her like an eagle, but does not dare touch her for she is a white swan. It seems to me that instead of Biber, Elena Makarova should have been tried for this role.

—"Russkii tanets," *Birzhevye vedomosti* (5 November 1912): 5–6.

"Raymonda"

A lexander Glazunov has inserted the element of symphonic movement into ballet music. It is as though he were justifying Wagner's idea that the symphony in general must be the dissolving of dance into sound. From this follows the conclusion, which Wagner himself never made, that ballet movement by its nature is merely a compression of symphonic sound. In this way the melodies of an orchestral composition, with their acoustical richness, harbor in themselves sculptural forms that provide the motifs for dancing. According to this idea, sounds in Glazunov, though they produce a far simpler impression, are joined in complex combinations thanks only to the artist's unusual skill.

Raymonda marks Glazunov's decisive step in the direction of balletic-symphonic creation. The ballet opens with a harmoniously beautiful prelude. Laconic in nature, the prelude is marvelously orchestrated. After this there follows onstage the acting and dancing of Raymonda's girlfriends. The dancing is innocent, gliding along straight and broken lines, and interwoven with the

---

* This national dance of Russia was memorably described by the writer Dmitry Grigorovich (1822–1890) in his novel *A Brief Happiness:* "He threw his head back, tucked up the folds of his coat and, swaying like a barrel that was let go in the water, began dancing the russkaya using mincing steps."

fleeting movements of the mazurka. Then comes the ballerina's entrée. Her friends have formed an oblique line and scattered beneath the flowers. Olga Preobrazhenskaya does this entire line on pointe. As the dancing continues, she gently and distinctly thrusts her leg forward, whirling and frolicking on stage. The orchestra's accompaniment here is interesting in its musical chiaroscuro.

After two mimetic scenes comes the big waltz, which is not composed in the broadly melodic manner of Tchaikovsky. The dance motif comes strikingly to the forefront. Elements of the small adagio alternate with the dance figures, the leg extended forward and the arms bent under the head. The waltz ends with the dancers in a wide semicircle. Raymonda enters the semicircle and begins her dancing accompanied by the pizzicato of the music.

Feminine in its rhythm and its girlishly youthful harmonic combinations, the music surrounds the choreographic design with astonishing beauty. Preobrazhenskaya's genius shines here. She performs her leaps with feline lightness and gracefulness and, cutting short her dance figure, she transfers to glissades in an oblique line without changing her feet, which are placed one behind the other. The pizzicato ends with a marvelous pas. The dancer crosses the stage diagonally doing jumps on the toes of one foot, doing battements with the other. When repeating this number, instead of battements, Preobrazhenskaya brings her foot back. And the musical and physical impression keeps growing with each movement without dissipating or falling apart. The dance figures are tied to the transitions of the rigorous patterns. And in the orchestra the same figures are intoned in the dissolution of sound. Only Preobrazhenskaya can fuse so completely with the music.

The scene ends with two dances that sound marvelously in the orchestra. The Romanesque is restrained, in the style of the eighteenth century. The music has a courtly character and is somewhat weighty and majestic. Agrippina Vaganova and Elsa Vill dance beautifully, with aristocratic elegance. Preobrazhenskaya performs the gentle fantasy with its broken chords. She gently extends her leg sideways to waist height and then she changes over to an arabesque with a graceful turn.

The appearance of the White Lady in the second scene of act 1 is defined in the orchestra by the juxtaposition of separate stages of scenic movement. The mood continues until the moment of Raymonda's solo. Then the orchestra begins to subside in the modulation of sound. Preobrazhenskaya and Nikolai Legat's adagio is thematically beautiful; charmingly performed arabesques alternate with attitudes. The dancing ends with two pirouettes on the left foot.

After the rhythmic, melodious waltz, with its suppressed sighs, the variations begin: two variations by Elena Smirnova and Elena Polyakova that do not add much to the audience's impression, and Raymonda's variation, which is full of difficulties. But the rotations of the whole body, which end in the wide fourth position of the legs, are full of poetry. Preobrazhenskaya does them effortlessly. She performs her movements first whirling around, then giving them up to the whim of her fantasy. The variation concludes after the dance on pointe in a straight line, with a new and delicate rotation.

In the pas d'action of the second act Preobrazhenskaya again dances a complicated variation. In particular, she does a circle of jumps with turns on her left leg, bringing her turned-out right foot above the arch of the left first in the front, then in the back; the turnout is typical of all knee movements in classical dance. She repeats this number to the tumultuous bravos of the audience, exchanging the circular leaps with dancing on pointe on alternate feet.

The main number of the third act is the Hungarian pas classique. Unfortunately, it was poorly rehearsed and comes off ungracefully. The Hungarian cabrioles, with their striking of heel against heel and with their clicking motions on the entire stage, are beyond the talents of the dancers. The character element is not accentuated by the equally typical poses of the body. But the overall adagio unfolds in the usual tempos, in the picturesque transfers of the women, and in the beautiful groupings. After the adagio come the variations. Here I will note Viktor Semenov's femininely light turns in the air. Preobrazhenskaya's variation is built entirely on dancing à terre without any particular choreographic difficulties.

At the beginning of the act the little children dance charmingly and youthfully, accompanied by the whirlwind of large leaping notes. The general coda is composed in an exuberant style. The entire third act concludes in an apotheosis of pure musical light.

—*"Raimonda," Birzhevye vedomosti* (12 November 1912): 5–6.

"Coppélia"

O lga Preobrazhenskaya dances beautifully in *Coppélia,* although the ballet in itself is old and not necessarily essential for the modern stage. Her talent, as she combines music and movement, is obvious at every turn.

The ballet opens with a waltz of passion. The simple dance on the toes, blended with leaps in arabesque and with the transferring of the body from one foot to the other, is full of gracefulness in her execution. The expression of despair in the gesticulation of the hands to convey the soul's tempest is incomparable. We observe this very brief variation with satisfaction, and it shows the artist in the splendor of her theatrical individuality. Primarily we have a dancer in the classical mold: the lines of her movements are maintained with mathematical precision, and even in combinations they provide forms of impeccable sharpness. Before us are dance patterns in the ancient sense of the word, and the physical manifestations of ideas onstage and in the beams of the footlights. And the dancing of Preobrazhenskaya's hands wonderfully conforms to the dancing of her feet. It is as if they are playing on invisible currents. I have never seen even a fleeting stroke in Preobrazhenskaya that departed from the musical line. But in the chaos of balletic forms that flicker before your eyes you always feel the special energy of her hands. They accompany her feet, relaying not an external rhythm but rather the beating of her soul, which is in harmony with the orchestra.

In the first act of *Coppélia,* Preobrazhenskaya dances an adagio with Nikolai Legat. Standing in arabesque and holding her torso for several seconds, she suddenly turns her entire body forward and sideways, bending her right arm in the air almost level to her waist. In general Preobrazhenskaya succeeds wonderfully in these poses. The change of straight lines to those that are deeply bent lets us feel the intensification of the psychological motif. Then, going off to center stage, she does attitudes, leaning on her partner. Attitudes alternate with dances on pointe and with different kinds of arabesques, concluding in a picturesque adagio. Though not rich in forms, this movement nonetheless contains several beautiful moments. The groupings with the male partners are created in lines of soft, warm sculpture.

The second act, with the exception of the comedy of the doll coming to life, gives us two dances with Preobrazhenskaya: the semi-character Spanish dance with small pirouettes, and the Scottish dance with battements frappés. The entire act continues amid the gay uproar of the doll. Here the specific dabs of color smack of buffoonery. In the fast-paced rotations of the body you continually feel the dancer's lively smile, you sense her eyes, with their radiant beams, almost laughing. Giving themselves up to the dancer's art, the entire audience laughs quietly. Glimmers of delight cross their faces.

In the third act Preobrazhenskaya performs an adagio, a variation, and two codas. The adagio begins with dancing on pointe, with the right foot brought forward in croisé. Her partner, Legat, follows her along a straight line facing the audience. Then follow the usual arabesques for the adagio (low, with circular movements repeated several times with the help of her partner) and charming attitudes, striving after the effect of a fleeting illusion. During the movement the dancer extends her right hand to her partner, then, taking it back, she gives him her left one. Her whole body is turned sideways, with her back to the audience. The adagio ends as she jumps with both feet, brought down with heel toward toe, into the arms of her partner, palms extended forward prayerfully. And in the arms of a partner such as Legat, Preobrazhen-skaya seems like a light doll.

The variation-pizzicato from *Sylvia,** Preobrazhenskaya dances alone. In the musical sense this variation, as she performs it, is a model of choreographic art. Those headlong leaps and circular sissonnes joined with the battements at the ankle, those transfers of the body onto one foot (with the other moved to the side, half-bent in the air) produced so easily, freely, effortlessly, seem, in the final analysis, more musical than the music of the orchestra. In any case Preobrazhenskaya's dancing is of a higher quality than Delibes's rhythmic creation, which is excessively vivid and flashy. The music of her movements is quiet and noble, like everything that is truly great, artistically polished, and full of ideas and inner ecstasy.

In the conclusion Preobrazhenskaya performs two codas. The first is developed by Legat. She does an arabesque, with her back to the audience, sideways, moving across the stage with quick jumps on pointe. Like a squall she rushes forward toward the wings, moving her foot along the floor with toe to heel and heel to toe. Vaganova won over the public with the same arabesque in *La Fille Mal Gardée.*

Glory to Preobrazhenskaya! Glory to her astounding talent! Glory to the genius of the work and to the music that makes her individuality a reality, an individuality that borders on magic and miracle. Only in art can one encounter such plasticity, such transubstantiation of the personal principle, such an ability to fuse oneself completely and absolutely with beauty, sound, and theatrical myth!

—"*Koppelia,*" *Birzhevye vedomosti* (26 November 1912): 5.

Vaganova's Variation

Of the three soloists' variations in act 3 of *Coppélia,* Agrippina Vaganova's offers the greatest choreographic interest. She performs it faultlessly. This variation is built on the tempos of elevation, so that when there is a slight jump it produces a beautiful impression. It begins with grand cabrioles forward along a diagonal line in deep plié, jumping with one foot beating against the other. In the spirit of the French school of classical dance, it is necessary during

*Presumably this variation was borrowed from *Sylvia* as a showcase for the ballerina, Preobrazhenskaya.

the jump that the lower foot beat against the upper one, the knees and toes be extended firmly downward, and the heel be very turned out. At the moment of the beat, the body has to be turned toward the lower foot. From these linear features of the step Vaganova does not deviate an iota. Sensitive to the movements of the violin bows, the dancer provides onstage an astonishingly pure interweaving of sculpturelike forms with the pattern of musical waves. The rhythm of her movement carries the rhythm of the dancing itself, which is detached from the symphonic elements of the orchestra.

Thus, continuing the variation with the brilliance of her technical mastery, Vaganova bourrées on pointe; again with knees firmly extended, she performs splendid assemblés, and, as she unveils her art further, creates a genuine choreographic masterpiece. Moving in semicircles in the middle of the stage, she lightly transfers her body from one leg to the other. Her configurations run and flow into one another almost imperceptibly. Finally, there are two or three sauts de basque. The extended knee is thrust forward and thus creates the upward flight and rotation of the body, which is all the time turned toward the audience. The back of the head is almost never seen, the back is straight. The variation concluded in whirlwinds—small figures on demi-pointe performed to the cheers of the audience, who demanded a repeat.

Vaganova is one of the most remarkable dancers of the Maryinsky. Precise in its take-off, perfect in its picturesque leap, able even in the most headlong movements not to deviate from the pattern of the balletic step and its geometrically fixed design, her aerial work is unparalleled. And besides her flying, with elemental jumps and leaps, Vaganova possesses both the elasticity of graceful plié and ballon, which creates the resolved chords of dancing whose beauty is picturesque. Without question her execution is always polished in her terre-à-terre style, which blows like a cold breeze, as well as in her style of airborne aspiration. And if God would enliven these gifts with a revelation from within, if he would brighten them with just one of his rays—the ray of heartfelt passion—we would have before our eyes an astonishing dancer of the Petersburg school. But one should not demand from a talented person what is impossible for her. Even the way she is, with all the inadequacies of her composition, with all her flaws in conscious moral substance, Vaganova is still a first-class artist, the premier soloist on the Maryinsky stage, the best of the custodians of the golden treasures of classical choreography at a critical moment in the decline of the great and in the searching for the new on uncertain paths. . . .

—"Variatsiia Vaganovoi," *Birzhevye vedomosti* (10 December 1912): 5.

The Tsar Maiden

A New Production of "The Little Humpbacked Horse"

ಜ಄಄಄ಣ

W ithout going into details I shall give only my overall impressions of yesterday's ballet performance. Alexander Gorsky debuted before the Petersburg public with his production of *The Little Humpbacked Horse* in a reworked form.* There is much interest and great beauty in this frank expression of emotion. Unquestionably, Gorsky is a talented, probing individual, with that large-scale touch we associate with Moscow. In the new directions of balletic art that are still only breaking through the surface, Gorsky's activity has some significance. Working with the great numbers of the corps de ballet, he does not, thank God, lose sight of the solo dances of the classical kind. In everything the thoughtfulness of an intelligent man is evident. He destroys nothing, but instead studies everything from various perspectives.

Yet like Fokine, Gorsky primarily prefers dancing by well-disciplined crowds. Thus, in the first scene of *The Little Humpbacked Horse* the choreographic action takes place in all corners of the stage, among Konstantin Korovin's sets. The groupings have no pretensions to originality, but rather smack of the simple-heartedness of the mood. The children's prisyadka, the brawl, the dance with Kusov, are wonderful. The boys drag the peasant woman, forcing her to dance. She beats them off and runs away. The Slavonic dance follows Dvořák's somewhat drawn-out music. Boris Romanov and Evgeniya Eduardova dance the russkaya. Eduardova would be totally great if she would avoid galloping with those slight jumps and instead move in floating lines without her personality getting in the way. But Romanov is incomparable. A quasi-nobleman is dancing, not a peasant. His legs are full of fire, and they move with unexpected spontaneity; there is nothing artificial in the rotations of the body. After Eduardova and Romanov's russkaya there's a new russkaya in Klavdiya Kulichevskaya's performance. This base and infernal peasant woman, as I have already written elsewhere, dances with the factory worker, herself becoming aroused, and arousing him, in plebian bravado. Turning out his heels, Alexander Orlov moves his shoulders and places his hand on his hips in a semi-circle. Evgeniya Lopukhova dances the role of the petit-bourgeois woman in a

---

* Volynsky commits a rare factual error here: Gorsky had made his premiere in Saint Petersburg eight years earlier (1904) with his production of *Don Quixote*.

red kerchief. She plays with the tip of her toe sarcastically to the accompaniment of the muddled music, a mixture of quadrille and polka.

These are the highlights of scene 1. Korovin's sets seem to appear through a prism of a fairy tale. The colors are dense, even slightly excessive. The lilac sky is too oppressive. The architecture in the background recalls Moscow; the cupolas are Muscovite, but they lack crosses. And they simply fall short. There should have been a play on the cupola's gold in the air, which is heavy with storm. The most meaningful symbols of truth are not material but the ideal ones of the theater. These simple dances—the choreographic reflection of popular life—that take place beneath the cross would then go beyond themselves and lead to the unique truths of the spirit spread over the flames of the globe without impediment or demarcation. When you convey a Russian fairy tale on stage from the perspective of the old capital city of Moscow, it is impossible to avoid a cross: it sparkles not only within the city but wherever you turn.

In the second scene, after approximately forty measures in a major key, [the curtain opens on a set with a] rumpled field of rye and trees depicted with extraordinary talent. But the scenes alternate in quick succession. The fairy tale unfolds in mimetic scenes that prepare for the cascades of dances in the following acts. In the khan's palace there are long blue carpetlike curtains. Pavel Gerdt plays the khan; his servant is played by Nikolai Legat. The khan's wives (Feliya Dubrovskaya, Antonina Belova, and others), those refined pupils of rhythmic hand movements, accompany Olga Fedorova's dance, performed to the accompaniment of Glazunov's music with interruptions and continuations of dancing, but the conclusion of the mimetic scene is accompanied by Cesare Pugni's old music. The dance itself is not very successful, but Fedorova has a beautiful look. In such trifles her talent is electrifying. She concludes her dance by jumping upward with both legs, toes together.

In the next variation, the Dance of the Frescoes, Anna Alexandrovna Fedorova, Olga Fedorova, Elena Smirnova, and Liudmila Schollar participate. The frescoes, made on flaps, are exposed and lie on the nearby piers, facing inward. The animated beauties come out on stage. Smirnova puts her best foot forward: she certainly doesn't conceal the power of her legs! Schollar performs brilliantly. Both Fedorovas dance with force, passion, and simplicity.

In the sixth scene we see the kingdom of the Nereids. Flashing by the khan like a specter, the Tsar Maiden must be here, among the daughters of old Nereus and the beautiful nymphs of the Eleatic Sea, in a silver palace with gold ornaments, immersed in silence. From the depths of ancient legend, the prototype of aesthetic and religious legends of the whole world, eternal Russian feminine beauty emerges onto the fantastic shore of Russian mythogenesis. What an illusion, not only for a ballet master and director, but for a musician considering the features of popular fantasy! The holy of holies of universal generation hidden somewhere at the bottom of the popular soul, in whose light all that lives is transformed and on the verge of dispersing its magic. The everyday becomes the ideal. After several moments of action Ivan the Fool, uncombed, unwashed, and dressed in shoes made of bast, will turn into a dashing gallant worthy of the Tsar Maiden.

The ballet master did not expose or develop these illusions. However, the Nereids themselves look beautiful. Among them, in the first group of six who run out onstage, dance such talented artists as Elena Liukom, Anna Ivanovna Fedorova, Mariya Leontieva, and Gali Bolshakova—Nereids with untwined hair that hangs down lower than their dresses. Unfortunately, the silver water flowers on their heads give their bodies a heavy look, and the impression of gentle fluidity is lost. From behind, at the top of the stage, water surges in an electrical light, creating a perspective for the overflowing currents and the splashing Nereids.

Mathilda Kshesinskaya makes her entrance as the Tsar Maiden and the audience flutters. Thunderous applause breaks out and greets her. Kshesinskaya dances as she always does: powerfully, vividly, with flashes of genius that translate into art of the highest quality. Her dancing follows Marius Petipa's staging, unchanged by Gorsky, with large rotations on pointe and flashes of different ballet steps. She concludes with splendid gyrations at a quick tempo, of which she alone is capable.

In the final scene of act 3 Kshesinskaya dances the adagio, a typical classical structure, with Nikolai Legat, both with and without his support, and then the variation Melancholy, which turns into a mazurka and concludes with a Russian dance on pointe. At this moment Vasily Stukolkin, who plays Ivan the Fool, runs around the Tsar Maiden, throws his feet across the floor, plunging back and forth like a veritable eel. The hall breaks into applause and Kshesinskaya repeats her variation three times.

In the Underground Kingdom, the play of light, though directed to one side, spoils the dancing. A new and rather ethereal adagio is provided here, the adagio of Elsa Vill and Petr Vladimirov, to the music of Boris Asafiev. The adagio is replaced by several variations, beautifully executed. Vill is as light as a feather. But Vladimirov dances like a feeble gymnast with the mannerisms of Nijinsky. As she leaps with one foot, Vaganova extends the other sideways, in an oblique line, with her characteristic technical perfection. However, the stage is too dark here and it's hard to see, even from the first row.

The final scene of *The Little Humpbacked Horse* opens with a general procession of nations. Ivan Tsarevich and the Tsar Maiden pass along the edge of the proscenium, surrounded by nobles and children. An enormous divertissement unfolds. The pupils of the theater school dance skillfully. Olga Preobrazhenskaya and Legat jest merrily in the Latvian polka, assuming crude poses.

Samuil Andriyanov and Liubov Egorova, along with a large entourage, perform the Ural dance with its secondary cabrioles. The variation would have
come off even better if Egorova had been given wings for her elevation. Tamara
Karsavina and Alexander Orlov's Ukrainian dance evoked rapture from the
audience. The world has never seen such a beautiful Ukrainian girl in a crown
of red poppies. In Liszt's rhapsody, with Olga Fedorova and Eduardova at the
head, everyone is absolutely wonderful. But the women's costumes are too
gaudy. The cream-colored silk skirts are sewn with gold. The bodices are velvet,
and the feet are shod in gold slippers.

Kshesinskaya dances the last russkaya in a long brocade dress. Her headdress
is golden, wide, and five-cornered. The Tsar Maiden dances gently, tenderly,
picturesquely, first lowering, then raising her dark blue eyes, which are now
moist, to the audience.

To sum up, there is too much "Russian" weighing down this ballet. Along
with the popular folk dances—trepaks, kazachoks, and hopaks—there are no
other elements of nationalism, of a higher order. There are insufficient motifs
in the Byzantine style, even if they are taken from *The Calendars of the Saints*
and *Podlinnik,** from the golden edges on top of the cheap alabaster on which
in ancient times the faces of heroes, women, and girls were drawn. On this
golden edge, amid the crosses, cupolas, and multifarious activities of daily life,
should have been placed the Tsar Maiden, the graphic image of Russian beauty.
In addition, Gorsky's classical dances are not distinguished by originality or
any revelations that add to the old technique. The traditional adagios and
variations somehow don't suit the Slavonic character. We need designs that are
extracted from the deep foundations of concrete reality. And to take a new step
in this direction Gorsky should have first recast the classical compositions of
Petipa and brought them into accord with the patterns of folk dance. Then the
two wonderful figures of the ballet, Ivan the Fool and the Tsar Maiden, would
have issued forth.

With hearts aflame, the simple folk proceed to the transformation of their
image through the difficult workings of fate. All around are dance, noise, and
guffawing. But in the distance, in the halo of the sun's rays, the people see an
image of beckoning beauty, toward which they strive with their souls. In the
people's eyes the Tsar Maiden eclipses everything in the world with her significance, not only the celestial pealing of the church bells, but even the roar of the
Tsar's cannon over the living and the dead.

—" 'Tsar-Devitsa' (Novaia postanovka *Kon'ka Gorbunka*)," *Birzhevye vedomosti* (18
December 1912): 5–6.

* *The Calendars of the Saints* is a collection of homilies and brief tales about saints and
   martyrs; *Podlinnik* is a handbook for icon painters.

A Circle of Immovable Stars

Alexander Gorsky and Mikhail Fokine

I n their attempts to reform ballet, Alexander Gorsky and Mikhail Fokine have not moved it an inch because each of them has taken a false path. For Gorsky everything comes down to dramatizing the corps de ballet in the spirit of the Moscow Art Theater,* to combining antithetical styles; for Fokine it is a matter of dramatizing the entire ballet performance and deviating as much as possible from the foundations of classical choreography. Thus in *The Little Humpbacked Horse* we have a compilation of contradictory ideas and an increase of action in the corps de ballet's dances. In Fokine's *Egyptian Nights,* as in many of his other works, the choreographic material is directed solely toward producing an impression through the overall structure of the piece. The dances either flash by or, following the traditions of old ballet, fill up the intervals between the various movements of dramatic action.

I have already written about how the idea of dramatizing the corps de ballet's dances could have arisen only from an erroneous conception about their genuine character—a dithyramb in the form of movement—which corresponds to the patterns of a lyrical orchestra. To dramatize this, to introduce here a psychology that is broken up into individual components, and to dilute it in dances that proceed in sharp bends, means to abolish ballet's foundation and emotional source. As a whole, the corps de ballet produces the design of a circle. It divides into semicircles. Sometimes the dances flow in parallel streams, one opposite the other. Like the strophes and antistrophes in the dithyramb of Arion,† they produce a picture of movement and countermovement in rhythmic tempos which sing. But the temporarily ruptured lines

---

* The leading Russia theater, founded in 1898 by Konstantin Stanislavsky (1863–1938) and Vladimir Nemirovich-Danchenko (1858–1943). Stanislavsky developed a system of training actors that is still used; he also stressed the importance of the ensemble over individual actors.

† Arion was a seventh-century B.C. Greek poet; he invented the dithyramb, a wild choral song or chant in irregular form, originally in honor of Dionysus. In ancient Greek drama the choral song and dance often took the form of strophe and antistrophe: in the strophe the chorus sings one stanza while crossing the stage in one direction; in the antistrophe, they sing the next stanza while crossing back in the opposite direction.

invariably coalesce in the pure line of the circle, equivalent to the circle of emotional experiences.

On the Petersburg stage we have one of the best demonstrations of Marius Petipa's genius. His understanding of the corps de ballet's dances not only resists alteration but actually enters into any structure of classical choreography as an organic element. He organized the entire movement of the corps exclusively on the basis of the lyricism of a single design, as a collective symbol of the spontaneity that accompanies the soloist's dancing. Everyone toed the line. Great talents flourished in the ranks of the corps de ballet but always stayed within it. They didn't break loose from their columns; individual elements did not protrude in any of their details, as is currently the case in the disintegrating corps of our times, because the entire movement was felt as one and was fused together with a single musical mood. With Petipa the lyrical dances of the corps de ballet had just the kind of meaning they have to have in the structure of classical choreography.

The dances of the corps de ballet and the dances of the soloists were the structure that Lucian* compared to the roving of the planets amid the immovable stars in the firmament. The circular motion of the heavenly bodies, given the fixity of their symmetrical parts, seems nonexistent. It is seen in its illustration but is almost totally unperceived in its process. The divine harmony of the world is quiet. All is in place. Amid the chaos of flashing details the cosmos remains unchanged, like a magnitude that keeps embracing, creating, and preserving. But the planets rove and weave patterns among themselves, creating their own legends among the magic of immovable truths. Lucian had no doubt that the earth's choreography was only a reflection of the picture of the firmament in its streams and sparks that sink into the expanses of the magic circle, although he wrote his article on dancing when its classical designs had already practically disintegrated.

Then, as now, these designs were destroyed by the thrust of barbaric pantomime, which served equally the rulers and the rabble, and substituted for the rites of theatrical liturgy the realism of ordinary themes, accessible to plebian taste. But with his subtle talent and inspired nature, Lucian still felt the source of plastic ideas. The language of the dance figures spoke not only to his imagination but to his intelligence. He still heard the religious melody of the soul in the style of complex movements, which were becoming extinct on the stage at that time. Unfortunately, I can say nothing laudable about the lovers of pantomime in the case of contemporary ballet. Gorsky combines the tasks of

*Lucian was a second century A.D. Greek rhetorician and satirist. Here, Volynsky may have meant the Latin poet Lucretius (c. 99–c. 55 B.C.), whose epic poem *De rerum natura* (On the Nature of Things) has extensive discussions of planetary phenomena.

choreography with the goals of realist drama in the spirit of the early Stanislavsky. Indeed early, because the contemporary Stanislavsky—a talent of extraordinary breadth, with ingenious insights into the perspectives of the future—has
gone far beyond this in his strivings. And Fokine, that ballet artist from the
pathetic school of Alexander Sanin,* who lacks any feeling for ideal, classical
form and who is devoid of any sense of dance's inner thought, its mythological
beauty and religious aspiration, carries out a policy that abandons the spiritual
for the everyday, the great for the trivial. It is clear that we are dealing here with
a catastrophe on the stage, one that is, however, arbitrary and avertable because
the opposition of society's cultural forces has already begun.

The Little Humpbacked Horse is running with less and less success, yet
Fokine's productions are studied from every possible angle.

—"Krug nepodvizhnykh zvezd," *Birzhevye vedomosti* (7 January 1913): 6–7.

Isadora Duncan

The Last Word

I have expressed my disapproval of those aspects of Isadora Duncan's talent
that allow us to claim she is a dancer who belongs to neither the contemporary nor the ancient theater. I have noted and stressed the specific shortcomings of her art. Yet, having followed my critical instincts to the end, I see
now that I have not said everything that needed to be said. A feeling inside me
requires me to praise her lovely artistry beyond merely aesthetic and philosophical considerations.

Duncan is beautiful in the purity of her emotions, which inspire the viewer
more rapidly than any other more perfect form of art. I especially love her
during those first seconds when she appears onstage. She stands by the curtains
in a small plié, with a bent or slightly raised head. Her hair is gently combed
and smooth. Her hands are crossed at her breast, as we see when she illustrates
the music of Wagner, or they are extended backward, as in her transmission of
Gluck's music. The minute we look at Duncan we immediately feel the individuality that makes a thing unique. We feel an outstanding level of culture, a
culture that has become flesh. She arrived in Russia and created a school of

*Alexander Akimovich Savin (b. Shenberg, 1869–1955) was a dramatic actor who also
directed at Saint Petersburg's Alexandrinsky Theater from 1902 to 1917.

intimate dancing and raised the individual experience of personality to the level of cult. She showed something extraordinarily important to everyone. Her art revealed, as it were, a new truth: what takes place to the accompaniment of music has in every aspect of life the character of a religious rite. Not the people, not the nation, not the world in the glow of its great ideas figure in the rhythms of her artistic instrument. No, from the paths of the superhuman and universal she has escaped to an intimate corner, to a person who stands outside the flow of history, to a happy girl, to a melancholy youth. From her ardent heart she has erected an icon to the personal. And even Orpheus, in her interpretation, is no more than a suffering man. Even through the haze of ancient myth, stretched out between legends of disparate cultures, Duncan has perceived the motifs necessary for her art. Tannhäuser for her is not a legend. She experiences his image among a multitude of personal sensations, even without the tinge of generalized thought inherent in the theme of love.

Coming onstage to the public's approving applause, Duncan throws on a dark cloak. Gratefully and gently she bows low to the audience. Thunder breaks out. But her eyes with their moist glow quietly look straight ahead. Before her is not something elemental but something sweet and personal, which is momentarily suspended from the aims of the universal. Having covered the nakedness of her intimate sacred act, she stands modestly before the public. Not a movement, not a spectacle. The most cultivated woman of the world smiles in response to the storm of applause.

—"Aisedora Dunkan (Poslednee slovo)," *Birzhevye vedomosti* (16 January 1913): 4.

Anna Pavlova

A nna Pavlova has a phenomenal arch, which she almost dares not bend entirely when she lifts herself on pointe. If she were to extend it, she'd break her foot. The arch, which promotes take-off, gives force to the push, although the muscles and tendons of the leg, heel, and knee play the major role here: the aerial throws of the body are managed exclusively by them. Nijinsky's arch is average, but because of the elasticity of his tendons, he flies across the stage like a bird. Mathilda Kshesinskaya's foot is almost flat, but in stockings she dances perfectly. There is no doubt, however, that at the barre or in the middle of the hall the oval of the foot, which is especially balanced, is beautiful. Pavlova's arch is only partly a result of her school exercises. Nature itself in its generosity endowed her with physical features which, as they developed, provided the external image of this major talent of our day. Yet more of Pavlova is from God than from nature. When you watch her dance you cannot help but feel that her art, though not perfect in all its details, is directly connected to her emotional makeup. Her choreographic features are wrapped in inspiration, which alone is evident. All the rest seems trivial.

Pavlova's foot is charming—small and narrow. The structure of her leg is right, but somewhat concave in the knees. Her kneecaps almost touch. This is why Pavlova lacks the perfect turnout one finds in Vera Trefilova; but her knee depressions do not give her a single line. Her small beat is not pure. Thus Pavlova does not manage her passage down- or upstage along the diagonal with the fleeting contact of the feet above the knee joint—called, in the language of ballet technique, simple or double brisé—as well as the rather low take-offs of her body, such as entrechats quatre and royale, particularly well. Her knees are not impeccable either in her attitudes or her arabesques; the kneecap does not make a horizontal line with her foot but often hangs much lower. The sole of her foot is therefore raised to the ceiling and can be seen by the spectator, which is totally alien to the classical dances of the French school.

Pavlova's legs are lanky and muscular, taut like a goat's. Their lightness is extraordinary. She can do any step she wants with them, any battement, any leap from one foot or jump from both. But for all the inadequacy of her turnout, her batteries during her movement in the air are brilliant. They become beautiful only at high altitudes from the floor.

Because she is able to fling and throw out her legs whenever she desires, Pavlova produces the impression of an artist with extraordinary elevation. But there is an illusion here that is easier to understand than to follow. The perfection of her dancing flows from another source. Her deep and even pliés, given the swiftness of her leap, her ballon, give the sensation of the fluttering of wings high in the air. But in reality, Pavlova's elevation, if strictly measured, would not outdo Vaganova's. In this regard, next to her even Elsa Vill could dance without a loss to her reputation. Of course, I am talking about the height of the leap. The jumps themselves are astonishingly beautiful, not only in the character but in the poetry of their lines. Before us is a major talent, full of hymns to Apollo and dithyrambs in honor of Dionysus.

Throwing her legs slightly back, Pavlova spreads herself in the air like a wild bird. And onstage she flies at rapid speed up and down, obliquely, near the floor, against all logic, against all the laws of gravity, with her widely opened, dark brown eyes, in which fire burns.

Given her resilient, though not strong back, Pavlova's pirouettes cannot be considered first class. In this respect Trefilova's art has achieved greater perfection. Here, obviously, besides an inborn talent and a natural equilibrium of the legs, which is not found in a passionate nature, a firm back is required. But in a pirouette with her partner, Pavlova spins so quickly that the spectator cannot count the number of turns. In the whirlwind of her movement, it always seems that a single circle has flashed before our eyes.

Pavlova's body is lissome and light. Her shoulders are ravishing; they slope down with soft muscles the color of ivory. Her arms are too extended at the elbow and lack the semicircular lines that make the arabesque and attitude beautiful, but they are lively and tremulous. Her hand is strong and not unfeminine, although the fingers are short, prehensile, and square, like a Botticelli Madonna or the late Vera Kommissarzhevskaya. Moreover, her entire image conveys the impression of an undeveloped little girl who is ready to twirl almost pointlessly, merely from an excess of enthusiasm. Before the ballet she does no exercises, yet she flies right onto the stage on her cold feet, warming them up during her activity. In general, she does not prepare on the day of the performance. She drinks champagne and chatters away capriciously and randomly. Other dancers have a bite six hours before a performance and then lie on a couch with their legs stretched out. Two hours before they go on stage they're already beating out their battements. Pavlova furiously flits around all day. She has breakfast and then eats nothing until the evening. But fifteen minutes before the curtain goes up, she quickly gulps down five ham or roast-beef sandwiches. And then she flies onto the stage.

I have said far from everything about Pavlova. The image of this inspired artist needs to be gleaned from her dancing itself, from her first-class art.

—"A. P. Pavlova," *Birzhevye vedomosti* (21 January 1913): 5.

Pavlova's Farewell Performance: "La Bayadère"

P avlova's first entrance in *La Bayadère* is beautiful. Covered with a veil, she descends the staircase of the temple and makes her way toward the Brahmin who is waiting for her. Her bluish dress drapes her every muscle. Intertwined with pearls, her two black braids descend along her back. Her head is adorned with little gold plates on barely noticeable wires. Her slender arms, decorated with bracelets, stretch forward and gesticulate with great charm. The tone of her face and shoulders is swarthy; her lower lip is sensuous. The almond-shaped slits of her eyes are set beneath the arches of her dark brows. Lithe as a snake, the dancer instantly captures the audience's attention.

The Bayadère begins her dance with a graceful andante, starting with her leg back in tendu croisé, in the spirit of an arabesque. Throwing her arms about in an oblique line, she bends her body in a low bow, with her face to the public. Then, within a second, she rises on her toes and dances to the beat of the orchestra, acting with her hands and saucily lifting them sideways. The picture here is unparalleled in the curvature of forms, which convey the sensation of enthusiasm. This was one of the dancer's most remarkable entrances. The public felt the presence of a major talent onstage and filled the hall with thunderous applause. Caught up in the storm of success, Pavlova continued to act within the flow of the drama, conforming to the requirements of the libretto.

In the second scene the ballerina has no dances. I do not like the pantomime on stage, and whatever traits of talent there are in this area, I do not value them highly. The mute expression outside the dance that plays on Sturm and Drang seems incomplete and provides no satisfaction. It is an entirely different matter with regard to the performance's dramatic movements, which are, as in *Giselle,* woven into the musical and dance figures. The pantomime here has a poetic character and is free from the clamorousness of the gestures that occupy the words. But the passionate scene of jealousy between the rivals in act 2 of *La Bayadère* is, thank God, not too long. Moreover, it is preceded by Dzhampe's beautiful dance, with long veils tied to the legs of the young artists.

The third scene constitutes a mosaic of dances of various configurations. The so-called Crooked Dance of Slaves, with its organized asymmetry, in which equal groups of the corps disperse up- and downstage, is followed by the Fan Dance and Parrot Dance, with the four Bayadères with low take-offs and entrechats quatres, and with Manu's dance in which Elsa Vill performs, having inherited this number—with descending grades of vivid execution—from Vera Trefilova and Tamara Karsavina. Immediately, Alexander Orlov, Vasily Stukolkin, and Olga Fedorova rush across the stage in a feverishly rhythmic Indian dance. Stukolkin whirls in a vortex, beating the drum with his foot from the bottom up. And Fedorova, among the multicolored ribbons, rushes toward the footlights like a hurricane. The act concludes with the solo number of the Bayadère, who dances in the final moment with a basket of flowers in a passionate arabesque upward, with her darkened eyes directed toward the audience.

The fifth scene, the Dance of the Shades, is one of the marvels of Petipa's balletic creation. The shades emerge from a mountain crevice and, as they descend in a broad zigzag, they all perform long arabesques. They remain on the ramp in four rows and perform a general adagio, slowly straightening their legs to waist height. After this the variations of the three dancers begin in jumps and beats—Vaganova, Vill, and Elizaveta Gerdt, who prepare for

Pavlova's adagio with Samuil Andriyanov, so beautiful in style but divided into two parts. The artist performs the second one among the corps de ballet, who are lying on the floor in a semicircle and accompanying her to the beat of the orchestra with the waving of their veils. The groupings of the two dancers are built here on the effects of a composed, self-possessed sculpture, on the unhurried alternations of movements of striking beauty.

After the beautiful adagio come the three variations of the soloists and then Pavlova's variation. With the technical perfection available only to her, Vaganova does four cabrioles with leaps of increasing elevation, terminating them with a fading arabesque en pointe. But Pavlova's variation, of the terre-à-terre kind, is based on graceful pliés, on pirouettes en dehors, on semi-leaps, on dances across a slanted line to the accompaniment of the sonorous sounds of the violin, and on the marvelous turns of the body with bended leg which invariably changes to arabesque. Thus, in the coda she also completes each of her jumps with lightning speed in rapid bends in the same pattern. And, finally, in the last act, Pavlova glides and flashes across the stage, breaking the tempos of her flight with movements on pointe, circling the bride and groom and whirling with them in a delirium of dream movement.

The curtain falls, accompanied by a final thunder of applause. This is Pavlova's last exit at the Maryinsky because of her year-long absence from Petersburg, which seems a difficult, almost tragic, break with ballet. Indeed, we recently had the occasion to be convinced with our own eyes of the kind of art this gifted talent cultivates on the stages of Europe among the degrading working conditions their nightspots provide. The rays of light cast into the soul of this artist by the Creator of the universe, by the Creator of all that is marvelous, will undoubtedly be replaced there with the pathos of market transactions from which one can mint a fortune. A column of dust circles the eaglet, which has fallen onto the road of vanity and deceit. And although it is particularly unpleasant, it nonetheless needs to be said that Pavlova's genius on this new path is fraught with danger. This is yet another dash for the mirage of universal fame along the path of golden, diabolical temptation, and her talent will smash to smithereens. It will split into little pieces, it will disperse into fragments, kindled from the stage for the crowd, but no longer providing elements of integral beauty.

Falls from such heights are shattering.

—"Proshchal'nyi spektakl' A. P. Pavlovoi (*Baiaderka*)," *Birzhevye vedomosti* (25 February 1913): 5.

A Kaleidoscope of Attire

Still More on Konstantin Korovin

⚜⚜⚜

T hematically, *The Little Humpbacked Horse* creates the impression of a ballet, but the constituent parts make up only a mosaic of motifs without any overall consistent complexion. It is a series of episodes lacking unity. To begin with, the ballet's music is a tangle of pieces that belong to different composers. The works of Tchaikovsky, Liszt, and Glazunov are intertwined with compositions by Cesare Pugni, Dvořák, and Boris Asafiev, so that the orchestral playing constantly hurls you from the acoustical images of a specific tonality to a completely different effect. It is obvious just from this that such a potpourri of tunes cannot contribute in any way to a ballet's success. Failing to evoke the sense of a continuous musical idea that permeates the entire work, this mishmash additionally impedes the dance components of the narrative from cohering into an epic picture of fairy tale. Generally speaking, such an impossible combination of orchestral styles, which inevitably creates a chaotic droning, represents a grotesqueness which no serious stage can tolerate.

The unusual gaudiness of the costumes, created according to Konstantin Korovin's drawings and lacking any particular artistic value, corresponds to the mosaic of musical motifs. Only some of these costumes are completely satisfying, despite the fact that their colors shout at you too much. Such, for example, is the costume of the ballerina who dances the russkaya in a brocaded sarafan* with a gold headdress decorated with beautiful little earflaps. This luxurious apparel of the Tsar Maiden (Evgeniya Egorova), who beams with happiness, emits a glow of exultation and festivity. Furthermore, we must acknowledge as splendid Korovin's costumes for the various character dances, such as the person who performs the Ural number dressed in a marvelous caftan that radiates cheerful colors during the daringly high cabrioles. In previous performances, this caftan was massive on Samuil Andriyanov, smoothing out young Apollo's figure in a picturesque and stylish way. Similarly, the costumes for the comic pair who dance the exotic polka are wittily conceived.

In a round yellow hat with a black feather on his head and a chestnut-brown jacket with a double-breasted waistcoat with gold buttons, the Latvian performed with his partner, who was past youth's first blush. She, in the

---

*A sleeveless dress worn by Russian peasant women.

meanwhile, was attired in a simple skirt with a double jabot and coiffed with hair parted in the middle and little braids on her ears. For some reason this number was cut during yesterday's performance, but in its day the well-built figure of the dancer in her comic attire created an amusing impression.

On the other hand, the costumes designed by this original craftsman for Liszt's rhapsody are too motley. The dancers are all dressed up in cream-colored silk shirts embroidered with gold, in velvet bodices with white sleeves up to their wrists, and hats with cornflowers and yellow feathers. The variation with Olga Fedorova in the lead is beautiful with its feverish rhythm of movements that are mastered to the smallest detail; but the breakneck flight of many of the pairs turns the mosaic of colors into a confusion of undistinguishable design.

However, the general composition of these costumes, which one way or another meet the needs of the characters dancing on stage, attest to the artist's rich, albeit excessively expansive and even somewhat unbridled, imagination. One way or another the costumes appropriately embellish the numbers based on the transmission of everyday Russian life in all its diversity. One inevitably senses a talent, a nimble imagination, and a power of creativity of extraordinary range. Here Korovin is undoubtedly working in the sphere of inspiration unique to his creative individuality. But one cannot say the same about his work in the area of classical action, the field of stylized dancing, which represents ideal beauty and wonder. We have recently seen the distortion that Korovin's heavy touch has given to the fantasy of *Sleeping Beauty*. The charming fairy tale, permeated by fragrant breezes, cannot endure the yoke of red- and black-haired wigs taken from faithful depictions of the epoch of Louis XIV. Petipa's dances seemed to be stricken with paralysis.

The costumes of the Nereids in the sixth scene of *The Little Humpbacked Horse* do not constitute such a cacophony. At the rear of the stage water is pouring in a sparkling electric light. The women dancers run out from the wings and begin weaving themselves into different groups, dressed in light dresses. But the hair from their dense wigs, with their large water flowers, descends lower than their waists like winding ivy, giving a heavy look to their figures and depriving their dancing of its rippling flow, as if it were a puff of wind. Consequently, the poetic value of the picture has disappeared from these visually bland trivia, which are offered without consideration for the specific theme or idea of the virgin Bacchic chorus of the Amphitrites.* The dancing of the Nereids almost entirely disappears because Korovin's imagination, so weighty in its designs, did not accord here with the idea of the legend or with the plastic schemes of the great master [Petipa]. These schemes have been squelched by the massiveness of the attire.

---

*In Greek mythology the Amphitrites (and Nereids) were sea maidens.

But what crowns the overall calamity of the orchestra's encyclopedism and the costumes' kaleidoscopic quality is the chaos of the dancing, which creates the impression of turmoil. There is no guiding conception. Whatever is beautiful in the ballet comes not from Gorsky, but from Petipa. Such, by the way, is the brilliantly conceived dancing of the Frescoes in scene 5. Marvelous also is Egorova's first entrance in the scene of the Nereids. The choreography is elementary here, but it is perfectly cloaked in a reflection of moonlight. Also faultless is the corps de ballet's waltz, done in groups along straight or oblique lines. The music and dancing are perfectly integrated. But all of this belongs mainly to Petipa's art. The large pas de deux, set by the Moscow ballet master in the scene of the Underground Kingdom (Elsa Vill and Viktor Semenov), for all the strikingly beautiful transference of the ballerina in its first section, still has a generally clichéd quality. Beyond the ordinary technique of classical dance there is nothing new or original.

—"Kaleidoskop tualetov (Eshche o Korovine)," *Birzhevye vedomosti* (28 February 1914): 4.

Elegy

One of the current season's ballets provides great interest for the critic, and because of the undiluted simplicity of its content it will always remain a monument of high art on the stage. I am speaking of *Giselle,* a fantastic work which, judging by legend, achieved its original success with the classical performance of Carlotta Grisi in the production of Jean Coralli, and which now is running with the apparently substantial reworkings of Marius Petipa. The newest interpreters of this ballet, Anna Pavlova, Tamara Karsavina, and Liubov Egorova, do not deviate a step from Petipa's adaptation, not only in the dancing but also in the acting and drama. There are no new features or colors. Even Pavlova does not allow herself the slightest liberty, although individual places in the adaptation could undoubtedly use reworking since in its current incarnation the piece produces no impression on the audience. The first act proceeds rather sluggishly and in general fails to provide a picture of gaiety against the backdrop of peasant life. On the Paris stage something like a popular bacchanalia unfolded before the audience with the crowning of the fifteen-year-old girl with grape leaves to award her for her beauty and dancing. With her childlike face and the expression of guileless joy in her eyes, Grisi was beyond praise.

Biographers recount that Grisi created a storm with her dancing among the village girls and with her mad scene. But nowadays these very moments—especially the latter—are being conveyed in an unusually hackneyed way. Karsavina creates a tempest in a teacup. She runs her palms along her face, which is framed by tousled hair darker than night. But in this spot Grisi provided tender, elegant, almost sweet confusion. The gentle creature has lost her support in the world. But the angels have carried her aloft. Her dancing stirs the spectator with its echoes of her previous waltz with her girlfriends and of her marvelous poses with her partner, and step by step it acquires an increasingly passionate character. Suddenly there is a halt, a momentary, radiant interval. Giselle is ready to throw herself on Albrecht's sword: on her face is a determination that gives way to an expression of formless reverie mixed with weeping, and a gesture of the hand that is firm and tragic. But instead of these details, not only Karsavina, who lacks the temperament of a dramatic actress, but even Pavlova performs a cumbersome and boring pantomime.

Generally speaking, not only the mimetic parts of act 1 but even its dancing seem to me poorly developed by Petipa. One undoubtedly senses reflections of Coralli's Paris production, but with diminished drama and acting that is more simplistically realistic. The choreographic movements are not broadly developed by the ballet master. The maneuvers of the corps de ballet are not colorful in their figures and are generally presented as too sophisticated in their designs. In a word, the ethnography is not brought to its necessary height. The pathos of the action, following Théophile Gautier and Coralli's design,* organized almost exclusively around the play with everyday effects, is continually broken by an abundance of dance movements that, though elementary in their construction, nonetheless poorly accord with the picture of life being depicted in the wholeness of its character. Finally, the divertissement pas de deux at the end of the act, a tangle of motley shreds of pirouettes and cabrioles, is marred by chords from a completely different world of art, assaulting the viewer with its unnaturalness. Only the dancing of Giselle herself is conceived by the ballet master with unusual rigor and constitutes a glorious mixture of everyday movements with those that are classical in pattern. These latter movements are emphasized by the artist and brought to the fore, perhaps, in an unconscious discovery of the work. In real life the fifteen-year-old girl actually does not feel herself to be a completely ordinary being. The minute she takes a step that step is idealized in and of itself. During the dancing her body is gradually lib-

---

*Théophile Gautier (1811–1872) was a French writer, poet, and critic, whose writings on ballet supported the Romantic school. Though Gautier's articles did not constitute a systematized body of choreographic criticism, Volynsky regarded his work highly. Gautier and Coralli co-wrote the libretto for *Giselle*.

erated from the accumulations of weighty reality in order to provide a response to the music playing from within and to harmonize with the rhythm of aspiring upward.

Individual variations in *Giselle* gush forth with a flood of choreographic colors worthy of Petipa's powerful talent. At first the ballerina dances without a partner, gently conveying the musical design with two rhythmic beats through oscillating movements from side to side. Then after several gliding steps along the footlights and a short pantomimic scene with Albrecht, Giselle repeats the same figure with her partner. Immediately the element of elevation should be felt—the quiver of girlish eroticism that requires leaps and jumps for its expression onstage. Unfortunately, in Karsavina's interpretation this moment loses all its theatrical effect. Petr Vladimirov's high jumps, his torso thrust forward, divert the audience's attention, so that the ballerina, for all her talented dancing, is lost and obscured, even at the height of the action, dissolving among the masses and generally failing to strike or excite anyone with her art: her effect here is minimally felt. Karsavina's dancing is even and smooth; her poses have an unchanging beauty but with no flash of genius, and they do not illuminate trifling details with nervous excitement. Without emotional beams of light in her eyes, the expression of her face is lackluster.

Then Giselle dances the variation and coda. Along an oblique line across the length of the corps de ballet that forms in a column, the dancer does rapid sweeps with her leg in the air. These sweeps produce an impression of rhythmical columns of smoke drifting upward, hardly perceptible even to the experienced eye. After this a stream of new figures with leaps downstage in the direction of the footlights completes the ballerina's solo with several extremely expressive features. The dancing of the first half of the ballet has ended. The image of Giselle is prominently noted. Although the action revolves around the effects of everyday life and characters who lack a fantastic and wondrous touch, the ideal essence of the fifteen-year-old girl seems to be defined by itself. Her movement turns into flying and fluttering. In her first appearance at the beginning of the act she cuts across the stage in leaps, leaps which are rather low, almost terre-à-terre. Later their level grows higher and higher. Finally they give way to whirlwinds of circles in all directions.

The staging of the dancing in the second act is the height of perfection in classical choreography. But even here elements of pantomime are somewhat reworked and narrowed in their scope when compared to the original adaptation by Coralli. Thus on the Paris stage Myrtha, the Queen of the Wilis, having risen from the bushes like a cloud, makes cabalistic figures in the air with her staff and so summons a ring of virgins from all parts of the world. They flock from everywhere, each performing a dance liturgy in the spirit of her personal faith before finally fusing with one another, acquiring a uniformly silver color through a single ray of the moon and submitting to the ritual of dancing without the slightest shade of folksiness whatsoever. For some reason Petipa dropped this magnificent detail and so deprived the second act of color and variety.

Finally, when the ring of Wilis is full and has completely lined up beside their queen, the latter raises up the soul of the deceased Giselle from the flowers on her grave. With her lifelessly folded arms on her chest, the girl approaches Myrtha with a slow step and freezes for a motionless second before her resurrection to a new life. Suddenly she begins to spin around in one place, leaving the ground with barely noticeable exertions and thrusts of her foot. In general this figure resembles an arabesque describing a noncontinuous circle that is somehow split into parts. But her pattern is so incorrect, constantly shaking and fluttering, that it is impossible to relate it to a specific design of dancing. In any case this is not a classical pirouette with a multitude of turns but rather a chaos of movement deprived of the culture of dance, an emotional storm whose delivery lacks a yet-to-be perfected choreographical technique. But at the same time, how magnificently this chaotic movement emphasizes the reawakening from decay and death! Here the leg thrown back into an arabesque is, of course, nothing but a symbol of consciousness in its forward rush. The will is already weaving the lace of its own strivings and demands without end or limit. And to this arabesque of Giselle's the corps of Wilis, in white dresses fastened with bouquets of myrtle, provide an accompanying arabesque without changing positions on the ground.

Overall, the entire second act from this moment on is filled with arabesques. The arabesque is at the base of all Giselle's dancing. The jumps and leaps end in arabesque. It glitters among the bushes, rushes across the entire stage, leg extended back, even and straight like a string. Pavlova leapt spread-eagled in the air and then remained there for seconds like a sculpted dream. She swayed among the leaves of the trees with the same graceful movement of her leg, which was phenomenally beautiful in her execution. She completed her rotations in pirouette with a pose in arabesque. But almost the entire accompaniment of the corps de ballet in this act has the same character of determined symbolization through dancing. The Wilis toss the hunter from hand to hand and throw him into the bog. But when he is already gasping for breath at the bottom of the lake, the chorus of virgins runs around the stage, leaping in an incomplete arabesque, which one might call an attitude, as if to nuance the internal agitation no longer being conveyed by direct strokes; then again it unfolds along an oblique line from top to bottom with hands held out for a new sacrifice. In a word, in the course of the entire act, from the moment of Giselle's resurrection, there are no groupings that are calculated merely to achieve pretty effects in the conveyance of emotions. The body's graphics have a fantastic tinge. The mystery of desire, geared somehow far from the earth to the boundlessness of heaven, is performed by jumps and leaps, which in the final analysis are also nothing more than attitudes and arabesques in the air. The rotations have only a pantomimic character as, for example, in the moment when it is necessary to grab, bind, and throw Giselle's murderer into the swamp. It is also worth noting that already at the beginning of the act, the dancing of the Queen of the Wilis herself—particularly in Elsa Vill's performance, which is marvelous in its lightness—seems to determine the act's character as a whole.

Conveying Gautier's designs onstage, the Paris ballet master Coralli, and later Petipa, placed an adagio in act 2 that is repeated twice. At first it is a warm-up adagio, unpartnered, and a bit cold in the soloist's performance, but then it is a complete and broad one, with every moment filled with expressiveness. Albrecht stands at the cross, protected from Myrtha's staff. So as not to tear him from his place of safety by the temptation of her beauty and so save him from the reprisal of the virgins, Giselle holds back from displaying her charms. She rises slowly on her toes. Without breaking off, she bends her torso in an arabesque. She turns en dedans, the flame extinguished in her heart. In this way the marvelous naturalness of the dancing becomes animated by an inner content and is permeated throughout by ideological substance in each of its elements. All this is the vocabulary of the spirit in signs, formed with the application of great logic and thus intelligent in all respects. When, finally, Albrecht moves away from the cross, ready to submit to laceration by the Wilis, the warm-up adagio is replaced by a pas de deux filled with color and animation. This is one of the most remarkable creations of the master of the stage. The figures alternate with striking consistency and are consistent as well in their details. But the tempos of the movements remain without alteration. The movement schemes are the same, only now they shine with inner burning.

Giselle fades among the flowers in the gold of dawn. The image is completed with its final strokes and surrounded by a halo of sunlight in the likeness of a martyr in iconlike anguish. From her first entrance onstage to her final quiverings in the arms of her partner, everything is wonderful. An elegy without words, without monologues or dialogues, without the eloquence of bookish poetry, but nonetheless stirring the soul with the visual charm of its symbolization of the themes of love and death.

—"Elegiia," *Birzhevye vedomosti* (12 January 1915): 8.

Mikhail Fokine

Some Lines Toward a Polemic

———

. . . Sympathy for Mikhail Fokine over the past years has come exclusively from poorly educated cultural lightweights without a smattering of talent. Their fanfares have resounded among the amusement park–attending public, who confuse clowns with artists. Yet the clamor around Fokine has always been great, so it has been easy to yield to the illusion and see him from a distorted angle of vision. In a short period this genuinely talented man, who studied at the school of classical dancing and who possesses an ear rare in its musical sensitivity, found himself in the same company as various suspicious characters in the dramatic world who also imagine themselves as reformers. . . .

. . . For all his mistakes and false notions in the area of theatrical movement in ballet, Fokine is nonetheless a genuine artist with a great career ahead of him, with reserves of creative possibilities that are far from fully exhausted. It would be unjust to place him in the same ranks as the directors of the dramatic stage in Russia. And how wonderful that suspect people from various corners of the ballet world, though for unwholesome reasons, have gradually begun to step away from him in order to adopt more petty causes and support them according to their abilities. Thus I am certain that on the basis of my independent, though admittedly fleeting, observations the name of Boris Romanov will shine in the pages of several publications far above the name of Fokine. Shameless publicists are already lavishing their praise on him with almost no cause whatsoever.

In the newspaper *Den'* (The Day) I recently read that in the production of *Francesca da Rimini** only one moment was magnificent: "The passage of Giovanni the Lame is the one truly successful, the single infernal and somber place in the ballet." They are talking about the appearance of Romanov, who portrayed Gianciotto Malatesta. From the dark strip of the stage, Romanov penetrates the illumined square on the floorboards of the room in order to finish off the pair of lovers. The passage is worthless both in the plastic and the mimetic sense. A fireman could have broken through with no less success. Moreover, it has no relation whatsoever to the scene in *The Inferno.* This scene

———

*A ballet in three acts, eight scenes, and an epilogue with music by Boris Asafiev based on scenes in Dante's *Inferno.*

comes from the events of Francesca's earthly life, about which Dante had absolutely no information. Nonetheless, the obliging reviewer unduly praises Romanov. In another instance, two dancers dance in *Stenka Razin:** Alexander Monakhov and Romanov. Romanov's performance is mediocre. The jumping is purely acrobatic. There is no trace of the humor of the court of Tsar Alexei Mikhailovich, as it is represented, for example, in Kireevsky's[†] priceless *bylinas* and historical writings. The makeup is neither Parisian-chic apache nor Russian brigand, although the Cossack assembly consisted of people who thought of themselves not without a deep sense of pride: "We're not merely thieves or brigands, we're Stenka Razin's helpers." The reviewer, however, proclaims Romanov's performance first-rate. Actually, it was distinguished by incredible pretentiousness and cannot be compared to Monakhov's great art.

I mention these trivialities only to underscore the new order of things in certain journalistic circles with regard to Fokine. Of course, in comparison to him Romanov is a downright pygmy of the stage, unworthy of the critics' attention: he has acquired and plundered everything from the productions of his teacher, that same Fokine. The man just doesn't have any choreographic technique, a technique which has become obsolete in the eyes of vile directors of operettas, whereas in Fokine we have an individual of culture and originality. As a dancer he is undoubtedly first-rate and beautifully picturesque, with astonishing elevation and pure, noble pathos, devoid of bohemianism and always maintaining the strict decorum of art. In general, he is an artist from head to toe. Even in his mistakes his talent is evident. For Fokine the slightest turning point in the artist's soul can yield broad new efforts in the field of classical ballet.

Fokine needs to approach his task by putting aside for the moment several principles of production. First and foremost he needs to give up his realistic conceptions of ballet dancing. Classical dance cannot and ought not express anything realistic. The facts of real life are accompanied by emotional surges in the soul which do not flow into words. These emotions are configured only by the sounds of the orchestra and the medium of stage movement, each stylized and symbolic in its own way. If one sets out, for example, to represent not the fact of love, with all its complexity and rich substance, but only its poetic motif, the intimate and mutual attraction of two personalities, so to speak, in the garb of ballet—then one needs the technique of classical ballet: the world of poses

---

*A ballet in one act, set in seventeenth-century Russia that was danced to the music of Glazunov's symphonic poem. The ballet, which relates episodes depicting Razin's famous rebellion of Cossacks and peasants, premiered at the Maryinsky on 28 November 1915.

[†]Petr Vasilievich Kireevsky (1808–1856) was a folklorist, archeologist, and pamphleteer and Russia's most prominent collector of folk epics known as *byliny.*

and gestures of a particular hue, the combination of designs of a visionary character, the pattern of movement on the floor with the precise stamp of every step in the manner of Trefilova or the leaps of Pavlova and Vaganova. The plastic vocabulary of ballet is similar to poetic speech. There is nothing ordinary about it in the crude sense of the word. But through its technique, the music of emotions—which are fantastic to the highest degree in their configurations but nonetheless constitute the foundation of our emotional life—changes drastically. No, I am not expressing myself precisely. The issue here is not the soul. The classical forms of ballet exfoliate, reaching the highest loftiness from which emanates not the psychological element of personality but rather the abstract and universal ideas of the spirit.

Only on this ground can the reform of contemporary choreographic art be accomplished. The instruments for this are immense in number. And the sooner one begins to rework the old into the perspectives of new tasks and goals, the greater the chances for success. Otherwise this marvelous spectacle is in danger of annihilation or of degenerating into pantomime and revelry, worthy only of nightclubs.

—"M. M. Fokin. Shtrikhi i polemika," *Birzhevye vedomosti* (8 December 1915): 6.

"La Jota Aragonese"

This is a new production by Fokine, which does honor to the ballet master. I heartily salute the artist. In the course of some ten minutes he showed great natural talent and beautiful virtuosity. Thank God there are no bacchanalias. The groupings marvelously do their jangling, radiantly and delicately. They not only wonderfully accord with the harmonic phrases of the violins but have their own poetic motif and design that contend with the orchestra. And the dancing of the thirty-member corps de ballet that accompanies the solo stars is not incidental. The two elements of the dramatization are inextricably linked. The delicate streams of individual figures surge in front like great waves against the background of a more massive movement. This is a real model of how one must combine the two elements of balletic art into a pattern of restrained execution and action.

One moment of the corps' dancing—almost at its ultimate limits—seemed particularly expressive. The mass of dancers fall to their knees and cheerfully beat out time with their legs extended along the floor. It is like the improvisation of a crowd that has been seized by a fit of playfulness and frolicking in the pure, warm air of a Spanish spring. It is unexpected and poetic. The timbre is vivid and rich. Despite the few opportunities for rehearsal, every detail is coordinated. Rising from their knees, the whole bunch line up in lively groups and then rush forward and backward in a rapid flow. There is still no tempest, just some innocent fun on a summer morning. But everything points to the possibility of a thunderstorm, with flashes of passion in the future. The men dance expressively, also gently and softly. There is none of the vulgarity of previous productions in the Spanish style.

The peak of perfection is the dancing of the young girls done by the best artists of the troupe, and at its base are the classical figures. But these figures are scaled down. The battements are of all sorts. The gliding steps are done in various directions. The legs are alternated low in the air. These little gems of genuine art are strung on the gold thread of a Glinka melody. Especially wonderful are the variations performed by Elena Liukom with the fragrant charm of elegance and taste. You did not want to take your eyes off her. She glided in straight lines without moving her body and an expression on her face that captured the spectators in the hall. Hers is a lovely talent with a multitude of facets. She is a classical dancer with exquisite elevation. And for genre dancing, what harmony and variety of tones! Mariya Leontieva and Vera Fokina vied with Liukom. Leontieva's variation was exceedingly simple and done sketchily, as was Liukom's dancing. There were the most miraculous patterns on the floor. Liukom negotiated her part masterfully. Fokina's dancing was similarly well planned, although its choreography slipped into grandiloquence. Thus the rotation of her hand, with her elbow remaining stationary, produced a rather strange impression. Finally, Evgeniya Biber and Inna Neslukhovskaya, then Alisa Vronskaya, Josephina Shimanskaya, and Feliya Dubrovskaya produced effects with exceeding diligence, completing the full picture of an Aragonese jota. And again, there was not a single feature of Fokine's former dramatizations of Spanish life. Everything vulgar and nightclubbish was discarded.

—"'Jota Aragonesa,'" *Birzhevye vedomosti* (31 January 1916): 7.

My Miniatures

"Swan Lake"

The Maryinsky has done *Swan Lake* these past days without much success. The ballet appears ill-suited to Elizaveta Gerdt given the lyricism of its dances in her first scenes and the dramatic upsurge of the second act, which requires that the dancer perform with evocative brilliance and communicate a diabolical passion. This is the way it is with the lavishly developed, graceful pas de deux in Lev Ivanov's production, and with Marius Petipa's staging of Odile's dance at the ball, which is technically complex and graphically ardent. As I write these brief notes I cannot recall a single captivating moment in the dual part of this generally excellent and even remarkably virtuoso ballerina. First the pas de deux in act 1, scene 2, which is the central moment of Tchaikovsky's work. Odette's tragic story is told in tender movements that are also audacious in their external sweep, as well as large and majestically consummate in their structure. Several moments of the pas de deux are filled with pure genius. The Queen of the Swans flaps first one wing, then another on the arms of her partner. The movement extends naturally along a horizontal line with a broad battement at waist level, which nothing better or more colorfully expresses than the acoustical surge and high-pitched violins of the orchestra. Such is this battement's staging, which focuses seamlessly with the music. Dancers of the former generation, of Vera Trefilova's epoch, adhered reverentially to Ivanov's contemplated plan of execution, and the most competent partner—Nikolai Legat—masterfully increased the effect of the poetic movement by means of his support. In the new productions of *Swan Lake,* Odette's difficult dance is performed in oversimplified, banal forms that leave the public cold because they fail to express the unfortunate girl's blazing, fiery soul. Instead of flapping first one and then the other wing, in place of the rhythmic alternation of battements in the air, we have boring poses with the leg thrown back that are unsuitable to the moment and visually unimpressive. This is the kind of reworking of our most remarkable classical ballets in the spirit of disarray that is setting in at the Maryinsky, about which I have recently written.

Then in the act 1 variation and its concluding allegro Gerdt's performance failed to elicit the thunderous excitement and tumultuous applause this movement usually produces in the theater. Here we also have picturesque features and details that stand out in their unusual charm as if depicted in fragrant, painterly hues. How beautiful Tamara Karsavina was in these scenes, with the charm of her innate femininity and the awe-inspiring beauty of her dance form, especially when supported by her partner! But Gerdt's irreproachable technique, which is unaroused by emotional fire, practically stripped of romantic feeling and systematically and mechanically exposed as a kind of soundless emptiness, must be seen as being unresponsive to the action's overall artistic challenge. In spite of the purity of the external traits of her performance and the scholastic correctness of its conception, the character of the dancing—especially with that lifeless waving of the hands in the air—seems unusually prosaic and ordinary.

The last scene of the second act, the seductively wild dance of Odile at the ball with her two partners, with its conception of vividly dramatic acting, fares no better. First of all there is no expression. The ballerina's face, which in itself is delicate and fine, with a helplessly childlike smile, remains constantly rigid. Nothing. Not a cloudlet. Second, the figures of the dancing are somehow limp and wobbly, as they splash all over the place, instead of being intensely compact and focused on one point. Finally, only an evil genius could have advised this marvelous dancer to try her strength on gimmicky rotations, which is done—according to the general rule—fixed to one place without moving a step to the side. This is so-called fouetté. From the first rotations the young ballerina slides and then quickly rushes downstage toward the footlights, helplessly twirling her small figure almost on the same level as the floor, instead of providing a free and elevated movement with a buoyant and beautiful sweep. Abandoning in the middle of the dance the absurd figure of a stark monster without kith or kin, the bewildered dancer rushes to perform leaps along a large circle of the stage reminiscent of a circus. I neither could nor wanted to look, so I closed my eyes.

Let me note several additional features of Gerdt's art. The play of her hands occupies a special role in her art. If we were to draw parallels and compare such different artistic giants, we would have to say that Pavlova accompanies the dancing of hands with an intense play of her eyes, during which her fingers accompany the movement of her body rhythmically and harmoniously. Gerdt does not create such harmony or unanimity. In themselves her hands are gorgeously placed. But their dancing is nonetheless mechanical, organically unconnected to the overall dancing of her entire body, unable to attract the dancer's eyes to themselves like a magnet and spread in the air with no poetic animation. And it is just this absence of playing with her eyes that spoils the spectator's impression. She is unable to fix the changing figures of open gesticulation with her eyes or to gaze into her partner's face or to intimately and coherently merge her glance with the audience when performing her large rotations and turns in the air. Ecstatic dancing in general consists of the body's impulse to ascend. Just a split second of the dancer's burning eyes—never disappearing from the audience's field of vision, even when she turns her head—fusing with the thousand staring eyes of the public can create a colossal impression.

And this is where Pavlova's greatness comes in. Her eyes are always intensely and persistently focused on a single point or, as when performing Nikolai Legat's variation in *Don Quixote,* soothingly accompanying the figures as they alternately float across one another. To be sure, her hands are not completely without fault. Their overall culture in any case is occasionally delicately and properly (*zierlich-manierlich*) of the German make we find in Gerdt. But there is no comparison between the two. Pavlova's hands play, breathe, and live as if she were an ancient bacchante. Thus in *Le Pavillon d'Armide* they sublimely pluck the chords of the weeping harp. There is nothing superfluous here. Her shoulder motionlessly turns yellow like a patch of ivory. Then the hands stretch forward with palms open in a devoutly fervent gesture. In Gerdt's execution these marvelous moments are performed palely, colorlessly, anemically. Her excessively long arms are flung feebly and unspiritedly back and forth without expression. The same thing happens in *Raymonda.* In her dancing during the final act her arms pulsate lymphatically, pathetically, consumptively, without an agitated upswing, when instead, during the turbulent allegro they should rake in the air with passion, with the rapture of self-intoxication, with a kind of inner "hurrah," in full weight and full strength in every turn and every step so as to provide clarity and expressiveness to the rotations along the diagonal of the stage, from top to bottom. The same in *Swan Lake.* The dry, rigid movements of Gerdt's arms—winglike and pliant in the ballet master's conception—lack any charm.

My miniature has come to an end, but I do not consider my assessment of this young and gifted ballerina finished.

—"Moi miniatiury: *Lebedinoe ozero,*" *Zhizn' iskusstva* (4 June 1920): 1.

Marius Petipa's "La Bayadère"

On Saturday, 11 March, *La Bayadère* was performed at the Maryinsky with a new set of performers to commemorate Petipa's centenary. First of all, I should concentrate on the dancing of Elizaveta Gerdt, who appeared in the main role and carried it through with great success. I mention this last detail solely in order to give the dancer her due as if through the public's mouth, which will allow me to present my own personal opinions more fully. Gerdt has already developed completely; her art has completed the full circle of its development and, for all its imperfections, it deserves our thorough attention. And so we shall begin our analysis with Nikiya's first appearance on stage.

[When Pavlova performed this role she] entered covered with a veil. She stopped on top of the staircase, which led to the entrance of the Indian temple, for only a few seconds. But this already signified a feature of her passionate and brilliant art. You need to know how to stand while the music is playing, the strings roaring, the violins singing, and the orchestra waving and sighing. Descending from the stair in a slow step, the dancer came out to the proscenium and, pausing for several new measures, threw off the dark veil covering her face. A storm was set off in the theater. But the peal of acclaim quickly died away and the audience became still at the first signs of the dance theme. How wonderful Pavlova was at this moment! Two black braids woven with pearls fell weightily on her shoulders. On her head were reddish gold plates on wires. The head was splendid and unique, with dark crow's feet around the eyes, patches of fire in the almondlike slit of her dark eyes under the arc of her delicate brows. Her swarthy arms were encircled with golden bracelets and glittering pelts which fell along her body. Her dress was blue with brilliant patches. The dance of fire begins—a ritual in the full sense of the word as regards the beauty of its lines and the inspiration of its poses and gestures—with a smooth and tranquil andante. The dance figures are not compact in their design; indeed, the dancing is even somewhat cumbersome in its individual nuances, but it nonetheless constitutes one of Petipa's masterpieces. The dancer nervously tosses up first one knee, then the other, each bent in the air, and she traverses the stage on pointe, drawing with them countless circles in all directions.

Among the figures of the dance of fire there is one that is exceptionally wonderful. Extending the leg back at full length, the dancer must lightly turn from a pose where she is rolled up in a ball to full height. This is a slow turn with the whole body to the protracted tempo of the violins, as if the body were going through the complete cycle of its growth and suddenly becomes erect, like a wonderfully strong sapling, before the audience's eyes. For this picture to be fully expressive and sufficiently effective, one needs a classical leg, a resilient waist, and the support of the head, which directs all the movement. In Pavlova's interpretation this figure produced an enormous impression. The intensity of the body, which communicates the same intensity in the soul and its extreme capacity for willful and passionate impulses, eases slowly and protractedly. Finally the tension disappears completely and frees the body, arms, and legs for a simple pose. The dancer has inserted into a snakelike, plantlike figure the fire and energy of her by-no-means Slavic temperament and, to a certain degree, has even reworked it in a spirit peculiar to her talent, in which the plantlike element was far less than the animal–human- or animal–bird-like element, with its tempests on the ground and exaltations in the air.

In Gerdt this remarkable movement in the first act, as well as the entire dance of fire in general, produces no impression. None whatsoever—zero! Despite all her efforts the figure is small, indeed lymphatic. It has no pizzazz. It is a nonentity, as empty and meaningless as Olga Spesivtseva's, who also tried her hand last year in *La Bayadère.* Only it came out better in Spesivtseva's attempt, not because she surpassed Gerdt in the quality of her dancing but solely because in it—as in several other scenes of the ballet—she was helped by the native beauty of her external forms: the faultlessly classical arch and the harmonious structure of her body, which is simultaneously picturesque and statuesque. The most important thing in this marvelous composition was lacking in both dancers—an internal force, a cluster of passions and illuminations, which at first is rolled up like a ball of impulses that within several seconds opens its sunny core and splashes its fiery rays in your face.

It is really not necessary to talk about the romantic scene with Gerdt's partner. We are dealing here with a magnificent dancer in many respects, and nothing more. Do not look for anything else. This emerges with special clarity in the second act, in the argument between the two rivals. Gerdt is simply out of place here. Although she poignantly waves her long arms with a look of unfeigned tragedy, although she constantly jabs the air à la Duncan with the same finger, an impression of grief and jealousy just doesn't come off. It is better not to take the knife in your hands at all if you don't know how to squeeze it in your palm and you hold it with a tenseness of the muscles that can be felt even from a distance. There will be no stabbing, but stabbing must appear possible, almost inevitable. In a similar fashion the dancer loses the famous hyporchema of scene 3. I call "hyporchema" a dramatic dance with a distinctively real content. In the parlance of contemporary classical ballet the dance is called otherwise: pas d'action, in the brilliant style of French rhetoric. Frankly, the nomenclature of Lucian and the Atheneum's Pollux* is closer and more comprehensible in its phonetics. *Hyporchema* sounds traditionally and liturgically more solemn.

[In Gerdt's dancing] the series of figures and poses, the long croisés on the ground, the glissades and the darting leaps, produce a limpid impression. The turning of the entire body and the rising on pointe, although flawless in shape, nonetheless lack a poetic inclination upward. The arabesques are not headlong.

---

*For Lucian, see above. Julius Pollux was a Greek lexicographer of the second century A.D., author of *Omnasticon,* a list of Attic words and technical terms with explanations and quotations from other sources.

The brilliantly formulated dance with the bouquet could have provided suitable material for another interpreter, such as Pavlova, who danced this variation with a basket of flowers in such a remarkably strong and expressive way that the theater broke out in wild applause as soon as the music died down. The dancer died at the footlights, falling headfirst to the ground, and lying flat with her entire body. The enchanted audience froze for several moments and awakened from the artistic spell only when the curtain finally fell.

To be fair, at that point [in the ballet] Gerdt's talent began to reach its peak, so I will abandon all parallels to Pavlova. With regard to classical dance in its pure form, in the tempos of melodious adagio with its lush garden of plantlike figures and its passionate orbits and picturesque poses in the arms of her partner, the best ballerina on the Petersburg stage fears no comparison with anyone. She would not lose the public's interest even if Tamara Karsavina or Mathilda Kshesinskaya danced alongside her. The classical material of her art, which has been refined in the magnificent school of the late Samuil Andriyanov, constitutes a real treasure. I will not examine separately all the components of the pas de deux in the last act of *La Bayadère* but will speak only generally to characterize the dancer. I am mixing together monumental elements with the pyrotechnical technique of the variations and codas that demands not so much the heart and soul of the artist as the mastery of practice. The reader will not hear in my words the slightest tendency to diminish Gerdt's magnificent art. I write these lines only to establish the boundary between two forms of balletic virtuosity, the academic and the passionate; and considering my view on the subject I pay a great compliment to this artist when, keeping in mind the past and present of the Petersburg stage, I call her the most extraordinary practitioner of classical choreography. Among the current ballerinas— those who are ready to pack up and leave for a measly dollar, those who are frivolous and buffoonish and who should really be put in their place—this is a genuine ballerina with a well-deserved reputation as a performer of the most demanding roles.

La Bayadère is so full of stylish variations, so packed with wonderful classical, character, and genre dancing, that I would have to go on endlessly in order to say even a few words about every performer individually, thus making my article impossibly long. Petipa's genius has manifested itself here with an unusual scope of creative force; it sparkles with all the colors of the rainbow and demonstrates an unprecedented variety of motifs. His was a real talent—the demiurge of the predominantly female art of dancing. He gave this art his whole life and loved it passionately with the whole of his genius; he fused its designs and themes with the delicious feeling of specifically female, rhythmically plantlike, ripplingly unstable and flowing beauty. There was not an inch of a woman's body that he would not disclose and stylize in his art. He was a classical ideologue of woman in ballet. What a variety of female dancing there is in *La Bayadère* alone! The dance with the long veils fastened to the woman's legs; the dance of the slaves with the asymmetrically divergent groups (the Crooked Dance); the dance with the fans, with the parrots, with the crowd of barbarians, with the Bacchante at its head; nearly ten purely classical variations distributed among the best talents of the young generation of dancers (Mariya Kozhukhova, Taisiya Troyanovskaya, Ekaterina Geidenreich, Lidiya Ivanova); and magnificent variations totally unrelated to one another, not only in their structure but also in their individual features and lines, such as Manu's dance. I cannot conclude my article without devoting at least several lines to this dance.

This is a combination of various patterns on the floor: pas de bourrée, polka which earlier were performed by Trefilova and Karsavina. Karsavina provided such a splash of fragrant colors and florescent charm that one can never forget it. A mother is playing with her children. With one hand she supports a pitcher on her head, and the other she waves around freely as if to ward off the hopping little chicks who are clinging to her legs. These circles on the floor depicted by the legs are extended in all directions of the stage, now to the outer wings and now to the edge of the lighted ramp, everywhere following after two Lebanese cedars of extraordinary beauty. If Manu's god himself had been able to watch Petipa's brilliant work as performed by Karsavina, he'd have kissed her lips passionately for her mastery of style and her conveyance of the greatest of all of life's themes—that of the family and of motherhood. In the most recent presentation of *La Bayadère* this variation was done successfully by Elsa Vill, a talented and deserving artist, though, I hasten to say, one without any of the deeply felt personal and intimate flutterings of the child's world. Thus, her generally marvelous dancing is somewhat dry and only superficially playful. The glance of her laughing eyes is directed exclusively to the pitcher when it should really glide lovingly over the children. Nonetheless, the dance elicited the public's loud approval and an ovation for the artist. An adherent of the classical traditions, I also warmly applaud Vill, momentarily burying in oblivion Karsavina's beauty and Trefilova's total art and brilliant polish.

—"Marius Petipa (*Baiaderka*)," *Zhizn' iskusstva* (21 March 1922): 2.

The End of the Season

Lida Ivanova

. . .

F ollowing the firmly established tradition of last season, an enormous divertissement was performed after *Giselle* for the amusement of the public, as if we needed empty and senseless games. I want to note at the end of my article the appearance in the divertissement of the fledgling and unquestionably gifted dancer Lida Ivanova. It is worth saying several words about her.

She has a Mongolian-type face: Her eyelids are slightly swollen, concealing her lively, narrow eyes, which glance from behind Malaysian silks, by an impermeable curtain. Her cheekbones are prominent, her arms are not long, and her fingers are not especially agile. Her bony frame is heavy. Her body is rather short and round with a noticeable and dangerous tendency toward plumpness. Unfortunately, her leg is not of the strictly classical type—it is rather muscular, it lacks a perceptible lift, and it has a fat ankle. If you look at this Mongolian from the audience you don't feel anything special. She does not have enough femininely plantlike, picturesquely colorful substance for the theatrical adagio, with its botany of extended, convoluted, fouetté-like alternating figures that surge to the drawn-out tempo of the music. Nevertheless her leap is large and her elevation is outstanding, though it is somewhat dry and lacks a fragrant ballon.

In the pas de deux she performed with Vasily Efimov there was no robust fluttering of lines, no inhaling and exhaling beauty of the body's tension and turning. The pas de deux was performed wanly. But the variation came off much better, much more expressively, thanks to its airborne movements. However, even here there was insufficient purity, an inadequate arch, and extended toes. Her body jerked forward and spoiled the design of the elevated flight.

There is too little decisive material to allow any critical conclusions about this dancer. She has to learn to dance in modest spaces so as to get used to the stage step by step, and to prepare for more complicated and essential work in the future. She has the necessary qualities for serious development, and there is no doubt about her talent for classical art. All that remains is for her to focus her will on this effort. She needs also to think—and think quite seriously— about her outer appearance. The body of a classical dancer can suddenly lose its elasticity and pliancy and grow coarse or become pudgy. This is why one needs to work at full strength, making every effort to love one's art above and beyond anything else. This is when there will be intelligence. Regarding this young dancer one can say with complete assuredness: she is at the start of a highly promising career under enormously favorable auspices and with the palpable support of her associates.

—"Zakrytie sezona," *Zhizn' iskusstva* (16 May 1922): 2.

Two Schools of Classical Dance

"Sleeping Beauty"

I have recently seen *Sleeping Beauty* performed by two ballerinas who have different temperaments and different theatrical experience. Elizaveta Gerdt is a typical example of what is known as the French school of ballet art. This school has rendered extraordinary service to ballet by providing a roster of exceptionally brilliant talent and establishing its place as an artistic enterprise of the highest order. But in the current period of historical shifts and the whirlwind of moral and aesthetic issues that we are now facing head on, the French spirit's characteristically fatal bias for dazzling prettiness and playfully coquettish eroticism is especially obvious. We should never forget this brilliant people's stunning achievements: they were once not only the leaders in matters of taste but also of thought. Their genius and strength triumph in the world of emotions; but in the area of moral and resolutely intellectual pursuits, the French—for all their passion—pale in comparison with other creators of culture. In Russia we have long grown accustomed to turning our gaze to the land of Botticelli, Michelangelo, and Leonardo da Vinci. This is a land of strong-willed passions, from the might of imperial Rome through the seethings of the Renaissance to Garibaldi's Red Shirts and our own times. It is strange, when you race across Italy by train from Lombardy to the South, cutting through Tuscany, Emilia Romagna, and, in Carducci's* words, the eternally verdant Umbrian valleys, how you constantly encounter the enormous display of acrobatic heroism that produced not only the commedia dell'arte in all its purity and rudimentariness, but also such contradictory phenomena as Goldoni and

* Giosuè Carducci (1836–1907), a historian of Italian literature and one of Italy's major poets.

Gozzi.* Beneath everything Italian, both present and past, lie physical force, a strictly disciplined carriage, and a fiery and healthy passion for engendering what is new.

In our historic times, filled with such great challenges, the French art of dance should be corrected and even recast by Italian methods: it is affected and coquettish, pretentious and refined, with its constant profiles and croisé positions, its constant tension in the nape of the neck and back, its gymnastic splits in the air without any bold preparation, and its all-engulfing turns in the air. Indeed, what does a French pirouette represent next to an Italian one? The pirouette's psychological task must be nothing less than the emotional movement of a whirlwind writ large. And this is exactly what the Italian pirouette is. The velocity of the turn is furious. In the frenzy of the tempest both profiles of the ballerina flicker before the audience's eyes. The legs flex slightly. The impression is enormous and gripping. Italian art demands what contemporary biomechanics calls animated standing: straight to the ultimate representational feature, with the participation of all the components of vertical posture and without the slightest breach or distortion. The head may be turned—though not according to the demands of the capricious and coquettish French croisé—even in the direction of the dancer's legs, in order to create the illusion of complete coordination of the action with the performer's inner mood. The torso goes at all times behind the leg without turns that sway to the side.

And how beautiful the Italian attitude! The dancer's entire body is actually directed upward, not with timidly effeminate emotion but with a firm, immovable will, like the gentle rippling of water. The back is held with assurance. The head sits on the neck confidently and proudly. In this apotheosis of verticality, the dancer—all one line straight up in the air, all ascent and heroic exertion, all attention and apperception—suddenly freezes for several terrifyingly long moments. This is a genuine miracle of beauty and morality. And from this daring height the dancer, with a soft and liquid glissade failli, goes on to another classical step.

Such is the Italian interpretation of the arabesque, with a straight and highly elevated torso. And such generally are the methods of Italian classicism when applied to the distinct tasks of ballet. The Italian croisé is completely unlike the French croisé. The leg is in front, slightly bent in the manner of Harlequin. From the point of view of Petipa's school this is a scandal, and constitutes sheer

---

* Carlo Goldoni (1707–1793), an Italian dramatist whose realistic approach challenged the commedia dell'arte's device of using stock characters and loose plots; Carlo Gozzi (1720–1806), an Italian dramatist of the commedia dell'arte, was a staunch opponent of Goldoni's dramatic reforms.

horror on the stage. The leg must be perfectly extended and must correspond to the turning of the head toward the shoulder, which is brought forward! Meanwhile, Harlequin's pose—barely sketched and introduced like a gentle shade into this classically refined and icy cold art—suggests how possible it is to insert elements from the joyous theater of life. The hands wave forcefully over the head. The head faces the audience directly. This is also in its own way the marvelous Italian curling of the body into an elastic ball. In its actual execution it produces the effect of a daring, almost insolent challenge to the whole world, a summons to mount a bold and revolutionary leap, so to speak, a prologue to the upcoming and resolutely holy act as opposed to the curling of the body in the French way, which produces the impression of honey-coated lassitude and impotent stupor.

Olga Spesivtseva has not spent a year abroad in vain. She studied under the Italian master Enrico Cecchetti, known to all of Europe. Gentle and graceful in her articulations, she has now acquired traits that put her in a category all her own in the Maryinsky troupe. First and foremost, she is a classical dancer in the most rigorous sense. All her postures are perfect, her battements are restrained to the nth degree. Her turnout is faultless, and she is able to stand on her toes like none of her peers. If we add to this her exquisite body structure, the exceptional shape of her leg, the gradual tapering downward of her figure and the resilience of its ascent, the amazingly straight back and her absolutely delicate and sinuous waist, the plaintive curve of her neck and resplendently playful eyes—we have almost the complete picture of a gifted dancer. Her first appearance onstage has already produced several fine, though not necessarily absorbing, impressions. In Petipa's staging [of *Sleeping Beauty*], here is noted the so-called entrance of the ballerina, which is prepared for by the changing mise-en-scène. The dancer is provided with an array of different postures: beautiful pas de chat, extensive battements, circular leaps across the stage and some concluding ringlike patterns on the floor. This entrance is still unable to display all the dancer's reserves. Her leaps could have had a lighter, airier quality. The delicate battements, which are not autonomous, cannot be expressed by Spesivtseva here with all the strength she possesses.

But as soon as the entrance is finished and the dance with the suitors begins, there appears before our eyes that delightful art to which Cecchetti gives a new direction and which is still unspoiled by the distortions of the contemporary stage. Here are just the features I mentioned above, which are completely distorted by the flirtation of woman's culture with the theater's masculine elements. All the sharp bends of the body in bas-relief style, which at times become simply comical, should be abandoned once and for all. One should not forget in this regard several poses typical not only of Agrippina Vaganova, whose style occasionally suffered from a lack of pure artistry and craftsmanship, but of Olga Preobrazhenskaya: something here has become completely antiquated. And then there are the attitudes, the large arabesques, the gently exposed battements in second position, the rotations on the floor—all of which in Spesivtseva's performance should have been the embodiment of beauty and integrity.

In the variation of this marvelously performed dance, Spesivtseva exhibited several other features that reflected the spirit of Cecchetti's sparkling, playful technique. Before her complicated pirouettes the dancer does a frolicsome, rapid, frivolous and, in its design, even trivial beat of her legs pointed in an upward direction. With her fingers she slightly raises the edge of her dress, exposing her marblelike extremities. I am convinced that we are dealing here with one of Cecchetti's recommendations. If the dancer had allowed herself to depart from Cecchetti's precisely prescribed design or to exceed the minute doses of his recommendation, she would have inevitably lapsed into hopeless vulgarity. But there was absolutely none of this. The style of the entire dance was lovely and sophisticated. Alas, this was, if I am not mistaken, the only time the audience, which was otherwise sleepy during the entire performance, became animated. Unfortunately, the tours that followed were not especially successful. There were slips that showed insufficient firmness.

In the other acts Spesivtseva danced with varying success. In the scene of the dancing nymphs Spesivtseva's variation was excellent. Incidentally, at this point Fedor Lopukhov's staging, which was presented at the ballet's previous performance by Gerdt, was happily discarded: it was shabby, mannered, cold, empty in content, and inappropriately spread out across the stage. In Spesivtseva's performance, the old variation is a real masterpiece of classical art. It is filled with beautiful things tailored to the individual qualities of precisely the kind of dancer Spesivtseva is. She performs the ballottés, tossing the legs in a broad and physically expressive way in fifth position, covering the space generously and quite splendidly. This is a central moment in the old variation, and I know of no dancer who can compete with this young ballerina's artistry. But the later parts of the same variation, which require other poetic skills, as well as a playfully liberated soul, are performed rather blandly by Spesivtseva. In this case, Gerdt's equally polished and dignifiedly restrained art triumphs over Spesivtseva's.

I won't speak of the dances in the third act. We observe the same strengths and weaknesses that we constantly see in Spesivtseva's talent—one that is unquestionably attractive because it ordinarily gives the impression not of mere prettiness but of genuinely classical beauty in the broadest sense, which nonetheless knows its own limits. It would be nice to have a somewhat freer range of expression, which would produce not only a more picturesque staging but greater and more absorbing moral fervor as well. To abandon clichés and, most important, to emancipate our inner "I." More soul, more soul!

—"Dve shkoly klassicheskogo tantsa (*Spiashchaia krasavitsa*)," *Zhizn' iskusstva* (24 October 1922): 4.

Stravinsky's Ballets

༄༅༶

T he music of *Petrushka* is not only insufficiently danceable, it also lacks that special symphonic quality that can evoke lofty feelings within the audience. Torrents of aural and visual impulses flow between two equally low levels of musical sensation. Such is the overall impression one has of the work of this young and unquestionably talented composer. Added to these short-comings in Stravinsky's balletic output is a kind of malleability of the melodic design that the frivolous spurts and disruptive jolts of certain poorly coordinated motifs invariably violate. The drums cause an especially upsetting impression, nervously and chronically interfering with the orchestral harmony, which even without this lacks a rich and flowing wholeness.

Such peculiarities in Stravinsky's music make it impossible to dance to: it disturbs the dancers, and the dancers disturb it. The dances in *Petrushka* break down into two categories. On the one hand are character dances—various kinds of noisy Russian dances of the marketplace that incline toward raucous and ebullient bravado—on the other are variations that are similar to classical dance as performed by a puppet ballerina. Unfortunately, the character dances in the first scene of *Petrushka* are presented rather inadequately. Nothing flows, nor are the scenes interwoven into a theatrical whole; one gets the impression of something extremely meager, undisciplined, and disorderly in the ballet's overall action. In this festive scene with the popular masses, with its carousels, dancing bears, and masked youths, the merriment should have gushed forth and spurted in all directions. But this brio was totally lacking in the performance—it is even less in evidence this season than it was during the last one. The stylized dances of the puppet-ballerina as performed by Elsa Vill not only seemed void of the tragic meaning the ballet master wanted to assign to it; they also lacked charm or freshness. It is not fitting for artists at the end of their careers to undertake parts that call for the bloom of youth and demand fresh, resilient energy, particularly since even in an impoverished ensemble one can still find young members of the company with appreciable talent who are perfectly adequate for such relatively minor roles.

As a matter of principle we must note that if we consider how art evolved among the common people the fairground booth is not a source of classical dance. As a form of diversion the dances of the puppet theater are related solely to the movements of folk comedy and clownery. If we are searching for themes for balletic art in the world of puppets, we should look toward modern European literature, where we shall find these themes in the luxuriantly arrayed dolls of E. T. A. Hoffmann's tales. That kind of superbly dancing doll—the delicate and charming symbol of a lifeless girl—was marvelously portrayed by Jacques Offenbach in his beautiful opera,* and today it can still inspire a librettist to write an enchanting ballet. But returning to *Petrushka*, I must say in all seriousness that the puppet dances per se create a continuously irritating impression. They are insufficiently naive in their design to be interesting in and of themselves, and their excessive extravagance in terms of the action is an obstacle to the unfolding drama.

Moving on to the subject matter of *Petrushka*, let me note the following. Within the contours of metaphorical interpretation, it is witty, fresh, and original, yet nevertheless, overall it is unrestrained, exaggerated, and saddled with an ending that is almost comic in the impression it creates. The happy lover, in the person of the puppet Moor, strikes Petrushka with his sword. It turns out that Petrushka has a wooden head and his body is stuffed with sawdust. However, the soul of the dead puppet flies up to the roof of the fair booth and from there it threatens its master, the charlatanlike showman. If Petrushka had remained lying on the square like a lifeless doll, this tragedy in miniature would have achieved the status of a poetic episode within the world of the rowdy and reckless mob. But the mystical nuance which the artist emphasizes destroys the composition's sense of measure. It seems just as stilted and artificial as that other misguidedly included nuance, the scarf in *Le Pavillon d'Armide*—a real scarf, which descends from the bewitched Gobelin tapestry into the magical night. In both ballets Alexander Benois's artistic rhetoric has exceeded the boundaries of good aesthetic taste. Without these glaringly affected details everything would have been infinitely more successful.

The production of *Petrushka* was satisfactory only in a modest way. Although the stage set is not very large or bright—it fails to sparkle with the full variety of life's palette—there is nonetheless a sense that it was put together by a lively individual. Yet with greater inspiration the ballet could have acquired greater significance. Leonid Leontiev's performance as Petrushka at times produces an extremely winning impression. It is thoroughly realized and

---

*Offenbach's comic opera *Les Contes d'Hoffmann* (1881).

is sustained in all its sweetly palpitating tones; only at occasional moments does it turn into comic caricature and exaggeration. In any case the clenched fists with which Petrushka challenges fate and threatens the charlatan showman can only be attributed to the artist's keen imagination, which I have never denied when acknowledging his talent. But this is the single comforting thing one can say about *Petrushka*. In the general repertory of academic ballet it does not represent a notable phenomenon. It only trains the public to confuse light pantomime with serious balletic presentations, to mix up semi-character dances, which are conceptually impoverished, with classical dances whose goal is to strive upward. This is a show to be performed two or three times a season—and that's all.

But how does *The Firebird* fare in Fedor Lopukhov's production? I refuse to criticize in any detail this collection of trivial concoctions from a pompously banal imagination that is inclined everywhere to separate temperament and pathos. Lopukhov himself dances exactly the way he arranges ballets. In his character dances he is ready to fly over the head of his partner with an expression of extraordinary exaltation on his fully outstretched face. He screams of his emblazoned feelings, but the movements themselves display coldness and falsity. There is not one lively sensation. Everything is far-fetched. He keeps getting on your nerves with his high-handedness and unjustified rumpus. And this is just the way it is in this production of *The Firebird*. The unsightly dance of Kashchei's followers constitutes a collection of incoherent movements that are repellent to the point of disgust precisely because of their grotesquely invented figures. This is not the creation of fantasy but rather the lifeless arrangement of impossible positions with unheard-of bends of the body that generally leave the spectator deathly cold. What kind of Firebird is this— that most miraculous image from Russian folktales—in Lopukhov's bombastic interpretation?

The Firebird also produces intricate figures, although here one ought to provide something artistically simple both in content and form, something pure and sunny and beautiful to look at. But in Elsa Vill's performance this completely disappears. Everything is drawn-out, unhurried, and tiresomely dull. A negative charm emanates from the figure onstage: a sense of youth gone by and sad memories of the brilliant elevation that used to be characteristic of this dancer. In one spot, which represents a comic likeness to a ballet pas de deux, the ballerina's cavalier drops her headfirst and wipes her on the floor like a broom. But for ballet master Lopukhov this is a typical trick, worthy of his affectedly vapid and acrobatically unbridled art.

And if we eliminate this unpleasant feature from the pas de deux, then everything in it, as in many other parts of the ballet, represents a hodge-podge of generally familiar choreographic works. In its accumulation of tempo the orgy of monsters recalls the bacchanalia of *Islamey*. Themes from *La Bayadère* and even *Die Puppenfee* are found. In any case there is nothing original, nor is there a single feature introduced into the scene that partakes of a calm or genuine scrupulousness. That wild dance of unclean forces in Kashchei's kingdom will remain in the choreographic literature of our times as a specimen of a dance of half-witted monsters which it would be better not to show on the serious stage. To be sure, a character dancer with a style like Lopukhov's cannot be a ballet master: he tries all the time to make sallies even into the realm of choreographic philosophy, arranging all kinds of complicated transformations and putting into play his inadequate erudition, but this never makes any sense. Lopukhov has no soaring imagination. A penchant for constantly leaping upward and throwing yourself over the heads of your partners does not compensate for a lack of true creative artistic talent. All of this is only a surrogate, a glaring falsification that deludes no one.

The music of *The Firebird,* with its flutes, drums, and trumpets, at times recalls the music of *Petrushka*. The same jerkiness, the same endless stop and go in the orchestra, which gives no support even to the intricate acrobatic movements raging on stage. To dance to such music—at times long-winded, at others monotonously slow in its undoubtedly lyrical melody—is exceptionally difficult. But onstage, as I have already said, there are no serious dances. In the orchestra we have the hissing of Dionysus; among the dancers we have a disorderly commotion and racket.

The audience was tired and bored, and during the entire second half of the performance there was not a single round of applause.

—"Balety Stravinskogo," *Zhizn' iskusstva* (26 December 1922): 2–5.

The Birth of Apollo

I have been dreaming about a new ballet for a long time. For years I have been thinking about a theme which came to me one unforgettable night on Delos, when, because of rough seas, I decided not to return to Mykonos but instead to spend the night in a shack where members of a French archival commission were taking shelter. For a long while I was unable to fall asleep because of the excitement of the day: here is where Apollo was born; here stood the manger of the great sun god! It was at this time that I had just begun studying classical dance, and the thought of a ballet appeared to me in the vaguest of outlines. But now this question has been revealed to me in all its depth and magnitude, connected to the most diverse issues and with a historical perspective that I could then barely imagine. Nonetheless I still find myself returning to my original, and perhaps naive, impressions in order to recast them in light of the enormous experience I have accumulated in the area of ballet into newly resolute and more precisely defined form.

What does the birth of Apollo signify in that ethnic environment that could not help but impede the origin of his cult? The future mother of Apollo, Leto, could not find shelter anywhere. Everyone shrugged her off so as not to assist in the birth of the new god. In conceiving a new ballet on the subject of the birth of Apollo opportunities open up for scenes that are extremely rich in choreographic possibilities. The ballet master would have to present the everyday life and reality of various aboriginal peoples with their wild culture dating back to prehistoric time. In this amalgam one needs to distinguish between the different ethnic entities and to present them crowding onto the bustling coasts of Hellas.

First and foremost are the Pelasgians. Extremely powerful and severe looking, the builders of the fortifications of the Cyclops—giants of Hellenic pedigree who were temperamentally wild and Bacchic in their uncompromising cult to Dionysus—provide material for the most magnificent character dances. Here one could present a genuine orgy with ecstatic dancing around a sacrifice and include the speechless singing of an archaic dithyramb. This is still before Arion, before the first flashes of conscious culture, before the first attempts to inculcate in dance and song the principle of rhythmic harmony. Melodically, the music here must be elemental, crude, and weighty; a basic rhythm must predominate, one filled with physical, willful impulses. The music must be danceable in the purest and simplest sense, as if of its own accord it shoots up into a dance, a jump, an orgy of muscular tensions and resolutions. Such a bacchanalia, orchestrated and coordinated using all available ethnographic materials, could constitute one of the first scenes of this new ballet.

Leto herself in the midst of this wild chaos of hostile elements, with her hair coming loose from its bindings as if she were being pursued not only by the wind but by forest and mountain beasts, engages in dramatic mime with the highest degree of expressiveness. At times she stands on her toes and attempts certain dances, but the surrounding noise and chaos cut short all her initiatives. Classical dance does not yet exist, it is still in the womb of history, and the woman Leto—the prototype of the future incarnation of the new art—still appears in semi-chaotic darkness. Her toes only twinkle and then disappear immediately. She stands on her toes in fits of sudden joy, but at once hopelessly sinks down.

In the forefront is the characteristic Pelasgian dance, a powerful phenomenon that seizes the spectator. In the background, however, groups of other nationalities stand out visibly and picturesquely: local fragments of Japhetic tribes, splinters of Semitic peoples and Hamitic riff-raff brought in by the sea; strangers from the Lebanese hills of far-off Canaan; Phoenicians, merchants with purple cloths and vases, figures of Astarte,* multicolored glass and honeyed wines from Palestine. Here are envoys from Babylon, that Paris of the ancient world; Ninevite merchants with curly heads and beards and with the hooked noses of Hamites, trading in sumptuous fabrics, mirrors, and cosmetics; and, finally, Nubians and ancient Egyptians who trade in gold and ivory, leopard skins and Ethiopian slaves. The dance of the Egyptian woman could constitute a special variation in which patches of the sunlight of the future Apollo would flash through like prophetic signs. The Egyptian woman dances on pointe, with a wonderfully graceful back, assuming exquisite profiles and three-quarter poses. All around, her great art evokes generally hostile wonder. Only Leto, with rapturous enthusiasm, anticipates the coming joy of the new world of dance that has taken its motif from the valley of the Nile and rounded it off and completed it in flourishing Hellas.

This is the first act of the ballet, which represents the entire prelude to humanity's newest artistic expression, and in it three main choreographic moments predominate: the Pelasgian dances, Leto's supple études with the mime gestures that look into the future, and the classical dance of the ancient Egyptian woman. The orchestra works in tandem with the dance, incorporating roaring fanfares, drumbeats, the howling of wild beasts who pursue Leto, shepherds' reed pipes, the whistle of the wind, and Artemis's striking of the tympani. But the dance acting of the first act, concluding with the Egyptian woman's number, must yield to wonderful, measured melodies in the classical style.

The second act is performed on Delos, the place of Apollo's birth, among the plane-tree groves of this marvelous island. The island has accepted Leto. Here the first scene must be presented with particular splendor. From Olympus goddesses fly down to Leto, who is tormented by a difficult birth and an exhausted and unspeakable longing for a new source of light. But until Ilythia's help comes from Lycia, which represents a fixed point on the far-off land of the Hyperboreans,† Leto cannot be delivered of her burden. These constitute several beautifully alternating moments, filled with plastic poses and groupings,

---

*This ancient Semitic deity, goddess of fertility and reproduction, was worshiped by the Canaanites and Phoenicians.

†Ilythia (also Eileithyia) was the ancient Greek goddess of childbirth; Lycia was an ancient country in southwest Asia Minor that later became a Roman province; in classical mythology the Hyperboreans were a people who lived in a land of constant sunshine and plentitude above the north wind. Volynsky often wrote of them in his articles.

and with festive gaiety in the concluding episode of Ilythia's arrival. Apollo's birth is accompanied by the appearance of swans, who seven times swim around the island. The burning sun constantly spreads its bright rays across the stage. The orchestra must accentuate this by the increasing presence of string instruments, including melodious harps, whose harmonies are of a solemn nature. The winds continually fade, although on the periphery of the orchestra the diminishing motifs of the clarinets and reed pipes are still heard in the diverse variations. These diminishing motifs must communicate a feeling of sentimentality that at times reaches the point of infantile purity. Then the transition to Apollo's motifs will seem less shrill, built on the maximal coordination of the dominant themes.

Delos was the place where the Hyperboreans sent their gifts via Pelasgian Dodona.* The youths of Delos sang the hymns of the Lycian elder Olen,† and Lycia itself, as we have just said, was one of the transit points on the northern peoples' road to Central Europe. A sacrificial altar made of horns around which a prayer took place stood on Delos, and it contained a Semitic-like expression of penitence. All these circumstances give the ballet master the occasion to place on stage, after the birth of Apollo, several of the most interesting choreographic scenes. In the background on an elevated hillock is the sacrificial altar made of horns with objects to conduct a liturgy. The priest strikes the back of the worshipers with a bundle of twigs. In center stage young girls and youths perform dances known as hyporchema. This can be an entire dramatic scene whose plot expresses the conflict of the warring elements and the victory of the emerging cult of Apollo.

With its Hyperborean-Semitic strata, Delos was to a certain extent prepared to receive new creeds, and for this reason the native dance in honor of Apollo is filled with wild enthusiasm. Here one must disregard all of Petipa's clichés. There should be no pas de deux, where the dancers dance for each other and are bound together by the delicate ties of a fashionable romance. In Greece each performer danced with his eyes turned toward Olympus, as if only for himself or the sun god. In the staged hyporchema this trait has to stand out boldly and strongly. Let there be a mass dance; let there be jumps and leaps on highly extended demi-pointe. Let the men spin like whirlwinds in the air, making swift tours, and let the women, crowned with flowers, accompany them with their delicate figures and agitated pirouettes, straining their delicate strings in honor of the heavenly Apollo. Here it would be appropriate to introduce, in the manner of the Egyptian dance of act 1, a Semitic dance of a

---

*An ancient town in northwest Greece, site of a famous oracle of Zeus.
†In classical mythology, a Lycian poet believed to have originated the singing of hymns in the worship of Apollo at Delphi.

Jewish girl from Palestine. She also dances for the god with such a fervent moral sense that the spectator recalls the image of the captive Shulamite from the Song of Songs. Choreographically, this could constitute a genuine classical variation in the new style. The theme is completely fresh, and its execution should be designed in such a way that the dance in and of itself is not a conclusion but rather a prophesy of future forms of art. The Jewish girl stands out from the crowd that dances the hyporchema, and she performs her variation against the background of the rarely seen corps de ballet.

In general the action is permeated with the performance of a complicated pantomime, from the arrival of the goddesses and Ilythia to the sacrifices on the mountain; it is pervaded by the native masses who perform the dramatic hyporchema. The act concludes with the majestic flying off of Apollo on swans to Delphi. The day has been spent in rejoicing. Evening approaches, and the air is filled with the stringed singing of cicadas that will accompany Apollo on all his trips until he reaches Phocaea.* This singing of the cicadas should become the musical leitmotif of the ballet, and the overture should begin with it. For the first time we must feel the grandeur of the strings' harmony, which injects into our emotional realm not the brawniness of the sound but rather its visual, intellectual, and figurative sense. The strings sing and play—they speak almost in actual words, so that the spectator feels as he apprehends this part of the ballet that he is hearing the speech of Apollo himself, that he is seeing Apollo's spiritual power as he struggles for the benefit of humanity. While the cicadas sing in the orchestra, the drums, kettledrums, and cymbals keep silent The curtain falls to the protracted rhythm of vibrating strings in which the sound's brawny impulses—with their dancelike quality—are no longer felt, and the symphonic element gushes forth in spurts.

Apollo flies off to Delphi. In the orchestra peals of thunder and the flashing of lightning are heard. Amid the bursts of sound the din of a furious struggle flows like lava. The symphonic picture conveys the effect of enormous upheavals in nature, intertwined with the din and howl of the wind and brass instruments. Joyous melodies are glimpsed in the amalgam of sound. These melodies prophesy Apollo's victory over the difficult elements of the world. Apollo brings order to wild, rocky Phocaea, and he spreads over it a pure blue sky like a radiant carpet. He overcomes Typhon, the Titan of the terrestrial interiors, who shakes the center of the mortal world as if it were a feather. With his arrows he battles the clouds that hang over Parnassus; he chases away wild beasts with the help of his sister, the brave and fiery Artemis. All these scenes are carried into the music of the orchestra. Occasionally, during those

---

*An ancient seaport in Asia Minor.

moments when the sound brightens, the tenderly palpitating notes of the cicadas' leitmotif burst through amid the motifs of regeneration and rebirth.

Onstage are the Valley of Crisa, the Parnassian mountains with the Corycian caves appearing in the distance, the large spring of the Castalian waterfall, and, close by, the mighty, wide-branching tree of Agamemnon. Around the Corycian cave the final frenzy of the vernal orgies of the Thyiads are dying out.* One by one the torches in the hands of the Phoceaen and Attic girls are extinguished. Groups of women lie in exhausted poses, covered by skins of wild animals. The stage is half dark. Birds and beasts pursued by Artemis's arrows rush by like clouds. Armed from head to toe and surrounded by twenty-four female hunters, the goddess appears in the middle of the stage, which begins to brighten. Artemis is preparing the arena for her sun brother. Here one should place a large corps de ballet dance of a classical nature. This can also be a hyporchema that is danced as pantomime and performed like drama. The ballet master should not forget the true essence of the Greek hyporchema. The musical and dance element does not predominate in it; the music is thematic, as is the dance. The movements and postures have an allegorical significance, one that reflects essentially verbal motifs. This is why, for all the dramatic animation of the performance, the opening of the dance should lack any kind of special intensity. And this is precisely the way the dance of Artemis, at the head of the corps de ballet, must be. The dance is long and protracted, with monumental insertions and descriptive hunting episodes that can be presented in detail. At this point the music is fundamentally rhythmic, projecting the muscular energy of the Greek national character.

Toward the end of the dance the god Apollo himself flies onto the stage with a bold, high leap. The stage is already so illuminated that the night goddess's army should by now have disappeared. It becomes completely light; indeed Apollo's appearance is marked by the onset of a sunny day. This moment must be arranged with the optimal emotionalism in ballet. Light penetrates the entire stage. To the outpouring of violins and harps, the likeness of morning birdsong must be joined. The fluttering and rustling of birds' wings can be felt. Apollo appears at the head of his victorious troops, which also consist of twenty-four people. He has conquered the monster Python and is now celebrating his triumph over the dark forces of the earth with a choreographic liturgy.

*The Valley of Crisa was dedicated to Apollo by the inhabitants of the area, who decreed that it should never be cultivated. The Corycian caves were caverns on Mount Parnassus above Delphi, sacred to Pan and the nymphs. The Castelian waters, situated near Delphi, were held to be sacred to Apollo. The Thyiads were Maenads, female celebrants of the worship of Dionysus. The reference to Agamemnon is unclear.

At first the male corps de ballet dances. For the ballet master, the creator of new male dances, the widest possible field for all manner of innovation has opened up. The corps de ballet does not dance a hyporchema but rather a free-wheeling dance hymn in honor of Apollo. Here everything is possible and permissible, so that one way or another the feeling and quality of exaltation is conquered in its highest form. There is not one feminine, sickly sweet figure from previous ballets. Everything is done to the tempo of male leaps, rotations, and jumps, with powerful turns of the head and passionately expressive faces. These dances should not have a particularly Greek character. They can be borrowed from the arsenal of contemporary classicism, especially since in their choreographic application onstage the jumps, revolutions, and leaps are inherited from the same ancient world. Let the dances be old or, more precisely, eternal in their form; it is the animate way in which they are perceived that must be unfailingly new.

Every muscle must reflect an exertion of self-will, a self-conscious uplift and ascent, an explosion of internal striving, not toward the far and wide but toward the heights, toward the peaks of Olympus. This can be planned only in such general terms. But a future Christian Johansson, a fanatic of male dancing, will find the means for transmitting these cursory concepts onto the stage.

The dance of the male corps de ballet concludes with Apollo's solo. Here the literary man's pen must stop before the unrealizable task of describing what his spiritual eye sees as existing only in the distant haze. Apollo signifies not only the birth of the masculine in the narrow sense, but in general the birth of classical dance in all its applications, both masculine and feminine. On this note, the part of Apollo can be played by a female dancer as well as a male one because the power here lies not in the sexual motif but rather in the predominance of intellectual and formal grandiloquence, which is expressed equally by both sexes. The dance of Apollo places clearly before the spectator's eyes the complete science and strict technique of classical dancing. Here we can be instructed by the Homeric hymn: Apollo rises on his toes, preparing for flight. The corps de ballet responds to this figure with movements that have an elemental quality, as if they were clumsily digging up the earth. The figure of Apollo is firm and straight, like a delicate palm tree. The decisive turns of the head reflect a deep and fresh interest in the surrounding world. The curly head must produce the impression of a great mind, of thought that radiates with brightness. Homer does not describe Apollo's dance, but he prepares us for it in a few words. So here we grant complete freedom to the brilliantly inventive ballet master. If Apollo's dance only partially approximates our ideal conception and imagined model of plasticity, then a genuine event will take place in the world of artistic values. Ballet will come alive and be primed for new historical development after it reaches in its contemporary form the final steps on its continuum.

The dance of Apollo ends with the departure of the whole sunlike retinue for the construction of the temple at Delphi. The orchestra slowly fades into nightingales' trills and cicadas' stringed quiverings, accompanied by an offstage chorus. The crowd sings a dithyramb, interlaced with a hymn into one whole, as Dionysus and Apollo have mixed with each other in a cult of the new humanity.

In the interval between the third act and the apotheosis the stage is covered with muslin. Upon the removal of the muslin the landscape is the same as in act 3 at the moment when the sun is setting. A blazing sunset with the outlines of the cliffs of Parnassus and the Castalian waterfall in relief. The stage is completely empty, with not a living soul on it. There is only the orchestra, which evokes the sultry sounds of sunset amid the endless sea of cicadas' quiverings. The spectator has the impression of the past exultant day. The day is over, night has come.

—"Rozhdenie Apollona," *Zhizn' iskusstva* (3 January 1923): 2–5.

What Will Ballet Live By?

≈☜੨◑≈☞੨≈

T he life of the future ballet depends on different phenomena, general and specific, changeable and eternal. Society is entering a new phase of history, symptoms of which abound. After the fluctuations in so many directions, after the winds die down and the hurricane subsides, ballet's ineradicable higher instincts will awaken, instincts that we can call vertical culture. Everything will ascend upward, everything will rise on its toes, as in ancient Greece, where Apollo dancing on pointe* was the symbol of all that was poetically beautiful and sublime, where every citizen, every law, everything generally striving to the heights of duty, was designated by an expression borrowed from the choreography of the stage. Thus about good laws it was said that they stood, and are maintained, on tall legs—to recall Sophocles' expression. But what are tall legs if not those that stand on pointe? What praise for the dead letters of public law! Homer's Telemachus is called, for his proud and lofty character, one who speaks in a voice that resembles an erect gait. Again the toes—an allusion to a verticality that is always and everywhere elevated. In

* See "The Birth of Apollo," above, for Volynsky's image of Apollo on pointe.

general a person of more or less cultured bearing, with a tradition of lofty and eternal truths in his soul, constitutes a replica of the choreographic idea of standing on one's toes. . . . Kant saw in this phenomenon a manifestation of the supernatural, which had triumphed over the inert organic law of crawling and running on all fours. Life's regulating principle, its spiritual element, lifted man from the ground and raised his eyes to the heavens.

This is the ideological scale that classical ballet contains within itself—an art of the conscious spirit in its highest moral and individual soaring. It would seem at first glance that before us a spectacle unfolds that is not entirely comprehensible and is even artificial in its outer appearance. These dancers, running around on their toes, doing pirouettes on pointe with the help of their partners, cutting across the stage with floral patterns again on pointed toes, as their feet curve upward, these dancers seem to be the fanciful creations of fairy tales, when in reality we have here the expression of the highest vertical tendency that exists within us. Such a tendency is inherent in us from child-hood and runs through our entire life: to rise on our toes whenever we feel profound emotion, uplift, or joy. If ballet, which is equipped with verticality as its most intrinsic instrument, is deprived of this singular quality, this exagger-ated ascent upward, this dynamic and lively standing on one's toes, all of its lofty magic would disappear, and with this, the essence of its classicalness would be undermined.

Along with the toes, all the other acquisitions of the body through centuries-old culture would disappear, turning the flesh into a veritable fiddle, which expresses through its strings the gamut of man's unutterable emotions. Precisely because of the technique of the classical exercise, our body has been trans-formed into a scroll of ideas and feelings whose rival in expression is neither literature nor the word but music.

With a turn in the direction of vertical culture, the ballet of the future will be firmly established on its classical foundations. If Russian society has never exhibited a tendency toward abstract philosophy in the spirit of German spiri-tualism, fate itself has nonetheless reserved for it a certain kind of philosophiz-ing in the mute symbols of classical dances on pointe. Interpreting the compo-nents, the style, and the laws of this dancing's forms and figures will introduce Russians to abstract theorizing, which may seem to be abandoning men and women's passionate and beautiful bodies. This will be done by truly under-standing human flesh in all its most minute manifestations, in its seams and gaps, in its harmonious fullness and inevitable dissonances and limitations. This will be just that culture the Russian genius lacks: a culture that has lit-tle association with Kant and his discursively rich interlocutors, a culture of the diverse perception of the whispers, fears, and ecstasies, the musicality and rhythmicality of the body—its lamentations and exclamations, its heroic ascents and physical exhaustion. Man will be entirely understood precisely when the culture of classical dance speaks its primordial words, and when it seeks the determining and expressive appellation for every battement, every movement, and every choreographic ascent. If this culture of which I am now speaking directs its eyes to the future that will arise in Russia, it will serve the great glory and pride of our country. For just this culture we are building ballet schools, at precisely the moment when ballet itself, with all its old traditions, is beginning to grow shallow and collapse.

With this new affirmation of classical ballet's foundation there must immediately appear a ballet master for the new epoch, not in the spirit of the old and naive Jean-Georges Noverre and his pleiad of mimics, but rather in the spirit of the new musical and choreographic tasks which confront the classical stage. I do not believe that the old synthesis of music, words, and dance will be repeated in the coming centuries because long ago all the components of this synthesis became differentiated. Combining these branches of art together, we would be narrowing the capacity of each individually. Music expresses more than words: in unison with the word it would appear unnaturally limited. Words would similarly constrain ballet with their concreteness and restrictive clarity, and such a union would be destructive for the classical art of dance. By dramatizing ballet, Noverre led it to the point of inevitable distortion and numbness. Rather ballet, given its related nonrationality, naturally joins with music in an integral and infinitely expressive harmony. On this path of ballet's symphonization, in the broad sense of the word, choreographic art will go from triumph to triumph in the future. The new visionary ballet master will demand the assistance of new music—specifically danceable music—and a librettist who will unquestionably supersede Théophile Gautier in the scope of his intellectual genius. The ballet can take on the kind of themes that one cannot even imagine now.

To repeat: after the winds and storms of sexual passion, after the extensive flood of all manner of eroticism onstage, with all its ruinous hypnoticization, a new and fresh historical dawn will arise. A new sun will shine and with its brilliant rays illuminate all the summits of human engagement. Under these rays vertical culture will be lifted higher and higher and finally will flourish and spread across the earth an infinite row of light-bearing carpets. And with this culture genuine ballet will arise and speak its inspiring and inspired phrases. Everything in classical dance, with its characteristic means and indigenous voices, will burst into an eternal hyperborean hymn. Everything will be explained and justified in the rays of Apollonian sunlight: the toes, turnout, the hidden wisdom of the human body itself, which has awakened to prophetic speech after a long, lethargic sleep.

—"Chem budet zhit' balet?" *Zhizn' iskusstva* (29 January 1923): 18–19.

The Maryinsky Theater, Imperial Russia's premier theater for opera and dance, around the turn of the twentieth century (Courtesy of Robert Greskovic)

A 1922 caricature of Volynsky by V. Kozminsky, published in *Zhizn' iskusstva* (*The Life of Art*), where Volynsky's ballet criticism appeared regularly between 1918 and 1924 (Saint Petersburg State Library of Theater)

Vera Trefilova as Aurora in *The Sleeping Princess* in the 1921 London production mounted by Sergei Diaghilev. Before emigrating to the West, Trefilova was one of the dancers who had attained the privileged status of ballerina at the Maryinsky. (Harvard Theatre Collection)

Portrait of Elena Liukom, Saint Petersburg, 1914
(Saint Petersburg State Archive of Film and Photography)

Mathilda Kshesinskaya, another of the Maryinsky's
premier ballerinas, as Esmeralda, ca. 1900
(Courtesy of Robert Greskovic)

Mathilda Kshesinskaya with her fourteen-year-old
son Prince Vladimir Andreevich Romanov at
her palazzo in Saint Petersburg, 1916
(Saint Petersburg State Archive of
Film and Photography)

Elsa Vill as Swanilda in *Coppélia,* ca. 1910 (Courtesy of Robert Greskovic)

Olga Preobrazhenskaya in *Raymonda,* Saint Petersburg, ca. 1914. One of the
Maryinsky's premier ballerinas, she taught at Volynsky's School of Russian
Ballet from 1920 until she emigrated in 1921.
(Saint Petersburg State Archive of Film and Photography)

Tamara Karsavina, a Maryinsky premier ballerina and the star of Sergei Diaghilev's Ballets Russes, in *Petrushka,* 1911. Volynsky's hope that Karsavina would return to the Maryinsky after she broke with the Ballets Russes in 1920 never materialized. (Harvard Theatre Collection)

Tamara Karsavina in *La Bayadère,* ca. 1917
(Saint Petersburg State Archive of
Film and Photography)

Tamara Karsavina at home in Saint
Petersburg, 1916 (Saint Petersburg
State Archive of Film and Photography)

Anna Pavlova rehearsing with dancer, choreographer, and pedagogue Enrico
Cecchetti in Saint Petersburg, 1907. Cecchetti worked in Russia from
1887 to 1902 and again from 1906 to 1911.
(Saint Petersburg State Archive of Film and Photography)

Anna Pavlova and Nikolai Legat in *Chopiniana,* after 1908. Volynsky vigorously
supported Legat's candidacy for artistic director of the Maryinsky Theater, but
in 1922 the position went to Fedor Lopukhov.
(Saint Petersburg State Archive of Film and Photography)

Anna Pavlova in *Papillons,* ca. 1911. Pavlova was the standard by which Volynsky judged all ballerinas. (Harvard Theatre Collection)

Alexander Gorsky in 1900, his last year at
the Maryinsky Theater before he moved
to Moscow (Saint Petersburg State
Library of Theater)

Mikhail Fokine, Petrograd, 1916, the year
he mounted *La Jota Aragonese,* one of his
few works that Volynsky approved of
(Harvard Theatre Collection)

Mikhail Fokine and his wife, Vera Fokina, in *Carnaval* with the Ballets Russes,
Paris, 1910 (Harvard Theatre Collection)

Agrippina Vaganova, date unknown. Vaganova
taught at Volynsky's School of Russian Ballet for
several years before founding her own school
on Theater (now Rossi) Street.
(Courtesy of Robert Greskovic)

Elizaveta Gerdt, date unknown. Another premier
ballerina at the Maryinsky, Gerdt was one of the
few great classical ballerinas to remain in the
Soviet Union after the 1917 revolution.
(Courtesy of Robert Greskovic)

Lidiya Ivanova in one of her concert numbers, Petrograd, early 1920s.
Ivanova drowned under mysterious circumstances some weeks before she was
scheduled to leave Russia on a German tour with a troupe of young dancers,
headed by George Balanchine. The troupe never returned home.
(Saint Petersburg State Archive of Film and Photography)

Georgy Vereisky, portrait of Lidiya Ivanova,
Petrograd, 1923 (Saint Petersburg State
Archive of Film and Photography)

Olga Spesivtseva as the Black Swan in
Swan Lake, Petrograd, 1922
(Saint Petersburg State Archive of
Film and Photography)

Olga Spesivtseva, the last pre-Revolutionary Giselle, 1924. Spesivtseva's emigration that year dealt Volynsky such an emotional blow that he did not mention her name once in his *Book of Exaltations,* published in 1925. (Harvard Theatre Collection)

Olga Spesivtseva, early 1920s. Concerning Volynsky's relationship with Spesivtseva at
this time the composer and musicologist Valeriyan Bogdanov-Berezovsky wrote,
"He was tormented by her. He tried to get close to the object of his adoration. . . .
He tried to rouse her interest in him. It was clear that she had long had him
in her clutches." (Harvard Theatre Collection)

A Wretched Housepainter

"The Nutcracker"

❧❦❧

I don't find it funny,
When a wretched housepainter
Sullies Raphael's Madonna
—A. S. Pushkin

T he recent production of *The Nutcracker*, one of the finest ballets in the world, has not given me any satisfaction, although I greatly anticipated its production. In this Christmas ballet, children's eyes glow, a skein of fantastic motifs, figures, and properties unrolls, and beautiful music spills from the orchestra, heartrending to the point of tears. Two huge talents have invested their energies in the creation of this choreographic masterpiece: Petr Tchaikovsky and Lev Ivanov. The whole world knows Tchaikovsky, but Ivanov's reputation does not go farther than a narrow circle of lovers of classical dance. I am one of his most enthusiastic supporters. He is an astonishing genius, fundamentally pure and honest, full of moderation and inborn tact, harmoniously clear yet with occasional streaks of Slavonic melancholy and introspection. He is the creator of the best moments in *Swan Lake,* where he triumphantly worked alongside the Gallic genius of Marius Petipa.

In *The Nutcracker,* Ivanov has demonstrated his astounding musicality. They say that at the ballet's first performance thirty years ago, Tchaikovsky embraced the Russian choreographer and kissed him profusely before the entire audience. There is not a single rhythm or bar in *The Nutcracker* that does not flow into dance. Everything boils unceasingly onstage in the quiet splash of the gentlest patterns, with bursts of rosy childlike laughter, childlike delight and intoxication, interrupted by momentary chagrin. And all this is wrapped in the aroma of a Christmas tree, with its twigs here and there crackling from the fire of the candles. Indeed, of a fresh-cut Christmas tree, an illuminated coniferous Flora, in the style and spirit bequeathed by our Russian childhood's memories, and not its schematic representation, as I've seen in one of Chodowiecki's* innumerable engravings from the age of Goethe that hang in

---

* Daniel-Nikolaus Chodowiecki (1726–1801) was an engraver and painter whose talent was best seen in his more than two thousand engravings.

my School of Russian Ballet. Here the trunk of the tree is replaced by a mannequin. Candles and toys are secured in the candleholders and on the boards of the entire artificial scaffold.

The first act of this latest production of *The Nutcracker* was cloudy gray, without any inward fire or warm, festive heart. The children danced onstage, clapped, and tossed around the nutcracker. The battle of the mice was presented with the toy soldiers crawling out of the drawers; the semblance of the congenial assembly, in the German spirit, was shown. But an integral picture was still not achieved. There was no psychological center, and the action unfolded without a core belief. Indeed, the joyful children's eyes were nowhere to be sensed. The orchestra was exceedingly sluggish, and the dancing proceeded in a lagging tempo. Even the charming battle with the comic toy cannons was uninspired.

Regarding the second scene of this act, the famous Dance of the Snowflakes, it constituted a genuine profanation of our most beloved childhood memories. Every feature of Ivanov's production was maximally thought through and deeply felt. He gathered together the barely perceptible sparkles of frost, the hachures and patterns of snow crystals, the monograms and arabesques of frost into one well-proportioned artistically finished vision. In the production of the current rehearsal coach we get something anti-musical and splashily vapid in its external design. In Ivanov's production the dancers appear in white dresses in lines of three, with bits of fluff on their heads and dresses. In their hands they have icicles, which are also trimmed with light snow. These lovely details, which introduced into the scene the brightness and enchantment of the frosty element, were totally absent in the current production. The dancers appear not in compact rings but separated by large distances in a clear infringement of the workings of natural forces. The bits of fluff fall from above—wet, viscous, moist. This gives the impression of an unavoidable sticking to the ground, of a kind of pampered naturalism that, when communicated by the classical forms of dance, creates an irresistible impression on the ego.

This is how it was presented by Ivanov: dance circles of these women cut across the stage in zigzags, forming various figures—little stars, little circles, quickly moving lines, both parallel and intersecting. One section of the dancers forms a large, long cross with an interior circle of other snowflakes. In front of them, facing the audience, eight wintry sylphides dance in the rhythm of a waltz, making rapid and soft pas de basques. The circle rotates in one direction, and the cross in the opposite one. And once again, nothing but classical dance is used, with ponderous tempos alternating with their velvety conclusions. This marvelous scene was completely discarded by the new rehearsal coach, who replaced it with some vulgar, ignorant nonsense. His dancers perform high little jumps, flip-flop flights, as they rush across the stage senselessly, failing to group or form themselves in any kind of artistic combination. This is a genuine sullying of Raphael's Madonna by the hand of a crude and wretched housepainter! It is simply incomprehensible how such a blasphemous distortion of Ivanov's musical and plastic creation could be allowed.

Other scenes of *The Nutcracker,* in this last part of act 1, were also discarded with barbarous ruthlessness. Ivanov depicted a figure similar to the Russian letter П. Before our eyes is a thick, conjoined line of four rows, and lines at the sides of two rows. The dancers in the upper rows intertwine their arms and form a general circle. The lines at the sides disperse and rush after one another as they gather together and form small circles. The dances are again based on the same fine little steps of the balleticized march, which the pas de basque is. The jumps are barely noticeable—adhering, melting—and they moisten the ground with their snowy footsteps. Finally the last picture of this moment. The snowflakes form an aggregate star, with dancers moving inward and outward. A choreographic iamb is introduced into the dance, which is based on the realistic shifting and protractedly smooth flexion of the returning leg. The star is quickly transformed into a large dance circle. The circle opens, then closes. The snowstorm twists the huge group, this pyramid of dancers. Snow falls. The snowflakes quiver. The icicles also wave in the air from one side to the other.

This is the masterpiece of movement with which, in the elegance, intelligence, and perfection of its every stroke, only Pushkin's verse can compete. Even a talented person can find nothing to correct, much less a simple tradesman. Every little detail must be valued, like a treasured heirloom. Everything is untouchable here. Yet the whole thing, to my astonished sadness, was distorted, emasculated, and corrupted to the point of nonrecognition. Even people who had not seen Ivanov's production were at a loss and asked me why this part of *The Nutcracker* was so renowned. One could only throw up one's hands and for the thousandth time say that if the theater, the academic theater, the preeminent theater in Russia, is run by incompetent artists who don't know where to look first, then all kinds of artistic catastrophes are the order of the day. No one should have allowed such a sacrilege to occur from major talent to preserve the national reputation of a theater which, despite its decline, still draws large crowds.

The second act of *The Nutcracker* represents a rather large mosaic of classical and genre dances. But besides the separate children's numbers, coached more or less satisfactorily and making a favorable impression on the audience, all the rest passes rather palely and lifelessly. Even Elizaveta Gerdt's dancing was not especially good. I remember her performance in early 1918. It was artistically mature, something on the order of ripened wheat with a touch of exquisite classroom exercise. Her battements were sustained to the nth degree. She extended her leg and held it with exceptional mastery. Her attitudes in effacé conformed in the highest degree to her natural disposition. True, there was no special power or mellifluousness in her dancing. Her toes were bent as though they were grabbing hold of the floor. But there was a fresh purity and correctness in the choreography of her patterns. At times this design seemed to be permeated by the coolness of high academicism. This element of classical exercise, to my delight, has remained in Gerdt's current work, but what happened to that exciting element of ripened wheat? The dancer's fresh spontaneity has seemingly grown dim. Certain movements are artificially calculated, smacking more of a pedagogical presentation than a demonstration of truly vibrant talent. Her noble eyes still laugh. But the smile of her body movements, that plastic soul of art, without which one's impression always remains partial, is already diminishing.

I will not critique Gerdt in detail. For me her name constitutes a precious guarantee that there is still powder in the powder flasks of our academic staff! With Gerdt and Olga Spesivtseva, we have guardians of the art of dance, with whom today's public increasingly bonds.

. . .

—"Maliar-negodnyi," *Zhizn' iskusstva* (20 February 1923): 4–5.

The Weeping Spirit

I t is my duty to provide a brief evaluation of Olga Spesivtseva's dancing in addition to what I already said on the occasion of *Paquita*. But let me note at the outset that to write about the classical art of this dancer apart from the personality itself, to isolate choreographical issues from this artist's charm, is well nigh impossible. This is a talent completely harmonious, balanced, and consummate in its appearance, which is where all its wealth has gone. With regard to her art, we are dealing with a person who is so special and delicately individual that she has deeply impressed the public with the features of her unique and original beauty. Her gentle, slightly protuberant forehead— somewhat in the spirit of Carlo Dolci*—is feminine and charming, like an oval of a delicate plant. And of course it is poetic. This is Cecilia Dolci, but not Saint Cecilia in a realistic likeness, as if reduced to an affecting miniature. The permanent stamp of undying childhood lies in this artist, and this is all the

---

*Florentine painter (1616–86) of the baroque period.

more remarkable since we are dealing with a brunette, in whom the traits of childhood ordinarily disappear quickly, often at a very young age. And for this reason Spesivtseva's eyes also produce an unusually favorable impression. A little tear glistens in them, just as a note of weeping resounds in her voice, even in her laugh, to all those who know her. Yet her face is entirely dramatic in the elevated, innermost meaning of the word, and perhaps it is precisely in this attribute that the characteristic that most interests us about her appearance resides. Spesivtseva need only stand and smile with her mouth and eyes, and an unexpected radiance pours forth in all its gypsylike, Spanish charm. Some years ago, at the beginning of her career, Spesivtseva suddenly revealed this quality of her mimetic character in the role of Pierrette when she smiled her special smile and glided her childlike hand through the hair of her kneeling cavalier. The audience quivered with delight. At the time I thought (and said in print) that before us was not only a talented dancer but a rare jewel of dramatic art in ballet, the likes of whom the Russian stage had heretofore never seen.

What is dramatic acting, dramatic mime in ballet? This is yet another issue that begs for careful resolution. Extolling Virginia Zucchi, the late Konstantin Skalkovsky loved to underscore the Italian's sustained, incredibly expressive acting. She could show passion in all its authentic features. She was able to create and play roles in the ordinary sense. But if we are to believe Skalkovsky, it would appear that there was comparatively little material in Zucchi's acting that could be deemed balletic and classical in nature. In the best case she was an artist of high caliber, but in the style of Duse* or Sarah Bernhardt. However, this kind of expressive talent, no matter how valuable in itself, demands in ballet a complete transformation and adaptation to the peculiar conditions of the classical stage. On this stage there is no real, everyday decor. Everything is silent. There are no peals of laughter, no crying. The theme of the action is provided not by the libretto, which is usually stilted and banal, but by the musical suggestion of the orchestra and the immanent content of the classical staging. One who cannot read and translate these figures of classical apparatus, these immeasurable and diverse battements, these overhead leaps with circular rotations in the air, will never accurately understand what is really happening in ballet. And the dancer finds herself in the same position.

I ask myself, Was the vaunted Zucchi an imitative interpreter of the music's aural and figurative material, and of the dance's internal themes? I do not see this in Skalkovsky's numerous descriptions, and I myself never saw Zucchi dance. But what we see before us in Spesivtseva's mimetic talent gives a striking illustration of the idea I am trying to defend. Of course, all faces must be

---

*Eleanora Duse (1858–1924), the celebrated Italian actress, frequently starred in the plays of Ibsen and D'Annunzio.

animated on the ballet stage. All lips must smile. All eyes must burn with rapture and artistic emotion. But between the iridescent expression of the heroes and heroines of ballet's magic kingdom and the musical-choreographic motifs of each individual performance, there must exist absolute harmony. One must not only dance to the music, one must smile to it; one must mimic and gesticulate to the tempos of the orchestra. All the body's acting in dance is subservient not to the verbal material, of which there is none, but to the two key distractions—music and movement, which constitute the essential content of classical ballet.

In this regard Spesivtseva represents a rare phenomenon. All her acting is classical in the best sense of the word. There is not a single feature from run-of-the-mill drama. We have instead a direct reflection of the plastic motif of dance assumed in its most basic, internal form. Her face usually is focused in on itself, serious and pensive, as if preoccupied with a presentiment of approaching darkness or an imminent tear. She goes out onstage and assumes fourth position, and without any preparation the entire scene is ready. Nowadays such lovely moments in her art are becoming rarities, slightly past their prime in the growing richness of her natural talent. But the overall ability to carry with her the coming sound, the silent tangle of emotions on the verge of unfolding, the anguish and anticipation of artistic inspiration and intellectual wonder—this the artist has fully preserved. This is a spirit that weeps children's tears, that weeps almost in her sleeve, with the capricious and angry little voice of a child who is unable to grow up overnight and is powerless to let its inner "I" completely master itself. This is a spirit that weeps about its limits. In ballet terminology this is the purest croisé, the bud of a beautiful talent which has not yet experienced its complete flowering, and which, despite its frequent appearances, has still not presented to the public its consummate unfolding. Every ballerina has her invincible charm. Pavlova exhibits her spirit in grandiose proportions; the whole theater blazes from her art. The flutter of her wings is heard from on high. Spesivtseva is all promise, all upsurge to the unrealizable, all oohs and ahs of a kind of insatiable sadness with which she is also able to captivate the public. She does not ignite the audience with the fire of her talent but extends over them the palpitating cover of all those tears, as yet unborn but already tormenting her heart. Eternally young, she does not face the bitter fate of a flower past its bloom. And I pity anyone who has never seen this everlasting bud of beauty and talent.

How well Spesivtseva's unique artistic talent is reflected in *Giselle!* Onstage is a young girl, eternally dancing, dying from the disappointment that has overtaken her. In the second act she is a Wili, who continues to dance even in the world beyond the grave. I do not wish to speak about the separate variations in this marvelous ballet. From the point of view of choreography, Spesivtseva's performance in both acts stands up to the strictest criticism. She dances with Viktor Semenov, currently unequalled in the world in terms of the power, beauty, and lightness of his elevation and ballon. And what a captivating combination of two different talents we have in this unforgettable pair: the airiness of their leaps and the most delicate clinging to the ground. Much air is displaced by the powerful surge of masculine energy. Semenov is able to un-hinge the magic of genuine art, but what truly special earthliness, what unique realism there is in Spesivtseva's performance! This is the earth—and not the earth: something unsteady, unstable, and smokily incandescent ties her to the far-off sky. The impression is enormous. It would be impossible to describe the couple's fame abroad, especially in Italy.

In spite of my wish to refrain from details, I cannot help but note Spesivt-seva's first dance with Semenov. A classical ballotté is brilliantly mounted, as only Petipa could mount it. This is the innocent play and frolic of two young people in love. There is one moment—an imperceptible little feature, an in-stant, a point—when both artists seem to be hanging in midair. Now beyond this moment is the repetition of slight battements after a resolute shifting of the leg. The scene as performed by the artists comes off incomparably. Roulades of sweet-scented laughter pour from the stage. Of the other variations I shall not write, except to praise enthusiastically Spesivtseva's acting, especially the scene of grief, madness, and death in act 1. This is utterly splendid. Suddenly the gait slackens, the steps grow numb. The entire gaunt body folds into a white ball. What teary, childlike eyes, darkened with fiery specks of fright are under her thickly coiffed hair, which now falls loose! This is a wounded bird falling helplessly from a tree. Something miniature distinguishes this Giselle. But in its totality this miniature is marvelous, like the enamel work of a great master, it is a miniature which has already taken its rightful place in the showcase of choreographic art's greatest jewels.

Moving on to *Esmeralda*. To perform in this ballet after Mathilda Kshesin-skaya seemed a risky step. Nonetheless, at one point I firmly supported Spesivt-seva in undertaking it, although I did not for a minute renounce my high esteem for her famous predecessor. Kshesinskaya brought to the role of Esmer-alda a current of genuine tragicality. She dances the classical pas de deux at the ball with a deathly pale face and the expression of an incensed tigress in her eyes. The adagio with the cavalier is simply brilliant. And although Kshesin-skaya's dances are, generally speaking, rather crude and awkward, lacking in subtle classical polish and delicate and refined nuances, her art as a whole is inspired and powerful, of large scale and range. Spesivtseva lacks these traits. She presented Esmeralda not as a woman but as a child, and she offered a series of dances more perfect in their appearance than Kshesinskaya's. All her scenes occur in this miniature form and produce an enormous impression on the spectator. I was once afforded a pedagogue's delight in discussing several details of this role with the dancer herself, and perhaps I slightly influenced her by suggesting this remarkable image, which until now had been considered the monopoly of Kshesinskaya. But what I later saw onstage exceeded my expectations. My pale words took on flesh—and such a delicate, spiritual, and phantasmal flesh, once again saturated with those same childlike tears—that I stopped formulating my own conceptions and instructions and instead merged with the entire audience in the sheer enjoyment of the action onstage. But I cannot help noting a detail that has been etched in my memory.

In the pas de deux the ballerina keeps turning her head to the officer of whom she is jealous, who is sitting right there with his fiancée. How Kshesinskaya's eyes devoured the traitor! Spesivtseva, however, with her childlike eyes and her helpless weeping, stares at the man she is afraid of losing. Something intimate shows through the expression on the dancer's face. A fear of losing her inner support, a kind of childlike impulse to take her mother's absent hand, something inexplicably touching but tangled up in life's mists—all this showed through and left its mark in this moment of exquisite dance acting. And this acting can be compared with complete justification to that of Kshesinskaya as two different but equally precious stones on the velvet of the same showcase.

I once happened to ask Spesivtseva, without warning, which of the classical steps she loved most. I expected her to point to some of the figures of the world of Flora, in the spirit of her own inherent beauty and talent. But my expectations were wrong. Having thought for a bit, the dancer said: "Saut de basque." How remarkable! Saut de basque is a big leap in the air with a rotating movement of the body, with a sharp contraposto exertion of the head, only slight patches of plantlike gracefulness, a general predominance of elevation. The burning eyes must remain fixed on the audience. This is not a figure from Spesivtseva's choreographic repertoire, which is so rich and uniquely full of talent in all other respects. But the weeping spirit pines for distant abodes where the art of ballet can accommodate its no less elevated values. The ballerina spoke sincerely about something she loved that nevertheless eludes her. Recovering from my momentary bewilderment, I asked Spesivtseva about her recent and more determined convictions. She indicated a gently unfolding battement. Here Spesivtseva's answer accorded with her true talent. A gentle battement that slowly blossoms forth, extends into the current stream of overflowing movements, and culminates in an even and extended unpalpitating note—this in fact is the most supreme beauty of Spesivtseva's art. In this sense she currently has no rivals, despite the fact that her body is beginning to lose its plasticity.

With regard to *Paquita,* I should mention Spesivtseva's extreme leanness. It is not the job of the critic to dwell too long on such external traits, but I will express an anxiety that seizes not me alone when contemplating such, how to put it, growing dematerialization. One wants to stop this process in the name of preserving an art of such affecting charm. For all its soulfulness, ballet operates on flesh; it loves light bearing, yet at the same time solid materiality, which produces the impression of the nobility of marble.

—"Plachushchii dukh," *Zhizn' iskusstva* (22 February 1923): 4–5.

The Innovator

Mikhail Fokine

The beginning of Mikhail Fokine's career coincided with the early currents of decadence, which had already begun permeating literature and society. The final flickerings of this decadence revealed themselves in the circle that had gathered around the journal *Mir iskusstva,* centered largely on such artists as Leon Bakst, Alexander Benois, Eugene Lanceret, Konstantin Somov, and Mstislav Dobuzhinsky. I will not enumerate all the famous figures of the time who considered themselves set designers and scenic artists. They constituted a cultural milieu of educated and talented people who were graced with all the external qualities of the art of the time but who lacked what is special, important, and organically vital to any great creation—pathos. For them the cult of prettiness replaced the cult of beauty. I do not deny Benois's talent, his irreproachably subtle taste, his rare (even in Europe) instinct for the rococo, his wonderful sublimity in transmitting the green hues of Le Nôtre's* parks. But I altogether dislike his critical articles, which are so imperfect in their literary form and reek of a local, commercial rococo. If one were to consider seriously his large works on the history of painting, whose structure disintegrated even while they were being published, it would be a thankless, though easy task to show Benois's numerous errors despite his rich, encyclopedic erudition. . . .

Certainly Bakst, who has played such a large role in the recent phase of our balletic output, is brilliant and multitalented. He is a veritable Worth or Madame Paquin of contemporary costume design.[†] In the attire of Bakst a dancer resembles the creation of a delicately erotic fantasy; she is like an

_____

*André Le Nôtre (1613–1700) was a landscape architect and the gardener of Louis XIV of France. Benois created many sets and sketches depicting the Palace of Versailles.

[†] Charles Worth and Madame (Jeanne) Paquin were famous dress designers working in London and Paris, respectively.

artificial streak of summer lightning from the courtly age. How fine, delicate, and frivolously light she is! She does not incarnate the gracefulness of a Sevres porcelain figure, yet she can compete in charm with a good imitation of Saxon china. Moreover, Bakst is a genuine artist of the highest caliber, an enchanting conversationalist who captivatingly combines within himself epic Semitic features with the refined erudition of Aryan decadence.

This is essentially the atmosphere in which Fokine appeared. A complete child of nature, possessing the impoverished aesthetic competence of a youth who had just completed drama school and the inner strivings of a talented personality to whom no proper guidance had been offered, he—with his education in classics—was putty in the hands of the powerful clique who had given him refuge. The Fokine of that time poorly understood ancient culture. Antiquity meant a naked body. According to Fokine, if you discarded stylized dance—the toes, the turning outward, the ritual dynamics of the arms—and replaced it with the impetuous reflexes of free dance and running barefoot on demi-pointe, you would achieve a significant reform in the spirit of that very antiquity. Isn't that what the depictions of the dancers on the red and black ornamental vases of ancient ceramics and the fragments of Pompeian art tell us? It never occurred to this naive youth that we are dealing here with the depiction of the daily life and moments of everyday reality in the port cities of the Mediterranean, with the dances in taverns and street cafés, by which we can in no way judge the authentic, ritually festive dances of the people in the theaters of Athens or Epidaurus. The brilliant circle of Benois and Bakst poorly understood these matters, and I shall never forget the time when the charismatic Bakst, whom I often met at the renowned Ida Rubinstein's home, prevailed upon me to explain some picture on the theme of archaic Greece. It was difficult to hint even politely that he was hopelessly confusing phenomena of fundamentally different epochs.

Naturally, in the company of such instructors Fokine and his fledgling talent were doomed to errors that were destructive to ballet. Indeed, such works as *Eunice, Islamey,* Liszt's *Préludes, Eros,* and *Egyptian Nights,* which represent sad stages in his innovative work, testify to the genuine confusion in the ballet master's mind. Fokine obviously believed that he was working within the canons of classical art, when in fact all these works reveal a scantiness of imagination and scenic originality. The dances in *Eunice* are simply outrageous: they are confused and mixed up in a disorderly combination. The intoxicated, passionately unbridled chaos of *Islamey,* where the body is thrown onto the floor and the jumps are wild and frenzied (and thus uncharacteristic of the East), produces a repulsive impression on the viewer. Eastern movement is flowing. A woman from the East with whom I once spoke on this theme on Capri, who demonstrated her native art for me, said that on the banks of the

Tigris and Euphrates young girls dance sitting on the ground. We know that the Siamese dance only with their hands. All Asia and North Africa are restrained to the highest degree in their movements. First and foremost they exhibit flowing, plantlike zigzags, turns, and rotations of the body, not headlong, impetuous jumps.

It is painful to think about *Les Préludes.* The ballet master did not understand, and consequently distorted, a great man. Fokine does not comprehend the internal soul of music; he keenly perceives only its elemental rhythm, its athletic impulses without the auditory or visual halo that surrounds them, in which the musical work's entire essence resides. The brilliant composer sang of death as the opening to new biological transformations, but Fokine saw here the grave and gloomy ruin of an intoxicated consciousness. In *Egyptian Nights* the blunders continue, redeemed only by the music, and there are totally unnecessary bas-reliefs and an annoying paroxysm of completely unjustified convulsive movements. To speak about *Carnaval* and *Papillons* at length is senseless. These productions, with their cabaretlike unfortunate Pierrot and trivially joyful Harlequin at center stage, are suitable only for an intimate theater. On the academic stage, with its large-scale space and serious artistic tasks, they look completely misplaced.

Such are Fokine's innovative works in Russia. But he has presented many things abroad about which I can judge only by the critical responses in the foreign press. Lately Fokine's name has totally faded in Europe. The paltry foundations of his balletic edifice have been properly understood. After the fever of his first triumphs passed, a fever created in part by the precious juggler and manipulator Sergei Diaghilev, by the novelty of skillful publicity, and in no small measure by the participation of the most outstanding representatives of classical dance, Fokine ran aground. Now Europe as of old craves classical ballet, and the recent innovator has no choice but to return to Russia in order to engage in serious business on his native soil, to practice his genuine calling, which was interrupted by the glittering tinsel of his temporary and transitory undertakings.

Fokine is a man of undeniable talent on a rather large scale. He succeeds in mounting ensemble scenes like no one else, and they will always be tied to his name. The *Polovtsian Dances* are masterpieces of great choreographic art. The entire Scythian-Sarmatian element has found its monumental expression here. This magical quality is found in the dance of the buffoons in *Le Pavillon d'Armide:* everything exotic is radiant and tempestuous. *The Dying Swan* is lovely—a miniature expressed in classical tones. The simple bourrée is onstage for only a matter of minutes, yet it creates a complete and finished artistic impression. Not to mention *Chopiniana,* though over the past years this piece has been horribly danced: although it is only a suite of dances that are not connected to one another by a common narrative thread, its scattered blossoms produce moments of charm. If Fokine had only stayed with these classical themes! If only he would aim the power and reserves of his creative inspiration in our direction. Having passed through difficult trials and a period of self-denial, having experienced the terrible emptiness of pseudo-innovation's brilliant and momentary caprices, Fokine can now fly to the heart of real work, reconstructing and re-creating the pearl of Russian art—ballet—which is so urgently necessary for the Petrograd stage. Let him return to Russia. Old age and weariness can never threaten the ballet master who follows the classical ways of Petipa.

—"Novator: Chto ostalos' ot M. M. Fokina?" *Zhizn' iskusstva* (8 May 1923): 2–4.

"Don Quixote"

D *on Quixote* opened the fall-winter season with new talent in its production. Olga Spesivtseva danced Kitri. If I were interested in ballet only in terms of its essential features and not also concerned with living, eternally changing reality, I could limit this review to a brief account based on many of my former articles. This dancer has completely cast herself into a mold: her sense of perfection and completeness of movement have affected not only her body but, evidently, her entire essence. And a ballerina's essence is linked to her body in a most intimate way. In the early stages of her development, a dancer of this type moves intrepidly across the stage. Every impression she makes comes as a surprise and produces a feeling of joy—a joy which enters you and unlocks doors. Her suppleness increases and overflows with life's most thrilling emotions. Through daily exercises, which the dancer knows inside and out, she performs a given battement with the same spontaneity as those forces seething and surging within her. And her art, which constantly refreshes and renews itself, grows and grows. Now Spesivtseva has stagnated, just as Elizaveta Gerdt has. Each movement for them is produced out of habit and operates only as mechanical technique. In Gerdt—who never radiated with talent, but rather with youthfulness—the process of deterioration had clearly begun when Spesivtseva was still maturing. I do not anticipate any changes in her performance, and it is only sheer happenstance that might make it more or less pleasing. Within this general framework I can now proceed to the specifics of this production.

Like all successful performances of *Don Quixote* this one succeeded because Kitri's role was performed effectively. The dancer's appearance, especially given the dark complexion of her face and the slenderness of her slightly darkened body, was completely suited to the part, particularly in the first act. Her arms were too thin and undulated with a childishness that was out of place; her legs were raised too high. But in general the performance was vivid and colorful. Everything that demanded a purely classical aesthetic was foregrounded, and for brief moments gripped the audience. I could not say the same for the episodes of character dancing that required bravura, strength, and emotional daring in Kitri. Even Kseniya Makletsova's interpretation triumphs over Spesivtseva's, not to mention Pavlova's.

I shall mention several trivial details that require choreographic interpretation. One of the dancer's entrances is stunningly effective. There is a large pas de basque here that in a split second captures and focuses the attention of the audience. For this movement to fully express its organic logic, and in order for the legs to go up in a single unbroken movement, one extremely important principle must be observed: the legs lift and alternate, switching position as they hit the floor. Furthermore, in order for the contours of the movement to be appropriately soft and not to seem crude, it must not be produced with legs that are completely straight, as Spesivtseva does. The late Anna Johansson, a woman of great artistic sensitivity, advised adding just a shade of delicate plasticity, almost an allusion to a quick, soft battement. This immediately removes the sharpness from the movement and gives it a proper classical look. In the spirit of the dance, at the most diverse moments the straight lines must emerge from the palpitating zigzags like shafts of sunlight from the fog. Then the torso will not be thrust too far back, and a dignified impression will be created.

Another motif in the same long, complex passage needs some reworking. Kitri is playfully performing a step, flirting with her partner. Her foot must appear and disappear as speedily as a little mouse, imperceptible, elusive, laughing, and teasing. At this point the orchestra plays feverishly. Makletsova, who does not have a very agile foot, is a shrewd dancer and achieves complete success: she weaves into a basic battement a fleeting turn of her leg into attitude and effectively shifts through three different positions. This intensified the moment's sense of play because, within the contours of scenic art, the aesthetically calculated mix of movements is richer and more interesting than the individual movements in their purest form. Spesivtseva plays at performing this beautiful step, and if not for the mischievous childishness and sparkling eyes, I would consider this moment totally lost. It is too correct and therefore leaden and unwieldy in its design.

In the other acts of the ballet the star deals fairly well with the subject matter. The tavern scene does not stand out for its danceability; it is taken up by the entire ensemble, whose animated brio stifles the soloists' effect. The acting is as usual good but does not sparkle throughout. Spesivtseva moves through this scene as if in a constant stream of laughter, but she does not spread that stream far and wide. I don't know which of the two is better in this scene—Spesivtseva or Makletsova. But neither's art impresses me here as being great or authoritative. Looking closely at the ballet troupe, I suspect that among the beginners there is one dancer who will eventually perform this act of *Don Quixote* successfully.* For this we need the wholesome soul of a country girl whose undiluted enthusiasm is still intact, whose gaiety is unfeigned, and who shows no trace of internal hysterics. There are few such girls in Petersburg now, let alone in ballet, which has been overstrained by current conditions and is constantly harassed on all fronts.

In the final acts of *Don Quixote* I am gratified to note the success of Spesivtseva's highly expressive performance. The variation in the Dream provides motifs that come naturally to this dancer—flowing and elastic movements that contain all the coloraturas of the classical arsenal. Her poses are completely self-possessed. Her positions as a whole are finished—I can find no fault with even minor details. In the final scene of the ballet the dancer performs three variations, again with perfect mastery: a pas de deux, a solo variation, and a coda. In the pas de deux the usual positions of the body are presented flawlessly with the firm support of Mikhail Dudko. The complex pirouette is done with complete aplomb. The variation and coda that follow the pas de deux, the swift, upward-floating arabesques, the controposto rotations of the foot on center stage—all these completely accord with the set design and decor. The fouetté is especially successful. With the help of the long leg raised high above the floor, the tempestuous circular motions produce a great impression. In its structure Spesivtseva's fouetté is even better than Makletsova's, although Makletsova still prevails because her interpretation contains such stormy passion.

In this article I am unable to detail all the production's motifs. I have committed these to memory and shall return to them at my first opportunity. But I would like now to examine one of the ballet's variations. In her day, Vaganova performed it, and during the past few years Gerdt has done it, no better and no worse than her predecessor. The choreographic structure of this variation breaks down into three parts: in the first there are large and wide lateral leaps, done with alternating legs, which are repeated twice. Completing the leap and standing on her toes, the dancer does a slight battement in second position. The leap has to be exceptionally high. It is executed to the accompaniment of the gentle, drawn-out sound of the violin, without any other notes

* Volynsky probably has Lidiya Ivanova in mind here.

articulating the rhythm. The masculine leap, combined with a generous feminine flowingness, produces a dual impression which strains both the eye and
ear. There is something melancholic, oppressively dreary and at the same time
diffuse, broad, and sprawling about the entire scene. I love this moment of the
variation no less than I do the famous great sissonnes in the second scene of
Swan Lake. This is a real masterpiece of choreographic technique, which overflows into the realm of psychology, thought, and human will. After these leaps
the dancer moves back in tiny classical movements in two sequences of steps.
First she gathers herself into a ball, then she quickly blossoms.

The second part of the variation begins, full of bold and forceful battements, which in ballet are called batteries. There is something masculine,
forceful, and intensely passionate here, which takes possession of the audience
even when it is performed by a woman, if there is elevation. In its elevation and
force this leap should be equal to the original leaps, but the beats of the
cabrioles create the illusion of diminished magnitude. As a whole the movement is extremely rich in content, filled with choreographic nuances and a
mood of temporary agitation. The movement of a surging wave is created; for
several moments it appears to stand at its crest. But then it begins its rhythmic
descent in the third part, and this descent goes through various phases, which
are presented by the ballet master like little choreographic diamonds of the
highest order. The circular round movements of the legs, simple circles on the
toes en dehors, a softly rounded flourish, ending with a falling into position
with arms raised. Such is the variation in its three parts, which one could call
the variation of a wave: it springs up, it makes a frothy ascent, and it falls. This
is a bodily symbol of emotional events that repeat themselves daily.

The variation begins with a demi-plié, exactly the same plié that is felt
before any large-scale movement, as if the soul has been softened in a kind of
psychological plié. Having been primed, the soul has taken off—and in its
flight it has lost none of its tender and feminine emotion, just like the leap I
described above. The soul continues to play and rushes about in the air. In the
air it is always slightly masculine, with a slight patina of heroic will, which is
not characteristic of the female construction. The soul tenses up, is carried off,
and becomes bellicose in its skirmish with fate. This is the psychological
reflection of the entrechat sept. Nothing is artificial, everything is natural.
No acrobatic gymnastics—two languages, the physical and the psychological,
merge in complete unison. The ballet master senses every flutter of the soul,
but if the dancer has not been infected by this quivering, she can provide only
pure technique, which may delight the eye but not touch the soul. Finally, the
wave of inner emotion dies down to the level of the soul in its day-to-day life.
How delicate, how nuanced, how poetically affectionate is this presentation

onstage! The last dying flutter of excitement still lives on in the final movements of the variation.

I will not criticize the performer of this number, Mariya Kozhukhova. Those who were in the theater will themselves decide whether or not she got the job done.

—*"Don Kikhot," Zhizn' iskusstva* (2 October 1923): 2–3.

Classical Attire

T he ballerina's costume constitutes something extraordinary. The tights, which fit close to the leg, strike the spectator first and foremost, then the ballerina's flimsy dress, and finally the pink ballet slippers without heels. How is such extravagance justified? Innovators of the Russian style have tried, and continue to try, to expose women's legs in ballet. If we leave out Isadora Duncan, who is not directly related to ballet, we can establish, both in her case and in dance, the tendency over the past years toward nakedness—onstage, in artsy cabarets, on the roofs of modern restaurants and other up-to-date places which appeal to the enjoyment of a decent public code of ethics. I shall not speak of all these institutions of questionable aesthetics. I don't have Neptune's trident to command the elements! But ballet's attire has interested me for a long time.

Fifteen years ago I discussed this question in my correspondence with Mathilda Kshesinskaya, Vera Trefilova, Elena Liukom, and Tamara Karsavina. Their answers are preserved to this day in my archive. Kshesinskaya expressed her thoughts apodictically. She wrote in a minute handwriting, using short, attributive sentences. One of her remarks especially stuck in my memory: tights provide coolness to the body, which is necessary for dancing. Liukom expressed herself less definitively, and in general her letter to me, which was clearly formulated under a kind of trance, skirted around the issue. Karsavina and Trefilova also expressed themselves with complete precision, especially the latter, who never deviated even a step from the classical canon. Her letter is filled with elegant polemics against innovations in this area. To remove tights from ballet would be to denude it in all senses of the word.

Let us analyze the heart of the matter. Bare legs cannot produce classical figures. It is impossible to stand on one's toes when the foot is bare: without outside supporting coverings the toes will immediately spread apart and be unable to bear, for even a short time, the weight of the torso. Moreover, a naked leg, even one endowed with the most naturally beautiful shape, profits enormously when clothed in tights. The leg is smoothed out, it acquires support and assembles itself into a compact, artistically working unit. The roughness disappears; the flabby parts stretch and are distributed harmoniously; individual isolated defects, such as redness and even—horror of horrors—the body's hairiness, vanish. Clothed in silk tights the leg acquires its fullest possible perfection. The magnificent works of Greek sculpture always represented the human body free of all blemishes, defects, and peculiarities. These are bodies in general, universal bodies: there is nothing individualistic, no arbitrary features such as spots, pimples, moles, etc. Classical dance is sculpture in motion—consequently, in its statuesque as well as in its dynamic element it must answer to the demands of ancient art.

A naked leg would also suffer in terms of movement. Certain parts would flicker and shine with an unpleasant glow, would move forward disharmoniously in opposition to the task of the dance. The arch would not be delineated and would be deprived of the exclusive role it is called upon to play in the movement's overall effect. The female body loves coverings, even the finest and most weblike, because they make it easier for the eyes to see the natural play of the muscles. And through the gossamer of the tights the ascent moves forward, becomes resilient, oscillates, and subsides in its oval in an enchanting vertical climb—all with extraordinary beauty and expressiveness. But what could a bare leg do here, so shamelessly powerless, that bare leg that Kasian Goleizovsky's theater has shown in its evocative developments? Absolutely nothing in an artistic sense. Even Giorgione's naked Venus,* compositionally created by the subtle brush of a genius, were she to get up and move in front of us, would suffer in her captivating charm. Woman's beautiful body, ideally naked, is best in repose and not in motion.

What role does the ballerina's dress play in ballet? We must first note that in former times the ballerina's dress was longer and dropped below the knee, as we see in engravings and old lithographs. Nowadays the dress is high and exposes the dancer's entire knee. It is made of fine tarlatan, light and inclined to fly up and rise at the slightest puff of wind. Sometimes when swirling, running, or soaring passionately onstage the ballet dress surrounds the dancer in a genuine cloud. In general it corresponds to the etherealness of the impression, and in a certain sense plays the role of wings. In ballet there are variations that are apotheosized by nothing other than the dress. Imagine an artist who, bending with inclined head, hurtles upward from the footlights in a low arabesque. The dress rises above her head, and this head emerges in the tender accompaniment

* *The Sleeping Venus* by Giorgione (c. 1477–1510) hangs in Dresden's Gemaldegalerie.

of the enveloping element. Anna Pavlova had such inimitable moments. But even more, in the highly extended arms of Samuil Andriyanov, in the most magnificent pas de deux of her classical performances, Karsavina appeared in her coiling dress with unprecedented beauty. Even Elsa Vill, in the famous pas de trois in *Paquita,* thanks to the wonderful support of Petr Vladimirov, produced a captivating impression. Her dress nervously shook, fluttered, and emitted the tempo of elevation that adorned the artist's outstanding talent in its heyday. And I automatically ask myself, What would have happened if the dress were abolished from ballet? Ballet's poetry, etherealness, and wingedness would disappear. The figures would be prosaically massive, plump and heavy. Ballet would lose its fairy-tale quality. Here every reform is an amputation. The ballet dress and tights have existed, do exist, and will exist.

The shoe will exist as well as long as classical dance goes on. It merges with the dancer's foot, thoughtfully and lovingly tied with a pink ribbon around the ankle. In its padding it is suitable for standing on pointe, and in this form, with only a few variations, it existed along with tights and "knitted underskirt," even in ancient times. The Italian ballet shoe differs from the French—it is firmer and more stable in the padding, but it is inferior to the French shoe in lightness. As soon as a heel appears on the shoe, we are no longer dealing with classical ballet but rather with character or genre-historical dancing. Old minuets and farandoles, polkas and waltzes were performed in opulent noble surroundings with small colored heels. In these dances, especially character dances, the heel, by its rhythmic tapping, fulfills a task that is completely alien to classical dance. In mazurkas, the sole shuffles and the heel taps.

—"Klassicheskii tualet," *Zhizn' iskusstva* (23 October 1923): 10.

Naked, Barefoot, and Beltless

Alexandra Danilova performed in Mikhail Fokine's *Egyptian Nights* in a major space. She danced with bare feet, with her broad shoulders exposed, entwined only around the middle in some colorful fabric. Her naked and very rounded arms were thrown up and out, with twisted palms upward in an artificial contraposto effort—all according to the ballet master's affected and oppressive formula. This is the style of Fokine's Egyptology. On several striking drawings of the ancient kingdom inexperienced, antiquated artists who did not have the faintest clue about perspective depicted the movements of arms, legs, and torso in naively juvenile distortions. Huge numbers of such drawings, which later were somewhat improved, have come down to us from Egypt. . . . Disdaining real, three-dimensional Egypt and personifying it on the stage in the childish errors of the earliest archaic masters is a laughable undertaking and, from a scholarly point of view, an idiotic one. I beg not to offend anyone. I speak from the vantage point of Greek philology, according to which everything is idiotic that is not tied to the actual whereabouts of people and objects in three-dimensional space. If a work is not based on an exact correspondence of things, if it is torn from living life, from real history in its design, then it is idiotic and hangs in the air like a futile apparition and useless absurdity. Fokine's production *Egyptian Nights* is just such an absurdity. There is nothing Egyptian—not even in caricature—in it, only sheer absurdity. And I shall add this: ballet that is produced with sets in the style of contemporary life is horribly obsolete and incompetently reactionary, creating the impression of a crudely executed painting in the banal style of Henryk Sienkiewicz.*

And so Danilova danced in this ill-starred ballet according to Fokine's competent formula. I value this young dancer, who has begun her career with significant success. She has a capacity for work that has turned into genuine talent. In her classical dances Danilova sometimes radiates with youthful beauty. Her statuesque figure, all her lines, the position of her head, the shape of her neck—everything grows and flourishes. But in *Egyptian Nights* the performance of this artist can give nothing, either to her or to the public. Let us state first and foremost: a naked body is not beautiful onstage. In order for there to be a general harmony of movement onstage, without any individual deviations from the conventionally ideal design, the body must shine in the mirror of choreographic attire. Reflected in this true and obedient replication, it acquires the stamp of universal applicability. And it is precisely in this regard that Danilova committed a cardinal sin. She enraptured us with her attire and disappointed us with the bareness of Fokine's production. It is not good if an arm appears plumper, wider, and meatier than the adjacent leg. I caught myself thinking during this extremely boring production, Why not, for example, give Olga Spesivtseva's legs the plumpness of Danilova's arms, and Danilova's arms the lovely slimness of Spesivtseva's legs? This would be marvelous and advantageous for both artists.

I was able to occupy myself uninterruptedly with such thoughts because onstage such total monotony prevailed that my well-intentioned heart groaned. A torrid Libyan desert without a single oasis! Further, I cannot see any expressiveness in the dramatic motifs of Danilova's acting. Her face is round and detached, slightly oval-shaped at the cheeks, with delicate lines in its lower

*Henryk Sienkiewicz (1846–1916) was a Polish novelist; he won the Nobel Prize in 1905.

section. The main thing is that it is completely impenetrable, and its inner spring is hidden. Like many of our dancers, Danilova has not taken a course in the calisthenics of the face. Her face twitches and shouts, and its expression is reduced to a tense grimace. Tearing one's passions to shreds, plunking oneself on the floor, turning upside-down and spreading one's legs apart while toppling all over is not drama. Yet Danilova's performance was precisely this, and thus for all her native talent, it produced a painful impression. She plashed and flapped her hands. Personally I like a prudent classical port de bras, even if it is reflective of genre-historical dancing. The number with the snake absolutely flopped: with naked feet and a naked body, which was furnished with the proper attire, and with the absence of soft lines created by restrictive tights, all the movements and figures of Danilova's swaying dough splashed around in an anti-artistic twaddle.

Overall I have to say that the technique in *Egyptian Nights* is extremely elementary. Bas-relief predominates. The torso and head are thrown back. The hands are extended forward with open palms, parallel with the line of the feet, which are thrust with the toe of one foot toward the heel of the other. In all parts of the ballet there are distorted leaps, typical of Fokine. The classical tire-bouchon, which has penetrated Fokine's innovative acting since the time of Isadora Duncan, everywhere predominates. Everything adheres to tire-bouchon—the dances of the slave girls, the leaps of the youth at the beginning of the action, the dances of the artiste who leads the ballet, the dance with the sistrums, the dance with the veil—all, absolutely all. Tire-bouchon is, in essence, a forward attitude. The foot is lifted forward, is bent, and remains for several moments suspended in such a position. In the dance of the fauns and satyrs this figure is extremely appropriate. If you retain tire-bouchon for a long time, it cannot help but create the requisite comic impression, especially when executed without turnout. But it hardly follows that one should abuse this figure. In *Egyptian Nights* it is unpleasant to the point of being bothersome, and it is cumbersome to contemplate, like a bad habit. In general this movement is taken from ornamented vases, not from the pan-Athenian festival depicted by Phidias. An astonishing thing, and the same fatal mistake: one wants to reproduce and stylize something, but one learns from archaic monuments, not from the perfect works of Praxiteles, Skopas, or Miron, or at least from the Rhodian or Pergamon school! One could have taken endless lessons from the lovely statues of Tanagra.*

---

* Phidias (c. 500–432 B.C.) was a Greek sculptor. The pan-Athenian festival was an annual dramatic festival held in Athens in honor of its patron deity, Athena. Praxiteles was a Greek sculptor who lived during the fourth century B.C.; Skopas, a contemporary of Praxiteles, was a Greek sculptor of the so-called new Attic School; Miron was also a

The performance I saw consisted of three parts. In addition to *Egyptian Nights, Carnaval* and *Eros* were performed. But on the latter two I cannot squeeze out even a single sympathetic line. Everything was hackneyed, danced to the point of exhaustion, and confused in conception and manner of execution.

—"I nago, i boso i bez poyasa," *Zhizn' iskusstva* (23 October 1923): 8–10.

"Swan Lake"

The Swan in Music

W hat is a swan? It is a living aquatic flower. All aquatic plants, beginning with our own lilies and ending with the tropical lotus, have a round pliant stem, which carries the cup of the flower and has the sinuousness and character of a swan's neck. Of course, the swan's neck performs its own special functions: it separates reeds and thus catches the fish that swim deep within them. But there is a certain mimicry here whereby the appearance of the animal often conforms to the character of its environment. Snow-white fluffy beasts meld into the snow of the northern countries. The lion's color recalls that of desert sands, and its mane rises like grains of sand carried by a torrid sandstorm. The swan also corresponds remarkably to the aspect and disposition of the environment that surrounds it. The swan is characterized by a low and rare flight. It can flap over the water with its wings, but it would be difficult and unusual for it to fly above the water's surface, as seagulls do.

I have written a lot over the years about the predominance of the plantlike element in the structure of the female body. Delicately, pliantly, and with palpitating plastique, it assumes poses and figures that are distinguished not so much by force as by a flowing grace obedient to the susceptibility of a sensitive, plantlike being. It moves like a plant the wind has plucked from the earth, to which it continues to be drawn with all its fibers. This is why a woman's flight cannot be called great in any sense of the word. It is also a living plant that reaches above the chaos of water, flying and fluttering from place to place, leaping over small spaces, but not soaring high above the sky. There is a swan in

---

Greek sculptor who preceded the flourishing of Greek art in the sixth and fifth centuries B.C. Tanagra, a town in ancient Greece, was famous for its small terra-cotta figurines.

every woman, moving the reeds apart and gracefully gliding as it catches its meager booty among them. A swanlike neck is one of the favorite epithets of female beauty, and [to be compared to] a white swan is an ancient compliment among the common people. Here is a remarkable philological detail: to the masculine noun *swan* we affix a feminine adjective. The folk seemingly intuitively feel that a feminine soul resides in the swan.

In this sense, what immense significance the position of the head has—the French porte-de-tête—in a woman. If it rests on a high, delicate, and agile neck, it can freely tilt in any direction and with bold controposto turn on its axis. Here we find both the coquetry of gentle flirtations and the brief movements of semi-masculine audacity. But for all this great beauty if there are shortcomings in the porte-de-tête, then the entire charm of the head, with its most striking features, is cheapened. We can apply this principle also to the male, whose head, because of an insufficiently long neck, produces from its position deep in the shoulders an unpleasant and even painful impression. This is especially notable in dancing, in that classical display of the entire person.

Tchaikovsky made the image of the swan the central idea of his immortal creation, and on this score Tchaikovsky has outdone Pushkin. In his Tatyana,* Pushkin displayed with matchless craft only some psychological and everyday moments, and he achieved something enormously touching, at times even heroic, but without universal significance. As the basis of his feminine image, Tchaikovsky used biological features and by doing so he gave to it a universal character. The Swan is onstage, and its song sings in the orchestra through the violins. The entire music has a magical flavor. The introduction is tender and gracious in its melodic lines. In the first act we have a pas de trois which is imperfect in its rhythmic fantasy but magnificent in other respects. The first variation has a strongly balletic character with the realistic quality of classical movement. It provides motifs for simple par-terre dancing. Unfortunately, the dances, which are not distinguished by any originality, constitute a commentary on these musical moments. The entire staging, as a whole and in its separate parts, proceeds in schemes that recall the famous brilliant trio from *Paquita.* The second variation is more dreamlike in character and recalls motifs from Russian folk lyrics. In the protraction of the melodic line flash elements of possible elevation. The basic theme is enveloped in a haze of sound. According to the piano score, the variation ends in dreamy trills in which reflections of the female's anticipated appearance quiver. The remaining variations, broadly designated by Tchaikovsky, are of varied character: totally simple, rather elementary motifs and motifs in difficult continuous octaves and masterly modes, which are applied to the scenic tasks of ballet.

*The heroine of Pushkin's *Eugene Onegin* (1831).

Especially beautiful is the waltz. Despite the simplicity of its basic theme, it excels in its remarkable gracefulness and touching femininity. The waltz is built on the dynamic juxtapositions of its separate parts, with a hint of prenuptial animation. Tchaikovsky constantly prepares the background for the appearance of the dreamy thought about the Swan, which finally unfolds in all its melancholy radiance in the introductory section of the second scene. This motif has been somewhat "Lohengrinized": it seems to be a quotation from the musical phrases of the swan-knight of Wagner's conception. It is melodiously extended, languorously drawn-out in length, and with its acoustical sharpness it cuts through the musical fabric of the work, leaving on its surface a bright patch of light. For this reason it is poignantly sad, like everything that emanates from Tchaikovsky's intimate lyricism. The strings vibrate in a delicate haze. The waltz proceeds with an inflection of low flight, which characterizes the entire ballet.

Especially remarkable and noteworthy in this sense is the music accompanying the first phases of the pas de deux. In the entire literature of world ballet, I do not know of a better adagio. Here Tchaikovsky's biological interpretation is the entire philosophy, the entire soul, the entire languorous and radiant life of the Swan. The audience listens to this part of the ballet frozen in sweet rapture. The pas begins with the singing of the harps—an acoustic stroke from the kingdom of Apollo. The harp and the lyre are the instruments of the sun god, whose birth was commemorated by snow-white swans sailing around the island of Delos seven times. Apollo's life is entirely entwined in the softness of swan poetry, which never leaves it, for the very number seven signifies in the East nothing less than the perpetuity and fullness of strings. Seven days in a week, seven colors in the sun's spectrum, seven notes in the scale. The harp sings in soft, plantlike tones, which represent the rhythmic pattern for the collective arabesque of the corps de ballet. No greater artistic charm exists in the whole world. Hellas itself did not achieve in its great balletic art such potently sacred effects. We have here the lively and vivid interaction of the ballerina's solo and the corps' ensemble variation. One overflows into the other. Everything seethes as it harmoniously reflects what has just taken place.

In the beginning adagio the acoustical sequences soar and flow via the violins' playing on high notes, which support the classical patterns. Sometimes passionate exclamations of a gentle timbre are heard. Doing her grand, undulating lateral battements—the miracle of Ivanov's production—the dancer seems to be spiritually guided by the shimmering line of sound. The adagio is long and shifts from one place to another. The dancer is now in the arms of her partner, rather high up in the air, then in extended fading poses, which represent the image of the suddenly dying hours of love. One cannot forget the effects Olga Trefilova achieved many years ago. Tamara Karsavina also had her excellent moments. I shall write at a later date about how current ballerinas deal with this movement, but I cannot pass over in silence the recent performance of Liubov Egorova, the ultimate in plantlike beauty, which enjoyed enormous success among the public and critics alike. In any case, this is the dance and the kind of adagio whose test every artist must pass with flying colors. Jean-Georges Noverre and Carlo Blasis both admit that the adagio is the proving ground for classical talent. My personal observations in this area have strengthened my conviction that the female dancer can fully display her qualities of harmonious movement precisely here. This is not the testing ground of talent in the wide sense of the word, but rather of femininity and grace.

The small Dance of the Cygnets, which follows the monumental pas de deux, adds to the generally exquisite fantastic scene. This is a fine gem of sound, which accompanies the semi-genre dance in the spirit of the eighteenth century. Everything is gentle, everything is detailed. Recalling the motifs of a folk dance, the loose symmetry moves in flowing sounds.

The music of *Swan Lake* does not especially stand out in individual places, nor is it particularly varied in its thematic effect on the ear, but nonetheless it is a genuine masterpiece of Russian musical Romanticism. It is enlivened from start to finish by the pathos of self-renunciation, by the spirit of Slavic self-discipline. Tchaikovsky has forged the music with a single lyrical mood, clothing it with an acoustical and poetic image of the Russian woman, although the ballet's story has come to us from other lands. I have already said that in certain respects this image is more powerful than Pushkin's image of Tatyana, but it is also more incorporeal and softer than Rimsky-Korsakov's Snow Maiden. In the sounds that accompany the astonishing movements, this is a spring evening that is dying among the dreamy chords of the strings, like the fading smoke of the sun's rays.

—"Balet *Lebedinoe ozero*. Lebed' v muzyke," *Zhizn' iskusstva* (27 November 1923): 4–5.

"Sleeping Beauty"

I t is worth lingering on the costumes of *Sleeping Beauty*. A large expanse opens before the artist; he is not bound by the epoch that dictates the costumes and their color. Within the contours of pure fairy tale, he can give his complete will over to fantasy and taste. However, he must not forget that he is creating costumes for a ballet. Clothing in dance must be light but obedient to all the choreography's demands. If ancient costume is, in Goethe's words, the thousandfold echo of the human body, then the attire of dance must be the manifold repetition of the peripeteia of the body's movements. And since in classical dance these movements are stylized, the outer covering of the dancer must also have a corresponding character. But in stylized attire the vivid array of tones that floats in front of the audience has great significance: here the harmony of the color of the costume and the type of dance plays a big role. This significance has never escaped our marvelous costumier and artist Ivan Vsevolozhsky, who at one point headed the Maryinsky Theater. His sketches of the costumes for *Sleeping Beauty* are of lasting interest for the history of this period. Here is a genuine director of the ballet theater who knows and understands the finest details of what he is directing. With such a director the genius of Marius Petipa could spread its wings and produce an entire series of works for the Russian ballet worthy of the world stage.

Let us return to the question of the appropriate attire for *Sleeping Beauty*. We shall begin with the Prologue. In it the costumes form a pair and contain an unusual variety of colors. Konstantin Korovin, who discarded Vsevolozhsky's sketches, had one goal: to clothe everyone in faded colors. This was a fundamental and fatal error on the artist's part. One should not use the faded colors of the intimate boudoir pattern of the rococo for a pure and free fairy tale in the green forests of creative imagination, a fairy tale which in its very spirit begs for the luminous frame of classical dance. Here the colors, inseparable from those of the dancing and fused with it to the last detail, must sing, shine, and entice. But everything in Korovin fades and wanes. In the prologue, instead of a lively and vivid gamut of spring colors, the Lilac Fairy's clothes are a washed-out dark green. The grayish, lilac-silver wig with its long braids weighs down and ages the whole figure, turning the all-sweetness-and-light fairy—the young dancer Ekaterina Geidenreich—into a middle-aged lady. The same disastrous wigs on the other fairies of the talc, with ringlets hanging almost to their waists, also give these sweet creatures a somewhat weighty character. The fairy-tale qualities are completely eroded and replaced with a gamut of diverse colors that can be understood only by reading the program. Nothing flashes in our eyes, nothing speaks of itself without help from the program notes.

As for the king and queen, their royal attire, the symbolic solemnity of the man's chlamys and the woman's mantle, which drag along the floor, veritably oppress you with their heaviness. If you add to this the fact that the sets for the Prologue are painted in the same white-green colors and covered with wreaths of lilac, you see that we have the same monochromatically cheerless picture of the introductory action. In the orchestra the most marvelous sounds, vitreously translucent, buzz and billow: dancing to them seems like the easiest thing in the world. But onstage everything taken together is oppressively realistic and

moves slowly forward through the crawling movements of amphibious creatures. The fairy tale itself is not built on the lilac, but it is precisely the lilac—
moreover one that is still finishing its blossoming and fading, with all the
corresponding nuances of spring ending in summer's heat—that captures the
dominant role in the ballet and improperly prevails. And this is how everything
proceeds from beginning to end.

In the first act of the ballet the grand and complicated waltz is wonderfully
produced not only in a musical but also in a choreographic sense. The costumes of the corps de ballet are of a milky-pale and red color, which is at times
darker, at times brighter. Mid-length cabaret skirts with velvet bodices and
white gloves with puffs constitute the dancers' garb. The chic hats are adorned
with ostrich feathers. In theory these are peasants, but given their costumes,
they are French grand seigneurs—totally out of place in a crowd of simple folk,
who must accompany the king, queen, and Princess Aurora. How much better
in this regard is the previous attire, which I recall in its entire spectrum of color.
There were white shirts and blue trousers worn over blue stockings. The hats
were also of blue velvet. All this was simple, modest, and sufficiently dressy,
answering the demands of the action—no showy pomp but rather a charming
poetic background for the nobles who made their appearance. Vsevolozhsky's
amazing sensitivity manifested itself here without the slightest affectation. If
his sketches had been restored in view of the evolution of manners we have
experienced, an amateur artist would have turned out to be far more in accord
with contemporary times than the artist-professional who, with all his talent,
could only coat all the lively and magic splendor of the composition with a
monochromatically soft color. Korovin doesn't see anything, either in the dancing or in the classical minutiae that sparkle like diamonds, and he compre-
hends nothing in the play of the figures and schemes. Everything for him lies
in the artificially pompous scenery, the oppressive attire, and the brownish-
red wigs.

Aurora performs a wonderful hyporchema. I remind the reader that the
Greeks used this word for every dramatic dance, in the spirit of our current pas
d'action. Her attire is horrible. She wears a rust-colored wig and her dress is
pink, as is her bodice. Given her bare arms and neck, this color lends her figure
a certain monotony and stiffness. What kind of Aurora is this—the symbolic
image of the dawn with all the fullness of its tones and hues! The sky is all pink,
but the goddess of the dawn herself, who is carried on a golden chariot, hardly
merges with the background. She is completely within the fresh ardor of color
and light and of the morning's gentle rays, which shoot into a landscape that
arouses one to life. There can be no monotonous uniformity here. And Aurora's rust-colored hair not only oppresses, it distorts the picture. Again I must
say that in Vsevolozhsky we also had something artistically and poetically

beautiful. The costume was a vivid red, with gold spangles sprinkled all over, and it set the dancer apart from the crowd. And the four Frauleins who accompany the princess in elegant black dresses provided an intense background for Aurora herself. (Now, however, we have before us only a noisy crowd and an unjustified diversity of colors. And all the Frauleins have heavy dark wigs. I should add that in the first act, sixteen years after the prologue, the king and queen are in the same costumes! The scenery also fails to sparkle with originality: a wooden lattice overrun with greenery.) The four columns of the palace give off a soft purple tint. You can feel the colors. You can feel the scenery.

I shall quickly note the defects of the costumes in the following acts. In the hunting scene the women's attire, long and heavy, with its massive trains, interferes with the dancing. And again those inescapable reddish-brown wigs! The Lilac Fairy, as in a later scene of this act, is in a pure lilac dress, which hardly produces a joyful impression on the eye. The Nereids wear hideous wigs with their long hair hanging down. Then, too, the formerly marvelous panorama that elicited unanimous bravos from the audience in the ballet's first production has completely lost its luster. The second act, thanks to the unsuccessful choice of attire, colors, and either lackluster or tattered sets, as well as to the ugly background, leaves the spectator completely cold. There is no fairy tale, no enchanting spectacle, and therefore also no Aurora in the ensemble of the flowering and cheerful summer environment.

In the last act of the ballet the costumes of the entire cast change totally. The queen enters with a white cap on her head. The Jewels are clothed in attractive attire. The ballet dresses are light and of appropriate color. The headdresses are simply beautiful. Silver and Gold have a festive plume. Diamond and Sapphire have a radiant halo of bright and delicate stones. The Little Cat is in a grayish and rather dirty wig. On its head is a fleece with little ears. The Princess in the Blue Bird variation is in a wig of the same color; the sleeves with fluffy flounces hide her charming hands. Cinderella's costume is completely natural, somewhat in the style of Gretchen, with a cap on her head. Little Red Riding Hood has almost completely lost her fairy-tale countenance. She is wearing a dress that she doesn't need—a white silk shirt with a velvet bodice and a round hat made of glittering sparkles with little tufts of hair. This is too elegant for a poor peasant girl with a basket and a bouquet of wildflowers in her hands. This is rather an imp from hell than Little Red Riding Hood! Vsevolozhsky had it completely different. There was a real bouquet of well-chosen flowers. There was a peasant skirt up to the knee, a white cambric shirt, a little black bodice, a modest apron, and a charming child's hat of cheap felt on her head. It was not chic at all but rather simple, without expensive baubles. Aurora's costume also seemed unsatisfying to me: I am keeping to Korovin's drawings without considering any alterations introduced by contemporary artists. The pink bro-cade dress and the headdress with white feathers were little felt against the background of the gaudy corps de ballet, and at times they even vanished completely from view.

In conclusion I shall say only a few words about the modern Aurora who has replaced Elizaveta Gerdt and Olga Spesivtseva, the young dancer Taisiya Troyanovskaya. Her performance was not stellar, and I have a list of objections. Troyanovskaya's little head, with its beautiful face, is rather heavy. There are no bold or decisive tours, but as much bending as you like in a soft but colorless pattern. Although her eyes—and here I again object—sparkle, they do so not with an individual gleam but rather impersonally and pointlessly, just passably, as they glance rather coldly and emotionlessly from side to side. Her smile—and here I really object—is the same throughout the entire ballet: it is con-ventionally and sweetly motionless without directing anything, or ultimately being directed by anything, from within; it is hardly sunny, and it doesn't flow from the physical or psychological mists of existence. Troyanovskaya dances only in flat and open little scenes that do not originate from any depth. This is unadulterated effacé without any alternating moments which accumulate life. There is an emptiness within, and thus on the beautiful exterior there is no inspiring pathos. In light of such an inner structure, her performance, with its copious abridgements to make the acting and dancing lighter, and its stripping down of all complex technique, cannot capture and please the eye for a moment.

In the first act, immediately after the tormentingly long Prologue, Troya-novskaya does not complete the figures, and, though musical by nature, she cannot keep pace with the orchestra. The charming pas de chat of this act are clipped in their extreme contours by the shears of an amateur gardener: you have to be able to fill out the musical passage with dancing so you do not sacrifice any of the parts, and be coordinated with the subsequent figures, and not fall behind too much from the pace of the variations. Also unsuccessful in this sense is the disjointed dance with the suitors, from each of whom Aurora takes a flower. She rewards each of them with a thankful turn, as if to show that her talent is not insensitive to the gifts of love. Not keeping pace with the music, Troyanovskaya deprives the final suitor of the attention he is due. This is annoying because one would have expected from a young dancer who is sensitive to the rhythm and beat of the music the ability to accurately and fully convey complete phrases and whole monologues of the orchestral language.

In addition, a series of imperfections in execution mar the later sections of the ballet. The rotations are not firm or reliably constant, and there are blun-ders that distort the entire design. In this regard it is impossible to set Troya-novskaya next to any of the dancers from former times, beside Elena Smirnova or Kseniya Makletsova, not to mention Gerdt and Spesivtseva. The famous rotations of all these dancers, without the support of their partner, came off as dauntlessly pure and stellar. Finally, after failing to show focused concentration of a physical or plastic nature in any of her dance figures, Troyanovskaya suddenly displays this feature in the concluding episodes of act 2. She falls on the ground, carefully placing one leg over the other, possibly to hide from the audience the broad lines of her body. But here is where croisé is truly inappropriate and where, by the nature of things, one needs a generously open extension. In conclusion I shall add that the dancer seems heavy in her partner's arms; especially when she performs complex figures, which require contraposto rotations, the quality of the dancing is impure, weak, and extremely lacking in character. The external beauty is everywhere, but it has no internal countenance.

Such, in its cardinal features, is Troyanovskaya's emotional performance. I have noted only the defects because they are so glaring. But I would not deprive the artist of her innately feminine charm and unquestionable talent. This talent will some day find its form in the process of long, hard, tireless work—the price outstanding ballerinas pay for their fame.

—"Balet *Spiashchaia krasavitsa*," *Zhizn' iskusstva* (4 December 1923): 7–9.

"Swan Lake"

The Swan in Motion

I n *Swan Lake* music and movement fuse together. All the acoustical designs, nuances, little points, and parabolas are consolidated on the stage in equivalent movements. If we conceptually boil down, relax, and loosen the movement, we should present its musical outline in detail. In all likelihood, we are indebted to Lev Ivanov for such a perfect production. Marius Petipa was not himself distinguished by any particular musical sense, and in his works we often encounter episodic discrepancies between the acoustic and the movement. Moreover, the baroque grandeur and elegance so characteristic of this genius would not be completely appropriate in those scenes of the ballet where the Swan's gentle and languid theme predominates, that is, in the second and final scenes of this magnificent work. This is why Ivanov's collaboration in precisely these scenes was necessary. The other scenes were doubtless arranged by Petipa, with the distinctive resplendence of his large-scale, monumental classical composition. The pas d'action of the second act surely belongs to Petipa's best work, and, embellished by the Franco-Italian fio,rituras, it always evokes a whirlwind of delight among the public, especially in the last sections, which are built on the technique of fouetté. But the essence of the ballet is nonetheless in the Swan's orchestral theme, which Ivanov has reproduced onstage.

Let us linger on the main choreographic part of the production. In this regard, the adagio of the second scene occupies a central place, as we have already seen, not only in a musical but also a plastic sense. Here the Swan is in everything. Her broad, gentle battements in the arms of the danseur—fluctuating and undulating battements—recall the fluttering of a swan's wings. If the battement does not reach sufficient height, the complete artistic effect is not achieved. This means that the danseur has relaxed the demands of the choreographic moment and has not adhered to the bio-mechanical law which says that the ballerina's leg can be raised higher than the waist only if her partner supports her while she bends in the opposite direction. Mathilda Kshesinskaya's legs would spread impermissibly wide precisely because her partner would lift her above him in a straightly extended line. But even in the most faultless design demanded by the classical developpé, the fullness of musical illusion is necessary. The alternating grand battements must sing in unison with the orchestra. A noble melancholy is needed, which finds expression in the melodious tempos of the undulating extension of the legs. Otherwise one achieves a faultless technique at the cost of the inner emptiness of the content. This is what I would like my careful writing, which guards the rather fragile reputation of ballerinas, to do: to note those nuances that were unquestionably lacking in Olga Spesivtseva's performance of this crucial part of the dance. Her battement is pure and distinct. Everything is within the rules of choreographic technique. Her leg is long and attractive, formed by nature itself completely classically. Everything is impeccable. Only one thing was lacking—the Swan. The Swan was absent from the very beginning, from her first appearance onstage. And in her remarkable battement the Swan was also absent: there was all the formal and physical beauty you could think of, just not the Swan's beauty—plantlike and quiet, which strains the soul with its tears and sighs. This is why I, who love this ballet so much, could enjoy all the artist's subsequent dancing only with a feeling of desolation in my soul. Spesivtseva did battements whose designs were lovely, but I didn't feel the moisture of the swan's lake in them, or the drops of moisture on the swan's wings—only the dryness of an ideally perfect classroom exercise.

The adagio is long and complex. It is full of figures: double pirouettes with arms lifted upward; arabesques across the diagonal of the stage with aerial support from the danseur. The ballerina throws herself into the arms of her partner and extends her legs full length. This is the moment of the fading of the chimes of love. But how deeply the musical theme needs to be inhaled, embodied, and penetrated here! The body is in repose, but meanwhile it shakes with a silent, dying passion, basking and resting in the delightful peace of semi-existence. I do not consider Spesivtseva's execution of this moment particularly successful. Once again there was a beautiful line of the legs, which lavishly yielded to the general delight. There was a radiant marblelike effect—and this is rare, and it counts for quite a lot! But I want more and better from this moment in my beloved ballet. I'll forgive any defect or imperfection in plastique, but in the dancing, give me only a real Swan in *Swan Lake;* give me a sense of chaste seclusion in the stretched legs along which quiet, barely moving zephyrs blow. We don't need the indispensable month of June, the month of Swans, here. *Swan Lake* is also magnificent on a bright autumn day. But again, again: give me a Swan!

Yet none was present on the stage. The dancer leaned her head on her side, threw her arms back with a winglike waving, as if shaking off water; but although a soul shone through from another world, a feathered world, it was not an aquatic world, a world of lakes. It was rather a mountain bird's soul, albeit with clipped or wounded wings. In Spesivtseva's art neither music nor elevation dominates, although the bird's entire lightness is present. Her poses are vivid, the design of her agile dancing unfolds in a free choreographic manner. Her ability to hold her torso on austerely extended toes is exceptional. Her pirouette is not bad, although it often lacks emotional excitement. Yet for all these fortunate external features, the dancer's feminine charm is shrouded by a lackluster veil.

It wasn't always this way. At the dawn of her brilliant career, I remember several features which have sunk into oblivion. There was a smile on her face—in her eyes and near her mouth—which many dancers tried unsuccessfully to imitate. Once Liudmila Schollar stopped onstage and fixed her smiling eyes on her partner, who was facing her. This was totally in the spirit of Spesivtseva, but without her believability. Now it behooves Spesivtseva to imitate her image of those early days.

After the adagio comes the huge variation, constructed in a hybrid style, with the orchestral tempos predominating. This variation was in its time mounted for Pierina Legnani, but was later performed with great virtuosity by Vera Trefilova for her final appearance. The variation begins with a marvelous rotation of the leg and then changes to gliding figures on the ground, interrupted by short leaps. Spesivtseva performs the circular figures with legs pointedly extended in a masterful way. The variation concludes with an arabesque—open and picturesque—with arms thrown back. After the monumental adagio, such a hybrid variation, though encompassing various technical difficulties, cannot really grip the spectator. The act ends with the approving applause of the audience, which reacted to this glorious ballet with immense rapture.

The second act contains the outstanding number from Petipa's production. This is an ordinary pas de deux with a dramatic motif meaningfully adapted to it: essentially this is not the most classical theme, not one of form and choreography but an expressive theme transmitted by the forms of balletic art. Mimicry and technique are required here. Ordinarily ballet masters lay out the most complicated patterns here, which require enormous virtuosity from the performer. The mimicry, however, is driven not by the music but by the situation of the moment, and it exists in contrast to ordinary balletic action. For greater expressiveness words would be required, but there aren't any. You have to play this with a blatant expression on your face. I must say that this kind of acting— with the spreading of the arms and the eloquence of the eyes—is not completely in the spirit of Spesivtseva, who was created more for the lyrical genre. Even in *Esmeralda* her lyrical talent does not always cross over to expressive drama. Yet in *Giselle* everything in her is pure lyricism. To be sure, Spesivtseva copes brilliantly with her task in *Swan Lake,* but I did not see a particularly passionate elevation. Her acting is fine and delicate, and in places subtly beautiful—the stir and magic of her face stand out at times with a rare persuasiveness. There is something demonic here in the full sense of the word. The variation is stylish, strong, and steely. But the coda does not entirely satisfy me. The design of Spesivtseva's fouetté is beautiful in and of itself. She does it with her leg tossed up high and a lovely rotation around the axis. But the entire variation is supposed to amuse and captivate us with the gentle emotion of movement on a fixed spot. Ekaterina Geltser told me that this was done faultlessly by Legnani. She was riveted to the floor, and without leaving it during her rotations she constantly faced the public with her joyfully radiant face, which showed absolutely no fatigue. According to the sense of the entire act, a she-devil is before us, who entices another woman's fiancé into her net. This is where one needs to avoid every kind of corporeality, any tenseness, which is what would happen—in so cumbersome and heavy a way—with Kshesinskaya. The execution requires lightness. The fouetté, as a component of any pirouette, gives the circle its corresponding design. But a fouetté in its separate, independent existence, detached from everything else, like an instrument with blinding and hypnotic effects, is not within the means of every artist, even talented ones. After Legnani's fouetté, Trefilova's radiated with supreme art. Here one needs stamina, strong support, the fire of inner burning. Here one needs spirit and unfeigned, inherent enthusiasm. One cannot simulate such fire: you must have it within you.

Spesivtseva did not display these features of fouetté. Her figure was beautifully conceived. Having taken up her dress with the fingers of one hand, she turned her other one into an instrument of rotation. But the rotation itself seemed vague and dim. Her face could not be seen, and there was no play in her expression or in her eyes. Her figure did not disperse into components of artistic workmanship but rather, with obliterated borders, flickered erratically, smokily, dimly.

The performance enjoyed an enormous success, whose like I have not seen for a long time.

—"Balet *Lebedinoe ozero*. Lebed' v dvizhenii," *Zhizn' iskusstva* (1 January 1924): 17–18.

Lida Ivanova

T he current article appears too late. Its original publication met with difficulties of a totally arbitrary nature. And now, when those amazing difficulties have passed, there is something tragic and disturbing in a post-humous evaluation of the young artist who did not live to see this article in print. When Lida Ivanova* danced in *The Little Humpbacked Horse* for the last time, she asked that I be sent her "personal regards." Fate had it that I could acknowledge those regards only with a few words at her funeral service at the School of Russian Ballet.

Olga Preobrazhenskaya once told me that there was a young girl at the Maryinsky Theater's ballet school who had a great future. Soon after this, at one of the Maryinsky performances, a very young girl with her braid undone and slightly Mongolian features in her lovely face came up to my seat, curtsied, and introduced herself as Lida Ivanova. There began my personal acquaintance with the young dancer in the short period during which she attained rather considerable fame in Saint Petersburg. When my School of Russian Ballet was still on Pochtamskaya Street this young girl would visit rather often— sometimes alone, sometimes accompanied by her father. She sat in the first row in order to hear my lectures and conversations with the student audience. It was pleasant to look into her smart, sharp eyes, which had burned with light at each discussion that interested her. I suggested to Nikolai Legat, my close assistant at the school, that he try out the choreographic abilities of this young

---

*Volynsky uses the familiar "Lida" to replace the more formal "Lidiya." Ivanova drowned under suspicious circumstances on 16 June 1924.

dancer who, by the way, had just finished ballet school. The three of us went
into a large classroom and got down to exercises. At first everything went pretty
much ordinarily. She made some mistakes, but in general she dealt satisfactorily with the basic movements. When the exercise was moved to the middle
of the hall, Legat ordered her to do a saut de basque, a large jump with the
entire body rotating in the air. Ivanova moved off to the outer corner of the
slightly raised floor and from there, in two phenomenally high leaps, traversed
the enormous hall. This was so unexpected that Legat and I involuntarily
exchanged glances. His eyes gleamed with delight. After this, other figures
followed in the same tempo of elevation, and our surprise kept increasing.

Several months after this, having finished school, Lida Ivanova was accepted
into the Maryinsky ballet troupe. She stopped visiting me at the school, though
from time to time she came to me at the House of Art* in order to chat about
dancing and to consult with me about this or that book she should read.

Now, as I have said, Lida Ivanova is a rather famous person in ballet circles.
She has fanatical devotees among the public who greet her every appearance
with furious applause. At a performance of *Don Quixote* some time ago, she
received a genuine ovation for her wonderfully performed solo. Last year, in
her wonderful dance of the slave girl in *Le Corsaire,* she forced Olga Spesivtseva
to endure several awful and possibly even wrenching moments with the passion and glow of her miraculous leap. Though I did not see it, people I respect
have told me that Ivanova's recent entrance in the Pearl scene in *The Little
Humpbacked Horse* was totally out of the ordinary. Such are the brilliant prognoses for the young dancer who not long ago looked at me trustingly with such
childlike eyes. I think of this and am touched—all the more so that Lida
Ivanova is in no way my pupil; I invested no capital in her save for an occasional greeting, several words of praise, and precautionary reprimands in print.

What are my expectations? In terms of choreography I have something
quite specific in mind. On the floor Ivanova might not call any special attention to herself. I still do not see any outstanding feminine harmony of movement or any noteworthy plantlike hues. The pattern of her young body is at
times perceived as somewhat clumsy. There seems to be absolutely no prettiness, especially the mannered and saccharine kind. The rotations of her body
are not seductive. But her leap! It is young and high, and it seizes the sky in a fit,
with an impulsive take-off and a face that is all alit! There is a kind of tenacity
and surety in the air. All of this together yields not mere prettiness but real
beauty, which inspires in me great hope, whose like I have not experienced in a

---

*The House of Art (Dom Iskusstva) was the residence for Leningrad artists, writers, and
other cultural figures set up by the new Soviet government in 1919.

long time. This is Ivanova's choreography, with the irresistible charm of her all-promising youth, youth, and youth.

But Lida Ivanova is also a performer. Her acting is just taking shape, yet it is already noticeable to the experienced eye. Her great expressive gift for classical dance is mapped out in vague contours. The dancer is still only running her inexperienced fingers over the strings of her dramatic lyre, and the acoustical strokes that arise—asymmetrical and unplanned—obviously conceal the integral and melodious chords of future harmony. We are dealing with the soul of a great and intelligent artist. Now everything is scattered and dispersed in disorder. A kind of restlessness with its disturbing lines is traversing the overall design of her artistic growth. All is in a haze. All is unclear. But to our seduced glance a future Giselle is already sketched, the likes of which we have not seen for a long, long time. Everything is decisively in place for Ivanova's Giselle—the elevation and the expression of dramatic art.

With a heart full of affection and hope I recall the sweet girl of Pochtamskaya Street, and I wish her a joyful and happy journey on the great artistic road that is opening before her.

—"Lida Ivanova," *Zhizn' iskusstva* (24 June 1924): 2–3.

Adrienne Lecouvreur

Lida Ivanova's body has still not been recovered. One gets the impression that the girl has not died but disappeared without a trace. But already one wants to correct the word that has slipped from my pencil: for the ballet, Lida Ivanova has not disappeared without a trace. I see a deep furrow that has been drawn on our theatrical field by the sudden departure of this still not quite mature but extraordinarily remarkable dancer. . . .

From her first artistic steps this young girl was enveloped in an atmosphere of anxiety. Two years ago a rumor circulated that a carriage had severed her leg. I remember the confusion, my telegram, and the comforting response I received. This was right after she finished school, before she became a great artist; yet though the sensitive and greatly talented Olga Preobrazhenskaya valued her highly, there gathered around her certain unstable elements; the air around her almost shook with anxious whispering, fearful pride, growing envy, and convulsed reputations, which was the way it remained up until the last minute.

But not only the air shook. An epoch of intrigue began, toxins were prepared, and Florentine knives were sharpened. It is too early to name names. If Lida Ivanova had fallen while she was dancing, I would have been the first to think this was done deliberately, by a spiteful hand, as occasionally happened on theater, opera, and ballet stages. The power of envy is dark and threatening, especially when a bright and genuine talent comes to the fore among the chaos of degradation and decline. I am ready to believe that the motor of the fateful boat really did malfunction. But I would also not be surprised if, with another group of passengers and in other circumstances, the catastrophe might not have been avoided.

The word *motor* brings Ivanova's internal motor to mind. I remember her as a girl, tranquil and balanced. It was pleasant to talk to her. She strung her words in a quiet voice like large pearls on the thread of a free-flowing conversation. Her comments were thoughtful, and she asked questions in the slowly burning fire of her inquisitive temperament. Lately, and especially last winter, Ivanova was unrecognizable. Suddenly everything changed. Fervor appeared, along with an expectation and edginess that sometimes produced an unhealthy impression. Her internal motor had moved from its equilibrium and begun fussing about. All that surrounded her excited and irritated her. . . . All of this spoiled Ivanova's emotional motor and hurried it to death. If her history had turned out somewhat more successfully, if her internal motor had run more normally and peacefully, without having to push through the obstacles accumulated on her path, we would see a flourishing Ivanova before us.

Her talent grew with every hour. I shall long remember the impression I took away after her last performance this season. She made a brilliant display of her unusual elevation. Elevation was in general the major element of her fledgling art. I have already written on this subject and now I mention it only to delineate one special feature of this young artist's talent. When people generally speak about elevation, they have in mind something light, high, and beautifully airborne. A person is carried through the air with the grace of a butterfly. But in this instance we have something entirely different. Genuine artistic elevation is not like this at all. We know Pavlova's elevation to be something uniquely inspired, with wings powerfully spread in the air, in the glow of vigorous flames and in the light of a glowing dream. One important feature always caught your attention. Pavlova's elevation was never burdened by the determined will that was raging within her, or by the liquefied gold of a newborn person. No matter how highly I value this talent, this hurricanelike glory of our time, we are dealing here with the mind-set of former, antiquated times, a classical figure in the museum of the past.

In Lida Ivanova's elevations other traits and qualities manifested themselves. Another era has blown in like a storm on our scene. What a remarkable being

Adrienne Lecouvreur* was in the world of intrigues and machinations! [Iva-nova,] small in stature, with a high forehead and a pure, bright face without wrinkles and their possibilities; big-eyed; stridently monumental in her port de bras and like the preliminary sketch of a future great artist, soared in the air with a great take-off. Our epoch demands that the iron and copper—the true grit of the popular masses—ascend to the stars, not the ethereal reveries of individuals. Man himself has grown more severe, but even weightier: he yearns for the heights. And this is where Lida Ivanova's mission lay. She did not spread herself in the air like Pavlova, but performed en tournant in the arms of her partner as no other dancer before her. It is pointless to compare her terre-à-terre with that of today's miserable dancers. In *The Little Humpbacked Horse* she demonstrated a phenomenal rotation of her body in the air. Her arabesque was almost monstrous in terms of academic design. Her legs were stretched too widely. But there was no way to break loose from the figure. The theater rocked with applause. The willful enthusiasm that lifted her body glared like an entire sun high in the air. There was something even terrifying in the young dancer's take-off. Worried by this marvelous picture, I immediately whispered to her mother, "Tell Lida it's not done this way. But I adore her art!" "Not done" because at that moment the compositional design did not call for it. But one can still do it because the ecstasy that lifts us to the sky dominates over all canons of beauty.

I recall another incident that lovers of classical dance can never forget. Olga Spesivtseva was performing *Le Corsaire*. The audience became alert because, prodded by blind faith in the reputation of an accomplished artist, they ex-pected to see something perfect. There is a moment in the first act when the ballerina is sitting and waiting, while onstage the wonderful duet of the slave girl and her partner unfolds. Then the remarkable adagio, corrected and recon-structed by Christian Johansson, takes place. At the beginning of their careers Spesivtseva and Elena Liukom both enjoyed well-deserved success in this pas de deux. But times change. In this performance, Spesivtseva could only hope to retain her former reputation, but Lida Ivanova needed to acquire fame for herself, to burst into the future through her talent. And something extraordi-nary happened. The underaged girl created a movement that was purely ele-mental. When in her wild leap she found herself in her partner's arms—high and unattainable, filled with a determined fire in the spirit of the new historical

*The death of Adrienne Lecouvreur (1692–1730), the greatest French actress of her time, was also surrounded by mystery, many believing that she had been poisoned. For a poetic reaction to Ivanova's death, see Mikhail Kuzmin's "Dark Streets Beget Dark Nights" ("Temnye ulitsy rozhdaiut temnye mysli," 1926) and the excellent discussion of the poem by John E. Malmstad, "The Mystery of Iniquity: Kuzmin's 'Temnye ulitsy rozhdaiut temnye mysli,'" *Slavic Review* 34, no. 1 (March 1975): 44–64.

moment—all that surrounded grew dim, except her. A beautiful star was ig-
nited. True fame was born, for no artist can have it without elevation.

I shall not analyze any other performances by Lida Ivanova. In several roles
she revealed an astonishingly expressive talent. Dancing the Fisherman's Wife
in *The Pharaoh's Daughter* she demonstrated all the little wheels, and little
screws, of her miraculous mechanism. Her little motor rushed about the stage,
spreading its ardent emotional excitement. Her acting was utterly talented,
unfeigned, cheerful, and far from routine. But in the current repertoire she
still had not gotten the chance to prove her worth in all her brilliance. Of
course, we would not have seen Ivanova enter the pantheon of ballet idols in
Stravinsky's *Petrushka*—that musically and choreographically pretentious piece
of nonsense with its annoyingly false drum and exhausting fanfares. She was a
purely classical dancer whose soul contained the music of exalted moods,
adequate only for similarly serious forms of dance. I urged her father to send
Lida to Milan as soon as possible, where her growing talent would have received
the appropriate stamp. Oh, if that little motor had been in Milan right now!

If the sea returns Lida Ivanova's body to us the entire city will take part in
her funeral. Are there enough white roses in the flower shops for this occasion?
Something strangely intoxicating flashed by us in the evanescent fate of this
virtual child, who embodied the entire destiny of our now-orphaned ballet.
Her appearance inspired us with hope. Her death will add another pathetic
page in the history of art, where posterity will separate the artificial diamonds
from the genuine ones.

—"Adrienne Lecouvreur," *Zhizn' iskusstva* (29 June 1924): 9–10.

Tamara Karsavina

I first met Tamara Platonovna Karsavina at the artist Alfred Eberling's. I
entered his studio at the moment when he was painting her portrait. She
was sitting on a platform, posing for the artist. Her beauty struck and gripped
me at once. Her facial features were not without fault—her nose was somewhat
crooked—but the overall design of her physiognomy was full of warmth, tenderness, and gentleness. She was like the living aroma from a fragrantly smok-
ing incense burner. Like dark smoke, a halo of hair surrounded her radiant
face, whose beauty is impossible to forget. Her voice, her gestures, her sweet
smile, her whole figure in its entirety: everything, absolutely everything, left an

indelible impression. At that time Karsavina was not yet a prima ballerina, only a soloist. But her fame in Petersburg was already on the rise and every day it acquired greater and greater proportions. Our acquaintance immediately assumed an intimate and friendly character. I frequented Karsavina's place rather often, with complete informality. She had a charming family life. Her husband, Vasily Mukhin, a sensitive musician and a great and sophisticated lover of ballet, refined and well-bred, always took part courteously in our conversations on choreographic topics. At times a rare guest would come to tea, but most often it was the artist Savely Sorin, now known as the famous painter of Pavlova's portrait, which was purchased by the Luxembourg Museum in Paris, who visited with me. Karsavina received Sorin with particular satisfaction; he was a sweet and ingratiatingly pleasant person with the inborn talent of an elegant draftsman in his methods and themes. Sorin was much milder than I and not inclined to introduce conversations or arguments about principles.

In the earliest days of our acquaintance, when our friendly little group had not yet formed, it was possible to meet at Karsavina's such people as Valery Svetlov, Count Zubov,* and members of the young group called the Assyrian Beards.† I must mention here that at that time among the Petersburg dandies there existed a clique who trimmed their beards in the Assyrian style. Unfortunately, these were the shadiest and sometimes the most despicable characters of Petersburg's ballet world. They had their reserved box in the theater, where the dismissed dancers of ballet's demi-monde came to sit and make an appearance before the audience. These people, along with Svetlov, created and overturned reputations, arbitrarily planting in the newspapers whatever rumor about whomever their hearts desired. It is precisely they—whether at Svetlov's place or that of someone else from the ballet gang—who arranged those teas about which I have already written in these pages. These groups of people are the real plague of ballet, and one can fight them only with fiery means. This nest of poison vermin needs to be annihilated with heroic medicines. The presence of this breed at Karsavina's immediately struck me as unbearable. I did not conceal my opinions from Karsavina and, I recall, from that time on our friendly dealings became more relaxed, without the nasty intrusion of such antipathetic elements.

---

* Count Valentin Platonovich Zubov (1884–1969) was an art historian who studied in German and Italian universities before founding the Zubov Institute of Art History in 1912, located in Saint Isaacs Square in Saint Petersburg.

† Two months after his Karsavina piece, Volynsky wrote a separate article entitled "The Assyrian Beards," whom he identified as "fellow travelers of all kinds of escapades, a chic mix of balletomane-princelings with the kind of repulsive features of poor upbringing that are so characteristic of the majority of representatives of Russian so-called high society, as opposed to its West European counterpart."

And so before me was a real beauty—both in life and onstage. Onstage Karsavina sparkled with beautiful physical forms: a curved arch and a harmonious shape to her legs, which were classical in their very design. Like a storm cloud, dark hair covered her beautiful little head, and from her whole body there emanated an ineffable charm. There were also faults: raised shoulders and a somewhat bewildered, slightly saccharine smile on her sweet face. But such details were lost in the general effect of her acting and dancing.

Now is an appropriate time to emphasize the importance of personal beauty in balletic art. However great the choreographic capabilities of a dancer, if the face and figure are unsuitable for the stage, if there are distinct and serious defects of the arms, legs, or back, the aesthetic effect is destroyed in a fundamental way. What Olga Preobrazhenskaya could have produced if she had been beautiful! Agrippina Vaganova would have profited immeasurably if she had had different arms, if her head had been smaller or her legs longer. She shamelessly ruined *Giselle* but with different physical qualities she could have achieved success. Finally, Mathilda Kshesinskaya. She seized the hall with a kind of magic despotism, but pure ecstasy, in its exact meaning, pure tenderness to the point of tears and hysterics were just not there. However, if Kshesinskaya had possessed real beauty, then it would be difficult to calculate the heights her charm of acting could have reached. Of course, the face need not be flawless. But it has to be suitable for the stage. Or if it is unattractive it must yield to makeup, which often transforms the face's actual form. But returning to Karsavina, one must say that she was totally suited for the stage— from her feet to the last strands of her fragrant and lovely hair. She had no need to color it black in an adagio; it was her hair that inclined her downward with that grave inevitability necessary for the first part of the classical pas de deux.

But physical beauty alone is not necessary for ballet. Moral beauty is also needed, and although it is somewhat naive to pose the question of morality in ballet's current-day setting, this beautiful dream will come to light in the future, if only ballet in general does not perish or drown in the swamp of moral debauchery. I actively imagine in my outlook for the future, if not a pleiad then at least several, and if not several then at least one, true vestal of ballet who would pass her entire life ascetically, in atonement for the sins of the past and for the edification of the future. . . .

To return to the stages of my friendship with Karsavina. In our relations a rift quickly developed. This was when Mikhail Fokine's innovative experiments had not yet been discredited either by the current fashion or by the artistic crash of the theater itself. In those days everyone was attracted to him, especially in ballet circles devoid of serious culture. Karsavina was the main instrument and the herald of Fokine's success with the public, for the closest later bearer of his ideas, Vera Fokina, did not yet stand out from the ranks of the usual mediocrities. Karsavina appeared in *Carnaval, Papillons, Egyptian Nights,* and *Le Pavillon d'Armide,* everywhere arousing the audience's interest in the performance. Sometimes she provided bits of picturesque beauty that one could not forget even though they were barely noticeable among the trivialities of the overall adaptation. I am reminded of Karsavina's final exit from the stage in Schumann's *Papillons.* Everything was delicacy, everything was pathos; the dancer, in departing, sends her beloved friend her farewell greeting with the movement of her head in profile. There was nothing ever like this in terms of beauty and effectiveness of aesthetic impression. In *Le Pavillon d'Armide* several moments also shone, though not with such exceptional brilliance. But in general the performance of Fokine's compositions, with all their banal pretentiousness and dramatic pomposity, could only spoil the career of a classical dancer. My comments on this issue poured out in torrents not only in print but also in conversations with Karsavina, who at first reacted to them with perplexed dismay and later with bitterness and even tears. Karsavina's work on a translation of Jean-Georges Noverre, undertaken under my editorship, continued. I began frequenting her home less often, but when we met at the theater she occasionally threw me a salute. I shall never forget one of those sincerely cordial greetings, which she, returning from Moscow, bent over her box to give me in her black velvet dress. Nothing can sully or obscure my memories of this marvelous artist. At one time a cloud of principled disagreement covered our relationship. But then it disappeared.

. . . And suddenly she performed with unprecedented success in *Le Corsair.* Her playfully comic variation, the Little Corsair, is a masterpiece of style, and her male impersonation caused quite a stir among the audience. She runs around the stage in long emboités back, accompanying the movement with a symmetrical and sprightly throwing about of her arms. This is simply an artistic gem. But all the scenes built on pure classicism seemed faultless and, at times, incomparable. Karsavina's success, which had been wavering during the last years of the Fokine epoch, has now begun to increase from performance to performance. The production of *Giselle* furnished Karsavina with a real triumph, for which she is, at least in part, indebted to her outstanding partner, Petr Vladimirov. This was, if I am not mistaken, Karsavina's final performance at the Maryinsky; then she went abroad and her beautiful image left our stage forever.

—"Tamara Platonovna Karsavina," *Zhizn' iskusstva* (2 September 1924): 7–8.

2

The Book of Exaltations
The ABCs of Classical Dance

Principles of Classical Dance

Choreography

What is choreography? The word consists of two Greek words, one of which means "chorus" (*khor*), and the other of which comes from the word "to write." The Greeks labeled *chorus* any gathering of people who brawled, rejoiced, played, or traded at a bazaar, and even those who converged for some sad occasion or another. In ancient Sparta the bazaar square was called a chorus. The Greeks even said "a chorus of teeth"—and this expression is all the more remarkable since in an open mouth the teeth sparkle and take an active role in the expression of the face. In present times the concept of a chorus is usually connected to a notion of people who gather to sing in a church or on a stage. But by chorus one can also mean a group of musicians in an orchestra. In the figurative sense the word *chorus* is applied to several sections of a building, for example, to the spacious balconies in large halls intended for the multitudinous public. Making a verb out of the noun, the Greeks assigned to the former the same broad meaning the noun contained. In its general sense this verb, as transmitted into Russian, signified the concept "to rejoice." Let us pause at this expression.

In the structure of the Russian verb "to rejoice" (*likovat'*) is the root *lik*. In its ordinary usage *lik* means a face (*litso*), which is liberated from such arbitrary impurities as age, blemishes, or illnesses. *Lik* is the genuine essence of *litso*. If we say "a person's face," we can be asked what face we are speaking about: an old one, a young one, one before an illness or after it, a pretty one or a wan one. But if we say "a person's lik," then we are expressing its perpetual innateness. We can paint the historical portrait of Saint Nikolai, bishop of Myra, at one period or another of his life, and we can paint the iconic image of the man, representing not his face, but his lik. There is a legend that Saint Luke tried to paint Christ in a square, among a group of pupils and disciples. The painter studiously conveyed every little feature of Christ's face, but with no success. He went out into the street several times, changing and correcting his work. And each time the face came out differently. One day Christ came to Luke's apartment and explained the reason for the painter's lack of success. He washed all the dust off his face and when he put a towel to it, on the material there remained an impression of his lik in its essential features. This is how it is in the literary interpretation of the word *lik* as distinct from *litso*. In folk culture these two words constantly blur together. . . . If the folk make no subtle distinctions, they say "lik" and not "litso." According to this folk interpretation, *lik* also means a chorus, a dance circle, and even a collection of people of a specific category. A certain kind of sycophant is numbered among the lik of saints.

Here we need to note the enormously rich content that is consciously or unconsciously placed in the word *lik*. We have not only merriment but also sadness, emotional anxiety, and lofty melancholic thought. One can even say that it is by the fine sensitivity of their soul that the folk draw the boundary between *litso* and *lik*, now mixing them, now separating them from each other in their thoughtful locutions. And this is completely understandable: everything that originates in the depths of the folk spirit requires that we have an acute ear and perhaps even a gift for discernment. Noting this is extremely important for understanding everything that follows. From the noun *lik* we move to the verb "to rejoice" (*likovat'*). All the richness and variety of content contained in the root *lik* flows into this verb. *Likovat'* does not only mean to be merry, as many think. It is more than just a wild shout of joy. Shades of different and deeper feelings—even sadness—come into play here. . . . "No matter how much you rejoice, you can't avoid trouble," the Russian folk say. When the simple folk say, "An upright man rejoices all day," they mean not only sportive merriment, unworthy of a serious man, which is expressed in jumping and dancing but the merriment of another order, which is expressed in the exalted burning of the spirit. . . .

So this is what these three words mean: "chorus" (*khor*), "representation" (*lik*), and "to rejoice" (*likovat'*). They are connected with one another by an internal bond and in essence express a single phenomenon: a broad feeling with nuances of joy and sadness at one and the same time. In this way choreography is nothing more than the notation of such individual and broad feelings in all their variety of degree, tone, and type. Dance by itself, though it partakes of rejoicing, in no way exhausts it. It is only a small part of rejoicing and leaves wide room for other forms of expressing the human lik. However, when we speak nowadays of choreography, we are dealing with something narrower and smaller in scope compared to the generalized concept people invest in it. We mean only dance. Choreography is the science of dance, as any European authority can tell you without dispute. Nevertheless, standing on the ground of ancient and modern Russian philology, we are dealing with an exceedingly broad concept. We are speaking about rejoicing, as in a full-stringed orchestra. Everything sings, everything rings with the noise of the heart, everything manifests its lik every minute and every second, now in a mournful black, now in a bright red little border, now in noble and rich purple, now in bright and sad violet. All the trumpets sound as their voices overflow in a single, common, and inspired rejoicing.

This is the true richness of choreography in its fundamental concept. But in contemporary ballet everything has been shrunken, trimmed, and reduced.

Ballet

Ballet is a part of common choreography, a part of a common exaltation that thrills separate individuals as well as entire groups and crowds. The instrument of this exaltation is dance. Sitting in our seats, what do we see in ballet? Music is playing, people are dancing. From the first moment it seems that this is a form of complete and utter merriment. But after looking closely at the dance and listening carefully to the music, we realize that we are dealing not with merrymaking, or at least not with that alone. On the ballet stage, as on any other, what unfolds in its fantastic setting is an image of life that brings to people dangers, intrigues, violence, pleasure, and displeasure. Death itself sometimes figures in ballets, even entire cemeteries. Yet on the whole everything—sadness as well as joy—is presented not in the ordinary and crude form of everyday life but in a kind of ceremonial dress. It is all enmeshed in a bright haze of exaltation, where sadness has been softened and joy has become more thoughtful.

Yet this is only the outer cover of the presentation of ballet. Its real content is disclosed only in the dances themselves. Can it really be that something serious is taking place onstage? People are moving rather strangely, on the tips of their toes; they are throwing their legs up and back and are shuffling them along the floor; they are rotating, jumping, flying up and down—and all of this is done not in commonly accepted usual ways but in a way that is original to the highest degree. The thoughtless person who did not ponder the essence of what is taking place would call what is being performed to the accompaniment of an orchestra acrobatic gymnastics. But this is far from the case. We have become too accustomed to considering the human word as the only form of expressing thoughts and feelings. The body of the nonspeaking person seems silent to us. It can make involuntary gestures, which sometimes reinforce the meaning of words, but that the body can itself speak and, moreover, speak on lofty themes, is out of the question. This is how it seems at a superficial glance.

But this is completely untrue. In ancient Greece the people already knew that the body could speak. One need only look at the figures of the sepulchral monuments of the so-called stelai to see how expressive the body and its posture can be. The pleats of clothing can represent a full range of sublime feelings. The deceased woman sits in an armchair and with a pensive half-smile looks through her favorite jewels, which her servant holds before her in an open chest. The expression on both of their faces is not without sadness, but this sadness is touching, enlightened, and softened by an inner glow—it is so beautiful, and its beauty was accessible only to ancient art in its heyday. In the National Museum in Athens you pass through an entire gallery of stelai that evoke an inaudible sobbing in your soul. Sometimes it seems that if one could give these stelai living words, everything would immediately disappear.

Similarly the body by itself speaks, sings, and occasionally shouts more fully and sonorously than the human word. In the same museum you will find many figures without heads—they have fallen off over the centuries—and when you compare such headless figures with similar statues that have managed to remain intact, you stop regretting the broken-off heads, for the heads on the statues of the early period of Greek sculpture are usually not very expressive. How vividly these fragments of the torso live, how much they say to us through the waves of pleats in their tunics, which Goethe called the thousandfold echo of the human body. In the Athens museum there is no dead flesh.

And this was so not only in the art but also in the life of the ancient Greeks. The Greek could hear the speech of the human body; he was able to get carried away by it with unfeigned rapture and, of course, was able to appreciate it. He spoke of wise hands, thereby admitting that hands can be stupid, inexpressive, mute, and uncommunicative. The actor of Aeschylus's tragedies, Telestes,* was glorified throughout the ancient world for the play and the gesticulation of his unusually responsive and eloquent body. The body's eloquence is a purely ancient concept that at one point radiated to all of humanity and then died. People began hiding their bodies not in the clothing that provoked Goethe's delight but in some kind of indistinct casing, indeed in spacious boxes, as, for example, women's crinolines of Spanish origin. The body lost its language; it became mute. Moreover, the Christian church, with the extremes of its monastic delusions, placed upon the human body, as it did on everything earthly, the dark shroud of rejection and even contempt. The female body, with its extremely rich supply of expressive means, in particular suffered from this. Throughout the day this marvelous musical instrument fell silent, and at night it opened up only a little and only for a special purpose. And its eternal and unpretentious language disappeared without a trace! Hidden under clothes, condemned to enforced silence, the male and, especially, the female body lost

---

*Telestes was a Greek actor and dancer who was famous for depicting the war scenes—with the help of the chorus—in Euripides' *Seven Against Thebes*.

the art of speaking the delicate, plain, uncorrupted, completely natural language of sadness and joy, and instead gave itself up to crude instincts. Rather than being an instrument of rapture, woman was made the instrument of human nature's basest drives.

In the art of ballet the body rises like the phoenix from the ashes of the dark ages. Suddenly it is summoned to speak again and to rejoice—more accurately, to participate in the general exaltation of life. For a long time, through the efforts of successive schools, it has become necessary to slowly and gradually liberate the hardened, rigid, and stiffened body. We still have to give the legs freedom and ease of movement; ordinarily they are stuck together. The arms are given unrestricted movement in all directions. They must be able to leap up like wings, to fly up and down, to form a circle over the head, and with a tender caress to balance attitudes and poses. Every finger of the hand must be given meaning and dare not be dead. Now the fingers fold together, forming an expressive little ball, now suddenly one of them juts forward like an arrow that flies along with the body. And do not forget the lightning that runs along the back and accompanies the large turns of the body! And the natural play of the head and shoulders. All of this lives, sings, and dances in a common choreographic exaltation.

As I have already said, dances are only a part of the common choreography. Depending upon their nature, ballet dances are divided into three categories: classical, character, and historical (also called ballroom). The principal place in ballet belongs to classical dance. The word *classical* points to the origin of the dance in ancient Greece. One could just as well call classical dance "ancient dance": its essence and structure have been bequeathed to us by the ancient world. These classical dances, which occur on the toes and observe the most varied rules, introduce into ballet's ecstasy a special content. Here simple feelings are deepened and made brighter, as red light is deepened and transformed into purple. If you remove from a feeling all that is fortuitous and fleeting, if you take from it only its pure essence, then it will appear in that form in which we imagine it being depicted in ballet. The same applies to thought, will, and in general all movements of the human soul and heart. That is why ballet's classical dance, which communicates nothing accidental and local, is accepted everywhere; it is understood by all people and has a universal character. There is no Russian, just as there is no French, classical dance. All classical dance is built on one and the same rules.

Matters do not stand this way with character and genre dances. The former are genre dances, or dances of specific nationalities, or dances that are practiced in specific circumstances. Such is the Russian trepak, which is unknown to the French. Such is the Spanish fandango, which the Russians don't know. Finally, we have genre-historical dances. These are the dances of city folk, of various layers of society, that are borrowed by one nation from another and are per-formed at private parties or balls. The quadrille, the lancer, all kinds of old-fashioned gavottes and the by-now extinct minuets of French court times— these are examples of the last category. Many of them contain qualities of classical dance. But these qualities are in part concealed and altered, and in part used for movements that are alien to ancient forms of art. Yet there is much charm and much beauty to be found here—for example, in the tapping of the heels. Their stamping, their playful coordination, their rhythmical beating especially embellish several forms of genre dancing.

Such is the general classification of dances in ballet.

Verticality

In ballet women usually dance on the tips of their toes, and at first blush this posture may seem unnatural and nonsensical. In order to elucidate this issue, which is so essential for ballet, we need to examine the nature and significance of verticality in everyday life. What is a vertical line? It is a straight line, directed upward. Objects either lie on or are spread horizontally along the ground, or they rise above it, cut off from all unnecessary support. People are so constituted that emotionally they form entirely different impressions depend-ing on whether they see something lying down or standing up, horizontal or vertical. In one case things are perceived as tranquil and level, even; in the other the soul is drawn to the elevated. If I see the trunk of a tree floating along a river, somehow I mentally float alongside it, serene and calm. But it is enough for me to look at the same tree trunk soaring from the earth to the sky for my spirit to be seized by an involuntary surge, an involuntary striving upward. A crawling snake produces one impression, a snake that rises up produces quite another. . . . Soaring cathedrals, obelisks, columns, mountains—all of these draw the soul upward. As soon as a person's eyes glide from bottom to top, his emotions and thoughts, which are fixed on the earth and so often weighty and ponderous, follow his gaze and irrepressibly strive skyward. At one point man crawled on all fours and lived in trees the way monkeys now do; he lived then horizontally, without raising his eyes to the stars, and he also thought horizon-tally, crawling along branches or the ground in pursuit of his nearby prey. But in the course of development, stretching out over many thousands of years, man climbed down from the trees, stood firmly on his two feet, and freed up his arms to engage in a conscious struggle with his surroundings. This moment constitutes an enormous bloodless revolution in the history of the human race. Man ceased being horizontal and became vertical. And from that moment only does he begin to be called not a humanlike monkey or a primate, but a man. And he now becomes nature's sovereign, its master. This mastery is explained also by the fact that, as he managed his liberated arms consciously and purposefully, man set about improving his instruments of struggle. He sharpened stones, prepared arrows, drew his bows, threw a boomerang toward a bird that came back to him, used a lever, built a hut, induced beasts into his traps, and so on. With verticality begins the history of human culture and the slow conquest of heaven and earth.

Thus in his day the Italian physician Moscati* considered this question in his lectures on the natural advantages of horizontality in comparison to verticality. Woman would give birth more easily, he claimed, if she had walked on all fours. Moscati's lecture was taken up favorably by the founder of the new critical philosophy Immanuel Kant. Agreeing with Moscati that crawling would be natural, Kant declared standing to be an act of the spirit that had overcome nature and elevated man above it. That is how highly Kant valued verticality and its meaning and advantage in human life. Kant's idea provoked a whole literature in the scholarly and philosophical world, and in the recent past our Russian thinker Fedorov,† who died not so long ago, returned to this issue. Currently it can be considered fully elucidated and beyond any doubt.

Human culture has unquestionably its horizontal and vertical tendencies. The economic life of nations spreads along the ground. Everything social gravitates toward one's native soil. But even here there exist surges toward the vertical that create heroes, creators of more just and more universal ways of life. Science is entirely vertical—it straightens out life's crookedness and points toward the heights. It is especially important to note that the ancient world understood this issue clearly. For the Greeks verticality also signified truth, moral purity, and straightforwardness in words and deeds. The word *straightforward* was seen precisely from this angle of vision. "To hold the head vertically, straight"—was an Aeschylean expression that had the distinct meaning of independence and pride. "He went straight ahead," says Sophocles when depicting the tragic hero's decisiveness about killing himself. Once again, one has a vertically directed feature to which is attached a wider meaning.

The Greeks juxtaposed everything vertical to all that was slanted and crooked, not only in the geometrical sense but also in the wider, largely spiritual sense. To speak straight talk, to look someone straight in the eye—all of this is at once beautifully clear and heroic. A society that is straitlaced is one of virtuous and high morals which stands strongly on its foundations and

---

*Moscati is the name of many prominent Italian physicians, but only Pietro (1739–1824), who was both a political figure and the director of Milan's main hospital, fits the description and dates Volynsky has in mind.

†Nikolai Fedorovich Fedorov (1828–1903) was a utopian thinker whose philosophical and aesthetic views influenced many Russian writers of the early twentieth century.

partakes of political and economic success. Refined classical philology distinguished three categories of words: those that are straight or direct and energetic, those that emanate from the soul and are emotive, and, finally, those that are neutral and express nothing definite. This classification is remarkable and deserves especially intense study. Some words seem to grow out of the soul like delicate and firm saplings which gladden the eye. Here all is straight, optimistic, and open. One feels the charm of the vertical without any deviation or dips to the side. Other words gush forth from man's inner depths. They carry within them qualities of his genuine representation and crackle with sparks. Academic Greek lexicon calls such words passionate. But it would be more just to call them exalted in the above-mentioned sense. The agitated soul reveals its representation; and its words, which are also direct and vertically raised, express man from his internal, not from his external, side. It is astounding to what extent the Greeks sought the foundations of the ecstatic in everything—in life, words, and deeds. The third category of words needs no special interpretation. We sometimes conceal our thoughts, arranging vertical saplings for the mere purpose of embellishing our conversation. . . .

Only in ballet do we have all aspects of verticality in a form of expression that is exact, concretely realized, and graphic to everyone. A dancer will never bend her back, nor will she ever round it in any of her turns. This would distort her entire figure. Everything in ballet is straight, drawn upward, extended outward with a steadiness that provides perfect harmony. We are talking here about classical dance and not the character or genre-historical type that allows various kinds of curvature to achieve its particular goals and to impart its special meaning. But all else in ballet, dances on the floor and in the air, constitutes the direct heritage of that which the great, proud, and pure ancient world bequeathed to us.

The Toes

Human culture and history begin with verticality; in it the human being's essence is presented in the most fundamental way, albeit in a state of potential and protracted repose. In and of itself verticality does not require motion. You stand in place as long as you like, and when you move from a state of immobility so as to be able to walk, you can maintain in greater or smaller degree, by desire or out of habit, a vertical posture and not break it. Some people walk slightly crooked or bent. Others lean back, giving to their step a mildly arrogant or haughty character. There are people whose backs are always in flux, moving in all kinds of directions. Women often walk pleasantly swaying their hips, as, incidentally, Dostoevsky puts it in his description of Grushenka. A person's gait is so varied and individual, it so much reflects personal temperament, character, and mood, that a detailed description of the types and manner of walking is almost impossible. We can say only this: insofar as it maintains a vertical line, walking constitutes an essential part of the human persona. The gait communicates a person's emotional essence to the extent that the line remains true to itself—straight, directed upward, constantly visible through all the detours to the side, like a prevailing motif.

Yet if the vertical position most basically reflects the human essence, then standing on the toes represents man's apotheosis, that is, his highest conceivable and imaginable expression. But one can stand on the toes, unshaken and immobile, only for a second. This is not simply standing placidly and serenely. It is the result of conscious and heroic effort in which you breathe in with your chest and hold onto the emotion in a kind of momentary standstill. Here there is a kind of point, if only imaginary, at which the entire person enters; and even only a slightly awkward or undeniable movement—even of a finger, or an eye that looks askance, or an accidentally or incorrectly turned head—makes the point disappear and will make you sink down powerlessly on your flat foot. This remarkable point—invisible, but all-powerful, through which your line of balance passes from your head to the ground—demands from you unfailing movement and progression in space. It rouses you irrepressibly and indefatigably to this movement and will not let you freeze in lifeless repose. You need to move, exalt, and produce the vertical line with fervor and passion and with an inner striving forward and upward.

Here is revealed a singularly important law of dynamics: where there is exaltation, there is motion. Whenever one sets an important task, whenever one blazes with a lofty goal, there can be no inert freezing in place. Everything that is elevated above the ground, everything that rises up like a trumpet call, is filled with a summons to movement. Such is the alarm to whose sound the crowd rushes, be it the alarm of a revolution or a fire. A little girl runs to her mother with joyful news on her toes; in order to express her delight when meeting her parents, she jumps up lightly on her toes. This movement is also familiar to singers during moments of emotional uplift, when one foot somehow involuntarily juts out and touches the ground only with its toes. Such poses were known in the age of chivalry, when, kneeling before a lady whom he was courting, the knight presented her with a bouquet or a poem. Sensitive toes also react to situations that are sad or solemn. We approach or leave a coffin not stepping on flat feet, but rather concentrating the movement of our legs primarily on the toes. . . .

In Greece the cult of the toes was apparently substantial. We can assume this by the scant though graphic evidence of philology and literature. In the famous hymn to Apollo of Pythia ascribed to Homer, we observe in two places some remarkable words. Surrounded by a chorus of Cretans, playing on a cithara,

Apollo steps forth in a beautiful movement on his toes. This was the way Eustathius,* the commentator on the *Iliad* and the *Odyssey,* understood this movement. . . . There is only one moment of standing on one's toes depicted in Homer without any further embellishment. But to complete his characterization, Apollo is juxtaposed to the chorus of Cretans who follow him not on their toes but leadenly, tearing the earth with their feet. This single moment is sufficient to prove the significance the ancient Greeks ascribed to dancing on the toes. It differed as markedly from dancing on the whole foot as prose differs from poetry, as weekdays differ from holidays, as the face differs from the lik. The Greeks were imbued with such respect for this kind of dance that its appellation began to be applied to the most varied incidents and domains. They spoke about laws, about people, about human reason using expressions from the movement of dance, emphasizing their elevation over common phenomena as if they were standing on their toes. These expressions were widespread in the vernacular, but examples of them are also found in the Greek tragedians. All this points to the fact that the cult of the toe was sublime in the ancient world. And this could not have been otherwise in a society that ascribed exclusive significance to verticality in human exaltation. As we have said, the toes are the apotheosis of verticality.

A culture of dance existed among the ancient Hebrews, in all probability borrowed from the Egyptians. Of this culture only fragmentary characteristics have been preserved in our day. According to these characteristics, as seen in contemporary prayers, which are uttered in a standing position with a slight rising on half-toes to accentuate the especially holy words, we can surmise that at one time this kind of movement was part of an extensive liturgical service. Perhaps this pose was accomplished not on half-toes but on sharply raised toes, whereupon the need arose for the praying person to move further along the ground in the form of one kind of holy dance or another. . . . We know that in the present day the above-mentioned ancient movement is constantly observed in the daily Hebrew prayer service, although in a narrowly abbreviated form. Thus the lateral movements are replaced by rhythmical inclinations of the head, with the eyes turned in the corresponding direction. If the shoulder is turned to the right, then the head is also turned there, in opposition to the general classical canon according to which at right turns the eyes are directed to the left shoulder, which is drawn forward.

---

*Eustathius of Thessalonica was a twelfth-century writer and church figure whose learned commentaries on Homer had an influence on classical scholars for centuries. The Homeric Hymns are a collection of invocations to various deities that date from a variety of times and were written by a number of unknown authors. Some of the pieces were ascribed to Homer in classical times.

In order to rise to the toes one needs to make a barely noticeable little jump. We know from Lucian that the Greeks called such a jump a schematizing movement. Suddenly this movement lost its everyday quality and became poetic. But the jump also presages the further course of this dance, which will immediately have to spread out into space or to uncoil in the air and untwist upward. This is why Homer does not describe the second stage of the movement: it is easily imagined without any verbal explanations.

But one must immediately note something here. Only women dance on their toes; for a man to do so would create a grotesque impression. This is an understandable phenomenon. Woman's movement is predominantly plantlike in essence, possessing all the traits of a flower or a tree that has not been separated from the earth. The turf leans on the ground in various attitudes of inclination. Let a wind blow and raise up some grass, and the grass appears attached to the ground only in one spot. But a bird sitting nearby leaves the ground and flies upward. The same for a woman. Ordinarily she is fixed to the ground. It is natural for her to stand on her toes in order to express the exultant wind, which has risen up to her soul. She can also walk on her toes: the straight heroic line attains here maximal gratification and pictorial expression. On the plane of the stage this movement is filled with great charm, especially if the dancer traces with her legs, like sharp needles, gentle and diverse patterns on the floor. A man, however, will fly up from his place like a bird, in a bold jump, and exhibit his active heroism in the air through a series of figures that are partly inaccessible to a woman. The man has no need of toes—he has wings.

Turnout

The human body constitutes a panoply of faces and essences. Take just the hand. Ordinarily only the back of the hand is visible. More rarely is its palm revealed. What an enormous difference between these parts of the hand for our soul and our perception! The back of the hand expresses essentially very little and is subject only to aesthetic evaluation. In some people it is bony and gnarled, or wide and coarse. In others it is delicate, pale, equipped with long fingers and at times possessed of exceptional classical beauty. It can occasionally attain great spirituality and even try to speak, as, for example, in the case of Filippino Lippi's Madonna, who appears to the hermit Saint Bernard.* What a hand that is—with its long, extended fingers, with the slight hint of its joints and its almost ethereal and gently palpitating back, all of which is enveloped in the music of piety and creates a touching, affecting impression. Somewhat different in appearance, yet still full of life, are the hands of the Mona Lisa. We

*A reference to *The Vision of Saint Bernard,* by Filippino Lippi (1457–1504).

do not see her open palms. But the artist, having insofar as possible softened the osseous frame of the limbs, achieved a pictorial effect that was known to past masters of the Italian Renaissance. Before the viewer's eyes the hands' delicate cushions repose in crossed position, and no special elucidation is necessary: by the hands alone you can divine the artist's thought expressed in this remarkable portrait. But their living reality is made so tender, so feminine, that you really see before you the Neapolitan lady who has captivated the Florentine craftsman. If only we were able to look at the concealed palms of the Mona Lisa! Our guessing would then turn into a genuine reading.

The palm is rarely seen. It engages in gesticulation during those moments when it is summoned to enhance the expressiveness of a word or a thought. The palm is the innermost essence of the hand. When the palm begins to take part in conversation, its entire character changes to one of intimacy, cordiality, and eloquence. The ancient Greeks knew this to the most subtle degree. They forbade their orators to abuse such a device, believing that the use of an open palm rather befits actors, who operate chiefly via emotional moods. An orator, however, being the advocate of the practical interests of everyday life, must convince through the force of logical argumentation. To be sure, when the palm begins to be engaged in our speech, a new strand immediately appears, warm, gentle, and playful. Everything suddenly lights up from within with a heretofore unseen glow. Absolute exaltation begins, and the person's heart beats to its rhythm. The master of the hand, Leonardo da Vinci, understood like no one else in the world this great romantic facility. In *The Last Supper,* where the play of hands displays a veritable fireworks of expression, he represents Christ with extraordinary wisdom. One hand is raised slightly over the table and is visible to the eyes by its palpitating fingers and its bent back. Here Leonardo conveys the momentary confusion which has arisen in Christ's soul. The other hand lies on the table with the palm opened and immediately calls all our attention to it. All the beams of the picture are directed here. All the world's sunlight, all the tenderness of human love—all of this has given its pale, radiant glow to this panoramic gesture. Christ shows us the face and the essence of his hands at one and the same time through the contrast of the various feelings that have reached their highest level. And this portrayal constitutes a wonderful example of the hand's expressive speech. In modern times this device is used by preachers speaking from the pulpit, and also by certain political orators. . . .

When the palm is open to the viewer, we call that position of the hand turned out (en dehors). The phenomenon of turnout extends over all parts of the body and completely envelops human form. What we see in the hand, we see also in the eyes. They seem to be closed all the time, looking inside, watching but not seeing what is taking place around them. But as soon as the striving of the will, what psychologists call apperception, comes into being, the ostensibly closed eyes turn out to be open. Now they look and see. A person walks along the street with open-closed eyes and looks inattentively at a passing girl. Suddenly something about her strikes him and he turns his head and looks at her with a new, all-seeing glance. We usually say that such a person has experienced love at first sight. But this phenomenon is not love at first sight; it is actually love at second glance, when the flickering instinct of the will tears the veil from one's eyes and opens them to the perception of beauty. Beauty demands conscious delight and apperceptive steadiness and eyes that are turned out to light and truth. Only then, when the heart's command is fulfilled, is true exaltation in visual perception possible. The eyes exalt in their own particular way. Suddenly a flickering of a speck of light, a kind of misty gold flood, begins in the pupil, small specks start to dance, and contact is now made not only with the woman's body but with her soul. From the first seconds of the eyes' encounter with the latter, the hysterics of desire vibrate within us, passing through laughter and tears. This is what turned-out eyes are! The Greeks saw in turnout an element of pathos. And truly, from that startling moment when apperception opens the eyes to a new spirituality in life, a turbulence of passion and feeling occurs in the human body. Everything has come to motion and burns with enthusiasm.

The face can also be closed and open, turned in and turned out. It can be simply a face, but it can also be an essence. Often the essence of the face is hidden in the mists of transient moods, formed by a conventional grimace or an official courteousness. At times it is completely immersed in the depths of life's sadness, grief, and quiet despair. But blessed moments occur, and suddenly the face rushes off somewhere and its essence appears. Someone's breathing has seemingly torn away the clouds and opened the floodgates of ecstatic apperception. That is what the turnout of the face means, its ability to be transformed into new animated forms. It is a remarkable thing: we never raise our face to the sky. But the eyes need only turn to heaven apperceptively, and the face reveals its essence. This is especially noticeable in women, who in moments of helplessness invariably turn their faces and fill their eyes and all the surrounding space above and below them with aspects of the most elevated moods. We see many such pictures and portraits in the art of the so-called Accademia in Bologna, when artists loved to depict women and girls sitting in the pose of Saint Cecilia, with their eyes lifted up to the sky. This motif soon wore out, turned banal, and became the property of candy boxes. But there was always a dose of healthy truth in it. If artists abandoned a theme that was no longer appreciated, life nevertheless continued and still continues to provide examples of genuine exaltation, rapture, and delight. A person's face is an eternal arena for the perpetual change of feelings and moods, and, depending on its turnout, its external traits either are closed off with a veil or opened up in radiance.

Exposing the Essence

Classical dance demands that all of the body's essence be exposed. The face, the eyes, the hands, even the back must act, and they must emerge from their concealment and withdrawal into the self. If only the face is visible but not the eyes, then the overall effect of the dance is incomplete. The eyes must at all times be involved in apperception, vigorously and consciously penetrate the world, and remain free from passive, indifferent lassitude. Exposing itself in all directions, the body constantly plays with its own tongues of flame. People who do not understand ballet frequently claim that it possesses little feeling and scant temperament. Of course, this represents a great misunderstanding. For it is precisely in ballet, as in no other art, that it is impossible to make a move without setting into motion the entire mechanism of enthusiasm and rapture. This enthusiasm is not of a lower order, but rather of a higher one; yet only he who himself burns with rapture at this time, he who exalts in the same sensations as he shakes open all the doors, windows, and apertures of his soul, can apprehend this. Here we have a genuine devotion to ballet and not that balletomania that often conceals in itself profanation, lust, and blasphemy.

The exaltation of the entire body includes the exaltation of the legs. Ordinarily, when people speak of turnout, they have in mind only the legs, completely forgetting that in turnout the entire body participates, as we have already explained. Let us look at the legs. The stiff, bony front part of the leg is unattractive and boring. When it is out front and occupies the entire field of vision of the spectator, the picture is extremely prosaic and not terribly winning. The dancer is moving like a Bushman with his knees forward, and this produces a very antipathetic impression. There do exist such anxious and troubled people whose walk resembles this. They fix themselves along rigid, boring lines, not gazing sideways; their feet are drawn together, and they look straight ahead. This is what it means to walk en dedans—without turnout, not open in the classical manner but turned in and drawn inward. As he walks, a cultured person is characterized by turning out his legs in a delicate manner that requires no special discipline. Here the inner side of the leg is open, wide, bright, and sinewy. A playful highlight, which is especially noticeable on the ballet stage, is infused into the gait of even the most ordinary person. What unfolds is not arbitrary, partial, and unconscious turnout but genuine en dehors, which is achieved as a result of long and thorough training at the barre. Without such turnout one cannot take a single step in ballet. There is no movement onstage that can be done without turnout. You extend your leg forward, or back, or sideways, executing what is called a battement. This battement must be turned out, otherwise it will not be classical. Rotating the leg on the floor or in the air, you must show complete turnout, directing to the spectator's view just that animated, wide, and delicately resilient part of the leg. Gently sinking down, the dancer directs her knee as much to the side as possible, revealing the confined planes hidden in the darkness. And everything turns out pure, harmonious, and ecstatically illuminated.

We should point out one important fact. The spine keeps the body balanced with its muscles when moving back and forth. But the steadiness of the movement from side to side is not guaranteed here. In classical dance there is an immense quantity of such movements, and this is why they all are dominated by turnout, with the whole foot resting horizontally along the floor. But the necessity for turnout is more palpable in jumps and leaps, if these jumps and leaps are accompanied by the contact and beats of both legs. In the absence of turnout the legs would not be able to glide smoothly against one another without shoving, stumbling, and kicking. Wherever they occur, in the air or on the floor, turned-out movements carry with them the highest quality of light, inner illumination, and heroic pathos, which are necessary on the classical stage. Go ahead and throw up your knee in the style of Isadora Duncan. In ballet this movement is called a tire-bouchon. A turned-out position in tire-bouchon is not appropriate in Duncan's genre dances or in many character dances, in the dances of Punches, satyrs, or fauns, or in the round dances in the folk manner. Every time a theme from such a dance intrudes into ballet, a choreographic corkscrew begins to be glimpsed in different directions, as if bottles of wine were being constantly popped open. The dance turns into a character dance, cheerfully bubbling with the foam of life and seething with animation. We see these dances in tire-bouchon in *Don Quixote, Raymonda, Pharaoh's Daughter,* and *Le Pavillon d'Armide*—everywhere, whenever it is necessary to break the geometrically regular circle of classical art. A turned-out position in tire-bouchon is one of the most beautiful figures in the apparatus of classical choreography because it enlivens dance by its sharp, densely massive stroke. If the legs are formed in the classical shape, if there is a high instep and the toes are strong, then this kind of tire-bouchon can produce an enormous impression, especially if it can be maintained for a long time at sufficient elevation, as Anna Pavlova was able to do. One leg sparkles white in its full length, while the other flies upward and speaks to the public through its stormy pathos, which is nonetheless controlled from within. Here is a perfect example of genuine classical exaltation which is inaccessible to those who lack the instrument of an active, indomitable will.

Turnout is not the property of choreography alone. It is reflected in almost all areas of the human spirit and activity. We encounter it in verbal and fine art.

A cover is thrown over all of Tiutchev's* poetry—his words sound from beneath this cover quietly, in semi-tones, with hidden depth. Speaking in the language of classical plastique, we could say that this lyric genius had no turnout: he is withdrawn into himself. Nekrasov,† in the vast majority of his works, is all open—he blares, shouts, beats his drum, and is visible and obvious in his entire authorial essence. There is no shutting in of the self, no cover—all the turnout is in your face. Dostoevsky is the same way, despite the profundity of his experimental artistic technique and his individual thoughts. This man's entire soul declaims to the world in a turned-out manner.

If we turn from literature to painting, we easily find the same contrast. A richly shaded cover extends itself over all Rembrandt's creations, and even the yellow in his pictures appears as if through a secret, misty patina. Rubens is entirely different. In his work the human soul is loudly and clearly thrust open, adhering to the will's bright lines. And if you are able to see life from that angle of vision, Rubens will become your favorite painter. His canvasses exalt. His drawing is passionate. Nothing is hidden; he provides you with everything.

We could find countless other examples in different branches of art—in sculpture, in architecture, and especially in music, where Wagner alone with his *Siegfried* is sufficient to display genuine turnout in sound. The principle of turnout prevails where human creation is present. The creative act is by its very nature an act of turnout.

. . .

Croisé and Effacé

In the everyday life of people and nature there is no en dedans and en dehors. Two other concepts correspond to, and replace, these, and they are known by the French words *croisé* and *effacé*. What is croisé? It is the gathering of an organ or a thing into a compact ball before the transition into an unfolded or opened state. If you press all your fingers into a fist, you have croisé. A bird before flying does a croisé. But all of this is produced unconsciously and instinctively, via an inherited mechanism. There is no apperception or any kind of consciously willed effort. And this is what en dedans is in life and in nature—a croisé that is involuntary, unconscious, and reflexive, as opposed to en dedans onstage, which is always the result of conscious, willful effort. Croisé is observed not only in a person's private life but also in his collective one, in the life of the masses, either when they are tense and seem-

---

*Fedor Ivanovich Tiutchev (1803–1873), a leading Russian Romantic lyric poet who wrote under the influence of Schelling and German Romantic idealism.
†Nikolai Alexeevich Nekrasov (1821–1878), editor, publisher, and poet of the "civic" school of Russian poetry.

ingly charged with a sudden surge of social and political energy or when they are releasing their will in turbulent and impetuous movements. One notes a remarkable phenomenon here. This tension has hardly managed to release its liberating motion when it itself becomes the preparatory stage for a new release. And everything proceeds in such a charge-discharge manner, from station to station, from step to step, from conquest to conquest. Here the path is as endless as life itself. The state of croisé is a state of pregnancy in the broadest meaning of the word. Ice is croisé. It melts the water and it is effacé. But this same water now constitutes a kind of croisé for the even more fluid and diffuse steam. The steam in its condensed state is croisé. In a machine it provides effacé with its motion. And in its turn this motion in various forms and dimensions becomes alternately now croisé, now effacé. Such is the goal of natural phenomena. Constantly and everywhere before us pass two poles, two images, two types of action, but both are unconscious.

Let us take the simplest occurrence of effacé in nature. A snail moves out of its shell and crawls, carrying the shell on its back. Unquestionably, having crawled out of its shell, it has unfurled itself and shown itself to the world. In a certain sense it has emerged en dehors. Yet this is not the en dehors that we see on the stage, which is always carried out consciously, but rather another manifestation of it, devoid of apperception and thereby representing a case of instinctive effacé. Such is the movement of the hermit crab or hedgehog, displaying their appendages and quills. All of this is effacé, but not theatrical en dehors in the precise meaning of this word, which is always thought out and willed.

All croisé movements hypnotically affect the spectator and the environment. A cat that has gathered itself into a ball provokes horror in the dog that is attacking her. The sight of a fist or a hand grabbing the handle of a saber causes a disturbing reaction. In the not-too-distant past, the sight of troops whose ranks were closed for battle inspired terror in the enemy. . . . It is hard to contain croisé in specifically fixed boundaries, so irrepressible is its desire to overflow into the widest effacé. The same alternation of these effects, these bursts of impassioned croisé trying to turn into liberating and comforting effacé, takes place in erotic storms. If a calming effacé is not achieved, there is always the danger of brutal conflict and the spilling of blood.

On the classical stage both these fundamental motifs acquire a different coloration and character. Both croisé and effacé are apperceptive—both motifs are designed to reveal the dancer's essence and state. If this state is open, the choreographer will show it in the position of effacé. But if the essence is closed, hidden, confined, completely withdrawn into itself and deeply absorbed in its hiding place, then the choreographer will present it to us in the form of croisé.

If we apply to all of this the theatrical terminology of turnout (en dehors) and turn-in (en dedans), then we can say that on the ballet stage everything is turned out in its material and bodily forms, in its mechanisms, and only those movements directed inward and toward oneself can be without turnout. For example, one makes a rotation, a pirouette en dedans, directed toward the supportive leg and the corresponding shoulder. That is its direction. However, the entire body, including the leg producing the rotation, is turned out and reveals to the public its inner sides. In this way, not confusing related phenomena with each other—croisé with en dedans and effacé with en dehors—we should say that the two theatrical concepts that we have introduced, although secondary, make the theme of classical dance immensely deeper. The natural phenomenon of coiling and uncoiling, tying and untying—obscure and incomplete, deaf and blind, and, in any case, not emanating from the limits of material incarnation—here on the stage acquires an elevated meaning. It is cleansed, made to glisten, and becomes animate as it expresses its lofty essence.

In ballet croisé and effacé meet at every turn. Every position, every pose of the body or its parts, is either one or the other: either a gathering up or an unfolding—picturesque, delicate, and pleasing to the eye. Leaps, beats, all manner of rotations in the air, all kinds of battements tendus—all this is done according to the technique of croisé. One can end a pirouette by holding out one's leg in effacé position, but the finale can be given another form that is concentrated inward. A certain form of this movement is called attitude. In its essence attitude expresses a moment of emotional fluctuation and uneasy stillness. One leg stands motionlessly on the floor and the other is raised behind with a slight bend. And this bend can be done concavely and convexly in croisé and effacé, and then we will have two pictures with different outlines. The head and eyes either will move away from the raised leg or will turn toward it. The torso will also change its position. The entire expression of the body is modified. In one case, in attitude effacée, we have before us a plastic image of a light breeze in the air. There is expectation, tension in the body. But overall this is painless, calm, pleasant, and open. Dancers without fiery temperaments resort to these kinds of attitudes. In another case, the psychological effect of the attitude is painful and anxious. In attitude croisée there are willful points, red-hot with emotion, yet despite the fluctuating and lacerated pattern of the pose, it casts off and radiates in space a stream of ardent poetry. The same must also be said about the other figures related to the attitude—the arabesque, in which two kinds of artists achieve different effects. Pavlova sparkled and burned with her croisés, although dancers with talents equal to hers but less temperamental and with less profound and complex souls were inclined toward simple arabesques in effacé position. Here we are dealing with psychological motives. According to these motives a dividing line is produced separating theatrical croisé from theatrical effacé. Different types of exaltation alternate with, and flow into, one another: open exaltation, joyous and wonderfully delicate, and concealed exaltation, enraptured and deeply passionate.

Elevation

The concept of elevation in the literal and narrow meaning of the word operates only in ballet. But even in ballet this concept is a complex one. Elevation consists of two components: elevation proper and ballon. These two components must be precisely distinguished, although together they constitute a single, common phenomenon. In the true sense of the word, elevation is flight up: the dancer takes off from the ground and jumps high in the air. We then say he has elevation. But this is not entirely correct because such a jump can be totally empty, that is, acrobatic or gymnastic, lacking any purposeful idea. Any clown can jump or leap over a dozen people lined up in a row, but no one would call that elevation in the sense that the term is used in classical art. That is only a mechanical trick, made possible by well-trained muscles and a lithe body. We often observe this very thing in a gymnasium or in youthful games, especially in the South, for instance in Italy. From a high platform young people jump headlong into the water, occasionally using a salto mortale. In war and in hunting one also must jump across ditches and pits. But in all these instances we are not dealing with elevation.

In order for there to be elevation it is necessary to add the element of ballon to the jump. By *ballon* we mean a person's ability to retain in the air poses and positions he naturally assumes on the ground. It is as if the person were standing still in the air. He not only turns around in the air, he vibrates with his entire body as if he were still on the ground. He reproduces static movements on the floor while simultaneously having parted from it. He crosses his feet, he spreads his hands in picturesque shapes, he fastens his gaze afar, while feeling with his feet that spot in space on which he must land. In an ordinary dance on the stage the performer through plié perpetually bends and unbends the spring of his body, which gives to his dances a vibrant, liquid, supple gentleness. And he must retain these features even when he has already left the ground. This is what we call ballon: the whole structure and life of ballet, and all its outlines and patterns, continue above the ground with fixed periods of immobility. The ground is re-created in the air. And as heavenly bodies even when engaged in motion display a visible form of stasis, so a dancer in the air, for all his animation, must have several fixed points—what we call stateliness and monu-mentality. Only in this way does he attain the right to be called a ballet dancer. Suddenly he flies up and then freezes: one second of complete immobility, but how much drawn-out inhalation there is in that second, how many resonant notes for his inner ear! Suddenly he stretches himself across an invisible carpet in the air, as Anna Pavlova used to do, and lies like a swimmer on currents of water. These are the wonders of ballon in balletic art.

Birds and beasts also jump and fly. But in the air their bodies and extremities assume a position that is unnatural to them on the ground. Birds draw in their claws, beasts crook them; only man stays the same both above and below. In this regard he is really like a plant, which also retains its external appearance in the air when torn from the soil by the wind. Humans always need something to stand on, and if this support disappears on the ground, then its fiction or illusion appears in the air. In reality there is no support whatsoever, but nonetheless it is as if it existed. With his earthly poses and supple movements, the person who remains motionless in the air for a second reminds us of a plant. This is why a woman's elevation captivates us the most. On the ground the woman is in general primarily a flower. All her gestures, movements, and postures are plantlike. When repeated in the air they create the impression of something genuinely human because humans always retain their loyalty to their earthly form. A woman is gentler in the air as well. She glows there like a tender and resplendent rainbow. Men jump somewhat differently. To the extent that they retain their ballon they also display plantlike charm. Yet this is not only a plant, but some sort of a mixture, a beast joined with a plant. This animal element finds its basic expression in the origination of the man's jump: the woman soars more passively, surging as if against her will as she obeys the forces that carry her off. But besides the animal element in the man's jump there glimmers a spiritual element. The animal within that tears him from the earth seemingly transports him to a completely different realm—the realm of intellectual and utopian fantasies. He takes off from the ground with thunder and lightning. His flight is always catastrophic, terrifying, audacious, and daring. He is full of heroic pathos and his face appears in an instantaneous process of transfiguration. Transfiguration always requires height; one always needs to ascend to a Mount Tabor* in order to shine. One cannot be transfigured while drinking tea; it is easier to be so over a glass of wine if it raises a person to the lofty heights that already exist within him. If a dancer is not transfigured in flight this is a bad sign for his elevation. It means that spiritually he has ascended nowhere, that he doesn't exalt when in the air, and that his dance lacks artistic fire, for classical ballet is pure exaltation and the pure air of heights is the natural arena for human enlightenment.

Flight requires that height be felt by willful experience. What does this mean? Strictly speaking, the expression "willful experience" is a conditional and metaphorical expression that is rarely grasped in all its power and un-

---

*Mount Tabor, in Lower Galilee, is traditionally identified as the site of the transfiguration of Jesus.

charted depths. A person thinks he feels through all his senses except his will. Light he sees with his eyes. The vibration of airwaves, what we call sound, he hears with his ears. Smell he perceives by means of his olfactory apparatus. But what can a person grasp in his soul by means of his will? In a person's soul everything is in constant flux, nothing stays in place, everything rises and falls in an interweaving of various currents. Everything is in the process of coming into being. The will also moves, quivers, and quakes, agitated from within through mysterious motives of possession and self-assertion. Palpitating and shuddering, it gives off passionate waves that are perceived by our conscious-ness as sensations of the will. One of those sensations is the sensation of flight, the sensation of height that resides in people in an incomprehensible way. Man is born with Taborian cliffs within, with cupolas, steeples, and all kinds of heights, and from childhood his will crawls and clambers higher and higher unless its natural growth is prematurely interrupted by a bad education or tragic fate. And that is the basic source of elevation without which great artists cannot exist. Even if one has everything—if all the physical conditions are in place and one's muscles are in terrific shape—if the will does not feel Tabor, genuine elevation will not occur. Then it would be better to jump over chairs and people in a circus, astounding the crowd with your dexterity but not shaking their souls.

At first glance, a woman's elevation is weaker than a man's, although in its form it is more plastic. But in dances on the floor not one man can compare with a woman. On the floor she has the appearance of elevation that never forsakes her. Devoid of the adroitness of a crawling snake, she charges upward like a lily, she stretches herself into pirouettes, she firmly holds her back straight in all postures, and she flies with her arms. All the time it is as if she were carrying out elevation on the floor.

The Nature of Classical Dance

Three kinds of elements exist in classical dance: the plantlike (vegetal), the animal-human, and the spiritual. Let us examine each element in turn. The plantlike element is the plastic element in dance. We can justifiably substitute one of these words for the other, although with different shades of meaning. When we want to stress the naturalness of a movement, its basic principle, we say that it has a plantlike character. If, however, we have in mind certain secondary features that derive from the plantlike, we say that the movement is plastic. The qualification of a movement is thereby raised, but the line of origin remains the same. A person is conceived, takes shape, grows, stands erect, then bends to the ground—and dies. This is precisely the life of a plant. The Russian word for plant (*rastenie*) underscores the moment of growth (*rost*). A person has risen, grown, and become a sapling. In French and German the word emphasizes the movement of sowing and planting. But what is sown and planted is destined to grow.

Therefore the basis of a person's naturalness is the plantlike quality of his nature. This quality is expressed in various degrees, qualitatively and quantitatively, in different individuals. For the most part a woman is plantlike. In the common meaning of the word, the plantlike constitutes her essence. If she bends down she is plantlike, if she lifts herself up she is a plant, if she holds out her hands or throws them up together, again she is a flower that sways in the breeze, and if she half-turns her head, yet again she represents something from the fragrant botanical world. Such are the movements of the shoulders, body, waist, and legs as well. Everywhere we have the bending and winding from the kingdom of Flora.* When a woman walks, her legs caress the earth, enveloping it in their unique charm. Her whole body flutters and sways with an arboreal and deciduous luxuriousness, as if a young tree strewn with flowers had moved from its place. A woman's waist produces an especially plastic expression, and from here originates the endless fussing of different nations, tastes, and fashions over it. It is well-built, delicate, responsive, lithe, obedient. Everyone plucks a flower by the stem, and we all draw a girl to us not at her chest but at her waist: here instinct and aesthetics correct each other and fuse together. A kind of invisible aquatic element flows through a woman's body, and when you come close to her you feel the fresh spray of this everlasting cascade. When you find yourself among women, especially at balls, you literally begin to swim in the living, collective fluid of life that surrounds you. Somewhere invisible fountains are making noise: rivers, streams, and brooks are flowing. This is why people the world over are so drawn to ballet. From the ballet stage, where plantlike bodies undergo their most delicate shaping, cleansing, and polishing, the innate element of feminine enchantment floats into the hall in unrestrainable waves.

One must recognize the fine distinction between a young girl and a woman. Each expresses her plantlike quality differently. A girl is one who is not torn by internal conflict. In her the bud is whole and closed. A storm rages and fulminates within her. But on the surface there is ice—the coolness of inviolability which is as yet unshattered and undamaged by the tempestuousness of spring. A girl's tread is easily distinguishable from a woman's. A magical little flower drifts by. A woman, however, floats like a swan. A girl will turn and leap and jump in her own way. Everywhere the plant is free and primordial, unfrazzled by the wind and unplucked by the birds. She exists in a still unbroken crystal bell jar. A woman, on the other hand, is a luxuriant rose, planted in a

---

*An ancient Italian goddess associated with fertility and flowers.

pot. The rose is fresh, fragrant, and ample, but an experienced eye will notice on some of its petals traces of numerous bruises and localized withering. It is a remarkable thing: in a ballet pas de deux of a woman and her partner—the most lyrical part of choreographic representation—one can never, if one knows how to look at the stage, confuse a girl with a woman. A girl extends and draws back her leg in the air differently. She extends and lifts this leg for the first time—and each time is the first time—not in a routine way, not as if she was exhausted by dancing or past her prime, but pristinely and with maidenly spontaneity. What attitudes and arabesques! What distinguishes the bud from the rose is the purity of expectation, the purity of striving somewhere unknown. It is impossible to confuse a woman with a girl in terms of psychology or plastique, and the discriminating ancients had their own Artemises and Pallases along with their Heras and Junos. The major city of Greece was protected by the Acropolis, on which, among the numerous other temples, predominated the Parthenon, the temple of the Virgin Athena; and behind* this majestic temple stood a gigantic statue of Athena herself, but in military armor, on guard with spear in hand. The entire history of Hellas is found in the image of the warlike Virgin atop the Acropolis.

Being plantlike means being attached to the ground. Not for a minute do roots leave the earth. And as soon as movements occur that signal a change in place on the floor, we enter the second realm of plastique—the realm of the animal-human. Jumps and leaps, rotations in the air, running across the stage—the whole technique of glissades and movements en tournant—all of this belongs to the realm of classical dance. The plantlike quality never disappears for a moment, but a secondary quality—that of animal dynamics, animal urgency and initiative—is introduced. And the entire aspect of the dance changes, even in a woman, as soon as she rushes upstage and downstage, abandoning the captivating body movements of the plantlike pas de deux. In this plantlike pas de deux resides the entire likeness of woman, the flowerlike and fragrant quality of the Madonna. But as soon as the Madonna breaks loose from her place and flies away somewhere, she needs the fire of animal-human pathos.

We learn from the first part of the pas de deux how much plantlike beauty resides in the woman. In the remaining parts, in the variations and the final coda, we come face to face with her artistic gift. Here she blazes and burns, carried off in various directions, clamoring and bursting forth in the fire that embraces her. If the dancer performs with the corps de ballet, a majestic picture unfolds before us: the forest and grass are enveloped in tongues of flame which,

*The enormous gold-and-ivory statue of Athena carved by Phidias in the fifth century B.C. actually stood inside the Parthenon.

before soaring up to the sky, creep along the ground and tree trunks, higher and higher, in arrested but authentic and indomitable movements.

We need to say something about the spiritual element in classical dance. No movement can be specifically called spiritual. The spirit operates from within: it penetrates movement but is also expressed by it. Apperception is the instrument of the spirit. Nothing can ever be done in classical dance without apperception, and with it dance achieves its particular eminence and becomes spiritual in all its aspects. The plantlike and animal-human elements are as if reforged in this fire. And here again we encounter the enormous difference between man and woman on the stage, as in everyday life. The spiritual coloration of woman's dancing is undulating, diffuse, unsteady, passive, compassionate, and minor in key—whereas in a man, it is primarily active and in a major key. In men's dancing the plantlike allows itself to be felt very weakly, in remote hints, but the spiritual element on the other hand is expressed with great boldness and is totally self-conscious. If a woman's essence is fundamentally plantlike, then a man's essence is fundamentally Apollonian and spiritual. That is why we have two types of exaltation, which constantly alternate with each other in classical dance: feminine and masculine—rustling, winding, and iridescent, Bacchic and languid with languishing eyes on one hand, and energetic and willful, militantly aggressive and combative on the other. These are the two poles of balletic art at their highest levels.

The Arms

In classical ballet not only the legs dance, but all other parts of the body do as well, especially the arms. In ballet the technique of dancing arms is called the carriage of the arms (port de bras). Generally the law of opposition reigns here, whereby, for example, if the left leg and left part of the body are brought into motion, then the right arm, not the left, accompanies this movement. This principle of opposition as a general norm can be explained primarily by the conditions of mechanical equilibrium as well as the aesthetic demands of the movement's symmetry. Generally speaking, the arms are freer than other parts of the body, and in the mechanics of the dance they represent several individual elements that function according to their own autonomous laws. The look of the legs is smoothed over by tights: nothing original or personal is required here—a beautiful leg is one that is shaped according to the classical canon. The arms, however, are bare, and although they follow several general principles, they are able nevertheless to reveal the dancer's personality.

Choreographers have decided on a specific number of positions for dancing arms. The arms can be at complete rest: they are then lowered along the torso, dangling lightly with the palms facing each other and the fingers slightly bent.

This is the basic position of the arms in the classical port de bras. Thereupon the arms begin to dance. They are raised above the waist slightly rounded at the elbow in semi-circles, the fingers turned toward one another eight or nine inches apart. This is the first movement of the arms as they emerge from a tranquil state. From this point on the rule is that every position assumed by the arms must first describe this motion. This rule is observed everywhere—in dances on the ground as well as those in the air. The arms always float following a specific order, constantly moving through their initial position while waving upward in circular and gentle lines. A pattern is created which substantially increases the gracefulness of the dance.

From the first motion of the movement comes the second: the arms are extended in opposite directions, with the hands curved inward. This placement of the arms, in which the entire hand is spread, occurs in ballet only in specific places. In general the hands are coaxial and the fingers are gathered as if they were playing the violin. From the second position the hands proceed to the third: one hand remains in its former place and the other flies up in a semi-circle over the head. This is the port de bras for attitude: here there is a symmetry with the leg that is bent in the air, which provides the entire figure with perfection and integrity. Then there is a remarkable position of the arms, with hands in a crown, which seemingly adorns the head. In this position the arms are raised over the head in semicircles, with the hands held facing each other about five inches apart. This is one of the most beautiful moments of the port de bras, in which the idea of the flower finds its fullest expression. This movement often gleams in classical dance, giving it a soft and rounded character.

There are other positions of the arms for the arabesque, for the preparation for a pirouette, for various other figures, and all these positions are as regulated as those just described. In the arabesque both arms are either extended along an uprightly inclined line, the lower arm along the ballerina's skirt or energetically thrown forward in the concealed breathing of the willful impulse. Choreography lists seven of these positions. But as I said above, it is possible to have free movement that conforms to the demands of the moment. This free movement particularly applies to male dancing, which expresses spirit and energy emancipated from their vegetal source.

The port de bras is intended primarily for women, for the psychology of a botanical creature who is also magical: a sapling that has wings but cannot lift them. Let the arms be spread out along the sides in the above-described second position. If one does a plié at this point, the hands begin to breathe and turn with their backs upward, gently and attractively assuming the pose. It is as if the hands express an anticipated future movement—at one moment preparing for an embrace, at another lowered in plié in order to support and lift the body. The same with an arabesque, with an attitude, and with a pirouette: the arm expresses the character of a movement and alludes to it. The arm breathes in harmony with the dance, it breathes on it, and together with it creates that incomparable rhythm of coordinated movement that gives the dance the aspect of a musical and plastic symphony. The arms are now open, now closed; now closing in croisé, now opening and unfolding into the most beautiful effacé. And the plantlike essence of woman is especially perceptible: the arms contain the accompaniment to the exaltation—appearing round, shaking, waving, stretching lengthwise, rising and floating. In its visible and invisible quivering everything here is resolutely feminine. How carefully one must deliberate over even the smallest reform in this area! Any unconsidered movement can destroy the vegetal charm of the dance, which constitutes the main resource of choreographic aesthetics.

The movements of the shoulders and head conform to the arms. The head follows the shoulder, but the shoulder itself moves forward or recedes back following the leg. If the right leg recedes back into effacé, then the right shoulder moves forward in the same natural impulse. The head turns in the same direction. This is what is called in ballet épaulement: the play of the shoulders. Everything depends on the dancing legs and their various positions, which involve the play of the head. Mechanics and psychology are mixed here. In a beautiful effacé front, the eyes are averted to the side as if bashfully avoiding something. But when the body is revealed in effacé back, the eyes follow in the same direction with an excited gaze. Everything that is harmonious and perfect here corresponds to the secret whims of the soul on the straight and crooked paths of its constant exaltations. The eyes are in a sustained state of consciousness, pouring their observant and excited surveillance into a stream of perpetual motion. They are never silent. They either warm themselves in sun-filled smiles or grow dull in confusion, or, like little needles, pierce the spaces before them.

Finally the head. In its movements one needs to distinguish an inclination from a turn. Turning to the side on an axis is called controposto, in Leonardo da Vinci's terminology. This is a turn in the precise and narrow sense. The inclination of the head—straight and to the side—is a purely feminine trait that could be spotted at any time in classical dance. But one must turn the head as well, decisively and willfully, and in this regard women are far weaker than men. A man's turning is not natural to a woman, just as the graciously feminine inclination of the head is not natural to a man. We see this graphically on the ballet stage. Controposto movements, movements en tournant, are beautiful in male dancing, but they look slack among the vegetal figures in women's dancing. In his *Last Supper*, Leonardo gave only two figures an inclined position of the head—John the Evangelist and Philip—having drawn them with classically delicate features. All the remaining figures of the apostles turn their heads—

expressively, abruptly, and with a great surge of emotion which is ready to overflow willfully and passionately. But having imparted a controposto turn to the head of the Mantuan duchess Isabella d'Este, Leonardo departed consciously and paradoxically from everyday reality. Women do not commonly perform such turns in which the neck muscles are so strained. As later criticism has noted, the misuse of the controposto turns introduces into Leonardo's brilliant art a rhetorical, affected element. Here we have a kind of experimentation that has led the artist to exaggerations which are unacceptable in any harmonious art. But in ballet, although much is conventional and almost everything is stylized in the direction of abstract likeness, movement nonetheless never crosses the border of the organically natural. In contraposto movements men are magnificent but women use merely light, ornamental hues.

Music

Music is a realm of genuine human exaltation. That which is most profoundly sacred and vital in us, and which cannot be uttered by any word, triumphs in music. If we ask music to copy nature—the singing of birds, the sound of the wind, the din of battle, even the noise of a train—we are demanding that it forgo its essential aesthetic mission. But it does not follow that all music must be complex and difficult to apprehend. To begin with, we divide music into two categories. One kind expresses the simple rapture of the body, the other the general rapture of the entire person; in fact the rapture of the body is suppressed and the rapture of the soul and spirit comes to the fore. Let us turn to the simplest examples: soldiers marching in the street to the accompaniment of music in which the drum plays the major role. The soldiers walk in measured step, and everyone around, falling into the flow of this music, submits to a larger or smaller degree to the rhythm of the drum. In particular, children, who still lack the quality of conscious perception which would control and delay their responses, follow the soldiers to the accompaniment of the music and imitate the measure and beat of their movement. This is the perfect example of the most elementary danceable music, operating through the cerebellum onto the motor nerves attached to the muscles. These sensations set the whole body into motion, and the rhythm of this music, so essential in its overall feeling, must also be called elementary. It is entirely possible that the most ancient archaic dithyrambs, the so-called line-by-line dithyrambs, were performed by the masses to the accompaniment of similar marching music of this simplified kind. The very rhythm of this music is described by the ancient philologists as "wildly passionate" and "ardently purifying."

Such music, which is, so to speak, danceable, can be complicated and enriched in its rhythmic, melodic, and harmonic design, and if it is, we have various types of danceable music that are more or less captivating. This music is complicated by sensations of a higher order that, as they continue to bear upon the body, draw into its hypnotic sphere no longer just the separate, simple components of the motor mechanism but entire systems of muscular and neural combinations, thereby creating the possibility for quite elaborate dances. Into this kind of aural-flexional music fall extraneous waves of music of another kind, which should be called symphonic. When such waves predominate and the flexional sensations all but disappear, the dance becomes difficult, even impossible. We now have a special kind of music, which we call sonically spiritual, aurally cognitive, audio-visual, and, in general, symphonic as opposed to danceable. There is no way and no need to dance to Beethoven's Ninth or Tchaikovsky's Sixth, or to one of Scriabin's ecstatic compositions. The entire soul is shaken to its frightful depths here, far from any muscular channels or systems, so that the whole body can be likened to a vibrating box in which the soul rejoices. The entire outer person at this moment represents just such a musical box with various symphonic motifs hidden inside it.

At the present time we see constant borrowings transported from one kind of music to another. Either balletic, danceable themes erupt in symphonic music, or large symphonic strains are carried into ballet music. Sometimes a dance takes on a special life: a Chopin waltz is elevated into a gem of the concert hall, becoming almost impossible and indeed unnecessary to dance to. On the other hand, the waltzes of Johann Strauss and Lanner,* for all the variety of their themes, are eminently danceable and, indeed, attractive and infectious to the highest degree. The true goal of a ballet composer should be to create the kind of music in which the aural-flexional and sonic-spiritual impulses are combined, thereby providing the richest scale of choreographic experiences. The heterogeneous sounds must be combined in this way so that in the complex design of the interwoven motifs the delicate and transparent shell will allow us to sense the bubbling of the danceable impulse. This impulse never disappears; rather it is permeated and ennobled by symphonic matter. Symphonic music by itself has no living contact with ballet: it is undanceable and insufficiently stimulating for the motor flexors. And for its part, ballet music that lacks symphonic color is one-sided and basically banal and circuslike.

We already have at present superb specimens of such fusions in the marvelous ballets of Tchaikovsky, Glazunov, Adolphe Adam, and others. In *Swan Lake* the dance theme is not suppressed, although the music itself permits genuine—how to put it—biological tasks. The swan has a plantlike plasticity

*The Austrian composer Joseph Lanner (1801–1843) is regarded by some as the inventor of the waltz.

and bursts forth to unattainable heights in which the human spirit resides—such is the theme of this remarkably choreographic work. And dancing it—oh, and how one dances it—is still possible and irresistibly attractive. I can take the most difficult themes of this ballet, and they all beg to be danced solely because through the shell of symphonic sound the contours of the highest order of refined motor possibilities appear, reaching almost the maximal boundary which separates the two types of music from each other. Such also is Tchaikovsky's *Nutcracker.* Everything exists in the haze of elevated thoughts and moods. But the chimes of the dance never stop beating their pulsating rhythm in its hidden depths, and the scene is naturally filled with an endless number of classical figures.

In Glazunov's works we also have flashes of brilliance, and *Raymonda* must be counted among the outstanding works of balletic literature. But the symphonic shell here is nevertheless heavy and massive, similar to thick, luxuriant velvet, which at times muffles the propelling tick of the dance clock. One can dance well to this music but not easily. The dance here is beautiful, sometimes dramatically profound, but still it lacks complete inner illumination, even when an artist like Olga Preobrazhenskaya performs it. Of *Giselle* I shall not speak at length. Here the utmost beauty and purity of fusion is achieved, and despite its old-fashioned technique the dance theme is saturated through and through with the juices of symphonic poetry.

After ballets like *Giselle, Raymonda,* and *Swan Lake,* it is particularly painful to consider the balletic compositions of Léo Delibes, Cesare Pugni, Leon Minkus, and others. One feels their shallowness and obvious poverty, and one sees the future of ballet music in clear perspective. The future musical composer of ballet must grasp the nature, technique, and meaning of classical dance in all its breadth and depth. He must be able to dissolve into sounds the classical figures of dance—all of their plantlike, animal and human, and consciously perceived spiritual motifs. That is when music will be simultaneously symphonic and danceable. An adagio will unfold to the sound of the ringing of bells, respiring together and at one with the most profound themes on stage, just as these themes issue forth in their sonic environment. The future Pushkin will see before him not ballets with simplified music but authentic creations of a choreographic symphony.

Features and Forms

The foundation of classical dancing is the exercises. These exercises, which are performed in a large classroom, at the barre and in the center, are more than simply instructional. Ballet dancers constantly return to these exercises over the course of their career, deriving from them gratifying and systematic support for their work. Some artists are far more talented in the exercise hall than onstage. But the opposite also occurs. Despite imperfect exercise, many artists open up beautifully in all kinds of ways on the ballet stage. The exercise is performed to the accompaniment of music and consists of a specific series of basic forms and movements that make up balletic action.

For his part, the ballet master who is searching for new creative formations would derive enormous benefit from visiting the exercise class and picking up some features and plans for future creations.

The entire stock of balletic art is contained and developed here, and the talented choreographer will treat it as a primary source for his work.

Positions

The exercise begins with positions on the floor. There are five classical positions. The first position is: feet placed on one line, knees stretched and turned out, heels touching and toes apart. The position is attained by putting the feet in their ordinary position, toes to the front, and turning them out to both sides. This process of turning by means of rotating the foot on its axis is called fouetté in ballet and contraposto in Leonardo da Vinci, as I already noted. One should begin the class routine with this and thereby immediately acquaint children with the two concepts of turnout and fouetté. In the second position the feet are placed on one line, separated by a distance of one foot, again completely turned out, with the toes turned in opposite directions. After introducing the names of different steps, the instructor can now gradually signal this position of the feet with the term *échappé:* from being bound together the feet change to another position and come loose from each other. This position contains an element of freedom in it, which the French term expresses. . . .

The third position is done by placing the feet with toes turned in different directions so that the heel of one foot adjoins the middle of the other. In ballet this figure is transient and almost unusable because of its unsuitability and ineffectiveness for creating other figures. Nonetheless such an elementary position is possible and therefore it is included in the classical exercise. The fourth position makes the following outline: one foot is placed in front of the other in such a way that its heel is on the same line as the toes of the back foot. The distance between the feet must again be equal to the distance of one foot. This is one of the most popular positions in classical dance, and the instructor here can gradually and slowly explain to his pupils several additional concepts. He will emphasize that in classical dance the feet, despite the fact that they are uncoupled, spread, thrown out, and beaten against the floor, must never exceed a certain spatial dimension. The length of the foot constitutes such a gauge. Signs of a new concept in ballet that emerge in third position—what the French call croisé, the concept of rolling up, gathering together like a ball— appear in fourth with particular precision. Ekaterina Geltser's immortal phrase must ring out: "In the beginning everything is croisé." Finally, the fifth position: the feet are firmly joined together, heel against the toe. This is absolute croisé, more finished and complete than the croisé of the third or fourth position, in complete contrast to the absolute effacé of the first two positions.

These are all the positions in their established sequence. There are only five of them—the five embryos of all future movements—and every figure of dance is always reduced to one of them. For all one's desire to think up a sixth one, it is impossible to do so because each position, being purged in its design of all that is arbitrary, is related to one or another of the five positions described above. . . . From the five positions of classical dance the entire diversity of figures and schemes of balletic dance pours forth in a huge flood. We have already seen that in these positions are contained several fundamental laws of choreography, such as turnout, croisé, and effacé, for the latter is merely the result of the liberation from the state of a ball being rolled up and enclosed in itself. This state is organically tied to croisé as its antithesis, the reverse side of the same coin, like an act of dispensation from a clenched and constrained state. Within such boundaries the exercise of the five positions in their established and traditional sequence proceeds.

Speaking methodologically and following the general universal principle whereby freedom is not born but acquired by efforts of the will, we could have redesigned the order in which we study the positions, starting from the end. Here you are, children: your feet are in a real ball, in the fullest and purest croisé. Now the foot moves toward the middle of the other foot—and this is a new position. Then the foot moves forward at a distance of one foot from the back one. This is also a new position. We already have three positions, locked into the uttermost croisé. Finally, the two last positions. The feet join at the heels, and the toes turn out in opposite directions. In this scheme of classroom instruction the exercise would begin with the original fifth position, it would change successively to the third, fourth, and first position, and would end with the original second position. This routine in the class work would be more logical than the former one, but it may be that technically it would be more difficult.

Such are the fundamental positions with which work in the classroom commences. They are the same for men and women, but in the man they appear colder and more cumbersome, which is explained by the bulky features of his entire body, including his feet, with their low instep. Only the fourth position appears whole and gallant in the male dancer, especially at the end of a pirouette. It was just this gallantry, and even bravura, that Christian Johansson openly demanded from the artist, keenly understanding that the features of male dancing are first and foremost spiritual, willful, and passionate. Indeed in this position there is something for the man that is supremely demonstrative, showy, and flattering. As for the fifth position, it is rarely encountered in men. Only tours in the air, which represent no more than an alteration of the legs en tournant, conclude with a fully turned-out bringing together of both feet on the floor. Men's legs are less turned out than women's; they do not have that softness and flexibility characteristic of women's legs, and thus, with the exception I have already indicated, men's positions produce a less favorable impression in the artistic sense. Everything is dry, sharp, and elementary. Women's positions, however, already contain within themselves the rudiments of future music; they are filled with inexplicable nuances and are soft and smooth. Here arises the plantlike essence of the woman in its natural beauty and correctness. All five positions are therefore designed for a plastic impression. If the dancer completes an assemblé not in fifth position, which the design requires, but in deviation from it, she loses something of her plantlike charm, whereas the man can commit such faults without any particular damage. From its initial flight, everything in a woman's dancing is geared to creating and adorning her plant-like essence and to providing the corresponding choreographic exaltation.

Plié

The female's plantlike essence possesses one feature which by nature is its very own. A woman is constantly disposed toward different forms of bending and unbending of the body. Now she inclines her head, smiling in someone's direction, now she throws it back in delicate languor. Now she oscillates her soft neck with a swan's gracefulness, now she flashes her eyes with a pulsating light, as if they were inclining toward, but not quite penetrating you. A woman's torso, like a flower's stalk, is constantly bending and unbending. Her waist is dutifully sensitive to all winds. And all the other parts of her body participate in these tender, plantlike demonstrations. Woman is everywhere a plant—pliant, soft, trembling with excitement, and unable to be torn away from the ground.

These features are especially pronounced in classical dance. After the classroom positions the dancer does a plié in all these basic positions of the body. This plié constitutes the plantlike life of the woman's body. It is a smooth curtsey, a bending of the knees in a special rhythm. The straightening of the legs from this plié position is called relevé in French. The old choreographers said that all classical dances are built on plié and relevé. It is impossible to maintain plié in the proper posture for a long time, and one must immediately straighten up into vertical position so that the impression the plié creates remains purely classical. Sustainedly bent knees give a comic quality to the dance. In such sustained plié we imagine dances of satyrs and fauns, of the whole noisy entourage of Dionysus. But plié constitutes the most necessary ingredient of classical choreography. If a male or female dancer lacks plié, his or her performance is dry, coarse, and devoid of plasticity. Plié is particularly beautiful in a woman. A man has none of that curvedness of the body, that turnout of the legs, because the ligaments in his groin are stronger and tauter. Therefore male plié is not especially pliant, producing more of an impression of a spring in motion than of a passive, obedient flower at the moment of inclination. But precisely like a spring, the male plié is filled with reserves of enormous energy that is felt in elevation, in ballon. Male ballon is not only more powerful and noticeable, it is also more sustained than female ballon. Plié softens male dancing on the floor, but it gives it a confident soaring, with wings spread out in the air. A woman's entire body, down to the ankles and feet, is soft because of her pliant muscles. Therefore plié spreads like oil over all her joints. Plié is not a moving springboard to perform jumps, or a spring to achieve elevation and ballon, but something completely self-sufficient—valuable for its own sake and an end in itself. It is woman's eternally pulsating inner dynamic, her life on the earth and in those rare instants when she is in the air.

Plié positions break down into two categories: demi-plié, where the heels do not leave the floor, and grand plié, where the heels leave the floor and the feet are on demi-pointe. And here we should note that only in second position—in demi-plié and in grand plié—do the heels remain on the floor, in resolute contact with it. This detail must be understood. In the new grouping of positions I described above, the second position is the concluding one. Rising higher and higher at different grades of support on the ground, we finally reach that position where the maximum support is given. When teaching beginning dancers the techniques of plié, it would be natural and methodologically sound to finish the exercises with the kind of position which, by its very nature, can endure the entire weight of the body without the leg involuntarily trembling. For this it is extremely important to teach the children when they are doing grand or demi-pliés to bend the knees on a plane with the toes, on a parallel line with them, that is, while faithfully observing turnout. The plié can be slow with a slow straightening up. But when curtseying slowly, it is possible to straighten the legs quickly. It is also possible to go down quickly and straighten the legs slowly. These are the different variants of classical plié.

As I have already noted, male ballon depends on the elastic strength of the man's plié. This explains the significance of plié for elevation. Ballon is the dancer's life in the air. But this life is stipulated precisely on plié. Therefore, speaking in the technical language of ballet, one can say that ballon is the repetition in the air of ordinary plié. The dancer must live and be able to remain in the air during long moments. There are good dancers who lack plié and ballon. But the genuine beauty of dance, in an artistic sense, is inseparably tied to the technique and spirit of plié. Dance performance constantly occurs through plié and relevé, through bends and vertical flights, through plantlike realism and spiritually uplifting states, through the alternation of two elements in which the entire aesthetics of ballet unfolds. . . .

Plié is done before every jump. Without the moving mechanism of the spring, the leap would be extremely difficult, lacking in force, and sometimes simply impossible. This spring, as we know, acts similarly in the male and female body, although it varies in strength. The male dancer flies up as if from the inner spring of his own ball, and this ball continues to palpitate in the air. But when the jump is completed, another, concluding plié, is needed, other-wise the finale of the jump is not soft and moist but dry and sharp. The dancer returns to the plantlike aspect from which he has emerged for the heroic jump. Everything returns to the earth and, entering its bowels, becomes a part of its unlimited and diverse flora. For a woman, this is particularly easy and norma-tive; for a man this is less characteristic but nevertheless attainable within the limits I have indicated. But on the ground exaltation begins for both once again in the forms peculiar to each: the woman sinks entirely in the element of her swings and curves and bends, in her coquettish smiles and lowered eyes, but the man projects his spirit and character in his thrusts upward as he converts the moist, liquid, and undulating plié into a solid rock.

. . .

Battements

In its general sense the word *battement* means the extension of the leg and its return to its former position. One can extend the leg from fifth position to fourth front and return it to the same fifth, from fifth position to second and return back, and from fifth to fourth back and once again return to former position. One can do a battement from first position to second and at the conclusion move the legs as before. All of these are battements. Ordinarily, when the battement is done in slow tempo, the heel is placed firmly and solidly on the floor as the foot returns to its place. If a rapid battement is produced, then such contact with the floor need not occur. However, battement from first position requires contact with the floor whatever the tempo. Thus contact with the floor in battements par terre is included in the principle of returning the leg to its former position, and deviating from this principle is tolerable only as an intentional cut.

We divide battements into three categories: battement on the floor (battement par terre), medium battement (the so-called battement soutenu), and finally grand battement, which is done by thrusting the legs up high. The thrusting of the leg thus increases in tempo and height. Each of these categories has its own aspects. Ordinarily the exercise in the classroom, during the transition from plié to more advanced work, begins with battement tendu. Battement tendu is a typical battement à terre, which in Russian can be called extended battement. It is ordinarily done in different directions, but each time, when the leg is placed out one must properly extend the foot to the tips of the toes. By this means of execution one maximally reinforces the toes and gradually shapes the instep, which is not so obvious in its natural state. High instep is crucial for classical dance: it gives the woefully flat foot a lively and graceful shape; it creates a beautifully plastic arch, and even if the arch is too high it makes the foot seem smaller. This is why the instep is so highly valued in ballet. In good dancers the instep is not rigid. It is playful, elastic; it lives its own beautiful life, and it furnishes almost every position and movement of the leg with charm. At the same time, the shape of each individual instep is unique. The best instep is not too high but rather average or a little higher than average. In this kind of instep the toes can be fully extended without any sense of disharmony, like the instep itself.

The second battement that is practiced in class is usually the battement frappé, which is jerky, sharp, and throbbing. Indeed, one could call this a throbbing battement. The leg, slightly elevated above the floor, is thrown forcefully and energetically to the side. Though the working leg seems extended straight out, during this movement its instantaneous, slight, and barely noticeable bend flashes before us. Without this bend the leg would be dead. While I do not propose establishing a fixed order of alternation in classroom battements, I do think that after battement frappé one could do battement fondu—which is the one that floats and melts. With its weight all the time on the ground, the supporting leg does a smooth plié in harmony with the other one, and the latter is thrown out in a pliable design. This is a marvelous battement: the plantlike motif resounds quite distinctly in it. This is an essentially female battement, and in it the dancer learns to tie movements together through the strands of soft and gentle figures.

The battement soutenu is a medium battement, raised slightly above the floor. Without touching the floor the leg that is lifted joins the supporting leg in front or in back, leaving a certain distance between the hips. If the hip joint were not in a state of intense stillness, the working leg would be doing contraposto, rotating on its axis and making incomplete motions en tournant. This is why the working leg is extended sharply and in a straight line, like a taut string, and the figure as a whole acquires a picturesque and penetrating character. If one does this battement in a deep plié, with a rotation of the leg and the body, the resulting impression is exquisite and enormous. The result of great craftsmanship, the straightness and sharpness of the dancer's leg convey the charm of authentic, living plastique, especially in their diverse rotating movements.

The small, so-called petit battement is one kind of medium battement. The heel, also not touching the floor, is borne along, touching the ankle in short, rapid movements from front to back and in the opposite direction. Small battements teach the future dancer the technique of beats, which play such a large role in classical dance. This is the vibration of quick sounds, the fluttering and rustling of modulating leaves on the branches of a tree on a mild windy day.

Now to the basic, rich, and full battement développé. This is essentially the battement that to a larger or smaller degree permeates all aspects of battement I have thus far described. During this battement the leg is drawn from one position and placed in another smoothly, slowly, circularly, breathing deeply, movement by movement. The bending and unbending of the leg occurs in an undulating design. A series of wavelike movements flow into one another and one by one dissolve into these measured transitions. This is a typical example of the body genuinely blossoming, as we used to observe in the dancing of Vera Trefilova. For all her genius, Pavlova's développé was not distinguished by its complete impeccability. It was low, insufficiently turned out, and more impetuous than smooth. Furthermore, it did not merge with the sound waves in the orchestra or create their equivalent in movement. In any case, Pavlova's body did not open or unfold in harmony with the music. Even with the classical dancing of her arms, her développé was out of sync. This is especially remarkable in the artistry of such an exceptionally talented dancer. The plantlike forms of beauty receded somewhat from their natural position and gave too much space to the passionate and emotional human-animal motifs.

By nature développé is a purely female battement. Men do not have the beautiful instep, the pliant knees, the finished step that women do, and therefore this battement in them lacks its characteristic shape. A man can thrust his leg forward or sideways with precipitous force. His frappé is brilliant. His shift from one position to another is sharp and decisive. But moving the leg from a stationary position and taking it through all the modulations of the movement upward and along a straight line is not in the partner's power. This is why the adagio, which is built exclusively on the multiple forms of développé, constitutes the focal point of female dance art, with the male merely playing the role of supporting partner. And just like développé, battement tendu and, for the same reason, battement fondu, are inexpressive in men: no curved arch, no female pliancy of the toes, no high instep.

. . .

It remains for me to say that battement développé à la seconde represents a special charm when performed at the beginning of a grand and complex pas de deux. In the second scene of *Swan Lake* such a battement is done high in the air with the support of the partner. If he were to lower the dancer in the direction opposite the leg, and the battement were to be extended somewhat above the waist, we would have something that fully meets the goals of the pas de deux. The adagio represents the most melodious part of the ballet's action. Here the dancing is at its most musical, and the pattern of the undulating battement concludes, along with it, in the highest and tenderest tremolo. The final movement of the développé and the last chord of the orchestra fuse here into a single exultant sound. Thus this entire adagio in *Swan Lake* is fully and completely accessible only to those artists who possess outstanding musical sensibility and whose rhythmic dancing constantly reincarnates in itself the sounds of the orchestra. We have such a remarkable développé in the second act of *Giselle* and in several other ballets. It is always the central part of the pas de deux and a demonstration of its pleasant-sounding melody in the form of the movements of the leg, the torso, and the whole body.

Battement développé, hints of which we see literally everywhere, lives like an eternal blade of grass in the realm of plastic Flora and constitutes a complete opposite to battement dégagé. The leg is drawn to the side, forward, or back, on pointe or not, and insofar as possible, without any sign of slow extension, without any kind of undulation, and with no bending whatsoever. . . . Développé is a gradual unfolding, but dégagé is just the separating. The legs appear to be tied together—and then we free them from this state, quickly and decisively. We have here a moment of emancipation or resolution, whereas in développé a very different movement is at hand—one of slow and steady development. In développé we sense the quiet flow of the plantlike process, which is completely absent in the volcanic and willful act of dégagé. And this is why, if in women's dancing the soft, undulating battement, which constitutes the predominant motif of all her evolutions onstage, plays such a distinguished role, then in men's dancing the bold dégagé is so typical and characteristic, serving as a springboard of his heroic dancing in its entirety. Here, in what appears to be an insignificant trifle, are reflected two cultures of classical art, similar in their fundamental principles but widely divergent in their rendering by the male and female: the culture of the plantlike movement versus that of the animal-spiritual, aggressively forceful and masculinely willful. All the requirements of turnout, croisé, and effacé, which have been described in detail above, apply naturally to the technique of dégagé, as they do to all the other battements we have considered.

One extremely important battement needs to be considered, the battement battu, that is, the battement that beats. Ordinarily, battement is accented in the movement forward, and the return of the working leg to its former place occurs without hitting the supporting leg. But this touching actually occurs in the battement frappé. The leg hits the ankle and precisely in this movement its characteristic accent is found. The battement that beats is the one in which the supporting leg is struck. All types of cabrioles, all kinds of beats, all ornamented leaps—forward or en tournant—contain an element of battement battu. This is for the most part the springboard of heroic dancing. If one does a pirouette with numerous fouettés, we have nothing more than a plastic testing of rotary steadiness on the ground. The axis of rotation should in no way be shaken, but the fouetté threatens its equilibrium. That is the challenge of this kind of dancing in the second act of *Swan Lake*. But we shall return to this topic later. Just like the battement that beats, batteries of various kinds constitute the challenge for classical ballon, diverting certain energy from it and, with that, demanding that it be firm and inviolably focused. And this is why battement battu is so magnificent in male dancing, yet pales in the woman's performance. There is no better way to praise a dancer than to say that she has male beats, that is, that her battement battu is expressive, quick, and as forceful in its execution as a man's.

Rond de Jambe

This is a rotation of the legs on the ground and in the air. How is the rond de jambe en l'air, also called rond de jambe développé, done? Let us take the rotation of the leg slightly raised above the ground: in this aspect its pattern appears more rigid and characteristic. In general rond de jambe teaches you to describe arcs and circles next to the body, all the while developing its fluidity and pliancy. At first the leg leaves the floor and rises at approximately 45 degrees, half a right angle. After this the leg is stretched in a straight line or with a slight oscillation to one side. This is only a prelude to, a preparation for, the rond de jambe. At this point the development of the knee's rotation begins, the hip, like the hip joint, remaining immobile. The hip joint remains uninvolved in the movement; its motion is always rotary and thus it constitutes a certain kind of fouetté, of which the rond de jambe never partakes. As a whole the movement looks like this: the leg is thrown back into effacé, bends at the knee, and is drawn to the other leg in deep plié en l'air. After this the leg is thrown forward, taking up its initial position. This is rond de jambs en dehors. In this movement the following features are outlined: two open, free effacés, at the beginning and at the end; two battements to the second position en l'air; one circular movement with leg bent, which is resolved by a small undulating movement à la seconde. The basic character of these movements is plantlike. This is a flower twisted and untwisted by a light wind. The preparation for rond de jambe as such is not a typical part of the whole movement. But the bringing in of the fully bent leg allows for our impression of the entire figure, lending it a vividly plastic coloration. It is done softly and flowingly. Finally, the last movement. It should not be done with an abrupt thrust, loudly and with excessive flourish. The feminine plantlike figure must have a plantlike finale: this is more a firm caress than an aggressive shove.

Let us imagine the rond de jambe in a man's execution. Its final movement has a shading characteristic of male dancing. It must be done with gusto and energy, with spontaneous brilliance and piercing frappé. In its masculine interpretation, rond de jambe contains no particular charm. Cecchetti did it in his day, as did Johansson, and Nikolai Legat performed it with great stamina. Nonetheless, even in them this exercise was not distinguished by anything special because male dancing is not by nature passively plantlike and gently curving. Rond de jambe requires extended toes, arched instep, gentle movement at the knees in constant medium height and, finally, distinct turnout. The advantage of a female dancer is especially noticeable when the circular motion soutenu is done, as the whole body rotates on the floor en tournant. But one can do a deep rond de jambe in the same tempo, also on the ground, without rotating the body and keeping the pelvic muscles motionless—and again the entire beauty of this figure appears with unusual boldness in the woman's, not the man's, execution.

This is a veritable bouquet of basic bodily movements, the culture of which predetermines the dancer's future aptitude. Because from the beginning rond de jambe develops in the organism the perception of gentle tempos, it introduces the finest psycho-motor possibilities to the body. Thus, among classroom exercises, rond de jambe precedes the usually complex and difficult battements—fondu and développé. After plié at the barre, a simple battement on the floor is done, battement tendu. Immediately after this, the instructor proceeds to the rotation of the leg in which we find elements of the circular, undulating battement and the battement frappé. Consequently, rond de jambe is the building bridge for studying all the ways one extends the leg and all the types of turned-out soutenu, which will be mastered in the next stages of instruction. In adagio rond de jambe is magnificent. Thus, in the pas d'action in act 2 of *Swan Lake* the woman with a large semi-circular movement envelops and embraces her partner's back, and this is done without relevé on pointe, immediately after the pirouette. For a man this flourish would be simply impossible and even grotesque in appearance. In other figures we also encounter rond de jambe with warm and intimate features. In the large succession of brisés, among the mischievously playful beats against the calf front and back (dessous-dessus) that are performed particularly by the [male] partner, we have a touching allusion to an incomplete half rond de jambe. Everywhere the rond de jambe, whether it is the springboard of movement or serves as its adornment, preserves its feminine character. This is the nuanced quality of plantlike exaltation in which the idea of the circle is always implicitly or explicitly present.

I have considered only one type of rond de jambe—the rotation of the leg in the air. Let us establish its general classification. First and foremost, the rotation of the leg can be produced on the ground, which is how the study of this figure begins in class. Such rotation of the leg is called rond de jambe dégagé—a disengaged rond de jambe. It is straight, linear, and stiff. Rond de jambe can be done in deep plié, with the pelvic muscles tense and the utilization of temps de cuisse, in which case we have before us a wonderful rond de jambe, an absolutely plastic, absolutely soft, absolutely plantlike feminine rond de jambe soutenu. A man ordinarily does not do this kind of rond de jambe. The one that I described in detail at the beginning is called rond de jambe en l'air. But it would be more correct to call it rond de jambe développé. This rond de jambe, like the battement développé included in its design, serves the same principle and choreographic aim and, since it is identical to it in spirit, it must bear the same terminological classification. The body either opens or unfolds itself in slow evolutions. The opening is dégagé, the unfolding is développé. In this rond de jambe everything radiates, everything is revealed completely the way it is in ordinary développé. Finally, there is a fourth kind of rond de jambe—the grand rond de jambe—which also begins with an unfolding battement in fourth position en l'air.

These are all the forms of rond de jambe. In executing this figure the female spirit is separated from the male by a clear and distinct divide.

The Exercise's Finale

. . .

Alas, the exercise at the barre has its finale. The instructor teaches the fledgling artist to stretch sideways while holding the barre in one direction or another. The body receives yet another touch in the development of its plantlike essence: the pliancy of the back, the sensitivity of the nerves in the waist, the life of the stiffened torso increase; the leg is extended and prepares for future sharply linear soutenus. Then the instructor allows the legs to be placed on the barre so that the step can be developed naturally with the strictest care and observation in order to avoid the slightest injury. One may also allow the young artist to take her foot in her hand and describe a high arc with her leg with the same goal of developing broad circular movements. When the leg is raised high enough, the instructor may permit the hand to be removed for several seconds: the leg thus gets used to remaining comfortably balanced in the air. But the exercise still does not end here. At the barre, the dancer learns to raise herself to pointe and demi-pointe and also learns jumps, leaps, and beats. He separates himself from the ground while holding onto the barre and then returns to his previous position with the inevitable plié and relevé. This movement is repeated many times and accustoms him to elevation and ballon. Afterward the technique of rising to demi-pointes and pointe—always measured in its tempos—is developed, as is the technique of slowly descending onto the full foot. It is at this moment that the first bricks of the foundation for the future spiritual evolution of the dancer's body are laid. . . .

In the Center

. . . We begin the study of this second part of the class work in the center with the detailed analysis of the artistic and reflex movements called coupé. Coupé is the springboard and the stimulus—at times hidden, at others obvious—of all the figures of the dance. This is one of the main nerve centers of choreography. Then there gradually appear before us all kinds of glissades, gliding movements along the stage, and garland-tied forms and movements. Adagio is the third part of the class exercise in the center. This is the crux of the entire balletic construction in all senses of the word. Here we will analyze all forms of beaten battements, attitudes, and arabesques, all types and ways of pirouettes. Finally, the fourth part of work in the center is the allegro. Here we have all the jumps and leaps, all the forms of beaten battements, all the diverse beats—in general the entire apparatus of heroic dancing in the air, in which the male essence and male exaltation shine and boldly manifest themselves for the first time onstage. But classroom instruction also ends here: everything we have analyzed contains all the plans, patterns, contours, and forms of the classical art of dance. Rising gradually from the first shoots of elemental Flora, and passing further and further through its luxuriant realm to animal and human existence, we finally approach the spirit of the human body and its universal transformation. We shall see graphically the features of choreographic exaltation that in their immaculate purity pass naturally into the exaltation of the cosmos. This cosmic exaltation cannot be anything but spiritual. We must never forget what we explained in the first and general part of this work: ballet, the choreographic art of the dance, constitutes only a part of the universal manifestation of sadness and joy.

Coupé

What is choreographic coupé, the shifting and repositioning of the leg while changing the body's center of gravity in the direction of the movement that is being produced? One leg displaces the other from its position and assumes the support of the entire torso, simultaneously provoking the reflex movement of the second leg. Imagine the simplest coupé in place. The legs stand apart in fourth position, one forward, the other back. The back leg quickly rises from the floor and with a decisive stroke strikes the other leg, pushing it from its position. This is the first movement of coupé in its simplest form. The movement of the other leg, which can take various forms, is the answer to this first movement. The leg can be raised and brought to the leg that has done the coupe; it can extend forward, back, sideways in a gathered-up or opened-wide form, in croisé or in effacé. This coupé is usually anticipated by a full or demi-plié.

In this form coupé constitutes the movement of both legs—each cooperating with, and mutually influencing, the other as the dance proceeds. One leg acutely perceives the fading impulse of the first. In this way there is established an intimate solidarity of the legs, which are connected with each other in the execution of the common task. The perfect coordination of the movements serves here as an index of the sound composure of the body whose organic quality is maintained. We see a deviation from such harmonic coordination in paralytics, in whom one leg acts almost independent of the other. One leg drags powerlessly behind the other along the ground, completely violating spatial and temporal rhythm.

. . .

Let us examine the element of coupé in various classical figures, returning to their individual analysis later on. We must inevitably rush ahead in order to establish and explain the origin of that displacement, which is common to all other figures and binds them together in a chain of reflexive correspondences. What is that popular movement on the floor we call pas de bourrée? The

French school is uncertain about the etymological origin of this word. It is used as the name of a primitive two-beat dance from Auverne that has completely disappeared in our day. In its figurative use the word often serves as a hunting term. But when we look carefully at the technical design of the figure we note in it the following traits: the right leg is thrust to the side in strong, decisive dégagé. It does a coupé toward the left leg which, in its turn, is reflexively thrust to the side. For a moment both legs seem separated. This momentary interval is relieved by the gentle movement of the leg which has just done coupé. It concludes the previous swift surge with a refined velvety caress, truly reminiscent of the hunter's chase. This is a moment when the intense movement is resolved in a tender musical chord. Thus the pas de bourrée is nothing more than a displacement enriched by a glissade failli.

One cannot do a single jump or leap without a preparatory beating movement, which is also called coupé. This preliminary movement lends to all the movements of elevation a deeply turbulent, active character and works on the ear and the eye like a thrilling signal to choreographic exaltation. How does one do a high jump if the legs are placed in fourth position? Let us say the right foot is in the front and the toes firmly rested on the floor. The foot is raised slightly and energetically strikes the floor as far in front as possible. This is the first pushing act of coupé, which produces the distinct impression of a preparation for a flight—similar for both men and women. After this follows the second part of the coupé: left foot, standing in back, is thrown forward, turned in or out, into croisé or effacé, performing a jump in its entirety. The designation of the movement will depend on where the foot stops on the floor: a grand jeté forward or assemblé. For assemblé the legs must be crossed in fifth position on the floor. This is what a jump is in classical dance—a pushing coupé in combination with the reflected movement of flight, performed with large or small amplitude and completed in one manner or another. . . .

One of the most remarkable forms of classical coupé is the circular jump from low plié, ordinarily performed in certain complicated variations or codas. In the male interpretation this movement takes on the swagger, boldness, and challenge of a daring deed. In a momentary upsurge the back foot strikes the ground turning swiftly. The body immediately soars upward with extended leg in croisé or in effacé. With all of its features this movement in its entirety resembles a ball that is rolled and unrolled in the spirit of the playful Apollo. Of course it becomes classical only when the dancer maintains an exact proportionality between his efforts and their effect; otherwise the movement becomes grotesque and enters the realm of character dance with its emphatic lack of balance, its comic effects, its underestimated balance of power and resources, its subjugation to the chaotic cult of Dionysus. In classical dancing one should only employ an effort that brings about the desired effect. No more and no less.

Just as the female caryatids on the side of the portico of the Erectheum* carry a weight on their heads that is proportional to the exertions of their bodies, so here, too, the performers must not exert any stress that fails to respond to calculated goals or results. . . .

Let us take another illustration as an example. Pure classical style is extremely rare. It has various orders. But within the contours of a single order, for instance the Doric, it recognizes not only simple, weighty, and cumbersome Paestum† situated among swamp grasses and daisies, but also the severe, more aerial Parthenon on the rocky Acropolis. The magnificent Corinthian capitol plays a role both in classical Greek and in later Roman architecture, in the architecture of the Renaissance and in the imperial baroque. For the completeness of our aesthetic perception we must distinguish all the different elements of ancient beauty and at the same time be able to combine them, as they are combined on the Acropolis, where in the Propylaea, Doric and Ionic columns alternate with each another in definite succession. Everywhere in the creations of the ancient world we observe pure forms of balanced movement in which effort and its effects harmonize with each other.

What are the Acropolis and the Parthenon, which stands upon it? The crag of the Acropolis was lifted to the sky by a volcanic upsurge of the earth. It flew up and froze. Man built on it palaces, fortresses, and temples. To this basic surge of nature—the first act of natural coupé—man's creative surge responds: the second act of the same coupé, for an unbreakable bond and organic unity exist between man and nature. Nature gives the impulse, and man responds, and everything here is proportionate and harmonious. One does not build a magnificent temple on a small hill or construct a puny building on a high one. There is no harmony, no classical coordination between the two acts of coupé.

In exactly the same way we observe in classical dance figures that, like Corinthian capitols, appear time and again in a mosaic of different styles, all of which in their basic features are the creation of a pure form of choreographic genius. The so-called pas de basque can serve as such a specimen. Without overly anticipating the future, let us consider in general terms the graphic construction of this figure. First a half-circular coupé is done. Immediately afterward, with a reflective-reflexive movement at a distance, the other leg comes forward with a gentle, plantlike gliding movement called failli. This is a pure pas de basque. These are the two distinct acts of coupé, percussive and

---

*The Erectheum is located on the north side of the Acropolis and served as a temple to the guardians of Athens, Athena, Poseidon, and the legendary king of Athens, Erectheus. The caryatids are the statues of maidens that held up the roof of the temple.

†An ancient coastal city of Lucania, in southern Italy, which was occupied by the Greeks and the Romans and destroyed by the Saracens. Its extant ruins include three Greek temples and a Roman amphitheater.

reflective, with an unwieldy beginning and delicate conclusion. As a motif the pas de basque reappears in other dances, character as well as genre-historical, and the figure can be enriched by various grace notes. What, for example, is the gargounillade, an ancient figure of dance, nowadays rarely practiced on the ballet stage? This is a double pas de basque, decorated by the rotation first of one, then of the other leg. The tapping coupé of the initial act fortifies the impression of the grotesque on stage.

All the coupés we have considered are like springboards for the sweeps and amplitude of the movement that follows. But besides these purely masculine, impulsive displacements and replacements there are also the softly feminine and decorative varieties of coupé. There are coupés which do not serve as a link of one movement with the other, but rather create the final pose of the dance. . . .

A similar soft quality distinguishes the coupé cabriole as well. One leg hits the other with a flicking of the mid-calf muscles. The push upward forms the first act of the displacement in the air. After this the second act of the figure in coupé follows: the reflex of the leg forward in a soft movement. This tempo is especially beautiful when performed by the female dancer with adequate ballon. While she performs her push upward, one might perceive the movement with a certain pain and discomfort: the spectator is not sure that it is becoming for a woman to do it. But its barely felt gentle continuation, the coupé's second act—in sustained ballon—is full of real charm. The impression of complete lightness is achieved here even without elevation.

In general coupé combines with almost all the figures of classical dance. An adagio can begin with a determined, swiftly tapping displacement. Then the second act of the displacement appears as an intertwining of feminine battements, with the energy and force of an unfolding that is preordained by the dynamic of the initial beat. And here again the coupé in its totality represents a marvelous combination of female and male dancing in one harmoniously artistic chord. The figure we call ballonné appears to be the same thing. It also arises out of the initial, originating coupé, appearing essentially, in the second part, as the coupé's feminine reflection in the air. First the springboardlike beat forward, then the slow and fluid curving of the leg high in the air, with all the charm and beauty of the plantlike plié—this is the cadence of ballet's classical strophe.

Regarding pas ballonné, I should make some additional comments to explain exactly where the coupé fits in the diversity of execution. One can do ballonné by first striking the floor in springboardlike fashion, which is accompanied by the reflected movement of the other leg. These two acts make up a complete coupé. Ballonné relates only to the return movement of the leg in soft light plié upon the execution of the external reflex. This is one form of ballonné

with a distinctly delineated coupé. Now let us examine another form of ballonné. You stand in one place without performing the tapping springboard
initiating movement. But then you must do plié with the supporting leg, and
this plié already constitutes the first part of coupé. This also gives rise to the
reflex movement of the other leg, so that the general outline of the executed
figure remains essentially the same, only softer, smoother, and more harmonious. The very word *ballonné* reveals its kinship with the marvelous concept
of ballon. Indeed, as we have said, ballon is no more than a light reflection,
even a representation, of plié on the ground. The second act of the cadence
requires from the performer a constant and gently wavelike flow of that fragrant oil that permeates every decent plié. Indeed, if ballon is done without this
vegetal oil, we wind up with one of the most vulgar forms of can-can, which is
intolerable in classical ballet. . . .

Let us proceed to some instructive examples that lead us to the very laboratory of dance. What is ballotté—that playfully sportive, urbanely garrulous,
and aimlessly coquettish flippantly graceful movement that begins one of the
world's greatest ballets, *Giselle?* First do an extended battement in second
position. From battement transfer the leg to maximally bent position, called
tire-bouchon. The leg hangs in the air as if it were gathered into a ball.
Immediately after this lower the leg onto the floor and simultaneously rise en
pointe. This is the first act of the classical displacement. Following directly
after this, the second act breaks down into several stages. The leg from behind
reflexively rises into retiré position and from there it continues to be extended
in wavelike battement upward to the second position, so that later the movement of the first leg can be repeated. This is how this magnificent figure is
constructed, reminding us of a balanced see-saw. The element of coupé per se is
quite uncomplicated: one leg strikes the floor and the other responds in développé. Everything else is merely decoration, broken down into a multitude of
movements. This is a charming amusement, playfully sportive and roman-
tically amiable, like a childish prelude to love. The entire figure attracts you
with its feminine hue.

Let us follow coupé in another of its remarkable couplings, in the complex
figure of dance that we call saut de basque, again slightly anticipating what I
shall later develop in greater detail. This is an aerial jump en tournant. Where
is its coupé? The dancer stands in fifth position, right foot front. This foot,
slightly elevated, lightly hits the floor in a tombé movement that makes up the
displacement's first act. Immediately the left leg, gliding through first position,
responds with a reflexive sweep high in the air, in a strictly extended pattern.
The entire body takes on a circular motion near the transferred axis of rotation,
while the right leg presses against the knee of the left one or somewhat higher.
The figure ends by falling on the left foot while maintaining the necessary

balance. Embellishing this movement with a supplementary figure depends on an experienced dancer. She can do a new coupé with great virtuosity, lowering the leg from the knee back and gently extending her other leg along the floor or in the air in a barely perceived, softly wavelike battement. In its overall theoretical structure, the entire step could be called masculine. But its embellishment, which the female dancer introduces through her stylish execution, provides all the peculiarity of female charm. To feel the divide between the masculine and feminine principle in such complex combinations means to grasp the mysterious foundation of dancing, which the human eye has hardly penetrated in our current state of plastic perception.

. . .

What is emboité—straight, circular, and performed backward? First of all, from a philological point of view it is the placing of one foot in step with the other. Soldiers march with legs and feet moving straight ahead. In classical ballet the chain of uninterrupted coupés, with alternating leaps up, provides approximately such a picture. Performed by a woman, this figure attains the character of a skillfully coquettish playing. Ordinarily emboité is done right leg in croisé and forward. But one can also do it backward, alternatively throwing the legs out in a gymnastically Italian grotesque design, in a stormy and impetuous rhythm, in each act stamping in coupé with one leg or the other. Tamara Karsavina did such a marvelous emboité in *Le Corsaire,* dancing the semi-genre number in the second act. She threw her legs back, moving all over the stage with the gentle fervor of a young boy, doing coupé simultaneously with her arms in the same tempo of sportive playfulness. But usually the movement I am describing is produced forward in croisé. In the majority of cases it is the final part of a coda that is danced diagonally onstage after a large variation in several parts in the tempo of a polka which changes to a waltz and then flows into a swift gallop. And you can construct this gallop on such a furious croisé by abruptly throwing out your legs into a running step.

Coupé can be of the beating, masculine type and the plantlike, female type, connective and concluding, straight and telepathic, that is, projected at a distance. Sometimes it is produced by the direct contact of the legs, but at other times without such contact, as if suggested in space. These two categories embrace all its varieties, the preparatory springboard as well as the decorative final kinds, which conclude the dancing with gentle poses on the floor. One can construct an entire variation on simple coupé forward, sideways, and back. The marching of soldiers constitutes the sheer accumulation of the masculine kind of automatic coupés. A quick street gallop, with one leg hitting the ground like a trampoline and the other swiftly absorbing the space, represents nothing but a series of masculine coupés in a real-life environment. Here we can have the chasing after someone at the panicked fleeing from threatening danger. But on the whole this is merely a series of the simplest coupés rushing across the floor. . . .

Wherever force is required for swing, energetic displacement is inevitable. In order to do an entrechat with glissade, the second part of the glissade—the gliding movement to fifth position—must resemble the first springboard act of coupé. The leg hits the floor in plain, deep plié. The takeoff of the other leg constitutes the second act of coupé. The very beats, the intertwining of the legs in the air, represent nothing more than the choreographic theme of the body's movement.

We have analyzed all the types of classical coupé in ballet. But as with all the other basic forms of dance, in its theoretical construction coupé far exceeds the bounds of choreography and obtains universal meaning in its application. The art of dance takes place in time and space. But what is space? As a Kantian form of external perceptions, it is a channel for the phenomenal content of all our impressions. The notion of space takes shape in the soul as the result of two acts of normal coupé: the beating visual impression and the muscular tension that responds to it reflexively. If this muscular tension is considerable and broad in its reach, we say that the space is extensive. In the case of the tactile sense, the tension is insignificant, and our conception of the size and extensiveness of space decreases. That is why a disorder of the muscular system entails shocks to the psychological system, which can reach such pathological forms as claustrophobia and the loss of one's sense of direction. We are dealing with a phenomenon of movement that passes into the technique of classical production in all its components. Space is the result of visual and muscular coupé turned into a contemplated representation.

The other Kantian form is time. What is time? It is also the result of a certain kind of coupé. Mental and visual perception, the apperception of an object from the past, is accompanied by a reflexive flash of memory. The force of this flash also brings about the sense of time in the process of personal development. If the flash is vivid, fresh, and intensely real, then we say that little time has passed. The phenomenon occurred as if it were only yesterday. If the flash is pale and couched in vagueness, then depending on the degree of its weakness, we feel the passage of time to be long or short. An object is reflected in memory's mirror more or less distinctively. The combination of the mental perception of objects with their mirrorlike resemblances in the memory gives us the sense of time that justifies Kant's teachings. Of course, we must allow for the role of personal affect in this process: a given object touched by this affect can appear to us with a special liveliness even over the significant course of time. But this kind of clarity of mirrorlike experience will always be episodic; it will extend only to the object that specially touches us, leaving the context of the event as vague as the past in which it occurred. Thus time is also the result of the two acts of coupé in the apparatus of perception.

This is true from the perspective of the past. How is it perceived from the perspective of the future? Here it is completely intertwined with the concept of space that is formed from the two acts of visual and muscular coupé described above. It flows from within the same process. The sense of time phosphoresces in the muscle's sensation. According to the tension of this muscular sensation, we unconsciously make inferences about the magnitude of time required for the resolution of the collected energy. Muscular sensation—the second act of coupé—contains the venture and evaluation of two things: space, which is to be overcome, and time, which is necessary for the solution of the problem. From the power of his initial springboard push from the floor, the dancer will extract a motive for moving across a certain range and supporting this movement high in the air during a larger or smaller amount of time. Coupé immediately predetermines both elevation and ballon, constituting the essential key to both elements of classical dance.

What we call coupé in the individual sphere can be defined as detonation in the social milieu of mass experience. An orator provokes in the crowd to whom he is speaking a powerful detonator when there is enthusiasm and great emotional tension. It applauds him and is ready to take up arms if he demands it, as was the case at the National Convention after Robespierre's speeches.* This is detonation. This is the reflected-reflexive movement that carries all the features of interaction that are characteristic of coupé.

. . .

Yet coupé has not only a social equivalent but a cosmic one as well. The whole world of causality is a theater of action of various displacements in time and space, which are direct and reflected. Striking flint on a stone causes a spark. This is genuine coupé in the physical world. Somewhat more complex is the discharge of diametrically opposed electrical charges in two storm clouds or clusters. The whole enormously rich field of thermodynamics in nature, with its sudden conversions of concentrated energy into heat, consists of a series of phenomena of a similar type. This is also coupé in a universal environment.

Finally the law of coupé in its psychological reverberations. What is passion, love's affect, in its broadest scope? This is a consciously or subconsciously willful energy which responds to external influence. The entire study of the soul's reflexes, beginning with irrepressible laughter and the equally irrepressible tears

---

*The ruling political body during the French Revolution. Maximilen Robespierre (1758–1794), one of the principal leaders of the Revolution, made many speeches to the Convention calling for the execution of the king.

of emotion and shock—all this enters the gamut of the flaring and reflected fires that burn within man. In Clytemnestra, who prepares her husband's death, there also burns an inner conflagration from a series of successive external bonfires that blaze on the peaks of the mountains of the archipelago in commemoration of taking Troy. The joyfully impulsive act of Agamemnon as a result of a long chain of external effects brings about transgression and death. Here is a poetic coupé gleaned from Aeschylus's immortal tragedy. From ballet, as from any great art, as we expand our interpretation of the subject, we enter into the infinite realm of being.

. . .

Gliding Movements

If we consider plié as the starting point of a particular type of coupé in a somewhat generalized extended form, as the first act of that coupé, then we shall have to include in this scheme a whole series of movements that have a gliding character. First and foremost is glissade. What is glissade? It is the gliding motion of one's feet along the stage to change one's place. At no moment can classical dance ever become prosaic and lose its grandiloquent character. Everything is stylized and molded into precise and strict design. The legs do not shuffle or trudge across the floor; rather they glide softly as they transport the body from one place to another. This is glissade's simple task. One executes glissade rather simply. Feet in fifth position. First a demi-plié, a gentle bending, without which no figure of dancing can be managed. This is the drop of oil that moistens the movement and gives it the necessary smoothness. From this bending in a reflexive manner is born elementary battement tendu on the floor. The leg is extended as far as possible, to the tips of the toes, which rest on the ground with arched instep. The other foot lightly and almost imperceptibly leaves the floor, gliding and joining the first one in closed position. Thus both feet, before they once again join each other on the floor, glide, one after the other. Glissade can be done forward, backward, sideways, in different directions, depending on the choreographic demands of the moment. The springboard for the entire movement is plié, the primordial impulse of the kind of coupé which is expanded in the space of the shift. From this plié the leg is thrown out in a soft manner, as if from its source of plastic moisture. Without some degree of this moistness the genuine essence of dance—especially female, tenderly plantlike dance—cannot be managed. We have here the originating phase of coupé: the impulse is provided and a reflexive response is inevitable. Consequently, the second act of coupé is expressed in the already mentioned battement tendu. Only the final movement, the delicate sliding of the foot to fifth position, will be the real glissade. If the right foot glides along the floor then it does so slightly and unnoticeably. The smoothest moment comes only at the end, when both legs are brought together.

One can do a deliberately obvious coupé at the beginning of glissade. One can do glissade soutenu. But these are all varieties of the figure, which does not change its essential aspect, no matter what the movement's ornament or task. Several parts of *The Little Humpbacked Horse* contain such glissades—the animated Frescoes, for example. The figures of the Frescoes represent ordinary gliding movements across the floor, maintaining just those principles of bending and reflexive battement about which I have spoken here. Basic dancing, embellished by various plastic grace notes, produces an amusing impression. One can do a more complicated glissade that in its entire essence is only the preparation for the following flight. Feet in fourth position in croisé. After plié on front leg the dancer does a barely noticeable jump, throwing back the back leg. After this the back leg quickly returns to its former position. The energy for the impending elevation is now concentrated. You can execute glissade in fifth position with or without changing the feet. This glissade is usually done to effacé. When changing feet the head is bent first toward one, now toward the other shoulder. The shoulders themselves move slightly and softly, hardly noticeable. Finally, we very often see onstage glissades that are performed in fast time—the feet push the ground away.

The harmonious movement that constitutes the basic feature of female dance is cultivated in glissades of all types and forms. The female dancer learns how to move forward softly in space, departing from the immobility of the plantlike state but nevertheless bringing to this forward movement the element of dream and reverie. The woman's soul travels through the world as well with this gliding shadow; it does not occupy space by seizing it in a coarse and greedily impulsive way but rather by gliding along the floor noiselessly and smoothly, like a swan in the water. In this regard the woman remains true to her original element; and all of female choreography, with its elevation and ballon, is tied to the elements of daydream and semi-slumber. Female consciousness itself, which is so essential in classical dance, is merely a gentle groping for the right themes through the languid, half-slumbering stretching of the will's mechanism. All of this beautifully emerges in the setting of poetic ballet, where everything, even the triumphs of masculine heroics, is covered with the haze of heavenly visions. There is no dust here, no roar of earthly struggles. Everything shines in the vaporous design of fairy tale.

There is a hint of soft plantlike feminine glissade in the figure called pas de chat. When frightened or when falling, a cat makes a jump in which all the elegance and art of glissade find their natural expression. Of course, the danced pas de chat lacks the degree of perfection we find in the leap of a cat, but it also carries with it a likeness to the wild and graceful animal movement that produces such a great impression on the eye. Yet all this is furnished and contained in glissade. Glissade must not be diffuse and sluggish; its beauty cannot be spiritless. On the contrary, it is characterized by a deliberation and energy that are calculated in their elegance and whose internal motor is the will. This applies particularly to female glissade, which contains traces of the threateningly demonic. This is Grushenka's gait in Dostoevsky's *The Brothers Karamazov.* Everything is catlike glissades. Her tread is soft and gentle: it kisses the floor, but it harbors within it anger and vengefulness.

A glissade in fourth position is called glissade failli. The foot moves forward in the fragrant oil of glissadelike movement, slowly and carefully, playing with the nuances of plastique in all their diversity. This was the unique glissade of Olga Preobrazhenskaya, in which she radiated in the various ballets of her repertoire. For this glissade to be implemented properly all the plantlike delicacy of female dancing is needed. You need to be able to rest on your foot, you need to follow your velvety smooth movement with a coquettish eye. This type of male glissade does not represent anything: the man is too active, and his movements on the floor, especially in the system of classical ballet, are only hurried and brief respites before the large tempos of elevation. But a woman is in her native element here. In life a woman finds no great comfort in waiting a little, in lingering a bit, in suffering for a while and in making others suffer with a mildly agitated glissade, slightly slipping and almost falling. But when dancing glissade, this coquettish culture is presented in its everlasting symbol. Glissade failli is the lovely caress of a panther. It looks especially wonderful after a big leap, which requires the energy of the will for the move. Such a leap—whose softness conceals greater force, greater movement, and a more natural expression of the woman's entire essence than there was in the aggressive energy of her flight—is completed by stroking the floor.

This is glissade in its plastic design and in its psychological and ideological significance. It enters the essence of female dancing naturally, corresponding in the highest degree to the woman's distinguishing means of changing from the plantlike state to the mobile animal-human one. Even in her aerial movements the dancer retains a trace of the flowing and gentle shuffling of glissade with all its charm. The ground, which the woman has just abandoned with her foot, seems to draw her back to its invisible sphere as it still supports its flower. She cannot definitively break away from glissade, and it continually glides after her wherever she goes.

A whole series of general movements border on glissade. Ordinarily, dancers study these in the first phase of classical exercise in the center, which they do after the repeated exercises of the material they mastered at the barre. Temps lié and chassé are such figures of dance. *Temps lié* means the movement of connection. When the word *temps* is used, the step has a specific meaning. We are dealing here not with the entire scheme of dancing but with an individual part that has been singled out for some reason. Thus we say *temps levé, temps de cuisse, temps relevé* precisely to stress one characteristic movement or another. In temps lié the characteristic moment is the link between several movements. From basic plié, as from an active spring, is born battement forward and, dependent on this same spring, relevé on the toes of the foot that stands in the back. Thus, at the very beginning we have plié, battement, and the movement for standing on the toes. Essentially in the phase we have just outlined we have both acts of coupé plus the tempo of the vertical. After these follows the concluding movement of the legs from the back to fifth position. This movement, this glissade toward the leg that has come forward from the back, this connecting ribbon that reaches out to it, is temps lié.

If you continue doing the same movements in the same large volume, sideways and back, you merely prolong the temps lié rather than introduce any new element into it. It remains the same system of beautifully executed connecting ribbons in fourth, fifth, and second position of the class exercise. For the figure as a whole to produce the proper aesthetic impression, you need the entire culture of classical movement, with its delicate pliés, coupés with battements, and gliding movements. Johansson made this figure a bridge to the third part of the exercise in the center, called adagio, thereby familiarizing us with the harmoniously coordinated evolutions of body and movements in all their parts, systematically accompanied by the arms, shoulders, head, and eyes. Here indeed on the floor is a garlanded likeness to the class dance in the primitive forms of connectedness and coordination that will be completely developed in the movements of the pas de deux. In any case, all seven positions of port de bras must be mastered in complete detail at this moment in order for the student freely and easily to use precisely those needed to furnish complete accord to the glissade movement.

With regard to chassé, let us first note one of the word's philological meanings. In general *chasser* means "to hunt," "to pursue," "to chase." Applied to dance, especially on the stage, the meaning of the word assumes a secondary position, yielding a more nuanced symbolism. The word *chasser* is also applied to boats carried along by the wind and to clouds carried by air currents. The French use this word stylistically when speaking about a carriage that rolls smoothly along the road. Thus it follows that the transcription of this concept into dance movement assumes motion that is not only gliding and smooth but also rustles and whistles along the floor, constantly advancing farther and farther. This is something delicate and deeply stylized, in the ritual of the ballroom.

The step is done in the following way. Move the front foot to fourth position and begin the forward movement with a gentle gliding glissade. Following it, the back foot pushes sharply into third position and itself moves forward into fourth, taking the other's place. In this manner a consecutive series of movements from croisé to croisé occurs, with a barely noticeable oscillation of the shoulders, which move first right, then left. The movement of the shoulders, performed through seeming hints, replaces a real and expressive épaulement, whose application in this instance would make the dancing clumsy and vulgar. Simple townswomen who have fun dancing and give free vent to their emotions readily practice just this kind of blatant épaulement. They move forward, reeling and turning here and there with their shoulders. But in more sophisticated, stylized dancing we can intuit that the shoulders are moving only by the gentle and completely inconspicuous tilting of the head. Yet the woman's shoulders still pulse with life. Immobility can be alive or dead. In this case the immobility is alive and filled with potential ardor. The chassé I have described occupies a central position in genre dances, but here this figure is carried over from the unlimited storehouse of classical treasures.

. . .

Fouetté

Fouetté, a French word, means "to beat with a whip" as punishment, or "to increase the speed of running." For a normal strike the whip is usually lifted and then brought down onto the back of the horse or the person being punished. The hand does not turn on its axis when it begins to move. If the threat of a strike rather than the strike itself is the issue, then the whip turns by moving the wrist around its axis. This latter movement, which is common in lashing, is called fouetté in ballet. Fouetté is the rotating movement of the body's parts around their natural axes via incomplete, partial en tournant. The palm does fouetté in classical as well as character dances. The head does fouetté when it turns to the side. If it bends downward or in different directions, fouetté is not achieved because there is no rotation around its axis or partial en tournant. Even the eyes do fouetté when they glance coquettishly sideways.

But in ballet these movements of the hands, body, head, and eyes have no special names; the term *fouetté* is essentially applied to the specific movement of the knee. The application of the term *fouetté,* which is actually quite broad, is here limited to several specific cases. Yet meanwhile we observe fouetté in the art of classical ballet wherever there are contraposto movements along the floor or en dehors or en dedans. When the leg in its rotational movement along the floor in grand plié moves back as it describes the periphery of the circle, it invariably changes the direction of its turnout: if it did not, further movement would be impossible. This change of turnout on the extreme point of the periphery should really be called fouetté. We can see such fouetté in the simplest example. You extend the hand with palm open and move it back in a circle and back horizontally. When the extended hand reaches a specific point behind the shoulder, it inevitably will have to turn out the palm in the other direction, otherwise the hand will be restrained in its movement. But it is this turning of the palm that forms the purest example of fouetté.

There are many examples of this in life. When punishing a child by spanking him, not with a whip or birch rod, but with the hand, the palm constantly rotates on its axis in swift movements that form the slap. Slaps across the face are created in the same way: they are not caused by a stationary palm, but invariably by one in a state of swift and abrupt rotation, which reflects the aggressive plash of the soul. You have to realize quite precisely that nowhere more than in fouetté is the human soul less passively indifferent. Precisely here the soul becomes the arena of the most intense feelings, from healthy and natural to pathological and demonic ones. . . .

The instructor has done fouetté with a whip, having been seized by mad excitement and having lost the intended pedagogical understanding that gave rise to the punishment. Such cases are too common and need no sustained analysis. But it is important to establish the complexity of moods that accompany the sets of movements of fouetté. If fouetté is removed from the concepts that direct it, if in the rush of the general movement it takes on an autonomous character, it will turn into an instrument of hysterical rhetoric and will produce, perhaps, a dazzling but not purely artistic impression. The continuous fouetté of the hands in Russian dance that for some reason is performed in *The Little Humpbacked Horse* on classical pointe is rhetorical in the highest degree. This kind of fouetté constitutes a too obvious emphasis upon the Russian style and is a break from the general harmonious scheme. The dancer moves forward on her toes, all the time delightfully rotating her hands, and in so doing interfering with the audience's viewing of the choreography. In just this way the famous fouetté that is repeated thirty-two times in *Swan Lake* draws the dancer into a kind of choreographic delirium in which acrobatic motifs predominate. Of course, this fouetté needs to be done in one spot on the floor for we are dealing here essentially with a pirouette, with the rotation of the whole body around a stable axis in a complete and finished revolution. But the fouetté itself, which tests the force of a pirouette, screams and shouts too much in its rhetorical sweep, covering the pirouette. We find the same rhetorical danger when performing the high saut de basque. When she is up in the air, the dancer must keep her eyes on the public. This is what makes the figure special. For this one needs a resolute contraposto movement of the head during the general rotation. But for all its decisiveness, this movement must be firm yet moderate, restrained, and deliberate in order not to turn into a rhetorical scream. In general, wherever the element of fouetté and contraposto predominates or even participates, the danger of rhetoric is always present and great. Classic examples of this are Leonardo da Vinci's painting and Dostoevsky's novelistic art. The entire *Last Supper* is full of controposto movements which bear an obvious theatrical and declamatory character. The charcoal portrait of Isabella d'Este is an almost extreme example of graphic exaggeration of controposto motifs, all the more impressive because here we have presented a cultured, refined woman. The same is true in Dostoevsky's novels, which, for all their brilliance, abound in needless expressions of sentimental and declamatory rhetoric. The character of Marmeladov* constitutes a particularly graphic example of this.

The technique of fouetté as such is not especially complicated. The foot leaves the floor and is thrust forward in a determined dégagé. Pierina Legnani thrust her leg forward openly and picturesquely in effacé. You felt immediately that something rapturously beautiful was unfolding before your eyes, in the melodious Italian style. Roulades of a choreographic serenade would spill into the air. Vera Trefilova used to open her leg in croisé. This conforms to the Russian spirit of precision and concentration before the opening and denouement. At first the waistband is drawn and tied tautly on the body, and only later do you begin to passionately and impetuously unravel it. Mathilda Kshesinskaya threw out her leg en face—and this was characteristic of her dancing, which was always in your face and daring in its tone. Regarding the national peculiarities of all these dancers, the Italians, Russians, and Poles were marvelously original. After the introductory battement, the leg is raised, as high as possible, in tire-bouchon. At first extend the toes down rather gently and not very intensely. You do this in a calculated manner so as to accumulate and preserve your energy for the forthcoming rotating motion. Finally, from tire-bouchon you produce a fouetté of the knee, keeping the hip as stationary as possible and not involving the hip joint in the circular flow. When doing the fouetté, which is included in the general pirouette, the supporting leg does a rhythmic plié and relevé whenever it turns. And the arms, like a conductor's, always joyfully perform as they open and close, keeping the trunk aligned with the leg. This is the usual fouetté, which is performed without breaking away from your spot. But fouetté can be done with a diagonal run across the stage in a fast en tournant, as Liubov Roslavleva and, most recently, Kseniya Makletsova did. This kind of fouetté also thrills the audience with its impression of unique power and temperament.

---

*A character in Dostoevsky's *Crime and Punishment* who early on gives a long monologue filled with bathos and self-pity.

Straight and Crooked Lines

In moving to the third part of the exercise in the center we shall consider the graphics of ballet figures in their general and essential features, avoiding everything that is arbitrary and concrete in the adagio. Adagio is the weaving together of various soft battements and pirouettes so that the study of its graphic first principle constitutes a natural and instructive prologue. Lines are of four sorts: straight, curved, broken, and circular. A broken line is essentially a line consisting of several straight lines, but a circular line—in the elementary conception of lower mathematics—represents a particular example of a curved one.

Every line has its own logic and psychology. A straight line extends into eternity from both sides. It is the shortest distance between two points. It is the movement of a point in one direction toward its goal. Imagine a straight line made by chalk on a blackboard. It gives the impression of having a magical force over reality, in which curved and circular lines predominate. To express the process of thought in movement terms, we have a geometrically straight line—clear, even, and racing uninterruptedly toward its goal in the faceless darkness of the surrounding chaos of things. . . .

. . .

What is a curved line? It is a line formed by the movement of a line that constantly deviates from its direct path under the influence of certain powerful forces. This is precisely what constitutes the external form of life, where everything influences the other and accommodates everything to itself, but it itself endures the same influence of other adjacent things. Everything is in confusion and chaos, everything suffices not for the goal but for its own self. It is not thought but feeling and will that propel the world. Individual wills, which struggle among themselves, as well as diverse feelings form the world of crooked lines, which open and close in an endless kaleidoscope of diversity. . . . The very will that pulsates in man so capriciously, inconsistently, and vaguely turns into an obedient little horse if it is saddled with thought. And suddenly this chaotic person, who is aware of his aspirations and the paths that lead to their realization, becomes a reasonable person, integral and consciously willful.

We have already seen what a broken line is—a composite version of a straight line. It is a symbol of a person who changes his goals or transfers them to different points. Basically it is the same magically straight line, the movement of the lighted point in dark space, thought's flight over chaos and the abyss. But brokenness contains elements of complexity and richness. Man is captivated by different goals; he tries to approach what he considers the truth by various means. His consciousness rushes in different directions, carrying behind it his entire temperament and character. Everywhere, at any given moment, there is a direct striving toward a goal, but as a result there are tormenting zigzags with their constant deviations to the side. . . .

. . .

What is a circular line? What is a circle? It is the kind of curved line whose originating point, when moving, rotates near a definite center and always maintains an equal distance from it. This center is the axis of movement. Concluding its path, the curve closes in a circle. The point always returns to where it began. It does not shake or vibrate or rush from side to side but rather imperturbably sails ahead and, like a straight line, is also faithful—only not to the distant goal but to the chosen center of rotation. If we translate these observations into the language of psychology, then in the circle we find the graphic characteristics of the emotional world of passion and sensibly willful impulses. A person rotates around his own self, around a mysterious center, around the sensorium of the spirit, of his individual "I." Every feeling, every passion, every emotional experience, with the exception of pure thought, has the circular or whirlpool-like spiral character of a whirling snowstorm or blizzard. And no matter how fast moving the sweep and force of the rotation is here, the circle cannot for a second break away from the fixed center. The circle is described in one place, rooted by its center to a definite point of the earth. Passions are dizzying. The head can spin from joy and many other feelings. Children turn around in rushes of the simplest emotions. Nations dance round dances in ancient farandoles. The antistrophic dithyramb in Dionysus's cult had the form of a round dance. The original orchestra also had the form of a perfect geometric circle. We dance around a Christmas tree. Newlyweds are led in a circle around the lectern in the Eastern Orthodox ritual. One rides a horse in circles, training it to run well. The circle prevails in the circus and in a carousel. There are endless numbers of feelings and moods which form circles.

Thus, thought is straight and endless, while feeling is crooked, round, and usually enclosed (in a circle). When the will serves thought it is direct; when it serves feeling and passion it is curved and round. Ordinary thought and commonplace, prosaic feeling constitute the humdrum life of man. But if a storm seizes hold of a person's soul, it becomes enchanting in its directness, while feeling becomes confused and whirls in a blazing maelstrom.

. . .

Attitude and Arabesque

Attitude represents a broken line, arabesque a straight one, and the philosophy of lines investigated in the previous chapter finds its application here. Let us first see what kind of figures these are that are constantly glimpsed in the technique of adagio movement. Attitude ordinarily begins from fifth position.

If you move the left leg front and left shoulder forward, attitude is presented in croisé. Raise the right leg in the back in a slow tempo to the retiré position. From the knee in the same tempo lift it higher, maintaining a half-bent position and extending no higher than the waist. Toes must be somewhat above the kneecap. This is attitude croisé. Hands float slowly in a semicircle from first position parallel to the leg, which rises in the back in coordinated movement. At the proper height the left arm extends to one side, while the right arm forms a circle over the head within the eyes' field of vision. Épaulement also comes forward: the head is turned toward the left shoulder.

Everything in the movement that has been described—the lines of the arms, legs, shoulder, and head—has the character of a plantlike process. Everything is feminine. All the bending and unbending of the body recalls the rustling branches of a tree, with the supporting leg, which rests on the floor, giving the impression of the immobile trunk that preserves the finest vertical bearing. In the male execution on the floor this attitude looks somewhat affected because it does not have in its structure those qualities and peculiarities which are characteristic of a woman's body. In women plié of the leg is softer and more pliant. The instep, the toes, the whole manifestation en dehors are plastic to the highest degree, and the bending of the waist is deep and neural. Additionally the line of the neck is swanlike. In men attitude cannot be gentle or plastic in any refined way, as long as we are speaking about performing on the floor. But when transferred to the heights, in the movements that are proper for the male type of elevation, attitude acquires a majestic coloration. Here it is really alive and at times simply magnificent. During a strong jump and an elastic ballon the bent leg bears, in a sturdy bundle, the possibility of the future decisive form, the transition of the broken line into a straight one. The dancer strides along an aerial arc with proud, willful aplomb.

In the technique of its initial movements attitude effacé in no way differs from attitude croisé. Only épaulement, the position of the shoulder and head, changes. What does this beautiful, soft, tender attitude represent in psychological terms? It resolves all the tensions, all the potential Sturm und Drang of attitude croisé. The curled-up body becomes uncurled and is relieved of its inner languor. The arm hangs easily above the head. The eyes are directed toward it with an expression of satisfaction and even solemn tranquility. The other hand is extended to the side broadly and freely, not for the classical arrangement of any new and complete figure but as if with a beautiful gesture to set off the momentary and carefree steadiness of the entire scheme. In one case the broken line is given in a condensed and intense set. We are seeing how the female essence is sought after and striven toward in the tinges of inner, guardedly concealed anxieties. These are the difficult moments that precede exaltation, which in this instance can be expressed only in a straight line. . . .

Both forms of attitude are widely applied. Jumps entrelace done in attitude or in arabesque come out beautifully. Small leaps on pointe in a diagonal are especially effective whether they are performed in croisé or in effacé. But if you do such leaps in deep plié, across the diagonal of the stage in an upward direction, with your leg extended in attitude, the impression would not be totally artistic. Two bent legs create a flattened, warped dance figure. But you need only straighten out the leg in the air—that is, give it the form of arabesque—and the movement acquires complete artistic finish. With an extended leg and a horizontally spread body, the figure of mobile arabesque in a dancer who rushes downward along the diagonal of the stage is one of the most beloved themes in ballet. This is precisely a splashing dolphin that radiantly and passionately flies over the water's surface. A straight line expresses the will's passion more resolutely than a crooked one and allows the final thrust toward the definite goal to be more concentrated, natural, and light. The movement is free from all restraints. The straight line rejoices and exults. Amid the horizontal and vertical schemes the dancer's body seems transported to the animal-human kingdom with no bends or breaks, but rather with an expression of pathetic struggle and even passion in straightness and clarity.

As we have seen, arabesques come from attitude by straightening the bent leg. With this, the play of the arms in the eyes' field of vision changes. The leg is extended like a taught string. But the attitude's resonance, which is felt more by what the eye remembers than by what it perceives, still quivers—just as sometimes épaulement, which is essentially invisible from without, is felt. The leg could be straight and seemingly dead in its straightness. It is extended and flattened but devoid of perceptible lifelikeness. This is the way we feel the lightness of a growing trunk and the deathliness of a stick. We observe the same thing in the arabesque. The straight line exudes an inner quivering, and this quivering is conveyed to our sensitive auditory nerve, like the emotional rush of the line that passes from a broken state to direct striving. In the two individual types of attitude the essence of the female dancer is still only promised; it still only languishes with the anticipation of its future birth. But in the arabesque we already have the basic traits not of immobile essence but of the dance of true choreographic exaltation that has begun in a living action. The straight line, with its aesthetic enchantment and magic spell, has prevailed over the uneasy casting about in zigzags.

For the arabesque to be artistically finished, you need in the final moment to release your arch and tuck in the toes while extending the leg in a straight line. The pattern of the leg is directed upward and forms a circular line. The toes are nonetheless directed downward. This is the way it needs to be according to Johannson's and Petipa's demands. Everything is finished and rounded in classical dance, and nothing leaps out from the soft mass with sharp and stabbing lines. The line of the legs is rounded. Port de bras is rounded. Even the toes, which point downward from the completely rounded accompaniment, do not spoil the general impression of completeness and finish.

This is where the graphics of choreography principally part company with those of mathematics. In mathematics the straight line is extended into infinity on both sides. It is in flight from one infinity to another. In classical dance this is impossible. Such interminability would dampen the very existence of the artistic impression. Imagine a mentally extended leg in arabesque along the lines of a geometrically straight line. All the muscles are paralyzed with stress. Here is where the impression of the stick occurs. There is not a hint of essence or exaltation. But let that same leg change its position so that, starting with the ankle, the foot bends slightly upward. And the entire impression from such an arabesque becomes artistically finished. The straight line in its absolute purity carries in itself the coldness of abstraction and belongs solely to geometry. In life there is no such line. But the straight line with the slight takeoff of a curve, in the gentlest movement of the beginning curvature as if sighing from its unbearable sorcery, transports us from the world of abstractions to the world of living beauty and vital forms. In its psychological ardor the arabesque strives toward the distant charm of the circle. And in this circle is the dancer's entire essence, all the bodily and emotional exaltation that are accessible to her. The element of finiteness affirms the infinity of artistic perception.

Pirouette

The pirouette constitutes the central part of the adagio. It is surrounded by soft battements of all types, which form its frame. The origin of the word *pirouette* is not exactly known: perhaps it comes from the Italian word for a child's top, or perhaps it is a distortion of the Greek root of the word for fire. A fiery circle—that's what a pirouette is. It must be performed with emotion and animation, in a swift and passionate tempo. Imagine a pirouette completed before our eyes. Let us look at its individual components. The dancer has risen on her toes, straightened her leg and back, and kept her neck steady. The other leg, having left the ground, has occupied a place sur le cou-de-pied just above the ankle. All is directed upward, as the toes lightly and delicately touch the floor. Gathering momentum with her arms, the dancer turns around without moving from her place. These are the external traits of the ordinary pirouette. The supporting leg, the hip, and the knee form a straight line which constitutes the axis of rotation. With a straight back, neck, and head, and with the trunk adjusted for balance, the dancer in the initial phase of the pirouette in her overall look represents a willful striving along upward lines. Only the leg sur le cou-de-pied provides a bend in the movement, which is also felt in the slightly raised—again, for balance—thorax from one side. But the line of the precise, all-enclosing ideal circle envelops in the process of movement all these lines, the straight and the curved ones.

This line has command over everything, constituting the ultimate likeness and essence of the entire figure. Thus the movement of the pirouette, taken as a whole, combines within itself lines of all kinds—straight, broken, curved, and rounded. But the idea of the movement, all the beauty and force of the figure, is contained in the following two moments: the straight white leg captures the eye of the audience as it seems to penetrate the ground and stands unshakably on delicate toes while around it whirl pure and integral circles—infallibly complete in the general flow of emotional exaltation. Even a slight breaking loose from one's place, a barely noticeable shift of the toes, an insufficiency or overabundance of momentum calculated without mathematical precision creates gaps and blunders that destroy the purity of the classical design. The fixity to one's place and the movement's confinement to a definite point correspond psychologically to the willed idea of the executed moment. The circle gravitates to its center in its fixed and unchangeable rotation in one place. The circles of feelings also gravitate to their focus, to the personal origin, to their guiding magnet, which attracts everything to itself. The center remains immutable: it is one and the same, immobile and eternal in the rotary movements that are performed around it. . . .

These are the two supreme features of the pirouette: the immobility of the support and the perfection of the magic circle. If a dancer's circles lack those elevated qualities, what does this mean in everyday language? It means that she lacks a firm support, steadiness in her emotions, and also the sense of true coordination and harmoniousness with her own guiding center. It means also that the performer does not have a sufficient supply of energy and pathos, and cannot twist like a tempest within herself, balancing internal and external forces. This is what a dancer is like without a pirouette in which straight-forward thought, crooked emotion, fractures of doubts, and the complete circle of will and passion participate. That is why working on a pirouette in the classroom develops simultaneously the personality, the soul's inner structure, and the tendency toward consummate wholeness. Everything must aspire to the circle, to the achievement of artistic effect, to the emancipation from the cold mathematics of straight lines and the chaotic ecstasy of crooked ones. Only in the circle does the exaltation of the human soul acquire its peculiar beauty and aesthetic.

The extent to which the pirouette is an organic part of human nature is evident in the remarkable words Mathilda Kshesinskaya said to me some time ago: "Italian women are born with the pirouette." The Italian woman, heiress of the Roman matron who dates from the origin of the Apennine peninsula and those remarkable Etruscan maidens, appears even today filled not only with the volatility of the Roman-Latin race but also with that innate devotion to wholeness and roundness which characterizes the nation that created the arch and the vault. . . .

. . .

Is the pirouette characteristic of the Russian woman? Only in part, in very rare instances. I have personally seen only one Russian woman with a pirouette whose equal I do not know in modern ballet. With great, precisely measured momentum Trefilova in *Swan Lake* did pirouettes in several rotations without the slightest difficulty and with a harmonious and composed expression on her face, although she had the exceptional support of Nikolai Legat. I have never seen anyone else do such pirouettes. Ordinarily even remarkable dancers like Pavlova and Preobrazhenskaya perform pirouettes with a frightened-looking face and a feeling of insecurity that spreads across their entire body. For some reason dancers trained in the Moscow style have a certain talent for performing the pirouette, for example Elizaveta Gerdt and Kseniya Makletsova. Ekaterina Geltser's rotations were in their time perfectly remarkable: whirlwind, passion, force, movement, without a single blunder. But for all this, the plastique of the pirouette is not the typical property of the inhabitants of the Scythian-Sarmatian valleys. The Russian woman, marvelous material for psychological novels, is too capriciously unsettled and insecure in her aesthetic emotions, too bifurcated between good and evil in the internal structure of her character. Pirouette requires a monolithic character, the exultation of the infinite, and absolute integrity and faithfulness to the guiding center. . . .

. . .

En Tournant

There are three kinds of rotary movement en tournant: the forward transference of the body in space, the completed form of the pirouette, and, finally, the partial revolution of separate parts of the body. We shall analyze all these variants of en tournant in turn, with regard to the importance of their differences in the technique of classical dance. On a low level, with a small jump, the figures en tournant are characteristic of women's dances. Done in elevation, en tournant is what makes male heroic choreography so special. The most important thing in en tournant of the first type is the agility of both legs and the changing of their position, which distinguishes this figure from all the forms of the pirouette. I am taking *pirouette* in the customarily narrow meaning of the word here, not expanding the concept of en tournant to its final limits. In the pirouette the line of the circle predominates: here the curved lines that single out and underscore the classical figure being performed replace one another. It is significant that the male pirouette on the floor, because of its narrow move-ment and lack of the broad swing and tender plantlike qualities which charac-terize the par-terre female circle, is reluctantly called a pirouette—so slightly expressed, pale, and comically weak is it in comparison with the ideal outline of the pirouette in general.

But men do exquisite tours in the air, simple and recurring, which are mistakenly called pirouettes as well. This is a changing of the feet in the air, changement de pieds, in circular revolution en tournant. And here the male temperament and the male's heroic technique, with its hint of acrobatism, are fully present. These aerial and recurrent changes of the feet occasionally pro-duce an enormous impression, especially in their precise, undaunted, and stationary execution with pauses on the floor. Such tours are not in a woman's character, just as the emotional and willful pirouettes embellished by the grace notes of gentle plastique are not in a man's. A man has no genuine pirouette on the floor, but he possesses all kinds of dazzling circular revolutions, finished and partial, and a technique en tournant that provides fury and shine to the figure being presented. In the pirouette the geometric circle is most important, but in en tournant the figure of the dance itself, with all its lively individuality, is what matters. In the pirouette there is something stationary and stable; in en tournant the curved line of the bent body is thrust from one place to another. We have a pirouette with the ornamental design of a fouetté: this kind of pirouette, as we have seen, must be attached to one point on the floor and, without moving off it, the dancer must make circles with the leg and the body in a set number of beats. Everything is in place, everything is rooted. But you can do a fouetté as part of the movements en tournant, along the slanting line of the stage, moving downstage without stops or interruptions. This is also one of the most stunning effects in the practice of en tournant, and in fact the fouetté itself is in the forefront here, the rotation of the leg around its axis rushing more and more forward.

Let us consider several types of en tournant. You can do a simple jump with a circular revolution along a straight line. At the last moment you can add diverse figures to this jump. Jumps fondu are also done in a circular revolution. A woman sometimes performs a ballonné in such a circular rotation. For a man this kind of step is too splashy and fussy. But here is a figure of dance that in its circular revolution produces an especially vivid impression. . . . What is a coup de vent? If the wind spins by striking the air with its gusts, this is coup de vent. If someone enters a room with unexpected quickness, as if carried in by a whirlwind, we can say that he has entered en coup de vent. But we have this rare figure in classical ballet at well. In the famous coda of the first act of *Esmeralda,* Kshesinskaya does precisely such a coup de vent, a dazzling circular pas de basque in the air, while directing her dance to the wild tempos of the orchestra toward the footlights along the diagonal of the stage. This is en tournant, a complete revolution in the air around the axis, which creates in the public corresponding gusts of excitement that resound like a whirlwind from top to bottom.

The courante of *Giselle* is no more than an incomparable arabesque de tournant. What is saut de basque if not the continuation of a determined coupé with a large leap (jeté) in a complete circular revolution? But there is one purely masculine step which is now rarely encountered in the apparatus and technique of classical dance—the rivoltade. The mechanics of its execution are complicated and difficult. You need to turn quickly in the air, describing three-quarters of a circle with legs horizontally extended in a dead point and back curved. You fall on the leg that was thrown out with a sharp bend. Externally this pas resembles the saut de basque, but it differs significantly from it in some extremely important features. In the saut de basque you do a full circle, whereas in a rivoltade we have only three-quarters of a circle. In saut de basque one leg is slightly extended along a diagonal, while the other is in retiré position, whereas in the rivoltade both legs are closed together in one terrifying moment before their final break. In general the choreographic character of each is completely different. And the rivoltade masculine and heroic spirit differs decisively from the soft plastique of the woman's jump in full circle.

This figure is so hard to perform that Nikolai Legat prefaced it with an ordinary preparatory leap from both feet, with a firm springboard coupé on the ground. The contemporary dancer Viktor Semenov, preparing his sensational number for *Don Quixote*—the grand cabriole forward—selected an unexpected rivoltade for its finale. Of course, the cabriole in and of itself is far simpler than Legat's complex figure, with its leap—the glissade failli—and concluding coupé. But this is why Semenov's rivoltade seems especially manly and dazzlingly improvised in its heroic spirit. After a high cabriole with the back toward the public, the dancer suddenly turns to face to the public. You cannot do this figure without masculine energy or the pathos of an animal-like elemental force, especially if there is no preparation. Legat, after all, prepared his rivoltade for a female dancer.

. . .

There are several general situations that introduce a biomechanical foundation into the terminology of classical dance. In the choreographic culture of the Greeks, en tournant was especially popular. All the bends of the curved line, the entire philosophy of life's fractures, the strength of the performer are marvelously reflected in the technique of en tournant. You stand facing a person, en face, and his impression of you is solid and powerful. He may be disturbed by the expression on your face, but his impression is free of vague anxiety. However, turn sideways to that person, either on the ground or in circular flight, whipping his soul with your profile, and you create a harsh, unexpected perception. All Greece was somehow completely en tournant. Those passionate cambrés of the body in the marvelous works of sculpture, in the reliefs and in the vase paintings, contain an undoubtedly special expressive power precisely in their curved turns and en tournant. In the effects of en tournant Aspasia* had no competitors. And in general male and female Hellenic beauty, thanks to the culture of complete and partial circular revolutions, had to produce such an irresistible dramatic impression. In life there was no geometric circle, with its supremely soothing sensations, but there was a rotary movement either via the entire torso or via the body's individual parts, with a lively and spirited expression. . . .

These are the currents of rotary movements, with their contrasting ideas in the contemporary combinations of classic ballet. Contemporary ballet is heir to these great tendencies bequeathed by the Greco-Roman world, whose basic tendencies are not united but contrasting and dialectic. In later centuries this inheritance found its reflection in the French genius, which significantly softened all that was sharp and harsh in the conflict of ancient currents, providing the classical culture of dance with a touch of mannered elegance and sentimental sugariness. Circles on our ballet stage are no longer Italian or Etruscan, and en tournant is not authentically and completely Hellenic. The remarkable technique of our primary sources turned out to be constrained in corsets and farthingales of the early and late rococo, during which the fresh and pure classical delights had evaporated and in large part dispersed. Thus the idea of the circle was deprived of its unattainable poetry, and movement en tournant of its attractive and hypnotizing artistry. And it was in this belittled, diluted, and syrupy form we apprehended the ancient legacy through France. With rare exceptions, circles on our stages are weak and imperfect, and en tournant is constantly reduced to unpleasant, mannered rhetoric, even among our wonderful dancers, of whom there are fewer and fewer on our stages. . . .

    . . .

The Clock's Chimes

    . . .

Despite a course of study that lasts several years, few artists master the essence and technique of rotary movement to perfection. If the adagio as a whole exposes the plastic individuality of the dancer, then precisely this part of it, the pirouette, underscores its gravitation toward ultimate completeness.

---

*Aspasia was the mistress of the fifth-century B.C. Athenian statesman Pericles and a leading figure of Athenian society.

Everything else in the adagio can be done with a slackened interest of the will, with an idle pathos of the passing mood—only the pirouette requires the careful, conscious use of all the means at the dancer's disposal, not only choreographic but psychological. Here the essence of the female dancer radiates, and the dance enters into the moving frame of the circle. For some dancers, especially the most gifted, the pirouette often does not come off in the center of the exercise room. The person lacks the impulse toward genuine force, and her apperception is not aroused, not put into place by the necessity of the invocatory moment. But on the stage, amid the play of the diverse energies and rising currents emanating from the hall, the dancer suddenly finds internal and external strength. She pierces her eyes at a specific point in space and, bracing the floor with her toes and imparting to her back the necessary aplomb, she gives herself up to a circular eruption with all the energy allocated to it. But the opposite also occurs. The pirouette works in the exercise room and ends in a lamentable fiasco on the stage.

There is no need to describe all the parts of the adagio. It too develops as one studies further, combining all the forms of opening and unfolding of the body. The soft, open battement in all its forms constitutes the prevailing motive that passes even through the pirouette's finale. One can say that this is the chain of all the various développés gathered by the magnificent garland for this individual figure.

There are dancers who are specially endowed with the capacity for these développés, if their legs—long, shapely, classically formed, with a successfully animated instep—are extended with the proper skill and beauty. The idea that the absolute fullness of the dancer's talent manifests itself here is exaggerated. It is not talent exactly that is revealed in the adagio but the dancer's plantlike essence, which can be vividly expressed even in a person who lacks talent. Nonetheless, we must admit that while they are not instruments for discovering talent, the qualities of battement are still decisive in determining the student's suitability for classical dance because they represent the condition for achieving its main goal—to discover and expand one's choreographic essence.

One figure in the adagio in particular attracts our attention. Having done a grand battement forward in a flowing and undulating tempo, the dancer sometimes throws herself into the arms of her partner with extended, closed legs. This figure still does not have a special name. I would call it "arrested clock chimes." The chimes of life, having just struck their hour, have stopped, and their hand lies motionless. This is the languor of fantastic love and its momentary pacification. Rare is the success of such a figure onstage. Frozen in semi-oblivion, the body is saturated with an inner movement and breathes with the memory of the past. These arrested chimes represent a kind of arabesque extended along the floor and contain within themselves all the features, all the peculiarities of the remarkable figure of the choreographic prologue to every-thing that follows. Having regained her breath, the dancer must lift herself from the arms of her partner with the face of a newborn creature, passing from the closed life of a chrysalis to the more active, though still fantastic, life of an intelligent, animal being.

In the fairy-tale tempest of movements the characteristic of plantlike pas-sivity and plantlike dream never disappears, no matter how high the dancer ascends or how widely she spreads on the currents of the par-terre dancing. The chimes continually beat and stop, small bells ring and die out. These bells sing in the garden and are constantly drowned out by the grass- and flowerlike rustlings of the surrounding flora. This is exactly what adagio is in classical ballet. Everything sings, everything rejoices, everything whistles with the songs of nightingales. The music keeps humming in the high registers of violins. But all this is clothed in the smoky veil of dreams, everything disperses and melts while at the same time retaining the outlines of a majestic monument. The scale is grandiose both in its construction and its deconstruction. The clouds rush and float in heaven's endless vault.

. . .

Postscript

Such is the general type of adagio in our delineation. The students collect their physical and choreographic energy in order to enter with it into the final part of their classroom exercise—the allegro. In the allegro we shall encounter new motifs of dance, both on the floor and in elevation, which provide mate-rial for scenic variations and codas. In general one needs to say that taken as a whole the exercises at the barre and in the middle of the classroom contain all the elements of ballet, not only of classical dance in the narrow sense but of character and genre-historical dance, woven with the ancient forms into one bouquet.

. . .

Allegro

❧⚬❀⚬❧

. . .

Leap, Jump, Flight

We should not confuse these three words, which are often used interchangeably in our everyday language. In the science of ballet we are dealing with different subjects and with different types of movements that have different characters. Let us start with the leap. A leap is the separation of the body from the ground by means of transferring the torso from one foot to the other. The impulse and energy of the movement are scattered, and they contain qualities of equilibrium and throwing over. The leap itself must be strong, captivating, calculated, and purposeful, aimed precisely at a specific point of landing. In this aspect the man's leap is especially typical, and at times it is extremely beautiful. A youngster leaps over a ditch. Inhaling a stream of air before his leap and then hurling himself from the ground, he directs all his energy to the leg that is extended forward before preparing to fall firmly onto it. There is something attractive, captivating, and seductive in such exercises. One can sit for hours on the Lido in Venice admiring the leaps of the young boys who throw themselves in the water, at times with a substantial push-off, at others from a high diving board. The momentary period in the air has a magnetic effect on the spectator. What precisely captures the onlooker in the psychological point of the object? A human being is so steadfastly and indissolubly subordinate to the earth's gravity, so passively dependent on it, that even his momentary emancipation from it produces a magical impression. This is the root of all those delights and irrepressible raptures that accompany all the feats and all the triumphs of elevation. Without realizing it, the public is applauding the victory over the inert forces of nature, over the soul's free outpouring of will, which rejoices in the cries of the heart in the impulse to leave and fly off from the ground. A dancer without elevation, with only the beauty of her par-terre dancing, can never be compared in this respect with the aerial dancer, who with one leap along the stage in wide and extended flight suddenly carries the entire hall with her. Indeed, we stand here before genuine sorcery.

. . . In the very word *leap* there is already praise, a certain dithyramb of classical elevation, which the Greeks valued as did no other nation on earth. This Pelasgian-Achaean mixture of brawlers, mercenary traders, swindlers, and crooks were able to burn with enthusiasm and at great historical moments glide over the earth. Homer describes a national ballgame. Throwing the ball, a youth soars into the air and does not come down to earth until he catches it. That's a leap and a ballon that could be the object of national pride. There we have not a dialectical babbler or a mercenary tradesman but a hero and winner of the marathon. How beautiful and significant this is! One needs to leap according to the following unwavering method: first you leap in your soul and then in space—that must be the order in teaching and practice.

What is a jump? It is the body's parting from the ground with both legs, with a single simultaneous deep breath. This is how the jump differs substantially from the leap, which is produced with one leg and has a disconnected character. The jump is compact, limited to itself, and ties the whole body into a kind of invisible coat of mail. And from its tightness depends the entire impression that it creates. In its energetic form the jump appears beautiful and expressive in men's dancing. If one does a large takeoff (pas de poisson) with the torso curved, as the French dancer François Montessu did in his day, one can create an enormous impression: like a playful dolphin darting out of the water. A person flies in the bend of the crescent moon, in a gentle semicircle, freezing in the air for several moments. The freezing cambré is enchanting. You have the same thing here as you do in elevation: there is an element of struggle and seeming protest. Everything naturally strives to become straight or round, but here via internal ballon the deeply felt curvature retards its fatal disappearance. Such effects in nature and in art are perceived at the same time both depressingly and enthusiastically—with a wrenching exaltation worthy of classical dance in its essence and in its heroic air. Much is achieved but at the price of great and self-destructive transcendence. The effects of the classical jump— limited, integral, focused—are all provided naturally in the jump's very possibilities. . . . David prays and jumps. Saul rejoices and jumps. It is precisely written—"he jumps"—and it is written wonderfully. Here we have upward flight for the sake of upward flight, ascent for the sake of ascent, not for some extraneous practical goal. "Where there is dancing, there is jumping," say the Russian folk. We have here aimless jumping, but the kind that gratifies the heart. Similarly, nature makes merry in the spring, and young lambs merrily jump over the bright green grass of meadows. Horses clear hurdles by jumping. Religious zealots of various persuasions jump fanatically, for example Muslim dervishes who drive themselves to complete and oblivious ecstasy.

What, then, is a leap? To fly means to rush through the air, to sail in airy space. Rushing and sailing already require a more or less protracted sojourn on high. Birds fly; that is, for hours on end they remain in an airy environment. We say "a ship flies at full sail." By this we want to say that the sails, like wings, carry the ship almost over the watery expanse. "A daring troika is flying"; of course this is only an allegory which represents the insane racing of the troika along an open plain with a kind of upward flight above the snowy haze. "Time flies," "the years fly by"—these expressions marvelously convey the unimpeded rush of the elements forward, as well as their momentary respite at separate points in the air. If the leap's culminating moment contains a certain dead or lifeless point, then it turns into a flight. Flight needs ballon: the ability not only to freeze in the air, leaping upward from the tension of the elastic plié, but to live in it by means of the diverse motifs of classical dance. The choreographic plié seems to prolong its existence over the ground. Everything that happens on the floor is repeated on high. All earthly reality rises by means of elevation upward and ballon that is born in plié, and it is sustained at the point that has been reached. Such is flight. The jump and the leap constitute elements of flight if they contain ballon.

The phenomena we have analyzed—leap, jump, and flight—which are hardly noticed in our everyday routine, acquire a special significance in ballet. Here they occur and are perceived with all possible awareness, calculation, and intention; they constitute the standard and the limit of diverse temperaments, talents, and artistic personalities. Some male or female dancers can jump, but they cannot leap. One can have both jump and leap but not flight—that is, there is no elevation in the real sense of the word. Another has vivid ballon but not a large leap or jump. And let us note that it is precisely ballon that plays the preeminent role in classical choreography and in the overall assessment of talent, and that compensates for shortcomings in other areas. Kshesinskaya did not have a high jump or leap. But her ballon was extraordinary and allowed her to achieve great effects in complicated beats even though she was not very high in the air.

Earth and Sky

All dances on the floor are repeated in the air. In elevation we do not have anything we would not have in promenade or in par-terre dances, except elevation itself and ballon. Let us begin with five basic positions: we find all these elementary positions both on the floor and in the air. In the air they are transient, lacking the tempo of a protracted stop in one moment of the dancing or another. There is a magnificent aerial equivalent to dance on pointe. As soon as the dancer departs from the floor he must arch his instep and turn his pointed toes earthward. With their points the toes look downward, as if they were standing on the floor. Such is the principle of dancing in the air. This is a remarkable phenomenon. The idea of verticality, as absolute as possible, never disappears for a moment from classical choreography, even when the dancing is embellished by the elements of ecstasy and aerial whirling. The instep is still arched. The toes look down. The landing on the floor soon occurs and—still unrealized—places the body in a position required by classical dance. The element of elevation contains no departures from the general principle of classical art, equally intrinsic to both elements, to earth and sky. The sky here is only the aerial reflection or transformation of the earth. The dance on the floor must be gently plantlike and pliant. This is achieved by bending the legs in all possible positions, the bending being called plié. In plié, as we already know, all the basic motifs of inspired biomechanics are gathered together. If a dancer has no plié, it means that his art lacks genuine vitality. In the air this symbol of vitality is called ballon. If elevation lacks ballon, the dance is deprived of those properties which make the aerial leaps, jumps, rotary movements, and all the moving along the steep, high arc artistic phenomena and not simply a case of flinging oneself from one place to another, from the earth to the heights. Without the pneumatic echo of earthly plié we have a leap, or a jump, or some kind of venture en tournant, but not ecstatic flight.

Let us move on. All rotations of the leg are repeated in the air, and the rotations of the female leg retain the plantlike and gently plastic traits which are inherent in it.

In male dancing this fundamental choreographic element—ballon—sparkles with an instantaneous brilliance and acrobatism, that very acrobatism which is the necessary ingredient of every heroic movement. To throw oneself at high altitude across a trapeze or suddenly to hang on it in midair by one's firm and strong fingers—here are woven together two elements of male dancing, minimally plastic and maximally acrobatic. But the crowd, which is sensitive to higher truths, wildly applauds the acrobatism as the courageous overcoming of material difficulties. The acrobat should never disappear in the dancer, appearing each time in him in the critical moments of his art transformed and aesthetically transmuted. Various ronds de jambe in the air, losing their plantlike quality in the hues of the poetic Flora in the cavalier, gain in sparkle, force, and animation.

Proceeding further. There is no battement executed on the ground that could not be performed in elevation. Simple battements without the extending of the leg, especially beaten battements, come off magnificently in the air in male dancers. Beaten battements in general are the main feature of heroic male dancing. On it are based all the cabrioles, all the forms of entrechat, all the beats which sparkle with emotion and resoluteness. These are energetically reworked petits battements that are performed in the exercise class as a preparation for beats high in the air. But if the battement is combined with the extension of the leg, with the motif of unfolding and gentle evolution, then its execution becomes the property of female dancing. Aerial développé is the authentic picture in plastic art of the female dancer. No one who saw Trefilova will ever forget this battement; she provided the classically perfect image of the Swan in Tchaikovsky's ballet. She did développé in the arms of a partner like Legat, swiftly drawing out her leg and moving it to the side in a palpitating and undulating movement, with short but evident respites at every half measure. Although this artist was by nature devoid of elevation, she achieved exceptionally beautiful results with the support of her partner and through sheer stubbornness of will.

I will not speak of Pavlova's remarkable battement. This genius of the stage extracts things from her art, with all the special significance that *extracts* has here. Pavlova's head veritably breaks forth from the surrounding chaos into the light and air. Her hands dance and fly undulatingly upward in a transport of wild ecstasy. One need only recall her famous variation in *Don Quixote,* where, almost with her arms alone, she conveys the whole range, the entire music of the sweet and dreamlike mood via hands that float one after the other as they open up to the sky. Pavlova's entire torso always leaps forth from a furled croisé, communicating curvature and erectness to the back with extraordinary psychological animation. What is remarkable in the fact that the artist's développé is notable for its peculiar harmony? Her enormous talent, which palpitates, undulates, and displays itself like a dazzling diamond, continually strikes us with the ever new shafts of light that emanate from it.

There is no need to enumerate all the movements on the ground that are repeated in the air, but we must recall some of them. Aerial attitudes and arabesques sometimes produce a fascinating impression. In male dancing the attitude constitutes only a transitional stage to the concluding arabesque on the floor. Such an attitude does not carry independent weight here. But in the woman's execution we have all the charms of the transition of the broken line to a straight one, accompanied by the beautiful curves of the back. Aerial assemblés are ordinarily performed only en tournant. The leaps forward—erect or with a rotation high in the air—are beautiful, as are all forms of jumps, especially those produced specifically in elevation. The beautiful glissade resembles the leap of a cat. In some dancers glissade does not call particular attention to itself: it does not rustle or lie on the floor in a silky way. But in the air this glissade suddenly gains and blossoms, acquiring a harmonious musical quality. Such was Elena Liukom's pas de chat. She soared and extended herself forward in a priceless aerial glissade, and her small figure seemed justified in its size. But on the floor her glissade passed unnoticed—perhaps precisely because her short leg was unable to produce the effect of sufficient gliding force.

Female dancers perform pas de bourrée on the floor. But this alternation of the legs, transferred in the air, acquires the character of a special entrechat, called royale. Indeed, we have here the repetition of the same movements. At first the leg is cast simply to the side and then it returns in beats to its original position, which quickly gives place to a shift to another place—forward or backward, depending on where the coupé is done. But all forms of entrechat are only variations of cabrioles executed in quick tempo. In the same way we can execute ballotté, ballonné, and various other figures equally on the floor and in the air for, to repeat, all par-terre and promenadelike movements find their reflection in the air. There is nothing new, unexpected, or alien in comparison with the poetry and prose of the earth. The earth is in the heavens, as it had presented itself to Copernicus. All the matter of reality is in Kant's dialectical expression. All is the same—one little scrap, one coarse clod of earth. But in this scrap, in this clod are contained all the perspectives, all the expanses, all the possibilities, and all the plans and forms of perception. This is what classical elevation is in its essential foundations. Be on the ground as you are in the sky, be in the sky as you are on the ground. Only change your breathing: either narrow or expand your diaphragm in order to inhale and exhale the greatest amount of air!

Only the pirouette in its pure form, in its geometrical design, with its fixed leg of support, is unrepeatable in the air. It rests upon its axis, inseparable from the earth—stationary in its motion, round and perfect in its curvature, nature's only absolute en tournant. In the air we cannot have the kind of pirouette we do on the floor. Instead of the pirouette classical choreography gives us here all the variety of en tournant. However, the striving toward pirouettelike rotation, which we observe in several animals, leads to a kind of whirling, which we observe in sparrows and doves, especially among tumbler pigeons. All these creatures rotate in a kind of pirouette, occasionally like the tumbler pigeon reaching genuine virtuosity. But still it is not really a pirouette if a bird, as it rotates, lifts off the ground. It does not possess a clearly defined, stable attachment to any point, and its rotating movement merely looks like a pirouette. With regard to a human being, in the absence of any support he definitely cannot transfer rotary movements in the air to the category of pirouette. He has nothing on which to gain a foothold in order to describe a real circle.

Such are the terrestrial and superterrestrial essences in classical ballet which flow into one another.

Beats

The simplest leap in ballet is called jeté. This is the throwing of the body from one leg to the other. In this throw there is force and gust. With ballon this is not an ordinary leap but a flight along or across the stage. Its technique is very simple. Suppose the dancer is standing in fifth position. After doing a demi-plié, he draws out the leg that stands behind into aerial position. This is battement. After this there is a push up into the air, and the leg, which has done a battement, lands on the floor, taking on itself the body's entire weight. For completeness and roundness of design the back leg can be drawn sur le cou-de-pied. This is the ordinary jeté done in various directions. Such jeté can represent many varieties depending on the character of the battement and the sometimes ornamental, sometimes substantial movements which accompany it. It is done forward with the extension of the leg, with the leg thrown over the other in aerial revolution, with beats, straight, and en tournant.

Jeté is usually enhanced by several circular figures that give it substantial artistic content. Thus you can finish a leap assemblé en tournant on the floor. One feels in this throwing of the body a sharpness and force that are expressed in the movements of the hip joint, which is strained and then released. You can do a jeté in combination with a small pirouette en dehors: the circle always brings into the leap's movement a fullness and finished quality of the choreographic unit. Pas de bourrée, done en tournant at the conclusion of the leap, furnishes it with a quality of graceful and playful energy. Finally, jeté is beautifully completed if one adds to it a fouetté en tournant and a concluding coupé. In all these forms jeté bears an exclusively feminine character for the leap itself here is too low for male dancing. Everywhere this is fundamentally a throwing, saturated with energy and willful striving, which is lovely both in the man's and the woman's execution. Onstage jeté can sometimes be especially captivating when performed by a talented female dancer—shaped by willful effort, there is still a hint of natural grace which is as lovely and eloquent in the air as it is on the floor. Thus what is sometimes essentially a male movement is, when rendered by the female, arrayed with a charm that is inherent in human flora; as a whole, this has an intoxicating effect on the eyes. . . .

Jeté can also be done with a beat. If the leg, as it moves from its position, strikes the calf of the other leg in the front and in the back we have a beat: a beaten battement on the path of a dance movement. What happens to the choreographic figure with such a beaten battement? The jump remains without any particular changes. But there is a new element—a beaten battement, produced once or repeated many times, pouring forth in the air in diamond-like sparks. Here is what has been added to the leap: the leap could have been a mechanical movement from one spot to another, but it has become a flight that is sustained in an elevated ballon within the movement. The leap could have remained in its pure impulse without any complications, like the spirit's cry against a specific goal. But now it has encircled itself with the recurring masculine battements, speeding through the air in the instantaneous space of time, barely enough for its task. Beats finalize the heroicization of the entire movement. They introduce a heroic element into the performance, taking away the energy needed for ballon and sacrificing it in disinterested acrobatics.

This is a phenomenon analogous to fouetté in the pirouette, which also bursts into the perfect clarity of execution, requiring additional efforts to maintain a stationary axis. In both cases there is real choreographic heroism, by which the exultant motif of the dance, on the floor and in the air, is emphasized with special boldness. In both instances we are dealing with an acrobatic technique that constitutes the framework of the heroic deed onstage. In the circus we observe many leaps, which at times are insanely courageous. There are leaps across a long row of chairs. A man hurtles himself across tens of heads, sometimes accompanying this leap with a salto mortale movement. But we never see any beats here. Acrobatism is an ingredient of heroism but not its pure artistic form. In ballet, however, beats, especially in male dancing, play an exceptional role. They are disinterested by virtue of the absence of a practical goal and exist only in the name of affecting beauty. By their nature beats are not the property of female aerial dancing, and if they turn out to be beautiful in specific women dancers, then we really have an exception to the general rule. Even Pavlova could not manage to do the small beat, the simple and double brisé, entrechat, and royale, with sufficient precision. It was not in her beats that the power of her astonishing talent came out. In a grotesque dance depicting a Parisian apache, Pavlova could suddenly touch our senses, completely transforming into a street thug. But soaring in the air, she abandoned all likeness to a male spirit and captivated you only by the poetry of her exalted movement. Kshesinskaya, with her powerful ballon, could excite the audience with her almost masculine beats, lifting herself not very high off the floor. Saying that a woman can do male beats is rare praise for her.

How do you do jeté with a beat? Feet in fifth position, right one behind. Demi-plié. Battement of right leg à la seconde. The leap is on this right leg, during which it hits the left one from the front. The leap concludes with the landing on the right leg, with the left leg sur le cou-de-pied. The technique is of the ordinary jeté, but the beat, although it is a single one without multiple repetitions, gives it the look and force of a blatantly acrobatic figure. Female dancers frequently perform leaps without beats. But it befits the male dancer to accompany practically his every leap with a beat.

What is a jeté en tournant? Let us take the large leap with the throwing over of the body in the air, which produces an enormous impression on the spectator. Feet are in fifth position. Glissade backward with the left leg, bringing the right one up to it. After this the left leg, slightly raised, strikes the floor, that is, it produces the first act of coupé. Immediately after this the other leg responds reflexively, producing the second act of choreographic coupé. Straight and erect, it is thrust forward without any circle. This is a sweep of the leg for flight.

After this comes the turning in the air, which ends with the landing on the right leg. The left leg, passing by the right closely alongside, is extended in a strict arabesque. This is a jeté entrelace with en tournant that is animated and filled with fire and temperament. But in the forefront is the jeté itself among the curved, wavy lines that emphasize and single it out. Everything performed onstage in revolution shows the dance movement in its dynamic curve, especially if it provides the revolution itself—a flight en tournant—with a bold and decisive beat. Everything becomes more prominent, loud, and even clamorous precisely because, when rotating, not only the legs but also the body of the dancer work: the head, torso, eyes, back, and arms. The curved lines and the powerful cambré in the brilliant whirlwind of the beats entwine the basic figure with jingling chains, and carry it boldly and dauntlessly forward.

. . .

Let us move on to jumps. They also are divided into pure jumps, jumps with beats, straight jumps, and en tournant.

Sissonne (Sisol)

Jumps in balletic language are called sissonnes or sisoles. *Sisol* is a distorted form of the French *sissonne,* which signifies an ancient dance with two successive assemblés. Nowadays this word, when used in ballet, signifies a jump with both legs landing on one leg. In each jump we have two parts: takeoff and landing. Takeoff from both legs is called soubresaut. Every sissonne begins with a soubresaut, carried high with as large a ballon as possible. Sometimes in this soubresaut a whole figure is created, and the longer it remains in the air, held up by ballon, the more beautiful and perfect it is. In *Giselle* the dancer goes in a diagonal across the stage toward the cross, doing consecutive soubresauts with gently flowing arms. I cannot recollect any fully satisfactory soubresauts except Pavlova's. She stretched forward, undulating her marvelous arms, focusing her eyes onto a single point and lifting herself from the floor with delicate smoothness, as if drawn to the cross. We have a similarly remarkable soubresaut in *Swan Lake* in the famous adagio of the second scene. Here there are three moments that must be distinguished for their clarity of execution. The moment of soubresaut into the arms of the partner, the moment of gentle battement, and the moment of lowering one leg onto the floor for the realization of full sissonne. In soubresaut it is ballon, which is only highlighted by the partner's support, that constitutes the main spring.

Jumps are done with extended, straight legs. This is what the French school requires, as opposed to the Italian school, where the legs are at the back, usually bent, in a Harlequinesque manner, which gives the movement a slightly grotesque character in the spirit of the old commedia dell'arte. Generally speaking, by their nature jumps are not bravura, aggressive, or adventuresome in space. They are rather monotonous and fixed in their unique design. If a pushoff and a flying forward, or in general any choreographic prelude, are intended for the jump, then sissonne occurs, is executed, and concludes in one originating moment, devoid of comic effect. But Italy tends more toward sensational, impulsive, and capricious jumps that express willful energy than to the more muted jumps, which are so much less demonstrative and expansive. Performing them, Italian dancers indulge themselves with their favorite broken design resembling attitude.

The technique of these figures is the most common. Let us take the figure popular in class exercises—changement de pieds. Stand with the body in fifth position. Bend the legs in demi-plié. Jump up with a change of the feet in the air. Land on the floor, with a new, small plié, in the same fifth position. Then immediately straighten out the legs. This is a basic rule of classical dance. You cannot prolong any bending of the body longer than the time for which it is calculated. The goal of the plié is only to flicker, to flash, and to spread like fragrant oil over the body, not to stiffen in a protracted tempo. The final goal of any dance and any class exercise is erectness or roundness, which completes the curved and broken lines. In the same spirit, so-called échappé—throwing the legs to second position—is executed. Fifth position. Demi-plié. Jump and open legs to second position. Change legs and take them to the original position by means of the new jump.

In this simple design you do both small sissonnes in effacé and in croisé and large sissonnes with the picturesque extension of the leg, and with the conclusion of the entire figure with a marvelous velvety glissade failli to fourth position. This last sissonne is particularly beautiful and monumental, and if it has plantlike plastic elements it produces an endearing impression when executed by a woman. The entire figure unfolds in bright, gentle movements. Here we have a soubresaut with ballon, the swift outlines of an undulating battement, and the rustling and coquettish movement of the leg gliding along the floor. All these elements in the woman's dance can be molded into a perfect form which is inaccessible to the man's execution. No matter how plastic, gentle, and graceful the male dancer is, he cannot be compared in this respect with the female dancer, the natural possessor of all of these external and internal qualities.

The pas de chat begins with the same soubresaut. For this charming and purely feminine figure, both legs must bend back one after another in half attitude and at the last moment retain the design of the original position. As I noted above, by its very nature the pas de chat contains in itself something glissadelike. Doing a pas de chat means lifting the glissade in the air. Liukom used to be distinguished by the beautiful way she executed this figure. But I remember that she did not perform these jumps very precisely, with the half attitudes, and thus her pas de chat often deteriorated into a distorted pas de basque. Yet her execution contained a breathtaking gracefulness, and her figure appeared excellent.

This is the character and technique of sissonne, without any complexities and without being embellished by any special ornamental qualities. But in general nothing is done in leaps and in elevation without the participation of complicating details. Any simple sissonne ouverte is usually accompanied by the rotation of the leg—otherwise it will seem too prosaic and dry. The tendency to do beats is rooted in the nature of leaps and jumps. We have seen échappé. By itself, it is not distinguished by its beauty: at times it even seems comic. In Petipa's humorous ballets it is encountered rather often. But if échappé, the bold throwing open of the legs, is adorned with a beat front and back, and if the jump is executed here as high as possible, one gets a magnificent figure—strong, glittering, and sparkling, especially in the male's execution.

And the beat is generally designed primarily for masculine strength. In women's dancing you cannot have such strength or concentrated pathos, which are needed particularly in jumps. Female dancers certainly perform jumps as decisively as do male dancers, except tours in the air. But their jumps are not free of a certain affectation. In the male's execution, jumps which are supplied with beats, intertwined with ropelike plaiting and executed in an atmosphere of acrobatic heroism, produce an amazingly rich impression. The legs are extended and straight, in the spirit of the French gallant tradition. These brilliant sparks play quickly and animatedly in entrechat, in brisé, in leaps and beats, in sissonnes with beats because in the forefront we have not the leap or jump but precisely this element—the heroicization of dance in the air. In entrechat, in brisé, in leaps with beats, in sissonnes with beats, in flights en tournant with beats, in brisé fondu with beats at random a similar beauty opens up before us: the beauty of the beaten battement, which turns movements into a heroic poem.

Entrechat

Entrechat constitutes a special kind of jump. First we need to discard one misunderstanding. Entrechat has nothing in common with pas de chat. There half attitudes play a predominant role, whereas here there is no bending—all is vertical, extended, and straight. The name *entrechat* is a distortion of the Italian word *intrecciata*. In these instances when one entrechat or another is done onstage, the Italians call them *capriola intrecciata*—complex and intricate cabrioles, which completely conform to the spirit of the entire figure. We have here the consecutive beating of one leg against the other on the model of the classical cabriole. This is a goat's kick, taken from the orchestra of Greek tragedy, from ancient satire. Even now in the theater we still have preserved the genesis of this dance and this jump. If entrechat is performed with an even number of beats, the legs, when falling, remain on the ground; with uneven beats, one of them hangs in the air. If an uneven number of beats is done not in jumps but in leaps, then in the finale the legs always appear together on the floor because preceding the leap is a battement which is counted in the overall number of beats.

Petipa was able magnificently to produce the dances of satyrs and fauns. They perform complex goatlike leaps and jumps, with bent knees, for comic effect, and with numerous beats. In the last act of *Le Roi Candaule,** Petipa provides an excellent example of entrechat for the part of the satyr. A pas de trois takes place with the participation of Diana, Endymion, and the satyr. This variation was choreographed for the first time for Vera Nikitina. Nikolai Legat danced Endymion, and Lidiya Kyaksht played the satyr. As a whole and in its particulars, this was something quite remarkable. Nikitina displayed a classical step and a lissome plastique, a swift and brilliant technique. Whatever inadequacy of elevation, the dancer made up for it with her ballon and its capricious lines. In the adagio Legat demonstrated such sensitive, hazardous lift that the audience was frozen in rapture. In the wings Petipa, raising his eyebrows and removing his pince-nez, followed the dancing with an expression of both fear and approval on his face. Dancing her grotesque number, Kyaksht shocked the public with her aerial revolutions, her circles with bent body, and the ropelike plaitings of her endless beats. There was something really classical, which the brilliant choreographer intuited and the dancers embodied onstage.

Batteries have a clearly expressed masculine character. The woman's plant-like plastique is not completely at home here. We have seen that Pavlova's leaps, jumps, and sissonnes lacked a truly artistic beat. Her heroicism was conveyed by different choreographic means, by the general clamor of her dancing. Kshesinskaya's beats deviated from the French model and emphasized the Italian technique. Her knees were bent in the swift tempo of the movement, but the beats nevertheless produced a great impression on the public. Preobrazhenskaya's beats were similar to Pavlova's: gentle, feeble, weakly and unheroically attractive. Vaganova's beats approached the masculine kind. Karsavina's were better than Pavlova's but worse than Vaganova's. Her legs were not extended in a straight line and contained traces of impermissible rotation around the axis. Carlotta Zambelli performed beats in the Italian way—all of them, including the typically masculine beat: entrechat sept devant and en tournant.

---

*A ballet in four acts choreographed by Petipa with music by Cesare Pugni.

But absolutely the best beats I have ever seen on the ballet stage were those of Mikhail Obukhov. He did them randomly, brisé; he did every kind of entrechat and sissonne with amazing perfection, emphasizing throughout the cabriole motif of the beaten battement. As the Bluebird, Obukhov was at the peak of virtuosity. He proceeded along the diagonal downstage, jokingly swinging his torso, splashing like brilliant rain on the ground. This is entrechat in all its manifestations. The character of beats in jumps can be studied in entrechats in great detail. With a good saubresaut with ballon, as Kshesinskaya possessed it, one can do numerous beats at a low level. Elevation itself, the height of the takeoff, plays a secondary role here. The swift technique of beats, accompanied each time by a resolute coupé, appears with unusual vividness and in addition with clear-cut and precisely alternating movements. . . .

En tournant occurs more rarely in jumps than in leaps. It presents great difficulty because of the necessity of lifting oneself off the ground immediately with both legs. Any kind of soubresaut with a complete revolution in the air to some extent constitutes an act of tightrope walking. The most common en tournant is in the so-called tours in the air, which are executed only by the men. The revolution here is produced at full scale according to the rule explained above that when the axis of rotation passes through the entire body a complete rotation can be accomplished. When the axis of rotation is located in a part of the body, a complete rotation becomes impossible.

Here is the change of the legs en tournant. The movement begins with a forceful and resolute jump. The more energy, height, and ballon, the more perfect the jump. After it springs up, the body does one or several revolutions, depending on the talent and endurance of the male dancer. These turns, in contrast to pirouettes, are called tours. I have never seen three revolutions or three tours onstage. The usual number of tours does not exceed two, and if they are done purely, swiftly, and with appropriate steadiness, they produce, in the landing on the floor, a brilliant masculine figure. There is an element of pirouette here—the circle, which is the ideal form of the curved line— but the change of the legs and a vertical extension upward give the movement the special character of purely masculine resoluteness. It is interesting to ask why women do not do tours. The answer is rather simple. A woman can soar in leaps and jumps, she can do the most different beats, although this is not characteristic of her nature, but to take off straight up and thereupon perform a revolution constitutes first and foremost an act of exceptional strength, and thus is primarily a masculine one. Even the expression "tour de force" entered the European languages as an idea about something extremely straining that requires a robust male virtuosity.

Tours are formed in three stages: a straight movement upward, a circular rotation, and a distinct change of the legs in the air. In all of these movements the axis is mobile and support is absent. But this absence of the support of the trunk in the rotary movement deprives the figure of any plantlike character and thus removes its feminineness. Such tours, even if we were to introduce them into female performance, would not be attractive and would only serve as an irritant to the eyes. A jump or leap without support does not contradict the art of female dancing, as do many other of the animal-vegetal movements produced on the floor or in the air. But rotation without axis established on the ground and without a stationary foundation represents precisely the kind of acrobatism in which the plantlike element is completely excluded and where the spirit of male heroism comes to the fore. It is through acrobatics that the dividing line between the two elements of dance in ballet, the male and the female, passes.

The Line Upward

. . . In leaps, jumps, and flight a person is transformed. The earthy movement is transferred into a supernatural one, into poetic exaltation. There are various nuances here, but none of them obscures the main issue: the movement of the person revealing his essence along a line upward. It is distinctive in the various temps d'élévation, but its overall type—in men and in women—evokes no doubts. Everything moves upward in triumphant enthusiasm. Breathing expands more and more. In the thematic unity of the dance in all its figures and elements the increasing heroic motif predominates, placing a large barrier between the two representations of choreographic art. The woman's heroism never loses the quality of gentle plasticity. It smells of the forest, of plants, and of flowers. The fragrant wafting of flora accompanies the female dancer's every step—on the ground and in the air. Male heroism is entirely active, rapid, and aggressive. Beats play an exceptional role here, and bold revolutions in leaps, which require not only elevation but also ballon, sometimes produce a stunning impression. Entrechat sept along a diagonal in Samuil Andriyanov's execution, with aerial en tournant that ended in a dauntless arabesque, gripped the audience, riveting them with a feeling of rapture. This is how the elements of the male and female dance are differentiated from one another.

Yet despite their differences, all these elements nonetheless float together in the heroic waves of the overall animation. One of the greatest secrets of higher anthropology is affirmed here. A person is born a unisexual being. But in one degree or another in a single person there exist traits of the other sex. A man affects tenderness and smiles gently like a woman at various times in his life. A woman constantly feels in herself surges of masculine feelings and an aggressiveness of will beyond what is normal for her. All of this echoes a person's primordial, unified nature, which has come to us in the fragmented process of history only in shreds and shards. In the creative process of the world man has appeared primarily as a bisexual being, and the feature of androgyny is inescapable in him as an image of a past perfection and as a supreme goal for the future. This future goal rustles in our bones and is felt in the ecstatic moments of our greatest animation. It sometimes seems that even in our everyday reality the boundary between the two sexes has been effaced and life flows somewhere in the distance in a single harmonious current. But this distance is high up. We feel this in the great social movements which suddenly equalize men and women. Here man himself gives birth to new forms of life, while woman impregnates the elevated essence of events with her active participation and sensibility. And everything is at the top, everything is on high, in life as in art.

The line of dance is carried upward.

Technique

All the steps analyzed thus far belong to the third part of the exercise, in the center of the classroom, to the category of allegro. In our fleeting overview several classical forms have not received detailed explanation, so we need to attend to some trifles in order for our study of the subject to attain completeness. I have spoken of leaps, but I have not noted the technical similarity between two steps: the simple jeté and the assemblé. The structure of jeté is the same as assemblé—only their conclusions are different. In jeté we have primary battement tendu, the opening of the body on the floor. The second movement is plié—the preparation of the spring for takeoff, in proportion with the goals and available means for elevation and ballon. Then there is takeoff with a clicking motion upward that is called flic. Upon completion of takeoff the landing on the foot which has made a flic is pas tombé. For the completion of the entire step in a gentle plantlike design it is necessary to have a new plié and a momentary spring onto the toes, with the leg sur le cou-de-pied. Without exception these movements are repeated in assemblés, except the last one: in assemblé the feet are brought together in fifth position.

Such are jeté and assemblé. To describe these steps technically, we have introduced two new concepts: flic and tombé. With regard to flic or, more accurately, the figure of flic-flac, the term was introduced into French in the second half of the seventeenth century by Scarrone.* This is the whipping upward and downward at a sharp angle. Various combinations are possible here. Flic, the shuffling upward, can be in the air, and flac, the shuffling downward, on the floor. Both movements—flic and flac—are high in the air. Flic is in the air, flac on the ground. Moreover, flic is only the preparation for

*The French poet Paul Scarrone, who lived from 1610 to 1660.

flac. Johansson called the ordinary changement de pieds flic-flac, and this name does correspond to the essence of this movement. We should note that flac can be done simply, shuffling the leg down, but it can also be done in a contraposto movement of the knee, en tournant. In the same way, threatening a horse with a whip, the hand rotates in the air around its axis.

Regarding tombé, we should say the following. This term was also introduced into the classroom lexicon by Johannson. Essentially, tombé is nothing more than a variety of par-terre coupé in its first movement, a feminine coupé compared to its other, more masculine forms. This is a battement with a stamping of the leg on the floor, now in the spirit of frappé, now in the spirit of fondu and développé. From such tombé it is easy to move to attitude, to arabesque, to big second position, to croisé forward, to pirouette en dedans or en dehors. For example, the following task is suggested in class: Do three ronds de jambs en l'air; then, on completing the rotation of the leg, do a gentle tombé as a signal to the sliding reciprocating movement of the other leg in glissade failli. At the conclusion you can execute the pirouette with one or two rotations, en dedans or en dehors. Here battement tombé appears particularly expressive and vigorous for the velvety glissade failli: a complete coupé anticipating a pirouette. In this coupé there is less stamping and stress, less gusty sweep but more plastique, more diffuse and pleasant delicacy. This is a purely female coupé, filled with even force and making ready the marvelous pose in contrast to the sharp, sensational, and sometimes bravura springboardlike coupé, by which the subsequent pose is taken as if from battle. At times entire figures are built on the alternation of two types of coupé in a complex choreographic design; moreover, if the movement has the character of a pirouette, the illusion can be created that a change of direction has been accomplished from en dedans to en dehors, or vice versa. In fact the change relates only to the direction of the pirouette, which has changed supporting leg and with it causing the rotation of the body in the opposite direction.

Among the figures of allegro, the movement called brisé remains to be explained. Here is how children are taught to do brisé—a separated beat during a swift run across the stage. Feet in fifth, throw up the back leg, and immediately move it back. With practice you can do this movement swiftly and decisively. Then the movement of the leg becomes more complicated. The leg that is thrust forward must beat against the front one and once again immediately return to its place in the same feverishly quick tempo. In other words, one teaches children to do assemblé behind, interrupted or broken by a flying beat. Consequently, brisé is nothing more than a variety of assemblé with a beat, with a beaten battement. Brisé can be done single versus double, moving forward across the stage in half steps that produce a semi-comic, semi-genre impression. The ropelike intertwining enmeshes the classical assemblé in a cheerful and festive play. This is the plastic communication of a broken chord, most of the time in the orchestra. The music of brisé is always the same, whether brisé dessous or brisé dessus is being performed. The classical winding spools like fire, like invisible latticework, with the internal guffaw of amorous deceit. This is a gentle trill in movements, which corresponds to a musical trill. There is something affected in brisé, something languorous and sobbing, mannered and delicate, which recalls the slender folds on the Sevres or Meissen porcelain figurines of the eighteenth century. In ballet we constantly have the combination of monumental lines, calculated to create a heroic impression, with fine, delicately sweet lines without which the art of classical dance would become heavy-handed and didactic. This art, however, is integral, complete, all-embracing, and in possession of its own meaningful features, yet it nearly always turns into the poetry of aimless play and unconscious acrobatism, exactly the way this occurs in life itself.

. . .

We have still not described pas ballonné in appropriate detail. Without speaking of the preparatory moments for this step, which are common in the practice of classical dance, we shall mention its major features. The technique of ballonné is very simple. Stand in fourth position croisé. Do a demi-plié. Raise the back leg after plié and do the first act of coupé, striking the floor. After this first act of coupé throw the front leg into a simple battement dégagé. Afterward, when the entire body moves forward, this same leg consecutively does a whole series of fondus, depending on the space provided by running along the stage. This is the technique of ballonné, which represents no more than the combination of two acts of coupé with battement fondu. The leg vibrates in the air with a back-and-forth movement, initially decisive and slightly drawn out in the second stage. This step, which contains two basic parts in its main design, could be called a plastic iamb in honor of Dionysus. The makeup of the poetic iamb is the same as the classical iamb: two syllables, one of which is quick, the other accented and held in a somewhat deeper breath. We observe the same thing in ballonné. Here the simple exposure of the body and its slight, almost humorous unfolding is woven together in one bravura accord.

Sometimes the dancer traverses the entire diagonal of the stage, doing ballonnés with her leg and nothing more. One gets the impression of a slightly unbridled, slightly ambitious gaiety which recalls that of the can-can. If in the service of Apollo we are sometimes easily drawn into acrobatism, then when serving Dionysus, we are always on the border of wild and recklessly chaotic dance, among whose forms the can-can-like ballonné occupies far from last place. The public usually responds to the dancer doing ballonnés with thunderous applause. The crowd doesn't always recognize and appreciate Apollo, but its own ancient Pelasgian or Scythian Dionysus it recognizes everywhere and greets with stormy enthusiasm.

Passing on to other steps that have not received detailed analysis, I should note that entrechat six, which is obviously studied only in the fifth year of classical exercise, represents the greatest difficulty. This is "the most gallant pas," claimed Petipa. As we know, it is executed in place with three croisés en l'air on scrupulously extended legs in a swift jump. In preparation one must do a clear-cut plié of both knees in order to give the jump reliable élan and self-assured ballon.

About emboité, which represents a variety of ordinary leap, I shall say only that this step is done primarily in croisé. The legs are thrust forward in turn in an increasing bravura. Kshesinskaya and Elena Smirnova did this step particularly well. Both artists with their technical skill were sometimes able to turn to the audience with the vulgar sides of their characters, which were always present in the complexity of their artistic personalities. Kshesinskaya's emboités shone with absolute perfection, not in her last years but at the dawn of her career. She could turn into a vulgar servant girl the way Pavlova could turn into a Parisian hooligan. And again I must say that the mosaic of classical dance here also reflects the world in all its combinations, but it reflects it in a reconfigured, stylized, and disciplined form. You shake the choreographic kaleidoscope and before you is the endless diversity of its colored glass. At one point the recurring diamond of absolute purity shines before you: all is white and sparkles with penetrating rays. And everything is monumental and inspired. At another point you see the bright gems of everyday and genre-character dances, each one of which contains a particular folk charm. Now a precious stone laughs at you with the brilliance of its innocent jest. Now the stone flashes and cuts across your soul with its coarse and tempestuously vulgar effect. In this diversity of forms are manifested the vitality and force of choreographic art.

Pas de Basque

Pas de basque also belongs to the category of classical steps performed in the tempo of allegro. It is hard to translate this balletic expression into Russian. First is the reference to the Basque people who live on the slopes of the Pyrenees in Spain. The Basques are of ancient Japhetic-Hamitic origin and consider themselves Spanish. Although they are extremely poor and wrap themselves in their threadbare mantles, the Basques proudly say of themselves: "Every Basque is a hidalgo." Their sense of themselves is of impoverished grandees. If we look closely at the technical construction of the pas de basque we find in it several features that indeed give the impression of a haughty movement, one which, incidentally, is widely utilized with particular luster and grandeur in the Polish mazurka.

The figure breaks down into two parts, different in design and character: the first part—for example, with the right leg—is connected to a kind of circular motion with great force that has a heavy, southern, and passionate character. This first movement ends with a resolute jump in effacé, involving a reciprocal reflecting movement of the leg in croisé, to fourth position. The second movement is done gently (glissade failli), as if to compensate for the weighty vigor of the first. The musical accompaniment of the two phrases corresponds accordingly to the construction of the pas de basque—alternately aggressively pushing and gentle. The alternation of these two fundamentally different movements gives the entire figure its unique charm. In essence this is a complex coupé, according to such authorities as Johansson, Petipa, and Legat. In one classical piece two contrasting motifs are strongly intertwined with each other by an organic reflex: indivisibly and unblendably. If the failli were not velvety, the dance would lack all gracefulness. If the first movement, the combination of a rond de jambe and a jump forward, is insufficiently energetic and substantial, the dance is deprived of its masculine element. That is why in the marvelous Polish dance, characteristic of the entire nation and so valued by all civilized humanity, the men beat the first part of the coupé and the women beat the second. If the dance proceeds with artistic feeling and absorbing inspiration, and genuinely realizes the genius which has produced it, then the woman unfailingly responds to the man's gallant play with a captivatingly tender and gliding shuffle in which we sense the modest feminine involvement in the generally spirited flight forward. The Polish mazurka conveys the national character of these Slavic Basques. . . .

Of course, in its classical interpretation the pas de basque is presented abstractly. It is purged of all its historical and ethnographic elements, reduced to its pure form, universal and eternal. There is only a frame, nothing else. One must do the resolute first part of the coupé and the obediently gentle second one without any fioritura—this is the whole challenge. . . .

. . .

Besides pas de basque we have another expression in ballet terminology: saut de basque. What constitutes this figure, so similar in name to the former one? In the former we have a walking step; in this one we have a jumping step. Let us look at its construction. Legs crossed in fifth position, right one behind. The figure starts like so: the right leg makes a small, gentle, half-open battement tombé and rests on the floor. This is a feminine signal to which the left leg, standing in effacé, responds with a gliding movement thrown up in the air in croisé forward, brushing through first position. We spoke about this in detail in the chapter on coupé. Such is the beginning of the figure. As in the pas de basque, we are dealing with one of the forms of coupé, in this case, of an aerial quality in its second part. In the remaining part of the figure a full circle is done in the air, en tournant, during which the right leg, continuing its movement, is gently pressed to the knee of the other leg, and then the entire movement concludes with a lowering onto the left leg. For the saut de basque to be clearly and distinctly executed, it is incumbent during the leap to keep the left leg rigorously extended, toes pointed. Like the toes of the leg that is pressing to the knee, the other leg must also be pointed as much as possible. The back is straight. The arms are in first position. The eyes are riveted to a point in space from which the entire movement begins. Such is this figure. The femininely masculine coupé in the beginning; a fast-moving turn en l'air, similar to a jump en tournant, in the middle; and a resolute landing at the end. The plastic motif of the figure is observed only in the introductory act and through the movements of the rotational movement. The back, the hands, and the eyes constitute an accompaniment of the dance being executed.

If we compare the saut de basque to the pas de basque, we quickly distinguish the same essential features only in a different alternation. The closeness in origin of the two figures strikes one immediately and justifies the similarity of appellation. We can say hypothetically that the Japhetic tribe of the Basques had its own expressively grandiose gait and its haughty leap en tournant. But from these two foundations—real and spiritual—formed all the ancient culture of the Greeks of the Creto-Mycenean period which then reckoned significantly in the formation of the Hellenic civic political structure. Both steps have yet another common feature in that they begin with movement in effacé and conclude in croisé. The scroll unfolds and folds in the same order and sequence, signifying a similar emotion in various movements of the dance on the ground and in the air.

Summa summarum

Our classroom instruction ends with these enumerated aspects of allegro. The exercise is exhausted, and the work in the last years of training boils down to combining the most complex steps into phrases, choreographic and plastic dialogues in which the arena of future stage art is revealed. Classical dance has been given in its most essential principles. In the course of two-plus hours the student rudimentarily covers all ballets with the teacher. By the end of the practice session she should feel significant fatigue. Everything in her has been broken and bent, hinged and unhinged, twisted and untwisted. Nonetheless, the body keeps palpitating with newborn impulses and newly discovered possibilities. As I have often observed, the future dancer leaves the classroom reluctantly—as if something has not been fully imbibed, fully experienced to the depths. Many experienced ballerinas have told me that after a good practice session they leave much wiser. Everything becomes more comprehensible, everything is perceived more fully and vividly. And every person who has been instructed in the ideas of psycho-physical symmetry will believe this and will understand the mood of the dancer who enters life after such health-improving work. Ordinarily the instructor, having put the class through such substantial practice, ends the lesson with the easiest and simplest movements after all that has been accomplished: some kind of par-terre or en l'air flic-flacs or some thrown grand battements and movements across the entire room. In the field of physical exercises such a device constitutes genuine Italian *sfumato,* the reduction of sharp contours to vague and gentle outlines.

A Bird's-Eye View

Male Dancing: A Synthesis

Men do not dance on the tips of their toes because they retain their unique spirituality by remaining on their full feet. Relevé can only destroy the impression of lofty naturalness. The principle of verticality is so innate to men that no additional positions are necessary to corroborate or implement it. However, when he returns to the floor from a variety of leaps or jumps the man still tries to provide a classical design in its typical features. He touches the floor fleetingly with pointed toes and then presses his entire sole to it. The toes are glimpsed only fleetingly and appear as a transitional form of a starting or concluding movement, whereas for the woman this form is far from transitional or transient but can be fixed in the general scheme of a given dance as constant. At first glance it seems surprising that a being who so predominates in elevation, such as the male, does not dance on his toes; indeed every attempt in this direction creates a rather repulsive impression. If, in Homer's hymn, Apollo is standing on his toes, then this movement can be viewed merely as a preparation for flight. On the other hand, such a divinity as Apollo, given the universality of his significance, contains all the human elements in their entirety—male as well as female—and the division into two sexes manifests within him the same paucity of sharp contours as it does in the virgin Artemis, who engages in the male occupation of hunting. Man completely gives himself to flight. It is unlike him to linger on toes, or to walk and move about on them. Man holds to the ground completely normally, convinced that he can take off whenever he likes.

We should note that the male partner constantly tries to encourage and facilitate the female in standing on her toes. He inspires her to this lofty striving upward by extending his hand of support. Here in ballet is manifested the age-old mission of man to elevate the woman to his height and keep her obstinately and protractedly on this level. Sensitive artists sometimes intuit this peculiar interrelationship between man and woman—primarily characteristic of Russia—not only in intellectual life but also in art. In ballet we constantly encounter this valuable nuance without paying it sufficient attention. Thus in the final act of *Swan Lake,* Legat designed several moments that differed from the usual routine. The female dancer stands on her toes, thrusting her leg in an extended pattern. The dance with the cavalier is about to begin. Standing on her toes, the dancer extends her hand to her partner. Ordinarily, the partner circles the ballerina, holding her waist with his other hand without changing his pose or withdrawing his hand. But Legat completely rejected this banal device. He abandons the dancer's hand, and she must stay on her toes, in an extended arabesque, over the course of terribly long moments, while her partner walks around her. This might seem an insignificant and hardly noticeable stroke. But it is precisely in such strokes, emitted from the unconscious depths of the artist's talent, that we see his genuine brilliance. We are left with a truly profound impression as we unexpectedly contemplate that prolonged steadiness without support.

The pose in attitude in the same act of *Swan Lake* in the final moment of the adagio produces an identical impression. Legat swiftly gives the dancer a spin for two pirouettes and then suddenly abandons her. Left to herself, the dancer remains on her toes, standing firmly on them amid the whirlwind of movement created by her partner. She stands straight up in attitude, rising intensely high up. The pose is full of passion and inspiration. Something here is caught and produced from the realm of the male spirit. Nonetheless in this pose the vegetal charm of female movement visibly flows in the placement of the body, in the gentle port de bras, in the rustling beauty of the ballerina's light skirt. In this example, which I have pulled from the endless laboratory of choreographic art, we have an illustration of the same magnificent theme of male influence on the female psyche. It is as if the male dancer were pulling the woman from the boggy vegetal soil that she nevertheless cannot leave for good. No matter how she tears upward while being supported by her partner, she nevertheless remains organically and invariably a flower-plant. Yet this does not exclude her from the realm of Apollo. The sun god himself is indissolubly bound to the plant world. The olive, the palm, and the laurel trees are dedicated to him. Apollo's first temple was erected from laurel branches and leaves, and only later did stone and marble copy the vegetal motifs of the primitive wooden structures. . . .

Young men study the same classical routine young women do, under the guidance of a common teacher. Their positions are the same, but in men they seem more massive and even somewhat unwieldy because of their figures and their feet with their low arch and, in the vast majority of cases, even without any sharp curve. Only the fourth position, with its demonstrative stepping forward of the foot, looks noble and gallant, especially after a pirouette before the beginning of a new inspired dance. Johansson demanded from his students not only gallantry but even a certain bravura, as if anticipating in the future the establishment of a heroism on the ballet stage that was not affected and foppish but naturally dexterous and spontaneous. Men almost never use the fifth position. Only pirouettes end on the floor bringing the feet together in this position. This occurs because men's legs are rougher than women's and differ from women's by lesser turnout and are harder to place close to each other in this position. But even when it is realized, this position always seems to lack harmony and beauty. In women all positions are distinguished by genuine charm, but the fourth position is especially attractive by nature of its broad, individual shape. After the pirouette a woman sparkles with a variety of expressions. A hint of coquettishness is possible, with the head peeping out under the arm; a hint of supplication with arms crossed on the chest. A hint of showing off, with arms thrown back along the skirt and the body carried forward: a pose that is largely feminine and pictorial, musical in a major key, and nonetheless completely plantlike. Everything sings harmoniously under the sun's caresses! The leg moved to the back only touches the floor with the lightest touch of the toes. Sometimes the arms extend forward in a welcoming gesture. There is no such wealth of expression and nuance in the male dancer, only swagger, gallantry, and bravura. But this is in its own way magnificent and necessary in the overall scheme of balletic exaltation. From the first steps of the exercise, the heroic prose of the male genius is juxtaposed to Flora's poetry.

The bending of the knee—plié—does not give the man the kind of curved back, the openness of the knee, the softness and gentleness that we find in the woman. The ligaments in his groin are stronger and firmer. The female plié spreads across the entire body like warm moisture; the male plié does not contain this warmth or soft element, but for this reason it surpasses the female plié in nervous energy, dryness, and power. In a dynamic sense it constitutes the key factor in a strong and potent spring. In this sense a man possesses much greater resources. A woman can never compare with him in running; not only is her step smaller, but the speed with which she alternates the bending of her legs is less than his. When running, a man is completely transformed into a genuine spring, utilizing in a sustained and persistent fashion his muscles and physical resources. A woman on the run tires faster, losing the energy of the initial impulse.

But the arid pliancy of the man is not only a feature of his legs. His fingers are also more pliant than a woman's. Apollo quickly moved his fingers along the strings of his lyre from top to bottom and from bottom to top, and this caused the endless beauty of his legendary playing. . . . Going further in this study of the relative pliancy of both sexes, we note in men a greater wealth in the intonations of the voice that express the varied spectrum of emotional experiences. The female soul splashes in one place. It is pliant and gentle only on its own point. It does pliés and relevés, preserving a persistent attachment to the chosen point of support on the ground. In general a woman cannot keep pace with a man. Being like a magnet in her milieu, she does not move to faraway places; these places are constantly and invariably drawn to her. Man in his pliancy envelops huge spaces, and for this reason male ballon is more vivid and powerful than female ballon. The male is able not only to remain in space by seizing it with his elastic jumps and leaps but also to linger at full speed and in full flight and carry his spring with him without losing his impelling vivacity in the process. In the movements of elevation masculine plié displays an unusual endurance, worthy of a heroic spirit. Brilliant masculine variations are accompanied by innumerable pliés after each beat, and it seems for this reason that the person is not only floating and living in the air with all the energy and motivation at his disposal but is celebrating in flight the victory over earthly laws. He is the image of openness—lying exactly in the luminous expanses just as he does stretched out on the water. Feminine ballon, on the other hand, is, in the shortness of its duration, deprived of true exaltation. Seeing the woman flying upward, we are astonished at this miracle, and she herself is filled with a similar amazement. But for all the joyousness of this amazement, it has none of the proud self-affirmation that accompanies male exaltation. The woman's knee is soft because of her resilient muscles. In her plié she whirls herself onto the floor. . . . Any ballerina with a large step can throw her leg back almost to the back of her head, at the same time maintaining her elastic and smooth plié. The muscles of a woman's legs are distinguished by the great power in their support and in their sweep. But men's legs, though usually proportionately longer than women's, create significant springboards of support and thus in the sense of vigor and dynamism, seem superior to women's legs.

Let us now move on to battements.

Battement tendu, extended battement, is not especially characteristic of men. Men do not have a curved instep in their feet; their arch is low. Their toes lack soft female pliancy. A ballerina who does a battement ends it by touching the floor with her beautifully pointed toes. This is not even remotely possible for a man; he does not dance on his toes, and the technique of caressing the floor is foreign to him. He performs a battement tendu, as it were, under his breath, in an obscured design. Apart from this, we must note the following characteristic. In a slow tempo, with or without plié, the leg usually does not leave the floor: it glides forward, never losing contact with the ground. Here the rhythmic element is distinctly felt. If the extended battement is done in a quick tempo, even without plié, then the foot departs slightly from the floor and is thrust into one direction or another, dryly and in a straight line, with a strict vertical bearing of the hip and knee and a tautly curved arch. There is nothing plantlike here. In this battement the woman begins to copy the male beat. For the man, however, the battement has enormous significance when rapidly executed. This is his direct preparation for the upcoming beaten battement. In the sweep of a brisk movement the legs get used to going beyond the limits of normal croisé, beyond the boundary of fifth position. This is acceptable in male dancing, but only high in the air.

The battement développé, unfolding in the undulating design of the battement, is not particularly interesting in the male execution. This battement is thoroughly plantlike. Yet the man in a biological sense is least of all a plant. The arch, the ankle, the toes, the well-developed instep—all this allows the woman to realize the picturesque design of this battement. Rich and full streams of movement successfully enter it. The figure terminates the moment the leg is completely extended, and the toes are at the level of the kneecap. This is the final sound of the violin's air. But the man lacks a beautiful arch, he has no gently developed graceful step, and thus the delicate currents of the extended battement are missing. He can thrust his leg forward with great force. His stunning battement, battement frappé, is unusually brilliant. The male coupé is sharp and decisive. But to extend his leg with all the peculiarities and nuances of plantlike culture to the surging of the orchestra, to carry it through all the modulations of the growing plasticity, first upward then sideways or forward, along a more and more straightened line—this the male dancer cannot do. This is why the adagio, constructed not only onstage but in the classroom on the varieties of classical développé, cannot attain independent life in the man's execution. In this monumental composition the male is naturally relegated to the role of partner, the role of support. But within the contours of this role he can display the entire splendor of his talent, all his limitless energy and superior leadership, about which we have already spoken. He is dynamic and enterprising, and though he does not do any développé he constitutes a marvelous and fervent background for the entire process of unfolding to which the woman gives herself onstage.

Regarding the other battements, we should note the following. Some of them open up the dancer's body slowly or quickly, firmly or gently, with a tinge of passivity. Other battements do not reveal but rather unfurl the dancer's body. Such is battement développé or fondu, such is the petit battement, whose technique should be especially well considered. Petit battement is a purely female battement. The accent of the beat is cou-de-pied devant, and the beating leg is constantly bent in a plantlike design. On the whole we have here a kind of rustling staccato of leaves before a storm, a flowery tempest on a small scale. If the arch is curved, the toes lowered and tenderly embracing the neck of the foot, the impression is dazzling. Everything is fused together, yet each vibration is perceived separately and distinctly. Because of its plantlike nature, petit battement is completely inappropriate for the man's leg. In general battements that are meant to unfurl the dancer's body in a slow tempo and in consecutive stages of evolution do not constitute the domain of the male genius. . . .

Rond de jambe belongs to the number of unfurling movements and thus is not typical of male dancing. . . . A man's rond de jambe does not have the charm of a woman's, especially on the floor, for example in assemblé soutenu. Like the string of a musical instrument, the extended leg—we have already described this movement in its general aspect—makes a sharp sweep with a momentary plié at the turn. At first the back is kept straight. Then it bends, a surge from one side to the other which flickers for a second. These moments are meant for feminine softness. While the leg is in motion, while the plié is accomplished during the turn, while the zigzagging spreads along the back, the eyes are riveted on the public. Only at the end does the head make a resolute controposto in order to return to its former spot. In the man's execution this last moment produces an especially beautiful impression, owing to the fact that the controposto turns and the firm, headlong movements of the partial en tournant are to the highest degree in the spirit of masculine art.

The tension of the coaxial muscles, temps de cuisse, by itself is not particularly advantageous for the man: here there are no contours which adorn the female figure. But we are speaking about the turn itself—rapid and energetic. The turn of the man's head is rapid to an extraordinary degree. It is not the rond de jambe itself, the mixture of développé and frappé, but namely the circular path, its quickness, its sharpness that we have in mind in the scheme of motion we are considering that applies to male dancing. In adagio the large rotation of the leg can be an effective concluding chord of any pirouette as performed by a woman. Thus, for example, in the pas d'action of the second act of *Swan Lake* the woman with a large circular movement of the leg envelops and embraces the man's back without rising either on the toes or on demi-pointe. For a man this gesture of the leg would be ugly. But the woman exhibits here her particular strength. . . .

So the male rond de jambe in many respects is inferior to the female and only in some individual features corresponds to the tasks of male dancing. Everything in the rond de jambe that comes from the evolving battement is foreign to the male dancer: the vividness, the fluidity, the roundness, and the gradualness. But the energetic unfurling of the body and the element of enterprising initiative makes this a tool of masculine art.

We now turn to other figures of classical dance on the floor. We have seen that the attitude is distinguished by a special beauty in women whether it is closed or open. Everything is turned out, with its gentle images directed to the public. Attitude croisé corresponds to a reserved and tense mood with a hint of a gathering storm and imminent lightning; attitude effacé corresponds to another mood, lighter and more sociable. Through attitude on the floor a woman can say a lot both in a Romantic and a purely classical style. She sings and acts in this figure, and all the attitude's nuances are formed in instantaneous pictures. All movements have the softness and fluidity of thick oil. In the man all these characteristic features and peculiarities inevitably vanish. His entire body palpitates with the motifs of struggle and victory which seek to pour forth into a turbulently passionate movement, one that does not correspond to an attitude while it is being executed on the floor. But let the attitude be lifted off the floor to the movements of flight, and immediately, as if fulfilling the principles of the male spirit, it becomes resplendent and majestic. The ballon is confidently prolonged. The broken line of the leg contains the promise of immediately straightening into the arabesque. The male strides along a steep and high arc with determined poise. But all this is possible only up in the air, in the element of elevation, in the desire to break loose from the ground. Here, with its enticing magnetism, the man's attitude can compete with the woman's.

Despite its origin in the feminine plantlike battement, the arabesque—owing to its rectilinearity—creates the impression of a typically masculine position. Expressing a sense of upsurge and freedom, it is strong, intense, and powerful. But in the male's execution this is a momentary standing in one place after an airborne run across the stage. The dancer stops dead and freezes in immobility. The sword gleams and slashes in the warrior's hand. But the fight ends and the unnecessary instrument is extended in the resting hand. Such is in general the concluding male arabesque—aggressively alert and suspended for a second. A woman's arabesque, on the other hand, is especially beautiful in the tempestuous dances across the diagonal lines of the stage, in the spatial transferals filled with fleeting ecstasy, in the final moments of a coda when the dancer is rushing downstage facing the audience, extending her leg, stringlike in the cloud of her ballooning skirt in complete antithesis to the male. The male arabesque constitutes the consummation of the aerial whorls, rivoltades, and big jumps en tournant. Only when he ascends into the air does the man discover himself and, after returning to the ground and finding himself, he can issue forth into the rectilinear and anticipated arabesque. . . .

Let us round out our discussion of the pirouette with some distinct features. The male pirouette on the floor is realistic in the crudest sense of the word. It usually begins from second position but sometimes also from fourth. If there is no second position, the dancer, in order to attain it, does battement frappé or a jump to échappé, with legs thrown in rapid tempo. Standing in demi-pointe, the dancer makes a circle. The foot "embraces" the neck of the other foot with its sole while the toes are lowered to one side. The design rendered here is closed, stifled, and unattractive. The body is not stretched poetically upward, as occurs when the pirouette is executed on toes. The rotation of the body is limited, like a top, with narrow span. The pirouette in attitude is without any gentle elasticity. The pirouette in arabesque lacks any pictorial quality. With its bold plastic features, the pirouette renversée can hardly ever be imagined in a man's interpretation. Only two moments here can create any kind of artistic impression: the rapidity of the turning of the body and the swiftness of the turning of the head. But both these moments are of pure nature. The entire body completely turns around its axis, guided by a willful impulse. The head is turned in a powerfully fast apperceptive effort. Each movement embodies a kind of atom of desire, a kind of motif of consciousness, unlike the blessed spontaneity of the woman's plantlike gyration. . . .

A series of classical movements on the floor can be divided into two categories with the utmost clarity. Some of them are accessible to the male dancer, others are largely peculiar to the female. For example, the simple alternation of the legs on pointe in the movement forward along the stage. One leg from the slight plié rises en pointe. The other is in demi-attitude. This is the pattern of beautiful classical movement forward. In order to give it artistic finish one needs to throw the weight from one leg to the other. The turns of the head have a coquettish quality. The play of the arms is varied and eloquently expressive. All this comes from the arsenal of female dance. We do this alternating with the rotation of the body (jeté en tournant), modifying it with all kinds of combinations and inserting now an assemblé soutenu, now a pirouette, now some chassées en tournant, now fouetté en dedans. In all its aspects this step is exclusively feminine. Indeed, the very leap necessary for its execution is too low for the man's takeoff and his means. Similarly, the small jumps on toes, with beaten battement or not, have the same expressively female character. The pas de basque demands from the performer well-elaborated plantlike resources. Just to mention glissade failli—elegantly velvety and connected to the floor by a rustling whisper! This glissade is inaccessible to the male. In the final moment the back leg rests on the floor with the tip of the toes: again this is beyond the male's capacity and is not in his character. For the woman the pas de basque is an ordinary figure, common in various dances, mainly as a preparation for a pirouette. In men this is encountered primarily in character dances, in Spanish dances, in the mazurka, and in the tarantella.

With regard to glissade, as a preparatory stage for future movement it can be performed with equal success by men and women. But there are glissades which contain an element of another, purely plastic order, for example, a glissade on demi-pointe, as in the dances of the Frescoes in *The Little Hump-backed Horse.* Here we have a gentle plié, a small leap, and an extended batte-ment with pointed toes. One can perform this glissade from fifth position, alternating the legs or not. The glissade is done freely, in effacé. When chang-ing the feet the head is tilted first to one shoulder, then to the other. The shoulders vibrate almost imperceptibly. Epaulement is marked mostly by the beautiful turning of the head to the right and to the left in a totally feminine way, as if the ballerina were playing with a fan. Another glissade is performed in quick tempo. The leg appears to push the floor back. All these are only frag-ments of the female art of the dance, with which no other art in the world can compare within the realistic limits of the level of the floor.

. . .

Male dancing in the air must be analyzed in reference to three phenomena: elevation, ballon, and beats and turns. The leap is typical of males: there is much determined and exalted energy in it, and much striving afar and above. Even with his child's legs a boy loves to jump, to the surprise and delight of his sisters. It is as if a man were born with a determined sense of flight, with that inner atmosphere which tosses him up and constantly separates him from the ground. In his leap he organically maintains a vertical tendency. The Greeks said, "Ελλάς 'ορτή, "vertically erect Hellas," thus expressing its militantly aerial character and, in general, imagining all that is exalted as essentially vertical, as if in a fervidly male semblance. It is not a man's way to fly in a flattened position, with his body inclined horizontally. If in real life the male can deviate from his vertical deportment while remaining on the floor, then, while in the air, face to face with the sky, he naturally, almost instinctively, straightens out like a slender tree. His back is straight, his head proudly rests on his neck. His ballon is suspended in the air and formidable. The male dancer can show off his body, flinging himself from figure to figure, much longer than the woman. This is the fundamental element of the male art of dancing. Man does not dance on pointe: he allows himself to express his aspiration upward in other ways. But soaring up in the air, he is transformed in a second and becomes the bearer of that principle in the human spirit we can call Romantic. This is the first principle of male dancing in the movements of elevation.

But the male dancer's leaps would be empty if they were not accompanied by various batteries: beaten battements, the so-called beating steps of all possible varieties. We already know what these batteries represent. These are balls, consecutive croisés, which impart to each movement a heroic character. Everything is built around the beating battement. The beats by themselves can assume different forms. Now they rustle and glitter and flash in diamondlike flickers; now they shine like white lights. But a beat is not a beat if we cannot hear a vigorous strike in it. The leg must be firmly extended, completely straight with toes lowered down, without the slightest controposto movement sideways. The croisé must be completely distinct. And everything together is performed briskly, so that the impression on the spectator is that of a whirlwind, not a series of images. If at a given height one can remain for "$a + n$" seconds, then the beats in good ballon abbreviate this interval of time to "a" seconds.

At one time, when I assumed the study of this part of classical dance, I had thought that the beats themselves had no ideological significance, that they constituted only an ornament of the dancing—its second-rate fioritura—and in the best case yielded to the display of pure and random virtuosity. I thought, Here is that ingredient of acrobatism which, being indigenous to the male spirit as the playful expression of the excess of energy, finds its fullest application. But not mere embellishment is contained in these beats but the content of the leap, and without the beats we have only the carcass—the skeleton of dancing in the air. That is why male elevation, with its prolonged ballon, is more powerful and more expressive than female elevation. In an absolute sense, a woman's muscular structure is weaker than a man's. Her spiritual force is also less than the man's in the aspect of art that we are speaking about. This is why the man has an unquestionable advantage over the woman both in the physical coefficient and in the potency of the spirit. . . . It is thus with Pavlova's elevation. In it every moment flickers with an excess of choreography and plastique. This is not circuslike elevation or tight-rope-walking gymnastics as one flies over a set number of chairs, but the elevation inherent in artistic genius, where illusion is one with the loftiest aesthetic impression. But if elevation is only an episode in women, then in men, who infuse it with heroic beats, it constitutes a normal and defining phenomenon. Such is Nijinsky's ballon. Not handsome by nature, Nijinsky could be beautiful up in the air. He emanated the impression of transformation, which gives any person or object the appearance of heroic ecstasy.

Finally, male tours. In contrast to women's pirouettes on the floor, they express bursts of active, willful passion. We have already said that these are large changes of the legs (changement) with circular flights in the air. These are not pirouettes because the axis of rotation here is in a state of movement and is not fixed securely to one point, as in a top. The initial power is in the force of the arms, which rotate the body. Sergei Legat assumed such force with his arms that he could perform two-and-a-half revolutions. A characteristic motif of such a figure is the battement—a beat which is hardly noticeable and barely perceived by the spectator. These turns constitute the special property of the male dancer in ballet. Women do not do tours—they use other means for similar effects.

. . .

Thus we have male dances in all their abundance. One can divide them into three categories: par-terre dances; related female dances on the floor but yielding to them in beauty, such as dances with elevation but not very high—ballotté and ballonné, small leaps and sissonnes with beats, entrechats quatre and royale, brisé and light jumps en tournant. As we have seen, these dances are only relatively successful in competition with women's dances on the same middle level. Finally, there are dances with large ballon, with great elevation, which we have just reviewed in sufficient detail. If we eliminate from male dancing the mannered bends of the torso and body in the spirit of recent times, if we strengthen the heroic tone, if only in a complicated acrobatic design, and give it a broad sweep in Johansson's style, then providing every movement is perfect and every gesture is grand it enters the realm of art it occupied at the time of its height. All smiling is cast off. The face is inspired by the energy of tranquillity and male self-confidence. No demi-pointes, no raised shoulders, no hands that are bent and pressed to the face. Everything is in the quick and bold turns, in the controposto rotations of the head, in the intoning of beaten battements. Then we have a dancing youth, brave and daring as he is supposed to be. We have Apollo. We have the warrior-dancer of whom Homer spoke and thought. This warrior will perform big leaps, high soubresauts, double cabrioles, double sauts de basque, tours and rivoltades, large and small beats, clear-cut pirouettes ending unfailingly in croisé—all that the beating of the heroic pulse can more or less render. And next to him will dance the ballerina, combining the plantlike movements with all the yearning for elevation available to her.

. . .

Acrobatism

If a rope is thrown across Niagara Falls, then crossing the waterfall on it constitutes an acrobatic feat. Such a spectacle evokes wonderment among the spectators bordering on rapture. Before our eyes is performed something that on a smaller scale resides in the heart of every person like a dim dream. What, precisely, constitutes the acrobat's feat? By itself, the movement along the rope, if it is drawn low and the danger is removed, represents the simplest tight-rope walking, which any person can easily achieve. But here we have a person who is at a height, standing over the bubbling and seething waters, and the movement is tied to mortal danger. To fulfill his task the acrobat has to focus completely. He must concentrate all his attention and all the resources of his will, gathered into a compact bundle, on one point and not be distracted by the slightest outside association. Conceptions of motion, in contrast to all others, possess one extremely important feature: a peculiar and irrepressible tendency to turn immediately into corresponding action. If the conception of motion—say, of a jump—comes to a child on hearing a fairy tale, reading a book, or remembering something personal, he immediately begins to jump. The conception of motion turns into an act.

From this, the danger of looking down from the edge of a roof, bending over the guardrail of a balcony, peering into a deep abyss or well becomes clear: the quiet fluttering of the motor nerve can materialize into a motion that leads to falling, and then the person will rapidly crash down. Here a certain mental resistance to such a fate causes dizziness, which can save a person in such circumstances by inducing him to move away from the edge of the chasm. Thus we have two conceptions, two spiritual acts which compete with each other. Depending on which of these conceptions gains the upper hand, the person will either hurtle down or withdraw from the danger.

But let us return to our tight-rope walker. His motor perception must be free of any other competing idea. He walks completely removed from the waterfall across an aerial wilderness, along a straight path, without an abyss below. As if taking off from his own internal spring, he is carried away via his thought to his intended goal, distracted and confused by nothing. It is impossible to imagine more self-possession or self-mastery: converting the abyss by its luminiferous action, the spirit dominates over everything here. The man walks, but his spirit guides him! This is truly a heroic act from a formal point of view. But this kind of form can be filled with different content while the operating cause remains the same. This motif is isolated, vacant, self-contained concentration. Everything is banished from consciousness by self-hypnosis, and what remains is pure space that belongs to the bearer of the spirit.

As we have already said, the content of a deed can be diverse. It can be social, ethical, erotic, and aesthetic. Apollo's struggle with Python, Saint George's with the dragon, Siegfried's with the dark serpent—all these are models of an acrobatic feat that is not practicably futile, as in the case of the tight-rope walker, but directed toward the defense of weak and oppressed people. But here also apperception—clear and once again vacant and free of any secondary notions of fire-breathing maws or poison fangs—is concentrated on one point. And the feat has to be performed precisely in an acrobatic way that to the outward glance is incommensurate with the person's individual strengths. The same thing characterizes the lion's entry into his cage. The flying from one trapeze to another demands the same concentration. The successful outcome of a duel with swords or pistols also depends on a certain acrobatic self-mastery, with the banishment of foreign and disturbing motivations. Everywhere acrobatism—the basic framework of every heroism—plays a decisive role.

One more word about the tight-rope walker across Niagara. His feat seems free of ethical content. It is completely shallow, free of a practical goal. Aesthetic experiences are also useless in practical terms, yet they nonetheless lead to great emotional shocks and actions of the highest order. From the simple observation of such a blindingly beautiful spectacle as the fearless walking along a rope atop a gaping abyss, those points from which the spectator's internal wings grow begin to palpitate. But in its deepest meaning acrobatism produces an aesthetic impression in the framework of balletic art, especially when the great and complex technique of classical ballet flows like a stream across the stage. Where specifically is acrobatism primarily expressed in ballet? Namely where the laws of real life are heroically overcome. Walking on toes is acrobatic. But here is the alpha of the great art, the apotheosis of verticality from which originated a biological revolution in the history of humankind. Turnout is unnatural and acrobatic, but here is the spirit of the idea shaping the outside form, the value of which the ancients knew well. What a great feat of acrobatism is the pirouette, with its precisely calculated turning around a fixed axis! We have previously spoken of the emotional and willful exaltation contained in it. Acrobatic in the fullest sense is that fouetté in thirty-two turns which is apotheosized in the art of such great dancers as Legnani, Trefilova, Geltzer, and Kshesinskaya. Without a fiery temperament these fouettés cannot be done, nor can they flash with that acrobatic beauty which elevates not only the artist but also the audience over everyday reality. What is there to say about elevation, about the cabrioles and tours, about the complicated flights with beats, especially in male performance? Here we stand face to face with the purest acrobatism, but one adorned in the flesh of living and captivating art.

Thanks to the plantlike element in dancing, ballet appears to be covered in soft floral carpets. Like carpets, the plants cover the ground. In their design, battements also form a kind of fluttering carpet, along which the art of dance spreads. This inseparable closeness to Proserpine* is precisely what captivates the spectator. The world is covered with green carpets. How beautiful is the

---

*The Roman name for Persephone, who in Greek mythology was the daughter of Zeus and Demeter and goddess of the underworld.

green cover of earth: this is développé in nature. Everything is beautiful and light and smells of flowers. The bright carpet of the sky is an inspiration to our heart. This is a flowing curtain, a carpet of rags and glitter which separates us from the dark abyss of night. But the velvety night is the same carpet that conceals something from us with its everlasting starry flickerings. The contemplation of this carpetlike splendor can evoke in us a feeling of monotony, of weariness from the homogeneous impressions that lull the soul with their smooth and soft charms. Exaltation easily turns into a drowsy sleep. But the torpidity is broken by the sudden bells of acrobatism and elevation, and the heavenly garden is transformed into an arena of moral deeds. The female talent in all this complex phenomenon of art plays a decisive role. The woman's apperception is always somewhat diffuse and fears any strict deviation. Some moments in her adagio are filled with that plantlike juice of life which overflows the barriers of art. If only women danced in ballet, then sooner or later elevation and acrobatism would disappear from it entirely. There would be graceful, somnolent Flora—serenity and sweetness. But here male dancing injects its call, its excitement, and its ideological command.

The Ballet Master

At the present time we possess enormous choreographic capital, inherited by us from ballet masters of old. This capital forms the historical fund of balletic art. We still lack new materials of any significance in this field, so it is natural that the task of the ballet master should break down into two parts: he must preserve and cultivate the old ballets, and he must be the initiator and continuer of new creations in this area. Let us examine both parts of this activity, one after the other.

The technical role of the ballet master comes down to the following. He must rehearse the ballets of Marius Petipa, Lev Ivanov, Arthur Saint-Léon, Jules Perrot, and others, assisted by the director, who knows the troupe of male and female dancers well, selecting performers from the primary soloists to the last extras in the corps de ballet. Musicality in the ballet master is a prerequisite for successful rehearsals. He must feel the features and outlines of the acoustic combinations and convey them in choreographic terms on stage with all the sensitivity available to him. The dances of the old ballets must be accompanied by the music in tempo. But sometimes choreography must make up for certain gaps which result from the unfamiliarity of ballet composers with the technique and character of dance in general and classical dance in particular. Sometimes it is necessary to stop a dance that is proceeding poorly and counter to the music, and show new forms of execution, within the limits of the projected goal. Here the ballet master is not violating the concept of another but rather partially introducing into the picture restorational strokes. All the variations and codas, the various adagios, the dances of the individual soloists and ensembles, the acting and dancing of the corps de ballet—everything is positively restored in rehearsal with special care. Here accuracy of reproduction is all the more necessary since the old dances were notated very poorly, and one has to restore them for the most part through one's own—and the artists'—memory, following established tradition. Sometimes curious cases of reverse plagiarism occur: one's own work is presented as another's, not always to the advantage of the artistic whole. Nonetheless, at the present time several classical traditions, especially those connected with Petipa, are holding strong, in part by means of notation, in part through living oral tradition.

Rehearsing the works of the old art, the ballet master must also clearly assimilate the pantomime and gesture integral to the masterpieces of ballet. These flourished under the protection of old ideas and their typical features must be preserved with love and solicitude. Pantomime in ballet, for all its archaism and, at times, absurdity to our contemporary aesthetic taste, has its charm. Porphyry conceals shards of the eternal and the beautiful, torn from the inescapable world of intellectual exaltation. The old solo dances cannot be replaced by anything positive. It is impossible either to reduce or to elevate these sunny structures of Apollo in the momentary image of human creation. But to introduce here in exchange for the old pantomime an expression of modern times which does not conform to the themes of classical art would be to distort the whole with a blatantly disharmonious note.

At the rehearsal the ballet master makes all the artists dance in appropriate theatrical costumes. The women are arrayed in tricot, to which they adapt as if it were their own second skin. They constantly need the stimulating chill created by the touch of the silk fabric against their naked body. Here everything is made level and smooth, is tight fitting and flattened out. The individual details—such as the isolated roundness, depressions, angles, and blemishes—have disappeared, and a certain universal and idealized model of the individual body is created. From the earliest years of work in rehearsal and onstage, the artist needs to learn to look at himself from the world's point of view. He is the conduit of art and not the child of caprices—personal and transient. Men also work in special costumes, which comport with the character of their future creative work on the stage. A soft shirt with unstarched collar, a light waistcoat, high stockings and close-fitting trousers—this is the rehearsal gear of the male partner. Additionally, simple dancing shoes, which do not hinder leaps and batteries. In character dances this shoe changes to a shoe with heels, for female as well as male dancers. In his working clothes the male artist appears as a kind of acrobat who is ready for his heroic performances, and this accords not only with the character of his own dances but also with that feminine vegetal movement he must accompany and awaken and place on an elevated plane. In the rehearsal hall contrasting effects are prepared that constitute the essence of the choreographic whole. The ballet master follows everything here, helps everyone, and directs everything. And again, he does this through music and to its accompaniment so as not for a moment to depart from the internal content of the old ballet.

This is the preparatory work of the ballet master who arranges a work not his own. With regard to the creations of Petipa, which form the main property of the contemporary stage, he must be the guardian and preserver of all the notations, all the formulas of this remarkable art. Knowing no limits to his rich imagination, Petipa piled combination upon combination, increasingly complicating the overall design of dance. His ballets suffer from an excess of creative scope and seem at times almost chaotic. His canvas, as a whole, is picturesque, and the sculptured motifs of the dance, buried under the luxuriant dyed carpets of lights and glitter, are heard only occasionally, like unintelligible voices from a bottomless pit. As we have already said, if not for the upward sweeping acrobatic poetry of the male dance, the exultant paean of masculine art, everything in Petipa might drown in the full-flowing streams of gallant eroticism. At times everything is so exaggerated and overdone in Petipa that the ballet master, no matter how highly he appreciates his brilliant predecessor, must now and again take a scalpel to it. A particular big dramatic duet, a pas d'action, in *The Pharaoh's Daughter* constitutes a genuine choreographic lump. How many parading characters there are—necessary and unnecessary! The Pharaoh's daughter, her girlfriend, the Englishman, the two confidantes, a dancing cavalier, the Pharaoh's brother. Every one of these dancers, excepting the Englishman, has special dances, choreographed with the highest mastery of which Petipa was capable. These characters dance solo as well as in flying ensembles. There is no doubt that in today's interpretation such variety, especially if one considers that whole sections of the production have been completely erased from memory, would be extremely difficult to repeat. It is necessary to put everything into a calmer, more modest framework. The variations of Pharaoh's daughter can stay. The other dances need to be shortened to highlight the essential part of the work. One would then have an expressive variation with the modest accompaniment of the best soloists dancing together in a mosaic entourage. The same kind of extremely useful cuts could be made even in *Raymonda,* where a scattered mass of individual, concertlike variations exhaust the spectator, who is waiting for the ballerina's dances.

In general Petipa's adagios have a tendency to suffer from excessive length. Thinking back on these gems of great art, we invariably notice the same themes in various productions. Everywhere the fires of similarly beautiful diamonds glitter, but they do so in different necklaces. And these diamonds sparkle in endless rows in the same setting, overwhelming the spectator with their oppressive abundance. It sometimes seems that it would have been better to take a limited amount of groupings and extend them in time, thereby providing a quicksilvery glitter to this or that prominent detail. A sustained arabesque, be it in the Italian or French style, will provide the gripping impression of sculpture, frozen and hypnotizing. Like Carlo Blasis, Petipa looked for the picturesque in everything; but specifically in the adagio the impression of ancient marble, the charm of heroic Phidias, could have played the preeminent role. Although a monument of vegetal materials is constructed before our eyes, with the floral art of women in the foreground, not for a minute should we forget that along the carpets of balletic art walks Apollo's foot. Precisely in this spot the resourceful imagination of the ballet master can sparkle with sudden illumination. Let the ballerina stand for an extra second on pointe. This will not betray Petipa's design but give it artistic finish. Let her for one moment linger like a weary courante in the arms of her partner with legs extended forward, and not immediately rush to escape from her repose. When the courantes suddenly fall silent, by the force of auditory illusion, we still hear their rhythmic noise and beat. If we extend an attitude in a protracted tempo, in croisé or in effacé, we will again experience an intoxicating effect, interwoven with anticipation and anxiety. It is not even necessary to overdo the pirouette with an excessive number of circles: one circular line on an unwavering axis, with the appropriate expression on the dancer's face, can evoke a burst of enthusiasm; but an excess of circular lines can only dampen the impression by an exaggerated acrobatism. How important simplicity is in the art of the dance!

The reproduction of the variations and codas strewn by Petipa in endless multitude among all his works constitutes at the present time the greatest difficulty. The design of the adagio is simple in its monumentality. But the variations and codas, where technique is at the forefront, are in this sense bundles of tangled weaving, and not even the best memory can hold onto them in all their fullness, precision, and wholeness. We will note one factor which has fundamental significance. By its nature the variation must conform to the character of the adagio in a choreographic and a musical sense, even if elements are included in it which by themselves do not have a place in the classical pas de deux. All three parts of the pas de deux—the adagio, the variation, and the coda—form a certain classical mold, a choreographic novel in the silent symbols of balletic action. Petipa did not reckon with this aesthetic requirement of balletic composition in part because he was not particularly distinguished by musicality (and in this regard yielded to Ivanov), and in part because the idea of such a unity was not completely clear to him. At times, ignoring the demands of harmony, he introduced into the composition a kind of mosaic gaudiness—features and motifs of other works that were foreign to it—thereby creating chaotic amalgamations.

In his capricious combinations, Petipa did not generally proceed from the demands of the music but rather conformed exclusively to the character of individual dancers. To terre-à-terre artists he gave tasks that corresponded to their talents. To Trefilova he granted the exhibition of her pirouettes, her toes, her brilliant pas de bourrée, and her swift diamondlike beats. If the music of a particular composer, fusing with the overall substance of the work, did not coincide with the performer's assets, he would replace this music with a different one—violating the normal development of the theme and reinforcing at all costs the effect of the delivery. He presented Pavlova with combinations that were flattering to her elevation. And generally in the same spirit Petipa everywhere pursued one specific goal: a great performance, where every talent would find its appropriate application. At the start of his career Petipa presented solo dances rather simply, without developing in them a particularly complicated technique. Sometimes a circle flickered, toes appeared, there were simple jumps with beats, and everything ended with an ordinary and simple choreographic flourish, a circular coupé along the diagonal of the stage and the final position on the feet without any intricate takeoff. Several specimens of these compositions that have come down to us are distinguished by an amazing beauty. They are brilliant in every respect—one choreographic note, like the clear and pure sound of a little bell, seems to run its course and then stop.

With the passage of time Petipa's variations, under the influence of touring foreign ballerinas like Carlotta Brianza, Pierina Legnani, Virginia Zucchi, and Carlotta Zambelli, became more complicated, owing to new and intricate forms. The dancers began to display their talent in these works, which were adjusted to their own distinctive traits. A kaleidoscope of forms was given to these dancers, and in their talents great diversity overflowed with ecstasy and passion. In one of her variations Kshesinskaya was able to demonstrate a leap, though not a very high one; to exhibit a soft ballon, to do brilliant beats, to perform an impeccable dance on pointed toes, to circle in a quick pirouette with such a fouetté that wild storms of excitement were evoked in the theater. The former modest finale, a light circle-shaped flourish, was replaced by new choreographic effects which are not easy to convey onstage. Sometimes the variations ended with a marvelous fourth position: one foot on pointe, the other extended in croisé forward in the romantic French style, with the inviting solemnity of elegant pomp. Another variation concluded with a deep arabesque, with a half-turn from the audience to the wings: the public's eyes would dart in the same direction to catch the expression of the ballerina's face. The solo variation was finished in a curved pose on both feet or with a beautiful

pas de chat on the knees. All these intricacies, which are impossible to enumerate, Petipa added to variations and codas in every new work, astonishing us
with the endless diversity of his work. No new ballet master can gather all this
together. Such clusters and accumulations of diamonds cannot be revived
under contemporary conditions. One can speak only of saving and strengthen-
ing individual parts, more or less critical, in any given work. The modern ballet
master can walk with Petipa, but through sad necessity he must always depart
from him, for we have not one dancer today who could contain within herself
and convey onstage the whole range of brilliant art, the whole comprehensive
baroque and intimate rococo of Petipa's creation.

Everything I have said here also relates to the dances of separate ensembles
and to those of the corps de ballet. The restoration of these parts also creates
great difficulties. Petipa was a virtuoso in regard to the corps de ballet, and we
shall return to this later in a special chapter. The ensembles are real jewels in his
crown, brilliant intermezzos which momentarily interrupt the flow of basic
action. Modern choreographers have now completely lost the art of such intermezzos. Particular adagios are choreographed with greater or lesser success.
Composing this or that variation is done by gathering together the surviving
shreds of Petipa's legacy. The late Andriyanov undoubtedly mastered such
productions. But no one nowadays can gather several people into one group,
no one can wave their arms among them and force them to pass along the
magnificent carpet of dance in a row of animated and original figures. The
newly composed ensembles are good for nothing.

In my numerous notes over the course of almost twenty years, I find several
features which depict the old ballet masters in their unique characters. Petipa
composed the dances of the corps de ballet at home and the dances of the
soloists and ballerinas during rehearsal. In his study he arranged groupings and
wrote them down on paper. More accurately, he drew them with unsophisti-
cated symbols. He noted groups by little crosses, little dots, and zeros. Male
dancers emerged as little crosses and women as delicate little circles. With such
notes Petipa would appear at the rehearsal studio and set to work. Solo numbers leapt out of the retort of his boundless choreographic imagination as if
self-generated. Following his powerful teacher but not imitating him in everything, Nikolai Legat came to the stage without any papers or even preliminary
preparation, depending mainly on the music and the inspiration of the moment. That was how he staged *The Four Seasons** for an anniversary performance to honor Glazunov. Right there at the rehearsal he arranged the groups

---

*An allegorical ballet in one act and four scenes with music by Glazunov and
  choreography by Petipa that premiered in 1900 at the Hermitage Theater. Legat revived
  the Petipa production.

of corps members with long veils, and what emerged was a beautiful mass adagio totally in the spirit of classical art. The corps de ballet was broken into several groups, to which were introduced the coryphées, soloists, and students of the theater school. The figures wound in garlands and intertwined in groups to the rhythm and beat of the marvelous music of the composition.

I shall say a few things about the manner of old Perrot, the creator of *Esmeralda*. Perrot worked before Petipa and for a short while with him. He was a small man with a large head. With his expressive blue eyes, he was distinguished by a beautifully proportionate constitution and handsome legs. He was a first-class mime. He would arrive at the rehearsal hall, sit on the floor, and spread his legs. A bow to all and dead silence. Everyone would sit and wait. Perrot would take out his snuffbox and a colored handkerchief. After waiting a bit, he would demand that the musicians play several beats of the dance being prepared for the performance. He would take the tobacco and think. Sometimes he would ask that the music be repeated. Time would pass in tense but concentrated anticipation. This man was always able to surprise you with something unexpectedly brilliant and heartfelt in his fantastic nature because for all his external shabbiness he concealed within himself piles of unspent gold. An hour or more would pass but Perrot would still not produce any dances. He would get up and say, "Excuse me, mesdames, today there's no fantasy, no talent." And he would leave for home amid general silence. The Maryinsky broke with Perrot precisely because it took him so long to produce anything. In this sense he was a direct contrast to Petipa, whose work was animated, quick, and inexhaustibly fertile. Moreover, Perrot, with the rigidity of an old classic, was unable to maneuver between individualities or oblige their capricious demands and tastes; in his own work he followed only the music in accordance with the rigors of his own spirit. But new birds sang new songs! Modernity has allowed the cream of balletic art to rise to the top. It was Petipa who created the pleiad of Kshesinskaya, Pavlova, Trefilova, and Preobrazhenskaya, who have given ballet its extraordinary sparkle and charm.

Having surveyed the past and identified the present, let us turn to the future and ask what we can expect and require from future ballet masters.

Myth and Fairy Tale

Even ballet masters of old sensed that the fairy tale constitutes the plot of all genuine ballet. This is why the classical dances in *Giselle, Raymonda, Swan Lake, Sleeping Beauty,* and *The Nutcracker* are associated with various themes from fairy tales. They begin with a more or less magnificent and solemn opening, followed by the obligatory realistic plot. Then suddenly the realism is abandoned, and the fantastic features of the fairy tale in their abstract choreographic designs are revealed before our eyes.

The fairy tale as the theme of ballet is the achievement and special property of the modern age, which begins approximately with the era of Romanticism. Greek ballet, which was closely connected to drama, had an invariably mythological basis and therefore sooner or later had to become extinct, just as did its later perverted legacy, French court ballet of the seventeenth and eighteenth centuries. Myth is too ponderous for classical ballet. It is essentially tragic and thus represents a kind of cosmic epic that at all costs requires words, monologues and dialogues, just like the so-called heroic epic, which also originates in myth. If we remove myth's basic cosmogonic or theogonic kernel and leave only its fantastic embellishments, which have been introduced into it by centuries'-long popular or individual creation, then we are left with the fine sheath of the fantastical which is supremely adaptable to dance. Greek theodicy cannot be the subject of ballet, but its individual features, when they become the impetus for folklore creation, contain advantageous material for dance movement. Of course, included here are also the fruits of individual creation, which are joined with folklore and merge with it over the course of time. Such are Ovid's *Metamorphoses* and the fairy tales of the Brothers Grimm, Hans Christian Andersen, and others. The fairy tale is light, radiant, and essentially good. Through it newborn eyes look at the world and see that world in grandiose and unusual outlines.

A church or monument is standing on a square. The building itself is totally real in its detail. The church is heavy, crude, and oppressive in its stillness, even when it is wrapped in a veil of smoky light or in a fine brocade of snow cover. But in fairy tale such a church loses its heaviness and ascends to a certain height, and all else in it exists on this level. Everything soars, everything flows in a stream of light, everything is amazingly bold, despite the fact that the backdrop of the fairy-tale action is all a dreamlike fog. An ordinary man passes by in a soldier's armor. In the interpretation of a fairy tale or of a myth which casts off its cosmogonic and theogonic principles, this ordinary man is transformed into a triumphant knight, or a knight seeking adventure. Here all beautiful women are transformed into maiden princesses; and evil crones, with whom myths are filled, turn into the witch Carabosse or hostile fairies. A little girl goes through the forest to visit her grandmother—this is no sweet simple peasant girl, but rather Little Red Riding Hood, and near her lurks a talking wolf. A little rabbit walks with a drum, a cat wears boots, a simple bird turns into a Firebird, and a frisky foal into a Humpbacked Horse. A corpulent and horrible fellow appears as a man-eater in the company of a gang of young boys. A neglected sister who is left at home appears at a ball as Cinderella. The newborn eyes see everything in these singularly enchanting outlines. They present life's tragedy in all its diversity, but the tragedy is shown through the light and moving palpitations of fantastic forms which naturally flow into dance. One can say with total assurance that all folklore is danceable in the highest sense of the word. Shaped in the flesh and blood of scenic art, folklore acquires the charm of genuine poetry, which speaks with equal inspiration to the exacting spectator and the general public. This is not the heroism of Odysseus with his heavy bow, or of Ilya Muromets* with his club—steadfast, but severe—but rather a heroism which becomes softened and more gratifying when combined with beauty.

In his designs and compositions the ballet master of the future will inevitably turn to the rich and lively sources of folklore, with all its supplementary material provided both by the individual and the culture at large. Nothing must constrain him—neither time nor space. All modern life, with its new ideas and new historical tasks, with its new aesthetic taste and new achievements in science, is at the service of the ballet master. Only one thing is required here—and this constitutes the heart of the matter—that he look at the world with the big, bright eyes of the storyteller. There has to be in him a little of the old woman who is knitting a stocking and endlessly threading fine stitches on her sharp hook. Theme after theme, figure after figure, loop by loop, stitch by stitch: The great fabric of balletic art grows in the hands of the miraculous storyteller. He sees a heroic theme and softens it in his art. He encounters death and disperses its tragic spell, disclosing before our eyes the magic world of shades, which continue to exist somewhere and quiver with their earthly sighs. Not only are life's real horrors softened and reconciled, but everything is presented with a beauty that makes heroism desirable and amicable to man's prophetic heart. The ballet master–storyteller represents the true educator of new generations, the so-called choreographic rhapsodist of modern times; he stitches together his own and others' themes, his own inventions and borrowings from the depths of mythology, into a gold-brocaded fabric that is dance, which raises to the stars any imagination that is the least bit lively and sensitive.

The public loves classical dance precisely for its gratifying ease and heroic themes, which are presented through a naive and guileless story that partakes of sorcery. If the ballet master gives his own pathos to the story, if he is convinced that he is producing a conscious work of art, which pulls out of the depths of fantasy all its intuitive inferences, then he will unfailingly achieve the greatest results.

We need this kind of ballet master at this historical moment. Not only does

---

*A popular hero of Russian folk epic who was modeled after the Old Testament prophet Elijah.

life itself require him, but so does ballet, which has become stultified and frozen in its development. A visionary must appear, a dreamer-storyteller and inspired rhapsodist of old and new ideas who has the talent to turn any contemporary event into a fairy tale. Along with such inner qualities, which emerge from the culture of an entire epoch, the ballet master must combine a wealth of choreographic knowledge that is accessible only to truly exceptional talents. From the immense reserve of class exercise he can draw all the necessary means, and by combining them into a synthetic creation, he will create artistically finished and perfect forms. This kind of ballet master will reform the old ballet. All that is concertlike in it and chaotically interspersed in a single, in essence musical-plastic, fabric, he will abolish. The ballet master will draw a line between flowerlike female figures and male figures, which rely on other effects. He will reinvent and give new life to male dancing, which in general desperately needs repair. He will to the highest degree possible be one with the music that the orchestra is playing. However, following the violin bows does not mean that for a second he will lose contact with his own inner strings, which are produced and could not be expressed in any other way by the impulses of his spirit. This is the place from which he will take his attitudes and arabesques: from those subterranean strata where the musical image and choreographic image intertwine and merge together. Thus will the entire fairy tale of life appear in ballet, adorned with the magic of art. All the bells will begin to ring. All the monuments will rise up, dressed in the garb of clouds. All the firebirds will begin to sing tunes of the sun.

This will be folklore's regeneration in the heroic culture of modern times.

The Soul's Reserves

Every object that enters the soul casts a shadow on it called sensation. We take a cold glass in our hand and feel the sensation of glass. This sensation independently produces in the soul a trace called physical feeling. A physical feeling is the reflection of the sensation of the object our soul's screen receives. You imagine your absent brother. This image produces a feeling in the soul that is called aesthetic. This aesthetic feeling is only a delightful shadow cast by the imagination inside a person. Even sensations which contain an element of unselfishness and disinterestedness can give rise to aesthetic agitation and spill over onto the entire screen of the soul with delightful emotions. This happens to us when contemplating a storm at sea or a beautiful mountain view that unexpectedly strikes the eye from a train window. Such contemplation can be the source of great creative visions if a person is blessed with the talent of pure intuition combined with the ability to embody what is seen and heard in colors, words, and sounds. But aesthetic feeling that ensues from impressions half-erased in the memory stands out for its spectral beauty and integrity. A certain note of revival sounds in it, a deeply personal element of the conscious choice of subject and mood. Around such a specifically aesthetic feeling are grouped all the chaotic images awakened by it—visual, intellectual, and acoustic. This is the purest form of aesthetic experience in the smoky, semi-obliterated, and colorful contours drawn by the apperceptive stylus against the background of the inner being. This is how feelings grow in their multiplicity, imprinted upon the soul, now from concrete objects, now from the mental movements close to the real world.

But the soul's growth does not stop at experiences. A person masters concepts in which the concrete features of the world are leveled and receives only its true essence. It is not the changing exteriors of things that are reflected in concepts but their eternal essences. This essence, which is grasped inwardly, also casts a fluctuating shadow in the soul, which we call an intellectual sensation. There are people who stand high on the ladder of conscious life who are stirred up primarily by conceptual matters. The souls of these people are full of even, rhythmically alternating ebbs and flows and inquisitive agitation that sometimes lead to great scientific discoveries. Such people are usually enveloped by a kind of productive conflagration for the benefit of humanity. From this conflagration they snatch charred logs and burning embers that illuminate the further path of their work. Sometimes such people seem dry and rational. But in fact this is not so: these people are like mills, eternally grinding the kernels of impressions that strike their wheels from the surrounding environment. Everything in these mills turns into fine flour.

Yet the development of the human soul does not stop at concepts either. There is yet another world of concepts in it which constitutes an independent element. Such are the concepts of eternal life, of infinity—with a capital and small *i*—of love and harmony. These concepts settling in man also cast onto the soul's screen feelings we can call universal. There are no French or Russian concepts. All concepts are eternal and common to all humanity. This is why the feelings aroused by them also have an all-embracing and lasting character. Only in the soil of ideas is the world united in its parts. Without them it would crumble into antagonistic forces and hostile contrasting elements which would crash and destroy everything around them. A strange thing, the world—real in all senses—is not held together by a material thread, and the cross-stitches in it are sewn on an ideal canvas. If you tear away the canvas all the stitches disappear without a trace. Plato vaguely sensed this, depicting a fantastic mountain up which ideas hover at various altitudes. The wise ancient philosopher imagined that the world seen by us in its essence reposes on this mountain height. This is its immaterial framework, its unity in its endless diversity, its vital and rich synthesis.

Finally, the will. It arouses the most powerful feeling in the soul, which we call passion. This is the root of all force, of every creative act. All the prominent movements of man's soul have at base the mechanism of his will. But we need to be able to recognize and distinguish the will in its most microscopic and embryonic expressions. It is situated in the center of the soul like a small point, dispensing radii of endless desires from itself to the periphery. The smallest act of attentiveness is already an act of the will. Every conscious impression contains this element within itself. The sharpest point of consciousness is already the tip of the willful event. And all of this taken together in its wholeness and compactness engenders in man steadfast passions of various shades. The strong-willed person walks along life's road as the agent of inexhaustible creativity, and every step is marked by the features of his temperament, emotions, and actions. Creation in its every stage is apperceptive and will-based, especially the creation of great masters. Amid the chaos of raging associations these masters never cease picking up, through this apperceptive needle, the subtleties, minutiae, and details, casting them all into a creative cauldron. From Dante's *Divine Comedy* flow rays of inquiries and demands which are understood by every living will. The same must be said of our own Dostoevsky. In his work a similar needle operated, a similar acuteness of tensions of the will by which not one disinterested soul was left untouched. Everything merged and fused in him into one fire-breathing space.

Such is the ladder of feelings in the human soul. They are all situated, as it were, on its second floor, if one considers that on the first are located the sensations and perceptions of real objects. But even the feelings on the second floor do not disappear without trace. They also cast shadows, and we can call these shadows a person's spiritual reserves. Under physical feeling stirs a reserve of doubts, hesitations, and assessments which are inaccessible to any verbal rendering. These reserves of the third floor, unarticulated and secret, form a kind of cloud in which the human soul finds its high and ultimate expression. Here radiant peals and dirges are fused together in one beaming round of events. Here is exactly the material that music and ballet need. Ballet, with all its delicate and fragile forms, lives precisely by these magically cloudlike reserves; the greater the person's talent, the more they are present. Simple joy is banal. But the reserve of joy in a person's soul is his genuine pearl, with an iridescent light of heartfelt emotion. This pearl hides in the further depths of the soul's third floor, and it is not present in everyone. But it is this pearl which shines in an arabesque if the classical figure is performed with artistic beauty. Grief in itself is tediously boring. But its bright reserve lives in the perfect attitude. And so it is in everything. In the pirouette, in the saut de basque, in the courantes of love, in the jumps and leaps across the stage—everywhere before us is the hidden life of the human soul, with all its pearls, real and fake, with all its diverse musical and plastic reserves. If a ballerina is lively and talented she fills her art with the light of her pearl-like reserves.

A person's reserve fund is his gold standard. No emotion or movement of his soul would have any value if this invaluable fund of intellectual gold did not stand behind it. You accomplish an insignificant deed, a trifle has come loose on your life's journey, an innocent joke has flung into space. Yet if in all this a spark of pearly luster is detected, all will go down well with public opinion. Gold reserves guarantee and provide everything with an appropriate weight. Not only our everyday affairs but also the simplest body movements and gestures are managed by the same standard. In some voices we hear the rattling of these gold coins. Some gestures, some glances of perceptively open eyes, some gaits are not without the stamp and sanction of hidden superior norms. If we turn to ballet, we have to admit that in its variegated diversity classical dance demonstrates the same gold reserve fund in its individual aspects, degrees, and gradations that is accumulated in the soul. The entire stage is inundated with the radiance and sound of fantastic riches that have accumulated over the centuries. And in the magical illumination created by talent, music, and fantasy, we suddenly begin to love a person simply for his gait, for the verticality that is sustained on pointe, for a back held with proud aplomb, for a heroic turn of the head, for a port de bras. Choreographic porphyry, like the porphyry of all of the other arts, has its absolute value, not only in the aesthetic but also in the moral sense. It teaches us unselfish love, unselfish emotion, and unselfish exaltation.

Such is the value of the creation of the gold fund of reserves in the movements of dance.

The Ballet Libretto

The question of the ballet libretto is of great interest. Perhaps no other form of literature has been so ignored and neglected as the ballet or opera libretto. But in opera we have the quality of Wagner's librettos, and for Richard Strauss's works we have the texts of Hugo von Hofmannstahl. In ballet, however, we have got an absolute wasteland, with the exception of *Giselle,* which is built on a plot by Théophile Gautier. In the vast majority of cases no one reads ballet librettos. And the only person who considers the libretto without disdain is the director. This question deserves detailed analysis. What is the problem with the old librettos? Ordinarily we are dealing with a trivial story in which at certain points dances are inserted. A wedding is proposed: the ballet master arranges corresponding numbers. A magnificent ball is planned: again dances pour out onstage from the cornucopia of character and genre dances. Classical dances are adapted to fantastic moments of action which take place either in sleep or beyond the limits of the world or in the fantastic setting of daydream. In the libretto's text we find no correspondence to these production motifs. They are not related or explained by any commentary or remarks. The ballet master acts in complete freedom here, ignoring the history, the everyday life and spirit, of the times, and combining only the universal elements of his art and reckoning only with the musical challenges and themes of the orchestra. This is the essential part of a ballet production that has nothing to do with the libretto.

Under these conditions no true poet would be tempted to write a ballet libretto. On the other hand, no truly serious ballet master would turn to a poet with such a request, knowing that contemporary writers are almost completely ignorant about dancing in general and classical dance in particular. For this reason the existing situation will remain hopeless until the classical culture of dance becomes the property of intellectual society and familiar to Russia's creative talents.

Ballet's true content is contained in the music and the dancing. The meaning of *Swan Lake, Raymonda, Giselle,* and *The Nutcracker* is revealed only by analyzing the musical themes and classical forms of the dance. Indeed, Tchaikovsky's music contains the entire tragedy of the swanlike female soul in conflict with coarse reality. In this sense the pas de deux of the second scene of *Swan Lake* constitutes a veritable litany of romantic motifs typical of every woman. The figures of dance, like words, phrases, and sighs of the heart, must each be interpreted individually. Taken together, these figures are the real text of the ballet's action. A preliminary analysis must show the correspondence of the plastic symbols to the musical designs that accompany them onstage, and if such a correspondence is established, the main content of the choreographic work will be defined in every way. This is the kind of authentic libretto that ballet needs. It must be a translation of musical and plastic themes into the language of the poetic word. Creating such a libretto, the poet imagines its content in musical and choreographic images, step by step, over the course of a large evolutionary period, with constant transitions of one mood to another in a long chain of links lyrically connected to one another. For this one needs to have a complete knowledge of the classical means which the ballet exercise creates. But it is not enough to know all the moves. One needs to interpret them, translating the mute figures of dance into the language of general concepts, equally applied to all areas of life and art. The librettist must concretely imagine all the emotions which can pour into attitudes and arabesques. As we said earlier, not all anguish demands the form of an attitude for its rendering on the stage. A woman has lost her belongings and has consequently fallen into despair. On the dramatic stage such despondency can be transmitted with extraordinary exactness. But in ballet one cannot express this in the form of an attitude, which represents something completely stylized and disengaged from the material details of life. Anguish, but not quite. Despondency, but of a different order. Let us take another example. A person must make a snap decision: to leave or to stay. He freezes for several minutes and gathers his inner forces for the definitive act. This is not an arabesque, even though the moment of anticipation and the split-second freezing are present. Anticipation is there, but not quite. Freezing is there, but not exactly. And how many other forms are ahead?—poses, leaps, flights, all kinds of rotations in the air, all kinds of battements, beaten and open. All of this forms a multicolored fabric, an endless gamut of experiences, thoughts, and feelings. An ecstatic pirouette renversée can provide the motif for an entire lyrical stanza and multilayered verbal expressions. And the spirits of diamondlike beats can elevate in a poet a whirl-wind of passionate images which accompany the soul's flight.

I will mention one more detail regarding the construction of classical dance, a detail which also must be considered and understood by the librettist. Dance proceeds from move to move, through perpetual coupé, which brings about the continuity and coordination of movements. The entire body of the dancer constitutes a set of echoes, where the parts resonate with one another. One hand responds to the other in a chanting scale of classical port de bras. The turning of the head is conditioned by the movement of the body and the character of the figure of dance. And here again we have a system of those same moves which are subject to a definite biomechanical or aesthetic law. If the left shoulder is moved forward, the head must be controposto to the side. Why? In a dark room there will be no such coordination of movements. But in the light of day, where the eye is the extreme organ of perception, such a movement, beautiful and significant in its expressiveness, is completely natural and in fact expedient. The eye holds the lever of movement as if controlling its mechanical purity. If the right leg is extended in effacé forward, like a free liberating movement, the head will turn to the opposite shoulder, which almost un-noticeably has quiveringly moved toward it. Here something passes from the source of organic and everlasting bashfulness, according to which the head always turns slightly away from the naked body. It is as if a cover were cast off from the leg and the eyes are naturally drawn aside. But that very same right leg is extended in effacé back, and the apperceptive organ follows it coquettishly.

In the classical dancing of ballet, where everything is connected to the impulses of the will, nothing exists outside of some internal control. Here inspiration is specifically conscious, self-willed, intellectually uplifting; it is linked not with a person's periphery but with his central organs. The heroic motif of the classical art of dance consists precisely in this, in contrast to other kinds of art, which are filled with reflexive and emotional storms, chaotic pauses, and anarchic individualism. All is natural in balletic dance, and a secret coordination envelops all its movements. And this is precisely why an ideological alphabet of ballet is possible. Having studied it like a choreographic ABC, the poet can set about creating verbal compositions. Understanding the structure of the framework within classical choreography, literature can begin to seek in its depths equivalents for a new, miraculous language of the stage. This is the path on which we discover the possibility of the libretto which the ideal ballet anticipates.

But there is another side to the matter with which we are already familiar. All the real movements of the soul, all its effervescence and anxiety, leave in it a certain reserve or unused surplus. Every such surplus is painted in the color of the emotion that emotion has evoked, but the tone of this color is completely different. Everyday anguish generates anguish of another order, not everyday anguish but anguish that is eternal, long lasting, and not conveyed by an ordinary word. Only classical dancing can reflect the genuine content of this anguish. Drama gives its entire external expression, all its realistic fervor. Here are both hot embraces and the culture of passionate kisses. All this would be laughable in ballet. The emotion of love produces an ideal reserve which is also not expressible by any realistic means. In this reserve, if we look at it with maximal care, the elegiac motif is added to the joyful sensations of the moment. This very elegiac motif is conveyed in the classical pas de deux. We cannot sufficiently appreciate the circles assisted by the male partner with the ballerina's leg extended in arabesque that produce the impression of great classical significance. This is a figure of self-oblivion within the clear boundaries of the ideal reserve. Such motifs occasionally enchant the spectator, especially if the performance is inspired by supernatural animation.

I will not list other classical figures. We already know that there is no figure in ballet which cannot be made exclusively in the reserves from the diverse feelings which animate us. That is the originality of this art and what unites it with music and sculpture. And here lies the scale, the genuine criterion to which critical thought will constantly refer when dealing with the purity of a ballet composition. Everything that falls outside of this reserve in the construction of classical dance subjects should be sent down to the area of other related arts. . . .

To be a ballet master one has to possess the talent of thinking in the geometric resemblances of movements and poses that are the ideal core of all material compositions. Such thinking will invariably be musical and will play in the ballet master's soul with acoustical representations, naturally translating themselves into the realm of corresponding movements of the classical type. Only then will the attitude occupy its appropriate place, and the arabesque will do the same. . . . We need a ballet master with a gift for conceptual thinking, for any other ballet master will be unable to utilize the extremely rich technical apparatus at his disposal. The ideal reserves of the soul, and nothing else, need this apparatus.

The librettist must stand at the same level as the ballet master. What is the fundamental task of the librettist? He also constructs a ballet, only not in the movements of choreography but in poetic words and images. With an apperceptive needle the ballet master stitches one form to another, and everything comes out in a mistily magic halo. Before our eyes figures wind quiveringly in light and luster. The librettist is, in essence, a rhapsodist. With his poetic needle he beholds the aerial images of life in the vestments of verbal beauty. If he is a versifier, then he fuses together the living word with the violin's magic of sound, and what is not subject to realistic exposition receives subtle expression in the verse of the poet, which is removed from everything realistic but connected to the reserve of the soul. Here is where the figure and music of arabesque receive their greatest possible elucidation and interpretation: in the winged words of poetry. All the largely emeraldlike brilliance of the musical and plastic elements fuses easily with such motifs of literary creation.

The ideal ballet thus will be the result of the harmonious collaboration of all three active creative forces: the composer, the ballet master, and the librettist. I have in mind here exclusively the classical forms of balletic art. As soon as the motifs of the production go beyond the boundaries of reserve and find expression in real features, as soon as representation in ballet has in mind a living person, dance moves from classical to character. Character dance fills those parts of ballet where a place is set aside for the temporal, the everyday, the historical, and the ethnographic. Character and genre motifs enrich and supplement ballet. The harmonious combination and correlation of such heterogeneous dances will depend on the artistic taste of all these creators.

We have spoken about the ideal librettist, who has never existed and still doesn't exist, with a grain of salt. When the classical forms of dance are deciphered for everyone, no librettist will be needed, just as he is not required for the creation of symphonic music that does not carry a specifically programmatic character. All explanatory librettos for Beethoven's compositions, though they are used in concert halls, are unnecessary for the true aficionado of music. The sound is comprehensible by itself. It speaks not only in emotions but in the subtlest nuances of thought, expressing it at times much better than the most perfect word can. Explicative poetry is provided as a preface for the works of the most modern figurative music, in particular that of Debussy. But these kinds of librettos, which limit the imagination of the listener, in essence only hinder his understanding. The apt title of the corresponding musical piece—"The Naiads," "The Vanishing Bells," etc.—successfully replaces them. But a lyric composer like Chopin rarely needs such titles. Chopin usually called his pieces only by their type or form: "étude," "waltz," "nocturne." In time the same thing will happen with ballet. Precisely because a librettist must use primarily the same reserves that are comprehensively rendered only by music and movement, and which unfailingly require acoustical and choreographic realization, he will always find himself in the background. Even if he possesses the genius of a Pushkin, a poet cannot have in his descriptive arsenal the kind of rapture a musician provides, or the kind of brilliant shaft of light a choreographer can offer.

Poetry is still intimate, and it depends entirely on an inner eye, not an external one. In classical dance, given the depth of its inner content, we have the complete triumph of sound and form. At one point the librettist's task will pass into the realm of history, as happened with the old lengthy descriptions of Beethoven's symphonies, which no concertgoers are guided by today.

The Danseur

In balletic art the role of the danseur is extremely large and important. It has two parts—technical support and support that must create ideal impulses of dance in the woman. The work of the danseur in this sense is particularly meaningful in the adagio. I am concerned here with the essence of this matter for in reality during the past years in Russia a series of practices have appeared that have profaned the danseur's tasks. There have been occasions when dancers have turned the soul of ballet into a circus act. The woman was thrown extremely high simply to raise her way above the head without any aesthetic justification. Then she became the focus of tricks. She was adroitly lowered onto the knees, headfirst, after which she was turned upside down with speed and dexterity. All this is outside classical ballet and relates entirely to the area of sensational stunts, for which there is a place in the Cinizelli Circus* but not on the classical stage. Not for a moment should we forget that everything in serious ballet is based on form and determined by music, which one can force only mechanically into those dangerous stunts. But even now it is worth noting that a few critical fulminations were enough for such techniques to disappear and fall out of use. And taking several steps back in our historical review of this question, we can ascertain that male partners in the spirit of Nijinsky and Petr Vladimirov, though occasionally guilty of an excess of aimless and spectacular acrobatism, were able nonetheless to inspire their accompaniment with genuine artistry. Developing this further, Vladimirov could inscribe his name in the annals of ballet alongside Legat's and even ahead of it. At one time this gifted

*This famous cultural space in Saint Petersburg was named after the Italian performer and circus rider Gaetano Cinizelli, whose family came to the city in 1847. After the Russian Revolution the building was renamed the State Circus on the Fontanka, the canal on which it resides.

artist began to lapse into superficial virtuosity, not, incidentally, because of the true nature of his talent but solely because he became Kshesinskaya's partner— a Kshesinskaya who was not at the height of her career but a weaker one approaching her sunset. The dancer had to shake her, but this artist practiced such methods only when he danced with Kshesinskaya. When he danced with Karsavina or with Vill he sometimes created real miracles. In *Giselle* he was marvelous precisely as the danseur. Vladimrov could understand what no one had heretofore comprehended. He was intuitively cognizant of the uneasy beauty of poses which protractedly die en l'air. Lifting his partner high in the air, he held her with arms extended for several moments, during the course of which he seemingly infused her with his creative spirit and she, obediently complying with him, stretched like a vibrating string. This was true of Karsavina in *Giselle,* thanks exclusively to Vladimirov's inspiration. He achieved similar effects in the famous pas de trois from *Paquita.* Vill, then in her prime, fluttered in his hands. Leaping over the head of her partner, in a large upward flight, the dancer became rigid in frozen movement, if one can use this contradictory expression regarding such magic. There is no doubt whatsoever that we are dealing here with ballon in one of its purest manifestations. This ballon was especially perceptible lately in the partnership of Viktor Semenov, who was distinguished by great elevation but was a very weak danseur. His face was not taught how to show emotions, so his accompaniment was reduced merely to phenomenal leaps, in which he had no equal.

To reduce the danseur's role in the adagio merely to one of mechanical support and a show of gymnastic fioritura for the sake of the fullness of the picture essentially means diminishing its true significance. First and foremost the danseur is the initiator of the lofty verticality and spiritual inclination of the ballerina. He extracts the plantlike essence from Flora's persistent shackles and lifts it upward. This is the crux of the danseur's role. To hold the woman on pointe for as long as possible, to serve as a springboard for takeoffs and flights, to wind those clocklike chimes, and to support her when she her falls in his hands—these form the complex of tasks entrusted to a real danseur. For all this the danseur must show modesty, and, if you like, retire to the background, creating the backdrop for a lovely picture. He catches the movement of each of his lady's fingers, always concealing himself behind her back. Under no circumstances should he stand out. Though he is sure of his partner's agility, he still doesn't let her smallest movements pass by him. Everything passes through his soul inaudibly and evokes a protective and loving response. In order to create a harmonic effect the danseur and his lady must conform to each other in height, temperament, and contrastive build. An inordinately effeminate danseur introduces a disharmonious note into the adagio. Female dancers do not like such partners because they instinctively feel compromised by their accompaniment. The danseur must be masculine in the fullest splendor of that word.

We need to distinguish two types of adagios: an ordinary adagio, which can be called a plastic duet in music, and a dramatized adagio, a pas d'action, which is accomplished less in the music than to its accompaniment—that is, guided by its theme and program. The Greeks called the latter dances hyporchema. The dance illustrates a dramatic motif and demands from the artists not only harmonious movement and distinctive choreography but an outstanding talent. Complying with the inspiration of the literary productions in words, Greek dancers gave their hyporchema the highest possible significance: dance as such, dance in its substantiality, had still not received its differentiating individuality in ancient times. The dramatic motif still predominated in the popular theatrical productions. Nowadays the hyporchemas have lost their former significance, having degenerated into simple, not very intricate pas d'actions. A pantomime drama occurs onstage and the danseur is only a passive character in it, a catalyst for the exalted pantomime of the female dancer. In the simple adagio the dancer's function is, in any case, much more expressive and inspired despite all the features and peculiarities we have described. . . .

. . .

One should never reject anything in its entirety. The eighteenth century, which inclined toward extremity, nonetheless sharpened, developed, and enriched natural grace. The gallant danseur remains, and is always the bearer of perfected plastique. But gradually he too must be transformed as he moves onto a heroic path. A natural shift in the ideology of balletic art will invariably occur. The danseur is no longer a mechanical co-dancer. He participates in the first part of the classical romance as if he were invisible—a vision of the woman, an object of her emotional exaltation. She dreams of him through the mist of a romantic sentiment. He leads, charms, attracts his partner, at times showing off his face, but he is never embodied in complete reality in the tempo of the elegiac pas de deux. His pantomime and gestures are penetrated by enthusiasm. The extreme rapture which fills him remains behind the pale mask of his face. This is how we envision the danseur of the future ballet. The man is the heroic dream of the woman; the first monumental part of the classical pas de deux is based on this. It is as if there were no male partner at all. But he participates, disturbs, and directs in a supreme fashion. He becomes a real force only in the variation and coda. Here the artist dances in freedom, above and on the ground, manifesting his inherent masculinity in the most varied beaten battements which suffuse his ballon.

In the violin-sounding adagio, in this surging of classical ballet, the seeds and sprouts of feelings are encapsulated that later increase and expand in the other parts of the pas de deux. Here is the early spring of exaltation, its first lyrical sigh. The living plant bends, inclines, and stands at attention under the caring glance of the gardener. And the gardener himself digs, tills, and waters, cultivating for himself a beautiful sapling. Sometimes the danseur flings himself into two or three leaps in which the profusion of his inflated emotions is expressed. But he immediately returns to his partner in order to fuse his being with the rush of his heart. All proceeds together in unison and harmony.

The Corps de Ballet

There was a time when the corps de ballet played a very important role on the Russian stage. It breathed inspiration into productions and accompanied solo dancing with great flare. Choreographers directed their exclusive attention to its perfection, reaching the kind of coordination of arms, legs, and in general the entire body which we dare not even dream of today. Groupings appeared to be cast from bronze. Transitions and interlockings were produced with such smoothness and uniformity that shoulder did not touch shoulder, and the lines of the dance flickered with restraint and austerity, as in a Moorish ornamental design. . . .

In several classical works of the old period the corps functions rhythmically and harmoniously as one person with the dancing of the male and female soloists. In *La Bayadère,* for example, we have a series of scenes as a part of the elemental stream of mass movement. The attire of the female dancers is unlike anything else. White skirts with white veils, the ends of which are held in the dancers' hands, produce a fantastic impression. Before us are shadows of the world beyond the grave, rocking and swaying, undulating and whirling, with the aerial lightness of Dante's visions. The shades form four lines, eight dancers in each, and while they are floating in their line from the mountain gorge, the theater is submerged in ecstatic rapture. You await this moment from the very start of the ballet. The impression is absolutely solemn. It is as if you were present at a spectacle in the Eleusinian mysteries, revealed before esoteric humanity. We shall not trace the further alternations of movements, figures, and poses but only note that in the majority of cases the corps de ballet's material is arranged along horizontal and vertical lines, and only at the end . produces a group with veils that flutter over their heads. All of this together is an astonishing accompaniment to the ballerina's dances. But it is far from a popular-mythical commentary, which the ancient Greek chorus is, in relation to its Answerer.* Here the essence of the matter is that the soloist and the corps

---

* Volynsky uses here the Greek word *ipokrit,* the actor of the drama who answers the questions of the chorus.

de ballet perform on one plane. There are absolutely no national or individual delineations, no juxtapositions, no judgments or assessments: the entire essence is in the harmonious accompaniment of the musical melody of the individual dance to the polyphonic chords.

The same thing applies to other ballets. In the second act of *Giselle* we again have a marvelous plastic scene, perhaps even more perfect than the phantoms of *La Bayadère*. Again in white veils, with a green miter on the head and in the bodice, the Wilis emerge onstage in small spurts. Like gentle figures from Flora's kingdom, they enter the common dance in slow tempo. The lines vibrate with the staunchness of a ritual, portraying the element of savage cruelty that humanity professed during the time of ancient Moloch.* Again we shall refrain from a detailed description of this work's brilliant concepts. But we need to emphasize that the evolution of ballet unfolds like a ribbon which twines around the central figure of Giselle. One plane, one type, one creed, without a hint of dialectical discord and contradiction. There is some struggle here but only of the most rudimentary form, in the continuation of the interrupted plotline. And again, what we have is not an imitation of the Greek chorus, in which racial overtones resound, but only the choreographic accompaniment to the essential theme. I shall not speak of the superb corps de ballet dances in *Swan Lake, Sleeping Beauty, Raymonda,* and *The Nutcracker.* Everywhere we encounter the same motif—sameness and unison in ballet production. Not a single note breaks forth from chaos, drones in an invocatory or protesting manner, rejoices or weeps over what is happening. Everywhere a single motif, differentiated in the individual and synthesized in the mass episodes. Ballet is fundamentally musical, and it will inevitably retain its musicality in its future transformations. But precisely on this point a whole field for innovation opens up which stands to enliven and diversify the slight monotony we feel even in the first-rate creations of present-day ballet. At the present time classical ballet provides a repetition of the individual in the countless reflections of the magic mirror. In *Giselle* we have everywhere before us Wilis, one Wili multiplied by a specific number of equivalents. The dialectical moment disappears in the harmonic flow of the general action. In *La Bayadère* there is one shade which is repeated *x* number of times. In the second act of *Sleeping Beauty* we have the same algebra: a sea of Nereids. The same in the depiction of Raymonda's magic dream. Such ideological monotony undoubtedly betrays a certain poverty. But, one asks, can a contemporary work of ballet content itself with a similar artistic conception? It demands new depths and a combination of different levels which contrapuntal music demanded in its time.

---

*Mentioned in Leviticus 18:21 as the deity to whom child sacrifices were made in the ancient Near East.

The creator of the algebraic corps de ballet is none other than Marius Petipa. This ballet master felt the beauty of one group and of movements as had no one else. Everywhere he has lines and figures that correspond to one another, producing the impression of one line and one figure. The element of division and individualization was foreign to him, especially when applied to the corps de ballet's masses. Arms make the same movements. The torso and head retain one and the same position in the lines of the crowd, forming not something new or different but rather a spontaneous repetition of the soloist's dancing, with unsubstantial alterations in detail. In any case, in all the metamorphoses we have one movement phenomenon, split into two parts: the personal and the collective. This perfectly resembles an orchestra, where tens of violins play the same melody in unison. Individual solos are as impossible in the corps de ballet as for violins in an orchestra. Transitions from group to group in Petipa's productions appear momentary and are produced in a musical tempo as if on one beat. The choreographic designs flow from one group to another freely, smoothly, fluently, without intervening rustling or friction. The group in one freezes in a tableau at the sweep of the bow. Here everything accords with the soloist's dances—not only in Petipa's productions but in those of several of his pupils. Thus Nijinsky, dancing the hurricane in *The Talisman,** made large leaps against the background of the kneeling corps de ballet, and these leaps seemed even higher. Kshesinskaya's first entrance was accompanied by the same calculated effect, and even in the absence of elevation her leap in attitude croisé still produced an aerial impression. Petipa was sometimes able to diverge from his algebraic schemes and disperse the collective unity of the corps into small fractions. But he did this only in his mime scenes, when, as the action proceeds, the corps naturally turns into a lively crowd. The crowd mimics in diverse ways—with their faces, with a shrug of the shoulder, with a semi-turn of the head, with a half-step—without, incidentally, making any broad, unfurling gestures so as not to distract the attention from the production's central themes. In dramatic moments variety is needed, a mosaic is required, not a homologous refraction of the operating motif into a diverse mass. Indeed, imagine seventy-five people standing in effacé along the diagonal of the stage, simultaneously extending their index fingers with a challenge, in the same direction forward. This would be awful. There should be no straight lines here; broken lines are necessary. Petipa understood the possibility of transforming the corps de ballet into a raging sea of heads, characters, and temperaments, but he didn't go far in this respect. In general, dramatic con-

---

*A fantastic ballet in four acts and seven scenes with a prologue to music by Riccardo Drigo. It was originally choreographed by Petipa for the Maryinsky Theater in 1889.

structions were not his strong point. He was a thoroughly harmonious poet who did not go beyond the limits of symbolization and saw everywhere reflections of the same fundamental image in the variety of individual shapes. For this reason his creation loses in dramatic quality but gains in range and breadth. In him exaltation is whole, resonant, full-chested, and consummate. In essence a violin and a flute sing, and all the rest only adds to and embellishes the solo motif.

But balletic art cannot stop at Petipa. Looking ahead to new vistas, we shall make a few prognoses for the future.

There are different racial strata in any given individual. Some of them are buried deep within, others dominate. Some are in a dormant state, others are active. A person is essentially the same in all of them, but through his entire construction lies a watershed of two or more warring races. This is where the real foundation of his dialectics lies, which Kant analyzed ideologically. In art dialectics must appear in the heroic ensemble, in the apparel of flesh and race. In the future ballet the principle of the conquering race will find its expression in the dance of the corps de ballet but race-the-victor will be reflected in the soloists' dances. Here, by the way, various combinations and even transpositions are possible. If the corps de ballet represents race the victor, then the conquering race will be depicted by the solo artist. Some Polyphemus,* Lucifer, or Prometheus, an echo of Pelasgian culture, can be represented in contrast to the radiant hordes against whom he has arisen. In this way two goals will be achieved simultaneously: the heroicization of ballet, which the spectator's spirit so hungers for, and the destruction of aesthetic monotonousness and sameness. . . .

These are the principles on which the new corps de ballet must be built, conceptualized, and assembled. At present its dances are reduced to beggary. The rich heritage of the past has been squandered and destroyed. The corps de ballet barely exists. It has lost its importance even as an accompaniment. Lines are not maintained, groupings are meaningless and arbitrary. Not a shadow of former harmoniousness exists. Wardrobes are also in tatters. Everything has faded, everything has been reduced to insignificance, and we have to create a new corps de ballet from nothing. But here the widest field of opportunity opens up for the talented ballet master and future composers: to take from the past its discipline and breathe new content into it. One needs to build a corps de ballet on ideological principles, not everyday ones. Ballet cannot stop being musical. As in olden times it will swim in its own harmonic waves. But a prophetic horn will sound in it, proclaiming the new age more loudly and bravely.

*Son of Poseidon, this Cyclops appears in Homer's *Odyssey*.

Mime

Let us look at the issue of mime in ballet, which is nothing more than the demonstration of individual motifs of the libretto. Ordinarily the audience cannot understand it. It consists entirely of conditional gestures, preserved in the form of an absurd tradition that long ago died off and lost all meaning. . . . Let us portray in the language of ballet the short sentence "I love you." The gesticulation is as follows: touch the chest gently with the fingers of both hands. Then gesture the hand forward with palm turned upward. Following this press the right hand to the heart and with the left palm cover the right one. From this pantomimic communication, which is obvious to the degree of comic absurdity, a simple emotion becomes excessively schmaltzy, even cloying. It goes without saying that with this mechanical transcription, the possibility of individualizing the emotion in the slightest vanishes, and for artists the road toward genuine acting is closed. . . .

But more complex sentences are communicated with absolute solemnity. "Here you will be taken to trial." You need to begin with a familiar gesture of extending your hand with the index finger extended. Then you point your finger sharply in the direction of the floor. And to conclude, you imitate a scale with your hands—thus depicting the scales of Themis.* In order to understand such a pantomimic phrase, you need signal flags, as in the navy. The hands' movements are sequential or simultaneous. The components of an arc or whole arcs are described. All of this is conventional and intelligible if a lexicon exists. The same is true in this balletic sentence. It is comprehensible only to someone who has previously mastered the vocabulary and in addition has mastered an understanding of allegory. At one time allegory was widespread. The frontispiece of any book consisted of an allegory. Any compliment to a lady in the age of chivalry rested on poetic allegory. "The scythe of death," "the scales of justice," "the arrows of love"—allegory sparkled in images and words. Current balletic mime is the legacy of those times, and this is evident even from the arbitrarily chosen detail, where the woman's dress is conceived in no other way than with a long train. But all this has long ago lost all sense and significance. All the semaphoric mime of ballet needs to be thrown off the ship of modernity like so much garbage that is no longer suitable.

Let us leave sentences and look now at individual words of ballet. How does one demonstrate the word *mother?* The arms are crossed on the chest with the palms at the shoulders. An absolute semaphore! Who will understand anything here without the lexicon? How about the word *friend?* The right palm rests

---

*As she appears in Homer, Themis, the mother of Prometheus and goddess of justice, keeps order at the banquet of the gods, especially when summoning them to assembly.

favorably and confidently in the left for several moving seconds. How can one represent in balletic semaphore a bird, a butterfly, or something that flies? You need to wave your outstretched palms before you. The fingers invariably quiver. From the conditional and semaphoric, the gesticulation here passes to the purely imitative, examples of which are varied and often anecdotal in life itself. There are people who are obsessed by imitative gesticulation. In conversation the hand incessantly comes to the help of the word. One asks, How might ballet be reformed? We already said that the semaphoric signalization needs to be excluded and forgotten. It makes ballet not only conventional and incomprehensible but at times simply comic, especially at those moments when a comic aim is not being intended. The content of ballet is not supported by the libretto; its essential features are provided in the orchestral music. Even when a libretto is written by the likes of a writer like Théophile Gautier, it still unfailingly deviates from the poetic core of classical dance. The famous duets in *Esmeralda, La Bayadère, The Talisman (The Bengal Rose), Giselle,* and *Swan Lake,* of course require from the artists a certain mime for the expression of various feelings and for the accompaniment of profound emotional situations. Every artist must eventually take a course in basic dramatic expression to loosen his face and give life and movement to it, and to teach it to change expression. The artist must bare his face, which is usually frozen and immobile, or, as in the case of many young girls, has pouting lips that reflect no definite expression. But even with this newly acquired fund of mime, the artist faces a new challenge.

Most important, he has to synchronize his mime with the music, with the movements of the dance, and with the classical port de bras of the individual poses. This is a formidable task. In essence the artist is obliged to remember the following—and here we return to the theory of reserves laid out above—ballet does not depict real experiences of passion but rather the reserve of those emotions that precede its manifestation or follow it. This is either the dawnlike anticipation of the coming storm or the twilight reminiscence of it. In ballet there are neither kisses nor embraces nor any attributes of possession: there is only its foretaste, its aspiration in love's anguish through the ardent cloud of romantic fantasy and eroticism. Humans are limitless in their passions, but they suddenly become constrained. A bittersweet reserve and a surfeit of moods remain which cast their light and shadow on a person's face. Here is presented the richest gamut of expressions for the most subtle feelings. Let the realistic mime of Savina and Strepetova* celebrate its latest triumphs on the dramatic stage, with their enthusiastic handclasps and fading embraces, with

* Mariya Savina and Pelageya Antipovna Strepetova (1850–1903) were famous dramatic actresses who worked primarily at Saint Petersburg's Alexandrinsky Theater.

their deaths and startling sobbing. From this the ballet artist must have only an initial fund, a primitive ABC of facial expression and gesture. The musical and choreographic elements determine everything else. Let *Giselle* be danced and played in a nonsemaphoric way and we would not recognize it. Even Pavlova does not give everything necessary here: in her acting there are more than a few elements which have illegally migrated from realistic drama. In this respect Zucchi offers an example of such harmful borrowings. But in light of what has been said, similar mistakes would have been completely impossible. In future heroic ballet, which harmonizes with the music and the supra-real subject of choreographic composition, everything will answer the task of classical dance.

With regard to the above-described pantomime material, its reform boils down to the exclusion of all ridiculous and conventional conglomerations and the preservation of natural descriptive gesticulation. This latter fund, stipulated by the absence of living speech, will still remain even when ballet receives new inspiration on the way to its systematic symphonization.

Vis medicatrix (Strength, the Healer)

Classical dance is Apollonian. It is permeated by consciousness, and not one of its designs is built on the variegated elements of sensual life. The principle of classical dance, as opposed to dance of the everyday or character type, is not direct feeling—so vital in its momentary realness—but feeling conditioned by the intellect which regulates it according to the laws of logic. Everything is apperceptive precisely because not one of dance's patterns escapes the control of consciousness; rather each one contains a certain animated reserve. In this sense classical dance must be attributed to Apollo's realm. It is organically opposed to anything Dionysian. Bacchic currents can intrude only from outside, in momentary episodes which do not destroy dance's integral wholeness. We have traced over these pages the Apollonian quality of classical dance, from the first flickerings to its most minute details, from standing on one's toes to the most complex and intricate figures of contemporary ballet. And everywhere passing by the intoxicating elements and delirious exaltations of primitive instincts, classical dance rushes onto the straight path characteristic of all flow of thought. But it is precisely this which causes the fullness of supreme ecstasy, in which reason and will play roles appropriate to them. Even if we imagine character, genre, social, and historical dances performed with extreme perfection, we shall still see before us only the flashing of semi-precious stones—rubies, sapphires, emeralds—not the perfect radiance of snow-white diamonds.

Classical dance in ballet is just such a diamond. Colored stones lack spectral play. They succeed by the charm of their color and depth. The diamond, however, plays with all the colors of the rainbow, containing all tones in transformation. Thus in classical art each feeling that inspires an aspect of historical dance stands before us in splendid reserve, in a purified state. With its rays this feeling passes through these reserves, liberated from everything superficial and arbitrary, and then is refracted in classical forms, devoid of anything narrowly and locally concrete. That is how we would depict the Apollonian character of the classical art of dance. That is its aesthetics and its sanction for all eternity. It is not only apperceptive in its construction and logically natural in its course onstage, it is morally noble by virtue of its ideological material. Psychological reserve makes it valuable with regard to every real moment, whether it is expressed by the quivering of the body or in the moods or emotional outbursts of the moment.

But classical dance is not only consciousness and reserves—it is curative in the deepest sense of the word. Here it is a part of that paean, that graphic and life-giving exaltation which emanates from Apollo. In his tragedies Aeschylus uses the word *paean* to designate medically curative effects. "Let there be a paean for the troubles of the moment"—bring salvation and cure from passing misfortune—we read in *Agamemnon* in the first surges of the great trilogy. "Be a savior now and a paean bearer, King Apollo," we read in another section of the same first part of the *Oresteia*. Medicine is termed paeanlike in the same lofty sense. With their luminous tempests, hymns wash away everything that oppresses a person's body and soul. Such is the paean's healing power. In the culture of classical dance this feature emerges with particular vividness. A good dance class alone, as I indicated above, improves a dancer's body, giving it an abnormal strength and elasticity. The body is shattered and broken but is assembled anew and harmoniously bound into a higher unity. This is a bodily unity which radiates with rhythm and musical coordination and creates as a result a certain special inner atmosphere of a well-oiled machine in which the action of the pliable muscles conveys the feeling of complete health. A master steps away from his bench with the feeling of deep satisfaction. He has unscrewed something, taken it apart, adjusted it, and put it back. An inert, dead thing in his hands has been filled with new meaning and content. And he feels himself a creator who has sent something new and important into the world. This emotion needs to fill him with exaltation. Workerly exaltation is precisely that exaltation that is accessible only to the creative spirit. A person does something, produces something, and his soul brims with happiness and joy. The same with a dancer who goes into the street from the exercise hall. He has broken and built not some extraneous thing but rather his own body, has resoldered its parts and distributed and redistributed its constituent elements. The soul has received new spaces and new ways to display the stocks of gold in the external world that are hidden in it.

One other feature is characteristic of Apollo: sunlike purity and the clarity of his effect on the world. *Phoebus* means "pure" in translation. Pure water takes its source from Phoebus. The Castalian water in Delphi, gushing from the fissure of a cliff, was such a water. And to this day you see yourself in this water as if in a clean mirror, and when you drink it you feel yourself in the possession of life's sap, which is neither turbid nor contaminated. The Greeks spoke of Phoebus's arms, perhaps borrowing this image from ancient Egyptian mythology. In Egypt the sun's rays were extended down to the earth like long arms which brought heat and light to the dark earth. Pure outlines—legs, eyes, even spine—all of these are expressions which we borrow from the enormously rich lexicon of Apollonian culture. Apperception tears aside all the veils, throwing the scum of vulgar materiality off man and by this making him the vessel of almost a universal purity. Man's inner exaltations are not only nourished by the conscious will that leads to the celestial heights; they lie at the essence of Apollonian art in general. They shine with the golden glow hidden within and provide Apollonian art with its moral significance.

But these exaltations, which carry the light of reserves and a healthy workerly frame of mind, are pure and clear in their even and harmoniously salutary radiance. Indeed, everything in classical dance, the best of the creations of the Apollonian spirit, is only the creative reworking of that which nature gives us in its rich and complex composition. Nature abounds in healing powers. It drives out melancholy, destroys various disease-producing elements, strengthens and animates, makes us look younger, and revives us. Sometimes it fills us with unexpected energy, the source of which eludes our analysis. Apperception merely looks for, selects, and gathers in a person the hidden Apollonian funds of nature. It burns through all the world's physical reality with the sun's rays— gentle, resilient, and vegetatively indolent—and like a tree rises to the deep sky. On its elevated level a new structure continues to remain natural in its evident artistic supernaturalness. The grandeur of classical dance consists in its forging values from the simple realities of the world that appear to the eye.

Here is a simple step—businesslike, fussy, or voracious—and suddenly there issues from it a choreographic pas in which all impulses and obsessions of the moment are extinguished. Here a simple turning of the body, when something on the street piqued its curiosity; there a geometrical pirouette of lucid and desire-free passion with a stationary axis rooted in the ground. Leaps have turned into flights, into ecstatically beautiful, proud, and free ballon. In everything there is nature plus creative magic, which is nothing but a displacement and new combination of earthly forces. And along all the creations of classical dance flows a creative juice which also flows from the innate depths of nature through the efforts of the will's spirit. Artificially dividing the world into two antithetical elements of the natural and the supernatural, we essentially make an enormous mistake. By this we juxtapose the face of the world to its essence, whereas in the essence all elements of the face are present, but in a different synthesis, which transfigures them. One can show the same thing in the scanty light of a room, in the changing streaks of artificial illumination, and in the clear halo of sunlight which reveals forever its entire essence.

All these considerations overturn the current view of dance as a source of unhealthy arousal and stimulation. If this can appear fortuitously justified in regard to genre or character dances, from the passionate Spanish dance to the crudely sensual dance de ventre in Tunisia or Algeria, then it has no relation to classical dance whatsoever. By its very essence classical dance can only improve the health of—rather than arouse—the performer and the spectator. And if in the course of time the view existed (and it still in part does) that the dancer is generally a seductress, then this can be explained by historical conditions in which dance was performed as a diversion for rich people. Indeed, artists themselves, not only in the past but also in the present, have failed to understand the art they have cultivated, its foundations and objectives. To be sure, we are dealing here with one of the crudest forms of profanation. But with the increase in the numbers of people who knowingly grasp the art of ballet, its rehabilitation will become universally recognized and substantiated.

—*Kniga Likovanii* (1925; Moscow: Artist. Rezhiser. Teatr, 1992).

Glossary of Names

꘎꘎꘎

This glossary contains references to figures connected to the world of dance—performers, choreographers, critics, artists and designers, theater personages—both those who lived before and those who lived during Volynsky's time. For ease of reading and because most of the artists listed here performed only in the imperial theater, "Maryinsky" is used throughout for the theater, which was renamed the State Academic Theater of Opera in 1920 and the Kirov Theater in 1935.

Andriyanov, Samuil Konstantinovich (1884–1917). Dancer and ballet master who was known chiefly at the Maryinsky as the partner of such luminaries as Tamara Karsavina, Anna Pavlova, Mathilda Kshesinskaya, Agrippina Vaganova, Vera Trefilova, Olga Preobrazhenskaya, and Elizaveta Gerdt (to whom he was married).

Anisfeld, Boris Izrailovich (1878–1973). Painter, graphic artist, and theatrical designer who was born in Odessa but moved to Petersburg as a young man, where he worked with the Mir iskusstva group from 1910 to 1917. Anisfeld left Russia in 1917 and eventually settled in Chicago.

Asafiev, Boris Vladimirovich (1884–1949). Composer and musicologist who began working as concertmaster at the Maryinsky in 1909.

Bakst, Leon (Lev Samoilovich Rozenberg) (1866–1924). Painter, book illustrator, and theatrical designer, in which field he earned an international reputation. From 1908 until his death, he lived in Paris. While in Russia, Bakst was a member, along with Sergei Diaghilev and Benois, of the Mir iskusstva group. For the Maryinsky he designed the sets and costumes for *Die Puppenfee;* for the Ballets Russes, he designed *Schéhérazade, Le Spectre de la Rose, L'Après Midi d'une Faune, Daphnis et Chloë,* and others.

Belova, Antonina Fedorovna (1895–1922). Dancer at the Maryinsky from 1913 until her death.

Benois, Alexander Nikolaevich (1870–1960). Painter, graphic artist, and scenic designer with a particularly strong interest in ballet who was artistic director for the Russian Seasons of Sergei Diaghilev's Ballets Russes in Paris. Benois painted the sets for the premier of Stravinsky's *Petrushka* in 1911.

Biber, Evgeniya Eduardovna (1891–1971). Dancer at the Maryinsky starting in 1909 who also participated in Sergei Diaghilev's Russian Seasons from 1910 to 1913. She left the stage in 1954 and taught ballet in Leningrad until 1970.

Blasis, Carlo (1795–1878). Italian dancer, ballet master, teacher, and writer who grew up in France and whose dancing at the Paris Opera and La Scala was distinguished by a high level of technical perfection, beauty of line, and harmony of movement. He choreographed more than eighty ballets and wrote many volumes on dance, including works on the relation of dance to the other arts.

Bolshakova, Gali Yosifevna (1892–1949). Dancer at the Maryinsky starting in 1909 who taught at Leningrad's Malyi Theater from 1944 until her death.

Brianza, Carlotta (1867–1930). Italian ballerina who debuted at La Scala and danced at the Maryinsky from 1889 to 1891, where she created the role of Aurora in Petipa's *Sleeping Beauty.*

Cecchetti, Enrico (1850–1928). Italian dancer and ballet master who taught in Saint Petersburg, worked with Petipa and Ivanov at the Maryinsky, and was also a teacher for Sergei Diaghilev's Ballets Russes from 1911 to 1921. In 1925 he left London for Milan, where he died shortly after taking over the direction of the La Scala school.

Chekrygin, Ivan Ivanovich (1880–1942). Dancer, composer, and instructor who worked at the Maryinsky from 1897 to 1917, during which time he also studied at the Saint Petersburg Conservatory of Music. Chekrygin taught dance at the renamed Leningrad Conservatory until his death.

Coralli, Jean (1779–1854). French dancer and choreographer who was one of the greatest masters of romantic ballet; his most memorable creation was *Giselle* (1841).

Danilova, Alexandra Dionisievna (1904–1997). Ballerina and instructor who danced with the Maryinsky until she left Russia in 1924; she worked with Sergei Diaghilev's Ballets Russes until 1929. She then danced with the De Basil and Denham Ballet Russe companies and eventually settled in New York, where she taught at the School of American Ballet.

Diaghilev, Sergei Pavlovich (1872–1929). Founder and editor from 1898 to 1904 of the Western-oriented Saint Petersburg journal *Mir iskusstva* (The World of Art), who later became an entrepreneur, an impresario, and the founder of the Ballets Russes, a huge theatrical enterprise, over which he presided until his death.

Dobuzhinsky, Mstislav Valeriyanovich (1875–1957). Saint Petersburg graphic artist, painter, and stage designer who also worked with Sergei Diaghilev's Ballets Russes. He emigrated to the United States in 1937.

Drigo, Riccardo (1846–1930). Italian composer and conductor who worked at the Italian Opera in Saint Petersburg and in 1886 began his thirty-year association with the Russian Imperial Ballet, returning to Italy in 1920. His most famous ballet score is *Harlequinade.*

Dubrovskaya, Feliya Leontievna (1896–1981). Dancer at the Maryinsky from 1913 to 1920. Until 1939 she danced in France and the United States.

Dudko, Mikhail Andreevich (1902–1981). Ballet dancer who performed at the Maryinsky from 1920 to 1941.

Duncan, Isadora (1877–1927). American dancer who performed frequently in Russia between 1904 and 1913. Her credo "the freedom of the body and the spirit gives birth to creative thought" made her a central figure in the history of modern dance. Duncan reacted strongly against the classical school of ballet, and although her ideal also originated from ancient Greece—particularly its frescoes, vase drawings, and sculpture —Volynsky protested against every aspect of her art, including her rejection of traditional ballet attire.

Eberling, Alfred Rudolfovich (1871–1951). Russian painter who was born near Lodz in Russian Poland but studied and worked in Saint Petersburg/Leningrad for the rest of his life.

Eduardova, Evgeniya Platonovna (1892–1960). Dancer at the Maryinsky from 1901 until 1917, after which she taught ballet in Berlin, Paris, and New York.

Efimov, Vasily Andreevich (1899–?). Dancer at the Bolshoi Theater from 1919 to 1927 who also performed at the Maryinsky in the early twenties.

Egorova, Liubov Nikolaevna (1880–1972). Dancer at the Maryinsky until she emigrated to Paris, where she danced briefly with Sergei Diaghilev's Ballets Russes in 1927. She opened a school of ballet there, which she ran for forty-five years.

Elssler, Fanny (1809–1884). Austrian ballerina and one of the greatest stars of the Romantic period.

Fedorova, Anna Alexandrovna (1884–1972). Ballerina who danced at the Maryinsky from 1902 to 1922.

Fedorova, Anna Ivanovna (1887–?). Ballerina who danced at the Maryinsky from 1905 to 1914 and in 1922, and with the Bolshoi from 1915 to 1920.

Fedorova, Olga Vasilievna (1882–1942). Dancer at the Bolshoi Theater from 1900 to 1909 and at the Maryinsky from 1909 to 1923.

Fokina, Vera Petrovna (1886–1958). Dancer, teacher, and the wife of Mikhail Fokine. She danced at the Maryinsky from 1904 to 1918, interrupting her career there to perform with Sergei Diaghilev's Ballets Russes in 1909–1912 and 1914. She emigrated to the United States in 1921, and from 1923 until her death she taught dance in New York.

Fokine (Fokin), Mikhail (Michel) Mikhailovich (1880–1942). Dancer, choreographer, and teacher who worked at the Maryinsky and also participated in Sergei Diaghilev's Ballets Russes in 1909–1912 and 1914. An elegant premier danseur, Fokine performed major roles in the classical repertoire, and also danced to music not originally written for ballet, including pieces which came to be known as "plotless ballet." Classical dance for Fokine was not a universal system but rather equal in importance to character dances and other kinds of free movement, for which he incurred the wrath of Volynsky, who never ceased to remind his readers of Fokine's "heresies" and confusion.

Geidenreich, Ekaterina Nikolaevna (1897–1982). Dancer at the Maryinsky from 1915 to 1936, after which she was a teacher and coach at Leningrad's Malyi Theater.

Geltser, Ekaterina Vasilievna (1876–1962). Ballerina who trained in Moscow, where she danced with the Bolshoi. Beginning in 1896 she performed at the Maryinsky, where her major roles were often for productions created by Alexander Gorsky. In 1927 she danced in one of the first Russian ballets based on Soviet themes, *The Red Poppy.*

Gerdt, Elizaveta Pavlovna (1891–1975). Ballerina and instructor who performed at the Maryinsky beginning in 1908. Her style was formed in the tradition of the classical school of Christian Johansson and Marius Petipa, as well as of her father, Pavel Gerdt, who was also a noted teacher of ballet. She is one of the few great classical ballerinas of pre-Revolutionary Russia who did not emigrate to the West.

Gerdt, Pavel Andreevich (1844–1917). Dancer at the Maryinsky from 1864 to 1916 who taught at the Petersburg Theatrical School from 1880 to 1904. He danced the first Desiré in *Sleeping Beauty* and Siegfried in *Swan Lake*.

Goleizovsky, Kasian Yakovlevich (1890–1970). Dancer, teacher, and choreographer who studied with Mikhail Obukhov and Mikhail Fokine and worked at the Maryinsky in 1909 before moving to Moscow's Bolshoi Theater, with which he was associated for the rest of his life.

Gorsky, Alexander Alexeevich (1871–1924). Dancer, teacher, and choreographer who was born and trained in Saint Petersburg but professionally connected to Moscow where, from 1902 until his death, he was ballet master of the Bolshoi Theater. Known as a reformer who tried to overcome many of the conventions of academic classical dancing, Gorsky ran afoul of Volynsky, who nonetheless recognized his significant talent.

Grisi, Carlotta (1819–1899). Italian dancer and the first Giselle (1841) who was one of the most noted representatives of Romantic ballet. Grisi danced in Saint Petersburg between 1850 and 1853, where she formally ended her career.

Ivanov, Lev Ivanovich (1834–1901). Dancer and choreographer who performed under Marius Petipa. A gifted musician, Ivanov stressed the primacy of music in ballet. Ivanov's choreography of the White Swan acts of *Swan Lake* and the Waltz of the Snowflakes in *The Nutcracker* was his most highly regarded.

Ivanova, Lidiya Alexandrovna (1903–1924). Russian dancer at the Maryinsky who was supposed to have accompanied Balanchine and other members of the Young Ballet on a tour to Europe (from which they never returned) but died under mysterious circumstances shortly before their departure.

Jaques-Dalcroze, Emile (1865–1950). Swiss music pedagogue whose method, known as eurhythmics, was introduced into Russia in 1909.

Johansson (Ioganson), Anna (1860–1917). Dancer and teacher who made her debut at the Maryinsky in 1878 in *Esmeralda*. She was the daughter of Christian Johansson.

Johansson (Ioganson), Christian (1817–1903). A Swede and representative of the academic school of classical ballet who worked in Saint Petersburg from 1841 and was a virtuoso dancer and pedagogue. His pupils included Elizaveta Gerdt, Nikolai Legat, Mathilda Kshesinskaya, Anna Pavlova, Tamara Karsavina, and Olga Preobrazhenskaya. Marius Petipa attended his lectures and used many of Johansson's materials for his productions.

Karsavina, Tamara Platonovna (1885–1978). Dancer at the Maryinsky from 1902 to 1918 and the leading ballerina of Sergei Diaghilev's Ballets Russes. She emigrated to England, where she played a major role in the development of British ballet. Her memoirs (*Theater Street*) were published in English in 1929.

Kommissarzhevskaya, Vera Fedorovna (1864–1910). Actress who from 1904 to 1909 was the head of Saint Petersburg's Dramatic Theater, which was more frequently known under her name.

Korovin, Konstantin Alexeevich (1861–1939). Moscow-trained and based painter who worked closely with the Bolshoi Theater and, starting in 1900, collaborated with fellow artist Alexander Golovin on Alexander Gorsky's production of *Don Quixote*. He also collaborated with the Ballets Russes. Among his most famous productions were *The Little Humpbacked Horse, Ruslan and Liudmila, Khovanshchina,* and *The Golden Cockerel.*

Kozhukhova, Mariya Alexandrovna (1897–1959). Dancer at the Maryinsky from 1915 to 1933, and from 1933 until her death a teacher of ballet in Leningrad.

Kshesinskaya, Mathilda Feliksovna (Mathilde Kshessinska) (1872–1971). Prima ballerina and instructor in Paris who was the daughter of the ballet dancer Felix Kshesinsky and the sister of the ballet dancers Evgeniya Kshesinskaya and Iosif Kshesinsky. Kshesinskaya, who had liaisons with various members of the Imperial family, danced at the Maryinsky from 1890 to 1917, after which she emigrated to Paris. Her reminiscences, *Dancing in Petersburg: The Memoirs of Kschessinska,* were published in 1960.

Kulichevskaya, Klavdiya Nikolaevna (1861–1923). Teacher and dancer at the Maryinsky from 1880 to 1901.

Kyaksht, Lidiya Georgievna (1885–1959). Dancer at the Maryinsky from 1891 to 1910. Beginning in 1908, Kyaksht lived in London, where, after leaving the stage in 1933, she taught dance.

Lanceray, Evgeny (Eugène Lanceret) (1875–1946). Graphic artist, painter, and theatrical designer associated with the Mir iskusstva group.

Legat, Nikolai Gustavovich (1869–1937). Instructor, choreographer, and one of the leading dancers and upholders of the "old" ballet at the Maryinsky. He was a noted teacher (of Anna Pavlova, Mikhail Fokine, Tamara Karsavina, Vaslav Nijinsky, Agrippina Vaganova, Fedor Lopukhov, and others) and left Russia in 1922, eventually settling in London.

Legat, Sergei Gustavovich (1875–1905). Instructor and dancer at the Maryinsky from 1894 until his death who was the brother of Nikolai Legat, with whom he produced *Die Puppenfee* in 1903. He studied with Pavel Gerdt, Christian Johansson, and Lev Ivanov.

Legnani, Pierina (1863–1923). Italian dancer and one of the great turn-of-the-century Italian ballerinas who performed at the Maryinsky from 1893 to 1901, and studied with Volynsky's idols: Marius Petipa, Christian Johansson, and Nikolai Legat. Her dancing was known for its exceptionally fine technique, and she long served as a model in her role as Odette-Odile.

Leontiev, Leonid Sergeevich (1885–1942). Dancer, teacher, and choreographer who began working at the Maryinsky in 1903 and performed there into the 1930s. He was one of George Balanchine's teachers.

Leontieva, Mariya Mikhailovna (1889–1972). Teacher and dancer at the Maryinsky from 1907 to 1923.

Liukom, Elena Mikhailovna (1891–1968). Dancer and teacher who performed at the Maryinsky, in Sergei Diaghilev's Ballets Russes, and in the Soviet Union, and who remained in her native Petersburg (Leningrad) until she died. Her most famous roles were Giselle, Esmeralda, Raymonda, Niki, and Kitri.

Lopukhov, Fedor Vasilievich (1886–1973). Dancer, instructor, and ballet master who in 1922 became the artistic director of the Maryinsky, where he served intermittently until 1956. His choice for this position over Volynsky's personal favorite, Nikolai Legat, infuriated Volynsky and alienated him even further from the Maryinsky.

Lopukhova, Evgeniya Vasilievna (1884–1943). Dancer at the Maryinsky from 1902 to 1924 who performed with Sergei Diaghilev's Ballets Russes from 1909 to 1911. Unlike her dancer sister Lidiya, and like her choreographer brother Fedor, Evgeniya remained in Russia after the Revolution, during which time she also appeared in operettas and plays.

Makarova, Elena Alexandrovna (1881–1912). Dancer at the Maryinsky from 1899 to 1907.

Makletsova, Kseniya Petrovna (1890–1971). Moscow-born and trained dancer who

performed largely at the Bolshoi Theater and about whom Volynsky wrote several short
articles. She danced with the Ballets Russes in the United States during World War I.

Monakhov, Alexander Mikhailovich (1884–1945). Dancer and teacher who performed at
the Maryinsky from 1902 to 1916. In the early 1930s he moved to Moscow where he
served as coach and choreographer at the Bolshoi Theater until his death.

Montessu, François (1796–?). French dancer who debuted at the Paris Opera in 1817.

Mordkin, Mikhail Mikhailovich (1880–1944). Dancer and choreographer who worked
with Alexander Gorsky in Moscow and traveled with Sergei Diaghilev to Paris in 1909.
Between 1919 and 1911 he formed a partnership with Anna Pavlova, dancing in London
and the United States. Mordkin left Russia in 1923 for the United States, where he
danced and taught until his death.

Neslukhovskaya, Inna Sergeevna (1889–?). Dancer at the Maryinsky from 1907 to 1916,
after which she emigrated to France.

Nijinsky, Vaslav Fomich (1889–1950). Legendary dancer at the Maryinsky from 1907 to
1911 and with Diaghilev's Ballets Russes from 1909 to 1913, and, with his sister
Bronislava Nijinska, one of the pioneers of twentieth-century choreography. After
breaking with Diaghilev in 1913, Nijinsky danced in London, New York, Spain, and
South America, rejoining Diaghilev's company briefly in 1917, when he performed
publicly for the last time. From 1920 until his death, Nijinsky spent much time in
hospitals and sanitoria being treated for schizophrenia. The complete version of his
harrowing memoirs was published in the United States in 1998.

Nikitina, Vera Alexandrovna (1857–1920). Dancer at the Maryinsky from 1873 to 1893.

Noverre, Jean-Georges (1727–1810). French dancer and ballet master who formulated his
views on ballet as an independent medium in his *Letters on Dance and Ballet*. Arguing
for plots full of intrigue, action that unfolds in a logical and well-developed manner,
and characters who exhibit strong emotions, Noverre advocated the separation of ballet
into self-contained dramatic pantomimes. A four-volume edition of Noverre's writings
appeared in Russian in 1803–1804.

Obukhov, Anatoly Nikolaevich (1896–1962). Dancer and pedagogue who performed at the
Maryinsky from 1913 to 1920, after which he lived abroad. From 1940 until his death,
Obukhov taught at the New York City Ballet.

Obukhov, Mikhail Konstantinovich (1879–1914). Teacher and dancer at the Maryinsky
from 1897 until his death.

Orlov, Alexander Alexandrovich (1889–1974). Dancer and student of Mikhail Fokine who
performed at the Maryinsky from 1908 to 1924. In 1909–1911 he danced in Paris for
Sergei Diaghilev's Ballets Russes, where he first performed the role of the Moor in
Stravinsky's *Petrushka*.

Pavlova, Anna Pavlovna (1881–1931). The most famous Russian ballerina in the West who
danced at the Maryinsky from 1899 until her final performance there in 1913; her most
famous roles were Giselle, Nikia, Kitri, and Paquita. Though closely associated with
many of Mikhail Fokine's productions (in 1909–1911 she occasionally danced with
Sergei Diaghilev's Ballets Russes), Pavlova remained loyal to the classical tradition of
Russian ballet, which Volynsky tirelessly propagated in his writings.

Perrot, Jules (1810–1892). French dancer and ballet master who worked in Saint Petersburg
from 1848 to 1859.

Petipa, Marius Ivanovich (1818–1910). Dancer and highly acclaimed ballet master who was
invited to Saint Petersburg in 1847 and remained to become the major force in the city's

ballet life for almost fifty years. Largely associated with the grandest productions at the Maryinsky, Petipa was for Volynsky the person to match for the revival and advancement of classical ballet.

Petrov, Pavel Nikolaevich (1881–1938). Dancer, teacher, and ballet master who worked at the Maryinsky from 1900 until he emigrated to France in the early 1920s. In the early 1930s he moved to Lithuania, where he was considered one of the country's greatest dance teachers.

Polyakova, Elena Dmitrievna (1872–1972). Dancer at the Maryinsky from 1900 to 1910.

Preobrazhenskaya, Olga Yosifovna (Olga Preobrajenska) (1871–1962). Ballerina and teacher who performed at the Maryinsky as well as with Sergei Diaghilev's Ballets Russes. Preobrazhenskaya taught at Volynsky's School of Russian Ballet until she emigrated, directing the La Scala School from 1921 to 1922 and then settling in Paris, where she trained generations of highly talented ballerinas.

Romanov, Boris Grigorievich (1891–1957). Dancer, teacher, and choreographer with the Maryinsky from 1909 until he was appointed ballet master in 1914 who also danced with Sergei Diaghilev's Ballets Russes. In 1921 he founded the Russian Romantic Theater in Berlin. He later worked at La Scala and eventually settled in New York, where he worked at the Metropolitan Opera.

Roslavleva, Liubov Andreevna (1874–1904). Dancer at the Maryinsky from 1892 until her death.

Rozai, Georgy Alfredovich (1887–1917). One of the most prominent male dancers at the Maryinsky, where he danced from 1907 to 1915. He also participated in Sergei Diaghilev's Ballets Russes from 1909 to 1911.

Rubinstein, Ida Lvovna (1883–1960). Dancer who studied with Mikhail Fokine and participated in Sergei Diaghilev's Ballets Russes. A millionaire, she founded her own troupe in 1929 as a showcase for new ballets and her own dancing, commissioning, among other works, Stravinsky's *Baiser de la Fée*.

Saint-Léon, Arthur (1821–1870). French dancer, choreographer, and composer who began working at the Maryinsky in 1859. His ballet productions include *The Little Humpbacked Horse* and *Coppélia*.

Savina, Mariya Gavrilovna (1854–1915). Actress who began her career in 1874 and became a star at Saint Petersburg's Alexandrinsky Theater.

Schollar, Liudmila Frantsevna (1888–1978). Dancer and teacher who worked at the Maryinsky from 1906 to 1921 and also performed with Sergei Diaghilev's Ballets Russes abroad between 1909 and 1914, and in the 1920s with Ida Rubinstein's company. She taught at the School of American Ballet in New York, and from 1965 until her death lived and worked in San Francisco.

Semenov, Viktor Alexandrovich (1892–1944). Dancer at the Maryinsky who began in 1912, and from 1913 to 1931 taught dance in Saint Petersburg/Leningrad until he moved to Moscow, where he coached and taught ballet until his death.

Sergeev, Nikolai Grigorievich (1876–1951). Dancer, teacher, and ballet master who served as the Maryinsky's chief regisseur from 1903 to 1917. He emigrated in 1918, taking with him the scenes in Stepanov notation that he used in staging *Giselle, Swan Lake, The Nutcracker,* and other works for the Ballets Russes, Saddler's Wells Ballet, and the Paris Opera.

Shimanskaya, Josephina Alexandrovna (1893–?). Dancer at the Maryinsky.

Shiryaev, Alexander Viktorovich (1867–1941). Dancer at the Imperial Ballet School in Saint Petersburg, who taught ballet there from 1918.

Skalkovsky, Konstantin Apollonovich (1843–1906). Famous theater and ballet critic who occasionally published under the pseudonym "Balletomane" in various Saint Petersburg publications.

Smirnova, Elena Alexandrovna (1888–1934). Dancer and teacher who studied under Mikhail Fokine. She was married to Boris Romanov and was the ballerina of his company from 1921 to 1926. She taught ballet in Buenos Aires from 1928 until her death.

Sokolova, Evgeniya Pavlovna (1850–1925). Ballerina at the Maryinsky until she left the stage in 1886, after which she taught and coached ballet; among her students were Mathilda Kshesinskaya, Anna Pavlova, Tamara Karsavina, and Vera Trefilova.

Somov, Konstantin Andreevich (1869–1939). Artist known largely for his portraits and book illustrations who studied in Paris in the late 1890s with Alexander Benois (with whom he was particularly close) and Evgeny Lanceray, and moved there in 1923 after leaving the Soviet Union.

Sorin, Savely Abramovich (1878–1953). Artist who mainly painted portraits, especially of famous Russian cultural figures (for example, Maxim Gorky, Fedor Chaliapin, Anna Akhmatova). Sorin painted Volynsky's portrait in 1905.

Spesivtseva, Olga Alexandrovna (1895–1991). One of Volynsky's favorite dancers at the Maryinsky whose hasty departure for Europe in 1924 caused him exceptional sadness. Spesivtseva danced at the Maryinsky from 1913 to 1924, while also performing in Europe and the United States with Sergei Diaghilev's Ballets Russes. The first Russian étoile of the Paris Opera, she spent the years 1943–1963 in a mental institution, and lived the last twenty-eight years of her life at the Tolstoy Foundation Farm in Valley Cottage, New York.

Stukolkin, Vasily Nikolaevich (1879–1916). Dancer at the Maryinsky from 1899 until his death.

Svetlov, Valery Yakovlevich (1860–1934). Ballet critic who began writing in the 1890s. He supported Mikhail Fokine's reforms and married Vera Trefilova in 1917, shortly after emigrating to Paris. He is the author of *Soviet Ballet* (French translation: *Le Ballet contemporain*).

Taglioni, Marie (1804–1884), Daughter of the eighteenth-century Turin-born choreographer and dancer Filippo Taglioni who danced the first Sylphide (1832), one of the ballets that defined French Romantic style.

Trefilova, Vera Alexandrovna (1875–1943). Ballerina who danced at the Maryinsky from 1894 to 1910. In the 1920s she returned to the stage, appearing with Sergei Diaghilev's Ballets Russes in productions of *The Sleeping Princess* and *Swan Lake*. She died in Paris, where she lived with her third husband, Valery Svetlov.

Troyanovskaya, Taisiya Alexandrovna (1898–1946). Dancer and teacher at the Maryinsky from 1916 to 1941.

Vaganova, Agrippina Yakovlevna (1879–1951). Dancer, choreographer, and teacher who danced at the Maryinsky from 1906 to 1916. She taught briefly at Volynsky's School of Russian Ballet before moving on to other positions in Petrograd/Leningrad and Moscow, where she gained international fame as a teacher and creator of the Vaganova technique.

Vazem, Ekaterina Ottovna (1848–1937). Ballerina who danced at the Maryinsky from 1867 to 1884. She taught in Saint Petersburg from 1886 to 1896.

Vill, Elsa Ivanovna (1882–1941). Dancer at the Maryinsky from 1900 to 1928. Volynsky wrote several short pieces about her.

Viltsak, Anatoly Yosifovich (Anatole Vilzak) (1896–1998). Dancer and teacher and the husband of Liudmila Schollar who performed at the Maryinsky from 1915 to 1921, when he emigrated to the West after working with Sergei Diaghilev and Ida Rubinstein. He settled in the United States, where he became an outstanding teacher.

Vladimirov, Petr Nikolaevich (Pierre Vladimiroff) (1893–1970). Leading male dancer at the Maryinsky, where he last appeared in 1918. From 1934 to 1967 Vladimirov was an instructor at the School of American Ballet in New York.

Volkonsky, Sergei Mikhailovich (1860–1937). Nephew of Prince Ivan Vsevolozhsky who directed the Imperial Theaters from 1899 to 1901. He appointed Alexander Gorsky as ballet master of the Bolshoi Theater and Sergei Diaghilev as a special assistant, and also commissioned members of the Mir iskusstva Art group to design for the Imperial Theater. An advocate of the ideals of Emile Jaques-Dalcroze, he emigrated in 1917 and died in Hot Springs, Arkansas.

Vronskaya, Alisa Frantsevna (1897–?). Dancer at the Maryinsky from 1914 to 1918.

Vsevolozhsky, Ivan Alexandrovich (1835–1909). Costume designer and director of the Imperial Theaters from 1881 to 1899, Vsevolozhsky brought the Maryinsky to its zenith. He designed costumes and sets for more than two dozen ballets, and produced most of the outstanding Petipa-Ivanov productions, including *Sleeping Beauty, Swan Lake, The Nutcracker,* and *Raymonda.*

Yakovleva, Olga Matveevna (1885–?). Ballerina who danced at the Maryinsky from 1901 to 1929.

Zambelli, Carlotta (1875–1968). Dancer who studied at La Scala and from 1890 was an étoile at the Paris Opera. In 1901 she was invited to dance at the Maryinsky, where she performed in *Coppélia, Paquita,* and *Giselle,* which she rehearsed with Enrico Cecchetti.

Zucchi, Virginia (1847–1930). Italian ballerina who studied with Carlo Blasis and toured Russia with great success from 1885 to 1892. Between 1885 and 1888 she performed a number of major roles at the Maryinsky (for example, in *Esmeralda, The Pharaoh's Daughter,* and *La Fille Mal Gardée*).

Index